D1555194

Publisher's Note

This book has been reproduced from the original by a photo copy printing process. Not only does this process pick up every desirable detail but also picks up undesirable qualities such as poorly printed words, old lead Linotype defects, blotches, and faint areas. Nothing has been changed to alter the original book. Improvements have been made, however, in the quality of paper, cover material and binding. We trust that you will enjoy this quaint reprint. It is a most important endeavor in the preservation of American Historical Literature.

Bill Schroeder, President
Collector Books
P.O. Box 3009
Paducah, Kentucky 42001

BEEF.

1. Sirloin.	**7.** Thin mouse-piece.	**13.** Brisket.
2. Rump.	**8.** Veiny Piece.	**14.** Thick Brisket.
3. Edge-bone.	**9.** Flank or Thin Loin.	**15.** Shoulder.
4. Round.	**10.** Seventh Ribs.	**16.** Neck.
5. Mouse-piece.	**11.** Middle Ribs.	**17.** Shin.
6. Leg.	**12.** Fore Ribs.	**18.** Cheek.

VEAL.

1. Loin, best end.	**5.** Flank.	**9.** Neck, best end or rack.
2. Loin, chump end.	**6.** Breast, best end.	**10.** Neck, scrag end.
3. Fillet.	**7.** Shoulder, or blade bone.	**11.** Breast, brisket end.
4. Knuckle.	**8.** Fore Knuckle.	

VENISON.

1, Haunch, or Hams.   3, Shoulder.   5, Scrag. or neck.
2, Ribs.   4, Breast.

MUTTON.

1. Leg.   4. Rack or neck, best end.   6. Breast.
2. Chump.   5. Shoulder.   7. Neck scrag end.
3. Loin.

PORK.

1. Leg of Pork, or Ham   3. Thin Rib.   6. Middling.
   of Bacon.   4. Spare Rib.   7. Chop, cheek or jowl.
2. Loin.   5. Hand or Shoulder.

THE

KENTUCKY HOUSEWIFE.

BY

MRS. LETTICE BRYAN.

CONTAINING NEARLY

THIRTEEN HUNDRED FULL RECEIPTS,

AND MANY MORE COMPRISED IN OTHER SIMILAR RECEIPTS.

STEREOTYPED BY SHEPARD & STEARNS,

West Third Street, Cincinnati.

PREFACE.

Believing there have been great improvements in the culinary art, and that there remains an immense space for more, has influenced the authoress to turn her attention almost wholly to the domestic economy of housewifery for the last few years. She has selected, perhaps, the greatest number of receipts that have ever been comprised in a similar work on the western continent. A considerable portion of them are original; some have been impressed by memory; and others taken from different authors, reduced to practice and improved, carefully avoiding the interpolation of accompaniments, seasonings, &c.; and the composition of such dishes, as the materials, and every condiment of which, are not common in her own country. She has endeavored as far as practicable, to arrange her receipts in the most concise, plain, and simple manner, making them so explicit, as for the inexperienced to comprehend, and practice them easily and adroitly. There are nearly thirteen hundred contained in her little work; some of which are quite plain and cheap; but if economy be consulted, none but what are well worth the trouble of preparing, and that will suit the tastes, and conveniences of many people. All unnecessary references have been avoided; also another practice in similar works that is far more objectionable, i. e., the too frequent repetitions of such directions as should be contained in the memory, as they not only swell a work unnecessarily, but make the receipts lengthy, and consequently irksome to look over. She has avoided inserting such directions as would prove injurious rather than instructive—one of which that is common in works of this kind, is the giving of the precise length of time to prepare a dish, which must be intuitively perceived by every reflecting mind, knowing there are varieties of quality in the the same tribe, or family of meats, and vegetables, and equally as much difference in the quantity of heat applied while cooking. It is justly complained of, for many a good dish have been badly prepared by the inexperienced following such directions. If I say a certain dish must be cooked for one hour, perhaps one will have a brisk fire, another a moderate one, and a third a very slow fire; what will then be the consequence? perhaps two out of three will be spoiled. In the place of such directions, the authoress has given infallible rules to ascertain when all made dishes are done, in their respective receipts. She flatters herself that she has so adapted them to the wants, conveniences, and pleasures of her country, that they will be a manual of equal benefit to people in almost every circumstance and situation. She has inserted some valuable pieces on preparations for the sick; and as she has so assiduously tried to make her little work useful and instructive, she sends it forth for an investigation before the public eye, not fearing but that it will receive as much patronage as it will be found to deserve.

INTRODUCTION.

You who have taken it upon yourself to be a helpmate for your companion, and a guide and governess to those who may be brought up under your care, discharge each devolving duty with care and precision, fulfilling the station of a housewife indeed, and not a wife only. Very much depends on your own conduct and management, to secure to yourself and family happy, and peaceful lives. Shun the deleterious practices of idleness, pride, and extravagance, recollecting that neither of them constitutes the lady. Never make your husband blush to own that you are his wife; but by your industry, frugality, and neatness, make him proud, and happy to know that he is in possession of a companion who is a complete model of loveliness and true elegance.

Have established rules for domestics and slaves to be governed by, and fail not to give them such advice as is really necessary to promote their own welfare as well as your own. Examine frequently your cupboard and other household furniture, kitchen, smoke-house, and cellar, to see that every thing is in its proper place, and used in the right manner, that nothing be lost, or wasted by the neglect of hirelings or servants. It takes but a short time each morning to secure such regulations; whereas, if neglected, hours may be spent in search of things which may be thrown out of their proper places: then of course in such regulations there is economy as well as comfort. Save your herbs and seeds; dry your fruits, and and prepare your sweet meats, catsups, vinegars, &c., in their respective seasons. Keep a supply of spices and peppers ground, and bottled: also sage, and other sweet herbs, which should first be powdered and sifted; corked up securely they will keep their strength and flavor, perfectly, and will be found very convenient, being always in readiness; besides there is no bustle, time lost, or retarded dishes, by the neglect of preparing the seasonings at a proper time, as they are often neglected till wanted for immediate use. Attend to the giving out of your meals, and proportion the seasonings to each dish yourself. This may be done at an early hour; and with the proper instructions to the cook, the lady may be relieved of further trouble during the day. Have your meals at regular hours, and in due time, and see that your table is set with neatness, and every thing on it well ordered, then there will be no danger of being frustrated by unexpected company. Never strive to have a great variety of made dishes on your table when you have but few to eat with you: perhaps half of them would not be tasted; it of course would only be a superfluous waste. Just try to learn what your company is fondest of, and have their favorites. A few things well ordered will never fail to give a greater appetite, and pleasure to your guest, than a crowded table badly prepared; and as there is a time for all things, there will be a time to crowd your table with delicacies. We should not only consult economy, but daily practice it; which is nothing more than a saving knowledge, carried into action. Such a course will bind up a lasting treasure for the rich, and secure a plentiful living to the poor.

KENTUCKY HOUSEWIFE.

SOUPS.

—◦✦◦—

BEEF SOUP.

Good soup may be made of any part of a fine fresh beef;
but the leg, or hock, is seldom used in any other way, and
makes equally as good soup as any other part of the beef.
Wash it clean, break it into two or three pieces, rub them
with salt, and boil it slowly and steadily till they are very
tender, carefully removing the scum, and keeping the pot
closely covered. When they get about half done, put in
some whole onions, white potatoes, turnips, carrots and tomatoes, and let them boil together till the whole is done.
Then take them out, strain the liquor into a soup-pan,
mash fine such of the vegetables as you wish to thicken
your soup, and put them into the liquor, which should be
about three pints in quantity. Add a tea-spoonful of celery
seeds, one of pepper, and a handful of shred parsley; simmer them together a minute or two, and serve it up. Be
careful not to season soups too highly with salt and pepper, as a lack of them can be easily supplied at table.

—◦✦◦—

A FINE BEEF SOUP.

Take any part of a fresh beef you fancy; trim off every
particle of fat, and boil the lean to rags, in a good quantity of water, carefully removing the scum, and keeping
it closely covered, to prevent the flavor from evaporating.
Pass the liquor through a sieve, to take out the bits of bone
and meat, that may be in it, and put it into a soup-pan, with

enough salt and pepper to season it. Flavor it highly with
tomato catchup, and any other kind you choose. Add two
spoonfuls of flour, mixed in half a pint of sweet milk, with
enough pounded crackers to thicken it, and boil them together a few minutes. Serve it hot, and put sprigs of
parsley over the top.

All soups should be introduced at the commencement of
dinner.

VEAL SOUP.

A knuckle or neck of veal makes excellent soup, and is
seldom used for other purposes. Break it into two or three
pieces, rinse them clean, salt and pepper them, and boil
them tender in a plenty of water, with a piece of lean ham
and such vegetables as you wish to flavor it. When all
are done, and there remain about three pints of the liquor,
strain it into a soup-pan, thicken it with a little flour,
beat up in sweet milk; or you may thicken it with ripe
tomatoes which have been peeled, and sliced onions, or
any vegetable you choose, if you have previously boiled
them tender in the soup. Boil it a few minutes with the
seasonings, add a small cup of rich sweet cream, stirring
it gradually, and serve it in a large tureen on toasts, crown-
ing it with sprigs of the green tops of asparagus or parsley. Some people like soup slightly acidulated with vinegar: do not season it thus yourself, but have a cruse-ful on
the table, to be used by those who prefer it so.

MUTTON SOUP.

Take four or five pounds of the rack or scrag of mutton; chop it up, season it with salt and pepper, and boil it
tender with a small piece of ham. When it boils hard,
skim it; then put in some whole carrots or turnips, or
both if you choose, and boil them gently together till the
whole is very tender. Have ready a clean pan, or rinse
out the same pot; place a sieve slanting over it, and pass
the liquor through it into the pan, which will take out
the small bits of meat and bones, if there be any; or you

may set it by the fire till they settle to the bottom, and turn off the soup from the sediments. Thicken it with boiled rice or barley, or mash some of the vegetables which were boiled in it, and thicken it with them; or, for a change, when the meat gets about half done, throw in some whole onions or tomatoes, having them neatly peeled, and when they are done quite soft, chop them small and stir them into the soup. Serve it up with dry toasts, and mash and season the turnips or carrots, and serve them in the dish with the meat.

Mutton soup is also good thickened with pounded crackers, very small suet dumplings, or noodles, boiled a few minutes to cook them, and seasoned with a little lemon juice or cream and parsley. Veal or beef soup may be made in either of these ways, and is equally good.

CHICKEN SOUP.

Take two half-grown chickens, clean them nicely, and cut them up; rinse them clean, season them with salt and pepper, and boil them with a few slices of the lean of ham. When it boils hard, skim it; then cover it and boil it slowly till the chickens are about half done. Have ready some noodles, or vermicelli, made in the usual manner, or small white potatoes, or onions neatly prepared and sliced; put them with the chicken, and boil them till tender, and the soup reduced to two quarts. Then take out the meat and stir in two spoonfuls of flour, mixed with a little sweet milk, till smooth; add a cup of sweet cream, a handful of chopped parsley or thyme, and serve it up with toasts. Partridge or pheasant soup may be made in the same manner.

SOUP OF GROWN FOWLS.

Having cleaned a fat young fowl, cut it up, rinse the pieces clean, and season them with salt and pepper. Put them into a pot, with enough water to cook them tender, leaving about three pints when done. When it boils hard, skim it; put in a small lump of butter, cover the pot, and boil the fowl gently till about half done: then put in a cup of rice, having first picked and washed it clean, and boil them together till all are done very tender. Then take out all the pieces of the fowl, select the breast, and some of the nicest of the other pieces; remove the skin, mince the meat from the bones, and put it again into the soup. Add a cup of sweet cream, and serve it hot in a tureen on sliced crackers. Grate a little nutmeg on the top, and lay round it on the edge of the tureen some sprigs of green asparagus or parsley. If you wish a larger quantity of soup, you should have more than one fowl, or it will not be rich enough for company. You may thicken the soup with vermicelli, noodles, pounded crackers, or small young potatoes: or, you may thicken it with the minced fowl and hard-boiled eggs, chopped small, adding cream and parsley.

FORCE-MEAT SOUP.

Boil a fine young fowl as before directed: when very tender, take it out and stir into the soup a large spoonful of butter, rolled well in flour. Add a large handful of force-meat balls, made about the size of a partridge's egg, dipped in the yolk of an egg and then in dry flour. Boil them a few minutes, and then put in a handful of little toasts, not larger than half a dollar, a handful of chopped parsley and a cup of sweet cream, or a glass of wine, which you choose.

HARE OR RABBIT SOUP.

Take a large hare, or two fine rabbits; case them, cut them into joints, and rinse them clean in cold water, but do not soak them in it; season them with salt and pepper, and put them into a pot with a few slices of ham and a good quantity of water. When it has boiled hard, remove the scum, put in a bundle of thyme, parsley, sweet marjoram, and a head of celery cut small, and some onions and white potatoes, if you choose; cover the pot, and boil it gently till the meat is ready to drop from the bones, and there remain two quarts of the liquor. Then take up the meat, pass the liquid through a sieve, pressing the seasonings, to obtain all the essence you can; put it into a pan or pot, and set it again on the fire. Stir in two large spoonfuls of flour, mixed in half a pint of sweet milk, with a large handful of force-meat balls, made about the size of a partridge's egg, dipped in the yolk of an egg and rolled in dry flour. Add a little powdered nutmeg, mace, and a glass of red wine. Just let it come to a boil, and serve it up on sliced crackers, toasts, or slices of light bread. Pick out some of the nicest pieces of the hare, and serve with the soup. Crown it with small sprigs of parsley, or green tops of asparagus, and send it to the table hot. If you choose, thicken the soup entirely with noodles, pounded crackers, biscuit, or boiled rice. Soup may be made in the same manner, of partridges, piegeons, pheasants, or grouse.

ANOTHER MODE.—Having prepared your hare, or rabbits, as before directed, boil them gently with a few slices of ham, till half done, removing every particle of scum as it rises. Have ready some small young white potatoes; scrape them, rinse them clean, split each one in two, and boil them in the soup till done, and the meat ready to drop from the bones. Then take it out, reserve some of the nicest pieces to send to the table whole, mince the remaining part of the meat from the bones, and put it into the soup, with a small cup of boiled rice. Add a small lump of butter, rolled in flour, a little powdered nutmeg and cloves, and a cup of sweet cream. Mix in any kind of catchup you choose; just let it come to a boil, and remove it from the fire; then stir in gradually the juice of one lemon; serve it hot, lay on the top some light sprigs of parsley, and accompany it with dry toasts. Squirrel soup may be made in the same manner, and is equally good.

⟶◦✦◦⟵

SQUIRREL SOUP.

Take two fat young squirrels, skin and clean them nicely, cut them into small pieces, rinse and season them with salt and pepper, and boil them till nearly done. Beat an egg very light, stir it into half a pint of sweet milk, add a little salt, and enough flour to make it a stiff batter, and drop it by small spoonfuls into the soup, and boil them with the squirrels till all are done. Then stir in a small lump of butter, rolled in flour, a little grated nutmeg, lemon and mace; add a handful of chopped parsley and half a pint of sweet cream; stir it till it comes to a boil, and serve it up with some of the nicest pieces of the squirrels. Soup may be made in this manner of small chickens, pigeons, partridges and pheasants.

VENISON SOUP.

Your venison must be quite fresh, as it is not fit for soup after the first five days. If it is a small one, take a whole shoulder, but if large, half a one will do. Chop it into several pieces, rinse them clean, and season them well with salt and pepper. Slice up a pound of ham, put it with the venison into a porridge pot; pour in enough water to cover the meat, add one or two sliced onions and a bunch of parsley, and boil it fast for a few minutes till scum rises; then remove the scum, cover the pot, and boil it gently till the meat is done very tender; after which take out the meat, reserve some of the nicest pieces to serve whole with the soup; mince from the bones a small portion of the other venison, and pound it in a mortar to a paste, adding a teaspoonful of celery seeds, one of mace, lemon and cloves, half a one of cayenne, and by degrees a glass of red wine. Strain the liquid into a soup-pan, and put in two ounces of butter, rolled in flour; mix the beaten yolks of two eggs in half a pint of entire sweet milk, and stir it in the soup; add the venison paste, stirring it by degrees; and before it comes to a hard boil, serve it up; put in a few small pieces of the reserved venison, and send it hot to table, with a plate of dry toasts and a dish of boiled rice, as both are much liked with venison soup.

FRENCH SOUP.

Take two pounds of fresh venison or veal, half a pound of ham, one chicken and two partridges, pigeons, or any other small birds; prepare them neatly, chop them small, and season them well with salt, pepper and mace; pour on a gill of molasses, and let them stand an hour or two: then put them on to boil, with enough water to cover them well, and boil them slowly and steadily till the meat is ready to drop from the bones. Afterwards take up the meat, and mince fine from the bones a small portion of each kind. Strain the liquid into a soup-pan; and if there are not at least two quarts of it, make that quantity by mixing in a little boiling water; stir in enough tomato soy to make it about as thick as cream; add a minced onion, two spoonfuls of currant jelly, and a tumbler and a half of claret or port wine; then stir in the minced meat, and before it comes to a boil, serve it up. Grate on the top a little nutmeg, lay on some light sprigs of parsley, or green tops of asparagus, and send it hot to table, with a plate of dry toasts and one of sliced crackers. The wine may be omitted in this soup, and sweet cream substituted, if preferred.

A FINE WHITE SOUP.

Take a pair of fat young fowls, and one set of calf's feet; clean them nicely, chop them into several pieces, and season them with salt, pepper and mace. Boil them slowly and steadily till very tender, removing the scum as it rises, and leaving about five pints of the liquor when done. Then strain the soup into a clean pot or pan, and stir into it gradually a pint of rich sweet cream. Remove the skin from the breasts of the fowls, mince the meat from the bones, and pound it fine in a mortar, with an equal proportion of boiled rice, the yolks of four boiled eggs, a spoonful of butter, a powdered nutmeg, a small handful of bitter and sweet almonds, and the juice of one lemon; stir it gradually into the soup, and in a minute or two serve it up. Send it hot to the table, accompanied with dry toasts and crackers.

BROWN SOUP.

Boil together four pounds of the lean of fresh beef or veal, a fat young fowl, having them neatly prepared and

well seasoned with salt, pepper and mace. Slice up half
a dozen onions, fry them brown in butter, put the onions
and gravy into the soup, and boil them slowly till the meat
is ready to drop from the bones, and the liquor reduced to
three quarts; then pass the liquid through a sieve into a
soup-pan, remove the skin from the breast of the fowl,
mince the meat fine from the bone, and put it into the
soup, with two dozen force-meat balls, not larger than a
nutmeg, and fried brown in butter. Add half a pint of
claret, two spoonfuls of currant jelly, two of tomato catchup,
a grated nutmeg, and a tea-spoonful of powdered cloves.
Just let it come to a boil, and serve it up. Send it hot
to table with a plate of dry toast.

MOCK TURTLE, OR CALF'S HEAD SOUP.

To have this soup in perfection, you must begin at least
six hours before you will want the soup. Having neatly
cleaned a large head and two feet, split them; put them
into a pot with a small piece of pork or ham, a good quantity of water, and enough salt and pepper to season them
well. Boil them slowly and steadily till nearly done, removing the scum as it rises; then put in four minced onions, four sliced potatoes, a handful of thyme, parsley and
sweet basil; boil all together till done, and strain the liquid into a soup-pan. Mince a part of the meat from the
head and feet, and put it into the soup, with a dozen force-
meat balls, about the size of a nutmeg, made in the usual
manner, and fried brown in butter. Pound to a paste half
a tea-cupful of boiled rice, the yolks of eight hard-boiled
eggs, a little grated nutmeg, mace and lemon peel; make
it into one and a half dozen balls, of equal size; roll them
in yolk of egg and flour, and drop them also into the
soup. Just let it come to a boil, then add half a pint of
madeira and the juice of one lemon, a tea-spoonful of
currie powder, and serve it up with dry toasts or crackers. This soup must be rich and highly seasoned, to represent what it is intended, therefore do not put in your
vegetables and other seasonings till the meat gets nearly
done, as by long boiling they will lose much of their flavor, and become almost insipid.

OYSTER SOUP.

Take two quarts of fine oysters from their shells; trim off the hard part, chop them small, and season them with a powdered nutmeg, and if they are fresh ones, sprinkle on a little salt. Strain their liquor into a soup pan, add a teaspoonful of whole black pepper, one of cloves, and half a dozen blades of mace; boil it till sufficiently flavored with the spices, strain it and return it again to the pan. Then put in the minced oysters, with their juices that may have exuded from them, and four ounces of butter rolled in flour; boil them five minutes, stir in gradually half a pint of sweet cream, and serve it up with toasts or slices of bread and butter.

A FINE OYSTER SOUP.

Boil a pint of water, till sufficiently flavored, with a dozen blades of mace, a grated nutmeg, a teaspoonful of whole black pepper, and one of celery seeds. Strain it from the spices, and return it again to the pan. Add a quart of entire sweet milk, and four ounces of fresh butter, divided and rolled well into four spoonfuls of flour; and having removed the hard part from two quarts of fresh oysters, mince them fine, and when the liquid begins to boil, stir them into it, and boil them for five minutes, or till sufficiently done; then stir in gradually half a pint of sweet cream, with the yolks of two beaten eggs, and pour it boiling into a tureen, on some bits of toasted bread or sliced crackers. Be sure you do not boil them too long, as it will render them tough and insipid.

LOBSTER SOUP.

Take a fresh knuckle of veal, break the bone in several places, rub it well with salt and pepper, and boil it till the meat is ready to drop from the bone, leaving about two quarts of the liquor, which must be strained into a soup pan. Having boiled two common sized lobsters tender, extract the meat from the bones and claws. Pound the coral, with an equal proportion of the meat, to a smooth paste, seasoning it with mace, cayenne pepper, cloves and grated lemon. Divide it into two equal portions; reserve one half to thicken the soup, and make the other half into little balls, the size of a partridge's egg; dip them in the yolk of egg, and roll them in dry flour. Cut the remaining part of the meat into small bits, and put them into the veal liquor, with two ounces of butter, divided and rolled in two spoonfuls of flour. Boil them together eight or ten minutes, and stir in the coral paste, and then drop in the balls; boil all together a minute or two, add a cup of sweet cream, gradually stirred in, and pour it boiling into a tureen. Grate a nutmeg on the top, lay on some light sprigs of parsley, and accompany it with slices of light bread, dry toasts, sliced crackers, or bread and butter

---

CLAM SOUP.

Put your clams into a pot of boiling water, to make them open easily, and as you take them from the shells, save the liquor. Having ready three pints of veal broth, made as directed for lobster soup, mix with it the liquor from a quart of opened clams; add twelve pepper corns, a few blades of mace, and a grated nutmeg; boil it a few minutes, skim it, strain it, and return it again to the pan. Mince the quart of clams, put them into the liquor, with four ounces of butter, broken up and rolled in flour, and let them boil gently for fifteen minutes. In the meantime, pound to a paste some of the veal, with equal proportions of boiled yolk of eggs, and bread crumbs, seasoning it highly with pepper, nutmeg, and grated lemon peel, and moistening it with yolks of raw eggs; make it up into a dozen little flattish cakes, not larger round than half a dollar; dust them with dry flour, and let them stand a few minutes, to dry a little. Then, when the soup has boiled the fifteen minutes, drop them into it; boil all together a minute or two longer, and serve it hot, with a plate of toasted bread. Another way is to have a larger quantity of liquor, and put in half as much rich force-meat, made in small balls, as you have clams, and a handful of toasted bread, cut into dice. Oyster soup may be made in this manner.

CATFISH SOUP.

Take a catfish, weighing six or eight pounds; skin and clean it nicely, removing the head; cut it up in five or six pieces; season them well with salt and pepper, and boil them tender, leaving about two quarts of liquor when done. Cut up some of the nicest of it into tolerably small pieces, and reserve them to serve in the soup; take another small portion, pick out every particle of bone, and pound the meat to a paste, mixing with it an equal portion of indian bread crumbs, boiled white potatoes, and boiled onions, moistening it with the yolks of eggs, and seasoning it with cayenne pepper, nutmeg, and chopped parsley. When it is quite smooth, make it into a dozen little balls, half as large as a hen's egg, dust them lightly with flour, and let them dry a little. Strain the liquor into a soup-pan; add a pint of rich sweet milk, four ounces of butter, rolled in flour, and if not sufficiently seasoned, put in a little salt, pepper and mace. When it boils up, skim it, and put in your pieces of fish, having sprinkled them lightly with flour, and then drop in the balls. Having beat very light the yolks of four eggs, mix them well with half a pint of cream, and stir it gradually into the soup. Stir it constantly till it raises the simmer, and pour it hastily into a tureen. Lay on the top some light sprigs of parsley, and send to table with it a plate of crackers, light bread, or bread and butter. You may for a change, have more of the liquor, omit the cream and milk, and slightly acidulate it with lemon juice or good vinegar. Eel soup may be made in the same manner.

ENGLISH PEA SOUP.

Take a fat young fowl, clean it nicely, cut it up, season it with salt and pepper, and boil it with a small piece of ham till about half done. In the meantime, gather your peas, which should be grown, but entirely green; hull them, rinse them in cold water, and boil them with the fowl. There should be about three pints of hulled peas, and three quarts of the liquor. When all is done, mash one pint of the peas to a pulp, return it to the liquor, to thicken it, and let the others remain whole.   Remove the skin from the breast, and some other nice parts of the fowl, mince the meat fine from the bones, and pound it to a paste, with an equal portion of the ham, seasoning it with pepper, nutmeg, and a few tender sprigs of mint, chopped fine.   When it is quite smooth, make it into small cakes, put over them beaten yolk of egg, and dust them with flour. Put into the liquor four ounces of butter, rolled in flour, and make it boil; then stir in half a pint of sweet cream, add the cakes, and serve it up hastily.   Send with it a plate of toasted bread.   You may substitute for the fowl, beef, veal, mutton, or any kind of nice game; ducks and pheasants make excellent soup with peas, and also pigeons and partridges.

ANOTHER MODE.—Having hulled three pints of peas, boil them with a few slices of ham and a little salt. When they are very tender, and there remains one quart of the liquor, take out the meat, and one pint of the peas; mash and press the peas through a sieve, and return them again to the liquor, to thicken it; add four ounces of butter, rolled well in flour, a quart of sweet milk, a grated nutmeg, and a small lump of loaf sugar, which many people think improves the taste of the soup more than any of the other seasonings.   Have ready some toasted bread cut into dice, put them in the bottom of a tureen, and when the soup has boiled a few minutes longer, pour it on the toasts, and send it to table warm.

FIELD PEA SOUP.

There are several kinds of field peas, some of which are unfit for soup, being very dark; there are two kinds that are white, and very nice for the purpose; the one is large, and the other quite small, being far the most delicate of this species.   They should be full grown, but not the least hard or yellow.   Take three pints of either after they are hulled, rinse them clean, and boil them with a small piece of pork or bacon.   When they are quite tender, take out the meat; and if they are of the large kind of pea, mash a part of them, to thicken the soup, but if they are small ones, do not break them, as they look much

prettier to serve whole.   There should be at least three
pints of the liquor, to which add four ounces of butter,
broken up and rolled in four table-spoonfuls of flour; season it to your taste with salt and pepper, boil it up, and
then stir in gradually a pint of rich sweet cream, and one
and a half dozen of little force-meat balls, not larger than
a nutmeg, made in the usual manner, and fried brown in
butter.

DRIED PEA SOUP.

Having hulled your peas, parboil them in clear water;
then drain them, rinse them in clear water, and boil them
with a small piece of pork or bacon, and prepare the soup
as above directed.   If properly made, it will be very near
as good as if made of the peas when green.

DRIED BEAN SOUP.

Take the small white beans, which are nicest for this
purpose, hull them, and parboil them in clear water till
they begin to swell.   Then rinse them in clean water, and
boil them till very tender, with a piece of salt pork; then
take out the pork and the beans; mash the beans to a pulp,
and season it lightly with pepper; mix with it an equal
portion of boiled rice, which has also been mashed fine;
make it into small balls or cakes; put over them the yolk
of egg, slightly beaten, dust them with flour, and spread
them out on a cloth to dry a little.   Having seasoned the
liquor with salt and pepper to your taste, put in a large
lump of butter, rolled in flour; boil it up, stir in half a
pint of sweet cream, and then put in the cakes or balls.
Serve it up immediately, or they will dissolve, and make
the soup too thick.   This is a plain, unexpensive soup,
but a very good one.

BUTTER BEAN SOUP.

Butter beans should be full grown, but tender.   Hull
them, rinse and boil them tender, in clear water, with a

little salt. Thicken the soup with butter, flour, pepper and cream, and serve it up with toasts or crackers.

ANOTHER MODE.—Boil a fat young fowl till about half done; then put in your butter beans, and boil them with the fowl till all are done, seasoning it sufficiently with salt, pepper and butter. Mash the beans to a pulp, make it into small cakes, and put over them yolk of egg and flour. Remove the skin from the fowl, mince the breast and some of the other parts, and put them in the soup, with the cakes; stir in enough flour and cream to thicken it, boil it up, and serve it. Dried butter bean soup may be made in either of these ways, after parboiling them in clear water.

ASPARAGUS SOUP.

Your asparagus must be young and tender; scrape and wash it neatly, and let it lie for a time in cold water; cut small some of the green tops, and put them also in cold water. Make a broth in the usual manner, of a few pounds of fresh veal or poultry, and a small piece of ham. Cut the stalks of the asparagus into pieces not more than an inch long, and boil them in the broth till tender, seasoning it with salt, pepper and butter. Mash to a pulp enough of the asparagus to thicken the soup, and let the other remain in pieces. Stir in a little rich sweet cream; just let it come to a boil, and serve it up with toasted bread cut in dice, dispersing over it some sprigs of the green tops.

OCHRA SOUP.

Make a plentiful broth in the usual manner, of fresh beef, veal or poultry. Put into it equal proportions of ripe tomatoes and young ochras, having sliced the ochras very thin, and pared and sliced the tomatoes. Boil them gently till completely dissolved, pass it through a sieve, and return it again to the pan. Have enough of the tomatoes and ochra to make it tolerably thick, season it to your taste with salt, cayenne and butter; and as soon as it comes to a boil, pour it into a tureen, on some small bits of toasted bread.

———⊙✦⊙———

MACCARONI SOUP.

Take five or six pounds of fresh beef or veal; cut several deep gashes in it, and soak it four or five hours in fresh water, to draw out the blood, changing the water two or three times; then break the bone in several places, boil it till the meat is ready to drop to pieces, adding a sufficiency of salt and pepper, and strain the liquid into a soup-pan. Have ready a pound of the best maccaroni; cut it up, and boil it in the soup till tender; then take it out, mash half of it very fine and smooth, return it to the liquor, and boil and stir it occasionally, till it is well mixed with the soup, which should be at least five pints. Then put in the remaining half of the maccaroni, with four ounces of the best cheese, grated fine; let it simmer a minute or two, stirring it all the time, and pour it into a tureen. You may make this soup with entire sweet milk, instead of broth, season it tolerably high with butter, and reserve the cheese to be served on a plate. You may also make it of poultry broth, by soaking the fowls in water after they are cut up, to draw out the blood.

———⊙✦⊙———

ONION SOUP.

Boil four or five pounds of fresh beef, veal or mutton, or a fat young fowl, with a small piece of bacon, having seasoned it well with salt and pepper. Remove the scum as it rises, and when the meat gets about half done, put in a dozen and a half of very small onions. Boil all together till done very tender, but be careful not to break the onions, as they look prettiest served whole. Pound a part of the meat to a paste, season it highly with pepper, nutmeg, mace and chopped parsley, and moisten it with a little wine; make it into small round balls, not larger than a cherry, and sprinkle them with dry flour. Put in enough butter rolled in flour to thicken the soup; add half a pint of cream and a grated nutmeg, and when it begins to simmer, drop in the balls, and serve it up.

POTATO SOUP.

Take a fine young fowl, prepare it nicely, seasoning it with salt and pepper. Boil it till about half done, with a small piece of pork or ham. In the meantime, scrape and rinse some large white potatoes, that are quite new, (old ones require a different process,) put them with the fowl, and boil them till all is tender. Then take out all the meat and potatoes; mash the potatoes to a pulp, season it with salt, pepper and butter; mix in the yolks of two or three raw eggs, to bind it; make half of it into small cakes, and flour them, and make the other half into small balls, roll them in flour, and fry them brown in boiling butter. Cut up the breast of the fowl, with some other nice parts, into tolerably small pieces; put them in the soup, thicken it with butter, flour and sweet cream. Just let it come to a boil, put in the prepared potatoes, and serve it up. To make soup of old, strong potatoes, they must first be par-boiled, otherwise the soup is not good, and is considered unwholesome.

PLAIN POTATO SOUP.

Having scraped and washed your potatoes, slice them up and boil them in water with a little salt till quite soft; then to each quart of the liquid, add a quart of sweet milk, or a pint of rich sweet cream, four ounces of butter, rolled in four table-spoonfuls of flour, and a little pepper and parsley; stir it till it comes to a boil, and then remove it from the fire.

TOMATO SOUP.

Peel and slice two quarts of tomatoes, and boil them till dissolved in two quarts of beef, veal or poultry broth;

then strain it into a soup-pan, put in a few more tomatoes that have been peeled and sliced, add a large lump of butter, and pepper and salt, to your taste; boil it till the tomatoes are done, stirring it frequently, and serve with it a plate of dry toasts or crackers.

GUMBO

Peel two quarts of ripe tomatoes, mix with them two quarts of young pods of ochra, and chop them small; put them into a stew-pan, without any water; add four ounces of butter, and salt and pepper to your taste, and boil them gently and steadily for one hour; then pass it through a sieve into a tureen, and send to table with it, crackers, toasts, or light bread.

BOUILLI SOUP

Having neatly prepared a fat young fowl, boil it with a small piece of ham, a head of celery, two or three onions and a handful of thyme and parsley. Peel and cut into dice some turnips and carrots; pare and slice some white potatoes, and put them all to boil in a separate pot, with a handful of butter beans, a little salt, and enough water to cover them well. Peel some ripe tomatoes and green cucumbers; remove the seeds, cut the thick part into shavings or ringlets, and stew them separately till done, adding a very little salt and pepper. Boil some red beets with the skins on till tender, and then peel and slice them thin and small. When the fowl is done, take it up with the piece of ham; pass the liquid through a sieve to free it from the strings of vegetables, and return it again to the pot; thicken it with a little flour, butter and cream, and season it to your taste with salt and pepper; then put in all the prepared vegetables in equal proportions, which should be cooked tender, but not broken up. The quantity of vegetables should be proportioned to that of the soup, making it as thick as you desire it.

Give it one boil up, and serve it with a plate of light bread or toasts. This soup is as much admired for its singularity as its fine flavor.

RICE SOUP

Pick and wash a pint of rice, boil it till quite soft, drain the water from it, and put it in tea-cups to congeal, filling them about half full. Make a rich broth of a piece of fresh beef, veal, mutton, poultry, or game; pass it through a sieve into a soup-pan, season it with salt, pepper and nutmeg, and thicken it with flour, butter and sweet cream. Just let it boil up, and no more. When the rice has congealed and taken the shape of the cups, turn them smoothly into a tureen, pour the soup boiling over them, and send it immediately to table. Barley soup may be made in the same manner.

MILK SOUP

Boil two quarts of entire sweet milk with a stick of cinnamon, a few cloves and a vanilla bean, till sufficiently flavored; then strain it, and return it to the pan. Beat the yolks of six eggs very light, mix them with half a pint of milk, and stir it gradually into the boiled milk; add four ounces of butter, rolled in flour, a grated nutmeg, and sugar to your taste. Just let it come to a boil, stirring it all the time, and remove it instantly from the fire, or it will curdle. Then stir in very gradually the juice of a lemon, and serve it immediately in a tureen on some baked apples, small bits of toasted bread, rusk, or pounded crackers.

CORN SOUP.

Take green corn that is very soft and full of milk; pick off the silk carefully, cut the grains about half from the cobs, and scrape off the remaining part with a knife. Have ready as much veal or poultry broth as you wish for your soup, and put in as much corn as will make it as thick as you desire; add enough butter, pepper and salt to season it well, and boil it gently till thoroughly done, stirring it all the time. Then stir in a cup of sweet cream, and pour it into a tureen. This is an excellent soup, cheap, and easily prepared.

ANOTHER MODE.—Take young corn that is full of milk, merely break the husk, and scrape out all the white substance of the grains with a knife. Beat very light the yolks of six eggs, mix them with a pint of sweet milk; add a small handful of flour, a little salt, pepper and nutmeg, and make it a thick batter with the scraped corn. Place a pan of boiling lard or butter over a bed of coals; drop in the batter by spoonfuls, and fry them a light brown on both sides; then put them on a sieve to drain. Having ready a rich poultry broth, season it to your taste with butter, salt and pepper, and make it a little thick with the scraped corn, and boil it till done, stirring it all the time. Then put in a little rich cream and the fried cakes, and serve it up.

—◦✦◦—

TURNIP SOUP.

Boil a nice piece of fresh beef or veal till about half done, carefully removing the scum. Have ready some small young turnips, a size larger than a hen's egg; scrape off the skin, leave on about an inch of the green tops, rinse them clean, and boil them with the meat till all is done. Then thicken the soup with a little flour and sweet milk, season it with salt and cayenne, give it another boil up, and serve it up with some of the turnips, which should remain whole. Turnip soup may be made of large turnips, but they should be sliced before they are cooked.

BEEF.

———◦✦◦———

GENERAL REMARKS.

In choosing beef, be particular to select such as has a lively open grain, an oily smoothness, a carnation color and white hard suet. These signs are always present with good beef.

The hind quarter of a beef comprises the sirloin, rump, round and leg, which, for practical convenience, are all subdivided, receiving other names, as is shown in the plate. The fore quarter contains the ribs, neck, brisket, and shoulder, which are also subdivided. The loin, round, brisket and ribs, may be cooked in many nice ways: the neck, leg and lower part of the shoulder, or shin, are seldom used for any thing else than soup. The separate pieces, which are the cheeks, heart, liver, &c., may be cooked in various ways.

The neatest and most genteel pieces for roasting are the sirloin and the fore and middle ribs, which should always be selected for nice company, as in fashionable houses other pieces are seldom roasted, but served up in some other way.

For roasting, it improves beef to lie in fresh water an hour or two; it serves to make it both tender and juicy. Then saw the bones or ribs on the under side, for the convenience of carving; wipe it dry with a cloth, and confine it on a spit, but be careful not to run it through a nice part of it, or through a part that will be exposed when served. Do not rub dry salt on it, as the outside will be disagreeably salt, while the inner parts will be too fresh. Stir as much salt as you think it will take to season it well, in a little cold water, with a small portion of pepper, and baste the beef with it frequently till you have used up the brine, or till the meat is sufficiently seasoned; then discontinue it, and baste with a mixture of fresh lard and hot water, until a sufficient quantity of essence has flown from the meat into the dripping-pan; then baste bountifully with it, till the meat is done, putting it on evenly with a large spoon, and turning the spit round occasionally, that every part of the meat may get done as nearly by the same time as possible. Roast it before a clear, steady fire, avoiding a smoke or blaze near the roaster, but supply the place or give sufficient heat with a bed of coals to roast it rather briskly. When you find it necessary, draw back the spit and enliven the fire by adding more fuel. If you are roasting a large piece, and the outside is likely to get too brown before the inner parts are done, pin a piece of white paper over it, to preserve the color. No certain length of time should be given for cooking meat in any way, as meat differs so much in quality, and there is so much variation in the quantity of heat applied to it while cooking. It is well enough to name the most common length of time required, but never be too positive. Some people choose their beef a little rare: in that case be your own judge: but if you wish it thoroughly done, try it with a fork; and if the bloody water oozes out, be sure it is not done: if it will admit the fork through with ease, and there is no appearance of blood, you may safely calculate that it is done. In the place of counting the hours by the clock, you will find it best to notice the fire and what you are cooking. When it is as near done as you wish it, remove the paper and sift on a little flour: shake it on very evenly through a dredging-box, and turn the spit very fast for a few minutes to raise a froth, basting the meat all the time with melted butter, which will make the froth much higher, lighter and more delicate every way, than to baste with the hot drippings. Avoid the appearance of dry flour, or its being put on in lumps, as either would spoil the beauty of the roast. When it is sufficiently rich, dish it with a light garnish. ·Skim the fat from the top of the drippings, season the remainder with any thing you choose, and serve it in a boat to accompauy the meat.

These directions should be remembered, that it may not be necessary to repeat it again and again in each receipt, as it is altogether superfluous.

TO CURE BEEF FOR SUMMER.

Beef for this purpose should be young, fat and tender, as the largest size is too coarse and tough for drying. It is best when killed late in the winter, allowing only enough time to cure it well before the weather gets too warm. Take a round from the beef soon after it is killed, and divide it into four equal parts. Prepare a good quantity of mixed spice in the following manner. Take equal proportions of allspice, cloves, cinnamon and nutmegs and cayenne pepper; pound them very fine, mix them together, and pass them through a fine sieve; then rub it well into the meat with your hands, and place it in a large tub; take plenty of salt to keep it well, and to every ten pounds add three ounces of saltpetre, three pounds of brown sugar and two quarts of molasses; mix it well, boil it for fifteen or twenty minutes, stirring it all the time, and skimming it well; then pour it over the beef, cover it, and let it stand till next day: then turn over every piece, rub the brine well into them with your hands, and cover them up again. Turn them over and baste them with the brine at least once in every two days, for two or three weeks; then hang it up and smoke it till well dried. It makes excellent chip for the tea-table, and is also very nice sliced thin, soaked for a few minutes in hot water, and slightly broiled and buttered.

Tongues may be cured in the same manner.

TO PICKLE BEEF.

Your beef must be recently killed: cut it into pieces of convenient size, and put it into a tub that is entirely tight, so that it will not leak a particle of brine. Take four gallons of water, mix with it six pounds of good salt, half a pound of saltpetre, a pound of brown sugar, a pint of molasses, and two spoonfuls of cayenne pepper; boil it a few minutes, skim it, cool it, and pour it over the beef; cover it, and put a small weight on the top, as the meat should be kept perfectly under the brine. This quantity of brine is the usual allowance for one hundred weight of beef. Look to it occasionally, and if the brine begins to have the least disagreeable smell, throw in more salt; and if a scum rises on the top, boil it a few minutes, skim it well, and when it gets entirely cold, pour it again over the beef, and cover it as before. This brine, if attended to as directed, will keep good for years. In two weeks the beef will be fit for use. Tongues may be cured in the same manner; also legs of mutton and hams. They should remain in the brine till well salted, which will take from two to three weeks—then hung up and dried. Tongues may be kept in pickle during the winter. Before the weather gets warm, they should be hung up and thoroughly dried, and put up in linen cases, and kept in a cool dark place, where the air can have access to them occasionally.

TO CORN BEEF.

When you corn beef in hot weather, choose the thinnest pieces, and if there are any bones in it, take them out. To every ten pounds of meat, allow a large spoonful of saltpetre, one of cayenne pepper, and half a pint of molasses; rub it well into the meat with your hands; then put on a sufficient quantity of common salt to keep it well. Have your tub of a suitable size, with several holes bored through the bottom, to admit the bloody brine to escape as it makes or exudes from the meat. Sprinkle the bottom of the tub with salt, and lay the meat in smoothly; then sprinkle a handful of salt on the top, tie a cloth tightly over it, and set in a cool place. In summer it will not keep well but a few days; in winter it will keep good for several weeks. The tender parts of mutton and veal, may be corned in the same manner.

Corned meat is generally cooked with vegetables, and better boiled than any other way it can be dressed. It is very good to serve cold, when boiled with enough mustard, horseradish and parsley to flavor it well.

TO COLLAR BEEF, IN COLD WEATHER.

Take the thin part of the loin of a fresh beef, rub it over with a small quantity of salt petre, and enough common salt to keep it well, and put it in a cool place for ten days; after which rinse it clean, and spread it out smoothly on a board. Mix together, and chop very fine, some parsley, thyme, sage, onions, and fat bacon, or fresh sausage meat, add a little pepper; spread it evenly over the meat, roll it up into a scroll, bind it up with tape, or pack-thread, to keep it close and compact, and boil it gently till very tender. Then remove the bandage; wrap up the meat loosely in a cloth, and place it between two smooth planks; put a weight on the top sufficient to press the meat flat, and set it in a cool place till next day; then trim the edges smoothly, and serve it with a light garnish of pickled radish pods, barberries, asparagus, or something equally suitable, and eat it cold, with scraped horseradish, mustard, oil and vinegar.

<hr>

TO STEW BEEF, PLAIN.

The ribby parts of a beef are generally preferred for stewing. Cut a piece of proper size, take out the ribs from the under side, wash the meat clean, and rub it over with enough salt and pepper to season it well; dust it with flour, put it in a pot with enough cold water to cook it tender, and when it boils hard, skim it, and then cover it, and stew it gently till about half done. Having some white potatoes ready prepared, put them under the meat, and stew them together till all are done. Transfer the meat to a dish by the fire, where it will keep warm; you may serve the potatoes whole, or mash them fine, moistening them with a little cream; thicken the gravy with a little flour, butter, cream and pepper, and pour it round the meat. Sweet potatoes are very nice, stewed in the same manner under fresh beef, after scraping them neatly.

TO STEW A ROUND OF BEEF.

Cut a piece as large as you wish, from a fresh round; take out the bone, and rub the meat well with a mixture of salt, cayenne, black pepper, powdered sage, cloves and mace. Extract the marrow from the bone, mix it with some hard lumps of fresh suet, minced fine, season it with salt and pepper, and fill the space whence the bone was taken with it. Lay some slices of fat bacon in the bottom of a stew-pan, strew on some minced onion and chopped parsley, and lay the round on that; lay some slices of bacon on the top; pour in enough cold water to cover the whole very well; cover the pan after removing the scum, and stew it gently till it is done very tender. Then strain the gravy, and return it again to the pan; add a small lump of butter, rolled in flour, a little made mustard, lemon pickle, and tomato, or any other kind of catchup you choose. Stir it till well incorporated, pour it immediately over the meat, garnish with little bunches of curled parsley, and send it to table warm, accompanied with mashed turnips or potatoes.

TO STEW A BRISKET OF BEEF.

Take a fresh brisket, saw off the ends of the bones, and saw them across on the under side in several places, for the convenience of carving; make several incisions nearly through it, beginning on the under side, and fill them with a mixture of chopped parsley and minced onion; season it well with salt and pepper, rubbing it on with your hand, dust it with flour, and stew it in a small quantity of water. About twenty or thirty minutes before it is done, put with it some small suet dumplings, made of a pound of minced suet, a pound of flour, cold water, and a little salt; they should be about an inch thick, and cut out with the edge of a small tumbler. When all are done, serve the meat and dumplings together in a dish, thicken the gravy with butter, flour, cream and pepper, and serve it hot in a boat. The ribs and rump of beef may be stewed in the same manner; they may also be stewed with white or sweet potatoes, or they may be stewed without any vegetables, and the gravy highly seasoned with the different kinds of catchup.

BOILED BEEF.

The round, fore, and middle ribs are all suitable pieces for boiling; and as it is rather a tasteless way of serving beef, it should be corned, or well salted.   Dust the meat with flour, and put it on in cold water; when it boils, skim it well, cover it, and boil it gently till at least half done, and then put in the vegetables, the most suitable of which are turnips, parsnips, carrots and potatoes.   They should be boiled with the meat till all are thoroughly done, as people seldom choose boiled beef the least rare.   Then skin and trim the beef neatly, and if the vegetable is turnips, or parsnips, drain them, mash them fine, and serve them smoothly in the dish under the meat; but if it is potatoes, mash them fine, and season them with butter, pepper and cream, and serve them in a separate dish.   Cabbage, cauliflowers, and broccoli are all common accompaniments to boiled beef, but they should be cooked by their respective receipts, as they are much nicer prepared in that way, than when boiled with the beef.

BEEF MORELLA.

Take a fine fat round, soon after the beef is killed, and rub it well with a mixture prepared thus: Mix together two ounces of saltpetre, half an ounce of cloves, half an ounce of allspice, half an ounce of mace, and the same quantity of nutmegs and cayenne pepper; pound them fine, pass them through a sieve, and mix it well with a quart of common salt, more or less, according to the size of the round.   Put it in a tub, cover it securely, and let it set for two weeks, turning it over once a day, and basting it well with the brine.   At the end of that time, wash it clean, fill the space from whence the bone was taken with a mixture of bread crumbs, butter, yolks of eggs, sage, and pepper; lay some slices of bacon at the bottom of a pan, put in the round, strew chopped suet thickly over it, and put two or three folds of paper over that, lest by long baking, it should get too brown.   Pour in a quart of water, and bake it with moderate heat, till thoroughly done, which will take several hours. Then put it in a large dish, pour over it half a pint of lemon catchup, and cover it securely with a cloth. It is eaten cold, with mustard, vinegar, &c. It should be prepared in cold weather, and will keep good a week. The gravy or essence will be found very fine for seasoning many dishes.

TO ROAST A LOIN OF BEEF.

A whole loin is too large to roast at one time, except for a very large company. Cut a piece of proper size from the thickest end, and soak it in fresh water for an hour or two, if practicable. Wipe it dry with a cloth; make several deep incisions in it, through a part which will not spoil the beauty of the piece when dished, and fill them with a stuffing made of light bread, butter, pepper, nutmeg and sage, and moistened with wine, or some nice kind of catchup; or you may fill them with a force-meat, made of oysters, suet, or bacon, bread crumbs and parsley, all chopped fine, and seasoned with sifted sage, salt and pepper, or you may fill them with mashed potatoes that are highly seasoned with butter, cream, salt and pepper. Wet a twine, or packthread, to prevent its scorching; tie it firmly round the loin, to keep the stuffing from coming out, and roast it before a clear, steady fire, as previously directed. While it is roasting, boil, peel and mash some white potatoes, season them highly with butter, cream, pepper and salt; make it smooth in a small, deep dish, and set it under the beef, to catch a small portion of the drippings, and then brown it lightly in an oven, or before the fire. When the beef is done, dredge and froth it as directed, and serve it up, garnished with scraped horseradish, or some nice kind of pickles. Skim the fat from the top of the drippings, season the remainder with a little brown flour and wine, lemon pickle, or catchup, and pour it warm in a gravy boat, to send to table with the roast; also accompany it with the potatoes. Sliced cucumbers, sliced tomatoes, cold slaugh, boiled rice, field peas, butter beans, beets and pickles, are all common accompaniments to roast beef.

TO ROAST THE FORE AND MIDDLE RIBS.

Take a piece the size you wish it; saw out the ribs on the under side, and soak it for an hour or two in fresh water; then wipe it dry, and spread it out smoothly on a board or table. Put evenly over it a mixture of grated indian bread, chopped suet, powdered sage, sweet marjoram and pepper, made moist with yolks of eggs, or any other stuffing you best like. Roll it up tightly, with the smooth side of the meat outwards; confine it with skewers, and roast it as directed. In the meantime, bake some fine sweet potatoes, peel them smoothly, set them under the beef at the last, to catch a little of the butter that drips from it, and send them up warm with the roast. Skim the drippings; season them with anything you choose, and serve them in a boat. You may substitute light bread crumbs for the indian, if you choose; or you may stuff it entirely with mashed potatoes, or for a change, roast it plain, without any stuffing.

BEEF ALAMODE.

Remove the bone from a round of fresh beef, and fill the space with a stuffing made of equal proportions of grated stale bread and minced marrow, or suet, seasoned with salt, pepper, mace, minced onions, sifted sage, and sweet marjoram, and moistened with yolks of eggs. Rub salt and pepper on the outside, dust it with flour, spread over it some small bunches of parsley and thyme, and sew it up in a piece of clean linen, to keep it in good shape, and prevent the stuffing from coming out. Put it in a pot with a small quantity of cold water, and a few turnips, carrots, and a head of celery, and boil it gently till the vegetables are done, turning it over once, and skimming the fat as often as is necessary. Then take off the envelopes put the meat in a pan of suitable size, strain over the liquor, add half a pint of wine, and a few spoonfuls of tomato or mushroom catchup, and bake it till done, and of a light brown on both sides. It may be eaten warm, or cold with mustard, &c. The essence is excellent for seasoning many made dishes, where such seasonings are required.

Alamode beef is often made without boiling, but it makes it much tenderer, and better every way, to boil it with the proper seasonings.

BEEF, MALAGA.

Take the thin part of the loin, or a rib roasting piece of a fresh beef; remove the bones smoothly, rub the meat with salt, pepper and nutmeg, and spread it out on a board. Disseminate evenly over it some grated stale bread, chopped suet, preserved currants and raisins, the juice and grated rind of a lemon, and a little powdered mace. Roll it up securely into a scroll, and confine it with skewers; stop up the ends closely with paste, to prevent the fillings from coming out, and roast it on a spit, as previously directed, only substitute butter entirely for lard. When it is nearly done, baste it with a thin batter, made of sweet cream and mashed potatoes; turn the spit regularly and rather briskly till the meat is done, and the basting a delicate brown, and serve it up garnished with grated bread, or small shells of puff paste. Season the drippings with brown flour and port wine, and send it in a small tureen. In helping round, fill the shells (which should be very small) with a slice of the beef, and some of the fillings to each.

BEEF, CASSEE ROLL.

Prepare a piece of beef as above directed, sprinkle over it a layer of minced oysters, grated stale bread, broken bits of butter, a little nutmeg, pepper, and if the oysters are fresh, add a small portion of salt. Roll it up securely, confine it with skewers, and lard it handsomely with slips of fat bacon, drawn through the flesh with a larding needle, forming diamonds. Dust it with flour, put it in a pan of suitable size; pour in a pint and a half of water, and half a pint of wine, or some nice kind of pickle or catchup; lay on some slices of bacon, and a piece of folded paper, to prevent its getting too brown, and bake it with moderate heat till thoroughly done. Thicken the gravy with butter and brown flour.

TO BAKE A BRISKET OF BEEF.

Select a brisket from a fat young beef, which has been recently killed, and remove the bones as smoothly as possible. Prepare a stuffing of minced oysters, shred parsley, grated ham, grated stale bread, yolks of eggs, salt, pepper and nutmeg; make numerous small incisions in the under side of the meat, and fill them with the stuffing. Rub it over with salt and pepper, and put it in a pan, on some slices of bacon; put round it some small force-meat balls; pour in a pint and a half of water, and enough wine or catchup to season it well; lay slices of bacon over the top, to prevent its getting too brown and dry, and bake it with moderate heat till well done. Then take off the bacon, shake on a little finely grated bread through a dredging box, put on some broken bits of butter, and brown the dredging a little. Garnish the brisket with the force-meat balls, and serve the gravy in a boat.

A PLAINER MODE.—Remove the bone, season the meat with salt and pepper, and bake it in a moderate oven till nearly done. Then having boiled some white potatoes, mash them fine, season the pulp with butter, cream, salt and pepper; make it into a smooth cake, and put it under the meat, or make it into rolls, or balls, as you choose. Bake them together till done, and a light brown, and enrich the gravy with butter, cream, flour and pepper.

———⟡———

A BAKED LOIN OF BEEF.

Take a piece of suitable size from the thick part of the loin; make several incisions in it, and fill them with mashed potatoes, which are seasoned with butter, cream and pepper; season it with salt and pepper, put slices of bacon over it, and bake it till about half done, pouring in a pint and a half of water at the first. Scrape and rinse some sweet potatoes, put them under the meat, and bake them together till all are done, raising the lid no more than is really necessary to ascertain how they are coming on. Baste the meat lightly with a thin batter, made of washed potatoes and sweet cream, and brown it delicately.

This is a plain but a very good way to bake a loin. A brisket may be baked in this manner with sweet potatoes, or any other nice part of the beef, first removing the bones.

BEEF OLIVES.

Cut smooth slices from a round of beef about half an inch thick, six inches long and six wide; beat them lightly with a rolling-pin, and spread them out smoothly on a board. Prepare a stuffing of fresh suet, bread crumbs, parsley, sage, pepper, salt, nutmeg and grated lemon, all chopped fine, moistened with the yolks of eggs, and worked together till well incorporated. Spread a smooth coat of it over the slices of meat, roll them up tightly, and confine them with little skewers. Roast them on a small spit before a brisk fire, basting them for a few minutes with salt water and pepper, and then with butter. Mix with the drippings a small handful of grated bread, a little minced onion or chopped parsley, and enough wine and catchup to flavor it well; and when the olives are thoroughly done, and of a light brown, serve them up with the gravy poured round them.

A SCOTCH FRY OF BEEF.

Cut long smooth slices, about half an inch thick, from a round of fresh beef; beat them evenly, and lay them for a few minutes in fresh water; then drain the water from them, sprinkle them with salt, pepper and sifted sage, and put them at full length into a stew-pan. Put on them some minced onion, chopped parsley and grated bread; pour in a mixture of water and currant wine, merely enough to cover them; add a lump of butter, rolled in flour, and a few small force-meat balls, and stew them with the pan closely covered till nearly dry; then fry them till a delicate brown in the same gravy, and garnish with the force-meat balls.

TO FRY BEEF STEAKS.

The finest pieces for steaks are the last cut of the sirloin and round. Steaks taken from the chuck and rump, have a coarse grain, and are tougher and much inferior every way to those of the loin and round. Cut them moderately small, and about half an inch thick; beat them tender, but do not break them or beat them into rags. Lay them in a pan of fresh water a few minutes, which will make them juicy; drain the water from them, spread them out smoothly, and sprinkle them lightly with pepper and salt, and dredge them well with flour. Have ready a pan of boiling lard, placed over a bed of clear coals, and fry the steaks in it till a light brown on both sides. Thicken the gravy with flour, butter, cream and chopped parsley, and minced onion, if you choose it. Serve them up with the gravy in a covered dish, and send them to table as warm as possible.

BROILED BEEF STEAKS.

Place a gridiron over a bed of clear coals, and clean and grease the bars well. Having prepared your steaks as for frying, with the exception of seasoning them, broil them on the gridiron till thoroughly done, turning them over frequently; then transfer them to a hot dish, sprinkle them immediately with salt and pepper, and put on a few spoonfuls of melted butter, and you may slightly acidulate them with flavored vinegar, or lemon juice, if you like them so. Cover them and send them up hot.

A BEEF STEAK PIE.

Butter a deep dish, and line it with rather a thick sheet of pie-paste. Cut some small thin slices from the thick part of a loin of fresh beef, and beat them tender, but do not tear nor break them to pieces; season them with salt and pepper, and put a layer of them on the paste in the bottom of the dish. Remove the hard part from an equal proportion of oysters to that of the steaks, and mince them fine; season them with a little pepper and nutmeg, and if they are fresh ones, add a little salt; put a layer of them over the steaks, dispersing among them some broken bits of butter, rolled in flour, and some small thin squares of the paste. Do this till the dish is full, strain on a little of the oyster liquor, and fill the dish with water; then put a sheet of the paste over the top, notch and ornament it handsomely with paste leaves and flowers, and bake it in a moderate oven. Another mode is to substitute for the oysters fresh beef's marrow, or minced suet, and for the dumplings, white potatoes, neatly scraped and sliced.

TO HASH BEEF.

Take cold beef, both fat and lean, which has been boiled tender; mince the meat from the bones, put it into a sauce-pan with a small quantity of water, and simmer it a few minutes: add one or two large onions, cut small, a good lump of butter, rolled in enough flour to thicken the gravy, three or four sliced biscuits, salt and pepper, and a gill or more of rich sweet cream, gradually stirred in. Just let it come to a boiling point, stirring it occasionaly, and serve it up in a deep dish with the gravy about it.

You may make hash of beef that is under-done, but then it must boil a while, and is never so good as if the meat was cooked tender at the first. If you have cold white potatoes, that have been previously boiled, you may slice a few of them, and warm them with the hash; but do not put in too many, or it will spoil the taste of the gravy, by absorbing much of its richness. No other vegetable is suitable to intermingle with beef hash. If you make it of boiled beef, some of its liquor would be preferable to water for the gravy.

ANOTHER WAY TO DRESS COLD BEEF.—Cut small thin slices from a piece of cold boiled, roasted or baked beef; sprinkle them with pepper, grated nutmeg and lemon; dip them into a common pancake batter, and fry them a light brown in boiling lard, turning them over once. Transfer them to a warm dish, pour out a part of the lard, (which will answer for other purposes, or for frying beef again,) stir into the remainder a lump of butter, rolled in flour, and a little gelly catchup or sweet cream, and pour it over the fry.

VARIEGATED BEEF.

Pick the strings, &c., from some hard lumps of fresh suet, sprinkle them lightly with salt and dry flour; tie them up in a small linen bag, drop it in a pot of boiling water, and boil it hard for a few minutes; then take it out, dry it, and rub it as fine as you can. Boil and peel a smoked tongue, cut it up, and pound it to a paste in a mortar, moistening it with a little wine or brandy, and oiled fresh butter. Boil till tender, in a small quantity of water, an equal portion of a round of pickled beef with any kind of nice vegetables with which you wish it flavored, and pound it also to a paste in a separate mortar, first removing every particle of fat, and moistening the lean as you proceed with some of the liquor in which it was boiled. Prepare a sufficient quantity of spice to flavor it well by pounding, sifting and mixing together equal proportions of nutmegs, mace, cinnamon, cloves, pepper and lemon peel. Stratify the suet, tongue and beef paste, in small potting cans, dispersing between each layer some of the mixed spice; press them down as closely as possible, that they may conjoin, so as to look streaked, or variegated when sliced. Pour a little oiled butter and brandy on the tops, tie a folded cloth firmly over each, and keep them in a cool place. It is used at the tea-table and at luncheon.

BEEF SAUSAGE.

Chop up the tender part of a loin of fresh beef, with some leaf-fat of pork, in the proportion of three pounds of beef to one of leaf. Pound them to a paste, season it with salt, pepper and sifted sage; make it a little moist with water, and stuff it into skins, having them neatly prepared and soaked in vinegar. Hang them in a cool place to dry, and you may cut them into links, and boil, stew, fry or broil them.

SAVORY BEEF.

Take the most tender parts of a fresh beef, mix with it one fourth its weight of the leaf of pork, and prepare it

..s directed for sausage. After it is a smooth paste, season it highly with sage, thyme, sweet basil, sweet marjoram, summer savory, nutmegs, cloves, pepper, and salt; all made fine, sifted, and mixed together. Work it till well incorporated, put it up in small potting cans, pour on a little brandy, or oiled butter on the tops, cover them securely, and keep them in a cool place. When you wish to make use of it, moisten it with a little wine, make it into cakes, sprinkle them lightly with flour, and fry them brown in lard, or butter, which should be boiling when they are put in, lest they become saturated with it; drain them, and send them up warm.

TO BAKE A BEEF'S HEART.

Trim the heart neatly, wash it clean, and rub it well with salt and pepper. Make a stuffing of bread crumbs, suet, or fat bacon, sifted sage, pepper and salt; all made fine, moistened with yolks of eggs, and worked till well incorporated. Enlarge the cavities of the heart with a sharp knife, and fill them with the stuffing. You may lard the heart with strips of fat bacon, or not, as you choose. Put it in a pan, with three gills of water, one of wine, and two ounces of fresh butter; make the remaining part of the stuffing into balls, and lay them round it; put slices of fat bacon over it, to prevent its getting too brown, and bake it with moderate heat. Garnish with the balls of stuffing, and thicken the gravy with brown flour, and any kind of catchup you choose.

TO STEW A BEEF'S HEART.

Prepare the heart neatly, and boil it till about half done, in a small quantity of water. Then cut it up in small pieces, put them in a sauce-pan, with a pint of the liquor in which it was boiled, or more, if the heart be a large one; add a little salt, pepper, and two minced onions, and boil it gently till tender. Thicken the gravy with a spoonful of flour and a gill of sweet cream, gradually stirred in; add a few small toasts, sliced biscuit, or crackers, and when it comes to the boiling point, serve it up with the gravy. Garnish with small force-meat balls, fried brown in butter.

A BEEF'S HEART FRIED.

Cut it in slices half an inch thick; beat them tender with a rolling-pin, and lay them for a few minutes in a pan of fresh water. Then squeeze out a part of the water; season them with salt and pepper, dredge them with dry flour, and fry them brown in boiling lard. Season the gravy with butter, flour, chopped parsley, and flavored vinegar. Pour it over the fry, and serve it hot.

TO FRY BEEF'S KIDNEYS.

Trim them neatly, split them in two, and let them lie in salt for at least twenty-four hours. Then slice them tolerably thin, and sprinkle them with pepper and flour; fry them in boiling lard till a light brown on both sides, and thoroughly done throughout, and transfer them immediately to a warm dish. Have ready a sufficient quantity of melted butter; stir into it a little brown flour, pepper and minced onions; add a small portion of tomato catchup, currant jelly, and red wine, or slightly acidulate it with lemon juice, or good vinegar, give it a boil up, stirring it all the time, and transfuse it at once into the dish over the fry.

TO FRY BEEF'S LIVER.

Select a good liver, and let it lie in salt twenty-four hours; this will draw out the strong taste, that is much objected to. Cut it into thin, smooth slices, rinse them in two or three cold waters, and wipe them dry, pressing them with a cloth, sprinkle them lightly with black pepper, and dust them with flour. Have ready a pan, with a good quantity of boiling lard, place it over a bed of clear coals, and lay in the sliced liver at full length, as it will not do to crowd them much; fry them hastily, but do not let them burn, for the liver of any animal is much more liable to scorch than any other part. When they are a nice brown on both sides, and done through, (which you may tell by taking up a piece on a plate, and cutting it,) place them by the fire in a covered dish. Pour out a part of the lard, and stir into the remainder a small lump of butter, rolled well in flour, a tea-spoonful of kitchen pepper, and two spoonfuls of tomato, or lemon catchup; and you may also add, if you are fond of the flavor, a minced onion, or a small handful of shred parsley; give it a boil, and pour it over the liver. It is excellent when rightly prepared.

TO BROIL BEEF'S LIVER.

Prepare it as before directed, only do not flour the slices. Having ready a clean hot gridiron, placed over a bed of clear coals, grease the bars well with a piece of fresh suet, or a lump of lard, which will be found most convenient to tie it up in a linen rag. Broil the liver on it till done thoroughly, and both sides of the slices a nice brown, turning them over as often as is necessary. Serve them up hot, with a very little melted butter poured over.

BEEF CHEEKS.

Separate the cheek from the head, rub it well with salt, and let it lie a day or two; then wash it clean, and boil it in plenty of water, with a piece of bacon; when it is so tender that the bone will slip out easily, then take it up, remove the bone, sprinkle on the meat a little powdered sage, and bread crumbs, put on some broken bits of butter, and brown it before a brisk fire.

BEEF'S CHEEKS HASHED.

After boiling them tender, mince the meat fine from the bone, put it in a pan, with enough water for the gravy, add a large spoonful of butter, rolled in flour, a minced

onion, a spoonful of lemon pickle, or of vinegar, one of
tomato catchup, a tea-spoonful of currie powder, and a
little salt and pepper; simmer a few minutes, and serve
it up. These are very good dishes when rightly prepared, though through prejudice, or for lack of knowledge how to prepare them, they are seldom used.

BEEF'S LIVER BAKED.

Take a thick piece of liver that is free from gall and
bile, and that has lain in salt twenty-four hours; wash it
clean, make several deep incisions in it, and fill them with
a force-meat, prepared in the following manner: Take
equal proportions of fat bacon, fresh suet and bread crumbs,
chop them fine, and mix them well together; season it
with salt, black pepper, nutmeg and sifted sage, and moist-
en it sufficiently with yolks of eggs. Having stuffed the
liver with the force-meat, bind it up with tape, to keep
it close and compact, rub it over thickly with lard, and
put it in a pan of suitable size, on some slices of bacon;
lay some more slices on the top, pour in three gills of
water, one of wine, and two spoonfuls of tomato catchup, and bake it till done throughout, with rather a slow
heat. Thicken the gravy with butter, brown flour and
currant jelly. A nice thick piece of beef's liver may be
roasted. Season and stuff it as before directed; wrap it
up in white paper, and roast it before a clear, but moderate fire, basting it frequently with butter. Have a rich
made gravy, highly seasoned with red wine and currant
jelly.

FRIED SWEET-BREADS.

Take as many sweet-breads as you wish, cut them of
proper thickness, and season them lightly with salt and
black pepper, dip them in common batter, made of flour,
milk and eggs, and fry them a pretty brown on both
sides, in boiling lard or butter. Thicken the gravy with
flour, cream and pepper, and serve it up with the sweet-
breads.

SWEET-BREADS WITH OYSTERS.

Fry the sweet-breads as before directed, and prepare the oysters thus: Select the finest oysters, trim off the hard part, rinse them and wipe them dry; season them with salt, cayenne pepper and nutmeg; roll them in yolks of eggs, and then in grated bread, and fry them a light brown in boiling butter; drain them and stack them in a dish with the sweet-breads in alternate layers. Season the butter with cream, pepper, nutmeg and yolks of eggs; stir it till it comes to a simmer, add a small handful of chopped parsley, and pour it over the fry.

TO ROAST A BEEF'S HEART.

Trim the heart neatly, enlarge the cavities, and fill them with a rich force-meat, made of minced oysters, chopped suet, bread crumbs, sage, chopped parsley, salt, pepper, grated nutmeg and yolks of eggs, all worked together till well incorporated; or you may fill them entirely with fresh sausage meat. Rub it over with lard, wrap it up in a piece of paper, and roast it by the directions given for beef. For gravy, take that of the dripping-pan, and enrich it with red wine and currant gelly.

TO STEW BEEF'S KIDNEYS.

After letting them lie in salt a day or two, boil them with a small bit of bacon till nearly done; then cut them into mouthfuls, put them into a stew-pan, with enough of the liquor in which they were boiled to cover them; add a good lump of butter, rolled in flour, and a large handful of small force-meat balls, which have been rolled in yolks of eggs and flour, and nearly dried; boil them a few minutes, stir in a cup of sweet cream and minced onion, or a handful of shred parsley, and serve them up with the gravy about them.

TO ROAST BEEF'S KIDNEYS.

In whatever way beef's kidneys are dressed, they should previously lie in salt for at least twenty-four hours.

Prepare them neatly, rub them over with lard or butter, wrap them up in several folds of paper, wet it to prevent its scorching, and roast them in hot wood ashes on a clean hearth. When thoroughly done, remove the envelopments, and serve up the kidneys with melted butter, highly flavored with red wine and currant gelly.

Many people think this to be the most delicious way of dressing beef's kidneys.

BOILED TRIPE.

Take it from the beef as soon as it is killed; empty it immediately of its contents, scrape and wash it clean, and let it lie in fresh water till next day; then scrape it again, wash it clean, soak it for twenty-four hours in weak brine; next day scrape it, and soak it again for twenty-four hours in water, with a handful of salt. By this time, if properly managed, it will be very white and nice. Cut it into several pieces, and boil it in a good quantity of water till nearly done, removing every particle of scum, and keeping the pot closely covered. It will take several hours to boil it tender: then put it into a stew-pan with some of the liquor in which it was boiled, and sweet milk, mixed in equal proportions; add a good lump of butter, rolled in flour, some black pepper, and several minced onions; stew them gently till all are well done, stir in a glass of sweet cream, and serve them together, putting the onions under the tripe and pouring on the gravy.

FRIED TRIPE.

Having boiled the tripe till very tender, cut it into tolerably small pieces, and sprinkle them with pepper; lay each slice in a plate of yolks of eggs, slightly beaten, and then in one of grated bread, making as much of it adhere to them as possible. Have ready over a bed of coals a pan of boiling lard, lay them side by side in it, and when both sides are a light brown, drain them, and serve them up with a boat of onion sauce. Or, you may slice a few onions, fry them brown in the lard, stir in a little butter, flour, cream and pepper, and pour it round the fry.

BROILED TRIPE.

After boiling the tripe till very tender, cut it into slices of proper size, and sprinkle them lightly with black pepper. No salt will be required, as they should be sufficiently seasoned before they are boiled. Place them on a clean gridiron, over a bed of clear coals, first greasing the bars well with suet or lard, to prevent the slices from sticking to them; turn them over once, and as soon as they are a delicate brown on both sides, transfer them to a warm dish by the fire. Having melted a small quantity of butter in a sauce-pan, add a very little chopped parsley and enough lemon juice or good vinegar slightly to acidulate it; pour it at once over the tripe, and send it up warm.

TRIPE WITH OYSTERS.

Having boiled the tripe very tender, cut it into small pieces of equal size, and put them into a stew-pan, with enough sweet milk to cover them; add a small lump of butter, rolled in flour, a little black pepper, and give it a boil up. Have ready an equal proportion of fine fresh oysters; rinse them clean, trim off the hard part, and put them into the pan with the brine; boil them a few minutes only, as, if boiled too much, they will become hard and swiveled. Mix the beaten yolk of an egg with a glass of sweet cream; stir it in gradually and serve them up with the gravy. Lay on the top some light sprigs of parsley, and garnish the edge of the dish with small toasts or little heaps of grated bread.

A FRICANDO OF BEEF.

Cut slices from a round of fresh beef about an inch thick, and sufficiently large to cover the bottom of a small dish; beat them lightly and smoothly, rinse them, and put on a little salt, pepper, nutmeg and minced onion; put them at full lengths into a stew-pan, with a lump of butter, rolled in flour, and enough water to cover them; lay on the top a few slices of bacon, cover the pan, and stew them gently till nearly done; then take them out, lard them over handsomely in diamonds with slips of the fat of bacon, about half an inch wide, drawing them through the flesh with a larding needle, and brown them quickly before a brisk fire. Thicken the gravy with sweet cream and finely grated bread, take out the slices of bacon, serve the gravy in a boat, to accompany the fricando, and garnish with sliced lemons and broken bits of fruit gelly, put round alternately on the edge of the dish.

TO BROIL DRIED BEEF.

Trim a piece neatly, slice it thin, pour boiling water on them, and let them stand for a few minutes, which will draw out the superfluous salt, and make them tender and juicy. Broil them hastily, but lightly, on a clean gridiron over a bed of clear coals, having the bars rubbed with suet, and turning them over once. Serve them up hot, with a little melted butter and pepper poured over them.

TO BOIL A SALTED OR PICKLED TONGUE.

Wash and scrape it clean, and boil it gently in a good quantity of water, with a small piece of bacon and some turnips, carrots, or any kind of vegetables with which you wish it flavored. Whilst it is boiling, peel and cut in the shape of flowers, some fine red beets, and stew them tender in a small quantity of water, seasoning them with salt, pepper and butter; prepare some white and yellow beets, if you have them, in the same manner, in a separate pan; or you may substitute for them turnips and carrots. As soon as the tongue is so tender that you can pierce it through with a fork without difficulty, draw off the skin smoothly, put the tongue into a dish of suitable size, put on a little pepper and butter, and lay the prepared vegetables around it alternately, resembling flowers. Accompany it with a dish of mashed turnips, carrots or potatoes, and a boat of melted butter, seasoned with pepper.

ANOTHER MODE.—After boiling it tender, peel it, sprinkle it with pepper, shake on through a dredging-box some finely grated bread, put on some broken bits of butter, and brown it delicately before a brisk fire. In the mean time, having boiled some white potatoes, peel, mash them fine, and season the pulp with butter, cream, salt and pepper; make it into rolls or balls, and lay them round the tongue. Send with it a boat of melted butter, seasoned with pepper.

TO BOIL A SMOKED TONGUE.

Select a large thick tongue, as thin ones are not good when dried: wash and scrape it well, put it into a small kettle of lukewarm water, and set it by till next day; then put it into a kettle of cold water, and boil it gently till tender throughout, which will take several hours: after which, peel it smoothly, trimming off the homely parts of the roots; put it into a dish of suitable size, put on a little melted butter and pepper, and garnish with bunches of curled parsley.

ANOTHER WAY TO DRESS A SMOKED TONGUE.—Having boiled it very tender, peel it smoothly, put it into a pan with some of the liquor in which it was boiled, a large spoonful of butter and a gill of red wine, and stew it for fifteen or twenty minutes, turning it over several times; then drain it, dredge it with finely grated bread, shaking it on through a dredging-box; put on some broken bits of butter, and brown it lightly before a brisk fire. Garnish it with lumps of currant gelly, thicken the gravy with finely grated bread and chopped parsley, and pour it hot into a small tureen or gravy boat. Have stewed fruit and mashed potatoes to eat with it. It is a nice accompaniment to poultry and game.

TO BROIL A BEEF'S TONGUE.

Take a fine smoked tongue, cut off a piece of the fat, or root end, which is not fit for broiling; peel the middle part of the tongue, and cut it across in very thin, smooth slices; broil them hastily, but very little, on a well greased gridiron over a bed of clear coals, turning them over once; place them in a warm dish, and pour over a few spoonfuls of melted butter, seasoned with currant jelly and red wine. It is a nice supper dish. If you choose, you may first boil it, and then slice and broil it as directed. Beef's heart, dried and broiled in the same manner, is excellent. It is also good served with butter and pepper only.

VEAL.

REMARKS.

The fore quarter of a calf consists of the neck, breast and shoulder. The breast and best end of the neck, which is frequently called the rack, may be handsomely dressed in various ways. The scrag is the thick part of the neck: it is a coarse piece, and is not admired by many people only for soup. The shoulder may also be cooked in different ways. The loin, fillet and knuckle compose the hind quarter. The best end of the loin, as is shewn in the plate, should always be roasted, as it is the nicest way of dressing it. The chump end may be stewed or baked. The fillet is an admirable piece, and may be cooked in many delicious ways. The knuckle may be boiled with vegetables, but is principally used for soup. The separate pieces comprise the head, feet, heart, liver, tripe and sweet-breads, which may also be cooked in different ways. The flesh of good veal is firm and tender, so that you may pinch it easily with your nail. The lean is of a lively, clear, light red, and the fat hard and white. In whatever way veal is dressed, it should be thoroughly done, as the least rawness or appearance of blood, renders it disgusting. It improves veal to lie in milk and water for an hour or two previous to roasting. Then wipe it dry, confine it on a spit at a proper distance from the fire, which should be clear and steady. It will require several hours to roast it well. At first it should roast slowly, and gradually moved closer to the fire as it gets nearer done. Put a little salt water, seasoned with pepper, in the dripping pan, and baste with it till the meat is well seasoned; then discontinue it, and baste with lard, till you have plenty of its own drippings, which should then be used. After it has been down some time, but before it begins to look brown, pin white paper over it, to preserve both the fat and color of the roast, as it should not get brown. When it is done, (which you may tell by sticking a knife through the under side,) remove the paper, dust the meat lightly with flour, set the spit close to the fire, and turn it very fast, till a rich froth is raised on the meat, basting it all the time with butter. Then serve it up with a light garnish, and put evenly over it a few spoonfuls of melted butter. For gravy, skim the drippings, season them in any way you like, and serve it in a boat.

TO ROAST A LOIN OF VEAL.

If the loin is very large, and more than you wish for one roast, cut it in two, and take the best end, which contains the kidney. After soaking it, roast it by the directions. Skim the fat from the drippings, and if they are too rich, add a few spoonfuls of boiling water; stir in a very little brown flour, and chopped parsley; just let it come to a boil, and serve it in a boat. Garnish the roast with sprigs of curled parsley, and accompany it with mashed potatoes, boiled rice, and sliced cucumbers, raw tomatoes, or cold slaugh. In carving a loin, help each guest to a part of the kidney, if it is ever so small a bit, as it is considered a great delicacy.

TO ROAST A FILLET OF VEAL.

Remove the bone, roll up the fat flap, confine it with skewers, and if practicable, let it lie in milk and water

for an hour or two, turning it over several times. Fill
the space whence the bone was taken with fresh sausage
meat, grated ham, seasoned with pepper, sage and chopped parsley, or minced oysters, seasoned with pepper and
nutmeg, and mixed with a small proportion of bread
crumbs, butter and chopped parsley. Make numerous
small, but deep incisions in the outside of the fillet, and
fill them also with some of the stuffing. [A very nice filling is slips of ham, about half an inch wide, and long
enough to put one end to the bottom of the incision, while
the other end will be at least an inch above the surface
of the fillet, and then confine the ends down with little
skewers.] Roast it as directed, covering it with paper,
to preserve the fat, and prevent its getting too brown, and
baste it freely at the last with butter. When it is thoroughly done, and handsomely frothed, serve it up; garnish with sliced lemon, or lumps of fruit jelly, and accompany it with boiled ham, mashed potatoes, or boiled rice,
and raw cucumbers, raw tomatoes, or cold slaugh. For
gravy, use that of the dripping-pan; if it is too rich, skim
it, and pour in a little boiling water, if not rich enough,
add some melted butter; season it with pepper, brown
flour, or grated bread and chopped parsley, or currant
jelly and red wine, either is good.

TO ROAST A SHOULDER OF VEAL.

Take out the bone, cut the shoulder of a proper shape,
and make deep incisions in it, not more than one inch
apart. Prepare a stuffing of fresh, hard lumps of suet,
fat of bacon, bread crumbs, or mashed potatoes, sifted
sage, chopped parsley, yolks of eggs, pepper and salt; all
chopped fine, and worked till well amalgamated; fill the
incisions with it, and roast the shoulder as directed for
roasting veal, trying it on the under side with a fork or
sharp pointed knife, to ascertain when it is done. As long
as there is the least appearance of bloody water oozing
out, it is not done, and should be roasted till the essence
which oozes out when pierced through with a knife or
fork, is white, and entirely clear of blood; then it is tho-

roughly done. These rules are infallible. Garnish with bunches of curled parsley, and thicken the gravy with brown flour, mushroom, or tomato catchup; or soy, have boiled ham on the table, also mashed potatoes, or boiled rice, and some kind of raw vegetables. Pickles and stewed fruit are frequent accompaniments to roast veal.

TO ROAST A BREAST OF VEAL.

Separate the joints of the breast for the convenience of carving, and trim it neatly; skewer the sweet-breads to the back, make numerous small incisions in it, and fill them with minced oysters, or grated ham, and chopped parsley, seasoned with pepper, nutmeg and lemon; skewer on the outside some slices of ham or bacon, cover it with paper, and roast it as directed. When thoroughly done, take off the envelopment, baste the breast for a time with sweet cream, then move it near the fire, and dredge and froth it richly. Skim the drippings, stir into them a small handful of grated bread, a minced onion, and a dozen or two of force-meat balls, not larger than a nutmeg, that have been fried brown in butter. If there should not be enough drippings for the gravy, stir in a little melted butter and boiling water; give it a boil up, and serve it in a boat. Garnish the breast with green pickle, and send with it some suitable vegetable. In carving the breast, help with it some of the sweet breads, as far as they will go.

TO ROAST A NECK OF VEAL.

Take the best end, which is called the rack, take out the ribs, and spread out the meat on a board. Lay some thin slices of light bread over it, put slices of butter evenly over them, sprinkle on some powdered nutmeg, sifted sage, powdered mace, grated lemon peel, and cayenne pepper; all mixed together, and passed through a fine sieve; lastly, grate on some ham, fat and lean together, roll it up, and confine it with skewers. Roast it as directed, frothing it handsomely at the last. Lay round it some slices of lemon on the edge of the dish, and season the drippings with currant jelly and red wine, or brown flour and catchup. Serve with it a dish of rice, and cold slaugh, cucumbers, or tomatoes.

TO BOIL A SHOULDER OF VEAL.

Having washed the shoulder very well, season it with salt and pepper, dust it with flour, and put it in a pot of cold water, with a small piece of bacon; when it boils hard, skim it, then cover it, and boil it moderately till about half done. Having ready some turnips, parsnips, or carrots, neatly scraped and rinsed; put them in with the meat, and boil them together, till all are done very tender. Trim the veal, lay it in a dish of suitable size, put on a few spoonfuls of the top of the liquor in which it was boiled, and spot it over at intervals with black or red pepper. Cut the bacon in very narrow slips, and lay them round it. Take out the vegetables with a perforated ladle, that the liquor may drain from them, mash them fine, season the pulp with butter and cream, make it smooth in a small deep dish, and sprinkle on some red or black pepper. The scrag end of a neck of veal may be boiled in the same manner. Onions may be boiled with a shoulder of veal, but they should be served whole, with melted butter and pepper. Butter beans and field peas are frequently served with boiled veal.

A KNUCKLE OF VEAL BOILED.

A knuckle of veal when boiled very tender, with proper seasonings, is admired for its numerous fat, sinewy tendons, but if it is boiled in too large a quantity of water, and not very tender, it is a tough and insipid dish. Select a large fresh knuckle, with as much fat about it as possible; season it with salt and pepper, rub it well with lard, and boil it till about half done, with some onions and celery, or some turnips and carrots. Then take out the vegetables, which by this time will be done very soft, strain the liquid, and return it again to the pan. Have ready a pound of the fat part of a ham, cut it into small, thin slices, skewer the ends together, and put them in with the knuckle; add a large lump of butter, rolled in flour, and boil them together till the knuckle is so tender that you can pick it to pieces with a fork. In the meantime, boil some rice or barley tender, in milk and water, to accompany it, and season it with butter, salt and pepper. Garnish the knuckle with the curled slices of ham, having withdrawn the skewers, and send the gravy in a boat. Have vinegar and mustard on the table, as they are much liked with a knuckle of veal.

TO HASH A KNUCKLE OF VEAL.

Having boiled it tender, cut the meat into mouthfuls from the bone, put them into a stew-pan, with a sufficient quantity of the liquor in which it was boiled, for the gravy; add a good lump of butter, rolled in flour, a minced onion, a tea-spoonful of grated lemon, one of cayenne pepper, and a dozen force-meat balls, a size larger than a partridge's egg, which have been rolled in yolk of egg and flour; add a spoonful of flour, and boil them gently for a few minutes. Have ready a deep dish, lined with small toasts, stir gradually into the hash the juice of half a lemon, pour it at once in the dish on the toasts, and send it up warm. Have vinegar to season it at table, if preferred so.

TO STEW A BREAST OF VEAL.

Separate the joints of the breast, and lard it handsomely and regularly over the outside with slips of fat bacon, drawing them through the flesh of the breast with a larding needle. Season it with salt and pepper, dust it with flour, and put it in a stew-pan, with enough cold water to cover it well. When it comes to a hard boil, skim it, then cover it, and stew it gently till nearly done. Have ready a quart of hulled green peas, put them under the breast, add a large lump of butter, broken up and rolled in flour, and stew them together till tender.

Stir in a glass of sweet cream with a little pepper, and serve the breast and peas in separate dishes, putting some of the gravy over each. A breast of veal may be stewed in the same manner with white potatoes, sweet potatoes or onions.

A FILLET OF VEAL STEWED.

Remove the bone, fill the space with slices of ham or salt pork; roll up the fat flap, and confine it with skewers; rub the fillet well with salt and pepper, dust it with flour, and put it into a pot with enough cold water to soak it tender. When it boils hard, skim it, and then cover it and stew gently till it is nearly done, which will take several hours, and which you may tell by trying it with a fork. Have ready a pound of ham or bacon; cut it into small thin slices, and curl them round little bones, or hickory pegs, and confine the ends together with skewers; dust them well with flour, and put them in with the veal: also put in some onions, green peas, white or sweet potatoes; add some butter, rolled in flour, and continue stewing it till thoroughly done: then stir in a cup of rich sweet cream, transfer the vegetable to a deep dish without mashing or breaking them, and pour on a few spoonfuls of the gravy; dish the fillet, remove the skewers and bones from the curled slices of bacon; lay them round the fillet on the edge of the dish, and put over a few spoonfuls of the gravy.

TO STEW A SHOULDER OF VEAL.

Rub it well with salt and pepper, and dust it with flour, skewer some slices of ham all over the surface, and stew it in a tolerably small quantity of water till nearly done, keeping the pot closely covered; then put in a head of celery, some onions or green peas, with butter, and stew them till tender: or you may put in some small suet dumplings, made of equal proportions of chopped suet and flour, a little salt, and made into a stiff dough

with cold water, then rolled into a sheet an inch thick,
cut out with the edge of a wine-glass, or small tumbler,
floured and put in while the water is boiling. It may
also be stewed without either, the gravy thickened with
butter and flour, and served up with a dish of butter-
beans, green or field peas, or stewed beets.

TO BAKE A FILLET OF VEAL.

Prepare a stuffing of bread crumbs, chopped suet, grated ham, minced onions, pepper, salt, grated lemon and
sifted sage, moistening it sufficiently with yolks of eggs,
and working it till well incorporated. Take the bone
from the fillet, and fill up the space with the stuffing;
make numerous small incisions in it, all over the outside,
and fill them also with the stuffing, pressing it down hard.
Rub it with salt and pepper, skewer slices of ham or salt
pork all over the surface, and put it into a pan with a
small quantity of water; put a piece of folded paper
over the top, and bake it in a moderate oven till more than
half done; then put under it some sweet potatoes, that have
been neatly scraped and rinsed, and continue to bake it moderately till done very tender; transfer the potatoes to a
small deep dish without breaking, dispersing among them
some broken bits of butter. Thicken the gravy with
butter, brown flour and tomato, or mushroom catchup,
or currant jelly and red wine; pour it into a gravy boat,
and garnish the fillet with force-meat balls fried in butter.

TO BAKE A BREAST OF VEAL.

Separate the joints of the breast, trim off the sharp
ends of the bones, and rub it over with salt and pepper. Make small deep incisions in the outside of it, forming rows or diamonds. Cut narrow slips of the fat of
ham or bacon, about half an inch wide, half an inch
thick, and between two and three inches long; season
them with pepper, nutmeg and grated lemon, and put
four of them into each incision, pressing them down
hard, so as to leave the ends only about an inch above

the surface of the veal. Put it into a pan of suitable
size, with enough water to prevent its burning; lay slices of bacon on the top, and folded paper on them, to prevent its getting too brown and hard, and bake it in an
oven with moderate heat. In the mean time, having
boiled some white potatoes tender, peel them, mash them
to a pulp, season it with butter, cream, salt and pepper;
make it into rolls, and lay them round the meat to brown
a little. When all are done, lay the potato rolls in a
small deep dish; thicken the gravy with brown flour
and butter, add a little red wine, lemon pickle or catchup;
give it a boil up, put a few spoonfuls over the potatoes,
and serve the rest in a boat. Garnish the breast with
green pickles, or pickled beets.

Pickles, boiled rice, sliced cucumbers, raw tomatoes
and cold slaugh, are all excellent accompaniments to
baked veal. A fillet of veal may be baked in this manner.

TO BAKE A NECK OF VEAL.

Take the thick part of the neck, which is the scrag,
a piece that is not much admired, being comparatively
coarse and tough; make numerous incisions in it, and fill
them with grated ham, chopped suet, or minced oysters,
that are highly seasoned with salt, pepper, grated nutmeg,
and lemon. Sprinkle salt and pepper on it, rub it over
with lard, put it into a pan with a pint of water and half
a pint of wine, or a gill of lemon, mushroom or tomato
catchup; put folded paper over the top, and bake it with
moderate heat, raising the lid and paper occasionally,
and basting the meat with the gravy. When it gets
about half done, lay round it some force-meat balls, and
bake them with it. When it is thoroughly done, remove
the paper, shake on some grated bread through a dredging-box, and put on an ounce of butter, broken up; brown
it a little, and serve it with the balls around it and the
gravy in a boat. Accompany it with potatoes and raw
vegetables.

A GRILLADE OF A BREAST OF VEAL.

Separate the joints, trim it neatly, and roast it as directed till nearly done; then put it into a stew-pan, pour over a quart of rich highly seasoned gravy, sprinkle on some bread crumbs, add a large lump of butter, rolled in flour, some force-meat balls, a minced onion, a tea-spoonful of curry powder, some wine, mushroom, walnut and tomato catchup: stew all together fifteen or twenty minutes. Garnish with force-meat balls, and send the gravy in a boat.

RAGOUT OF A BREAST OF VEAL.

Prepare it as for a grillade, score the top, rub over it a mixture of powdered sage and sweet marjoram, skewer on some small slices of ham, and roast it till nearly done; then put it into a stew-pan with enough highly seasoned gravy to cover it well, add some whole white potatoes, onions, turnips, carrots and a head of celery cut small, all having been boiled till nearly half done, and stew them gently together till all are done very tender. Serve the breast with the vegetables laid whole in separate piles around it, and send with it a boat of rich, highly seasoned gravy.

VEAL CUTLETS.

Cut large smooth slices from a fillet or leg of fresh veal, beat them lightly with a rolling-pin, and season them with salt, pepper, grated nutmeg and lemon; grate as fine as possible a part of a stale loaf of bread; make a thick batter with it, sweet milk and beaten egg, seasoning it with salt. Have ready in a frying-pan some boiling lard, dip each cutlet into the batter, and fry them brown on both sides in the lard. Transfer them to a warm dish by the fire, pour out a part of the lard, add to the remainder a lump of butter, rolled in flour, a small cup of boiling water, a small glass of wine, or some nice kind of catchup, two minced onions and the juice of half a lemon. When it boils hard, put in the cutlets; let them stew for four or five minutes, and serve them up with the gravy. It is a nice breakfast dish.

VEAL OLIVES.

Having taken out the bone, cut several slices the full size of the leg; beat them lightly, and lay them for half an hour in sweet milk; then wipe them with a cloth, and spread them out smoothly on a table or board; spread thickly over them grated ham or minced oysters, sprinkle on some salt, pepper, grated nutmeg and powdered cloves; add some finely grated bread and bits of butter, and roll them up tightly, confining them with skewers. Roast them before a clear but moderate fire, basting them with butter as they may require, and when done throughout, serve them up garnished with sliced oranges or lemons, and send to table with them a boat of drawn butter, flavored with nutmeg and orange juice. They may be introduced as a side dish at the dinner table.

VEAL COLLOPS.

Prepare several slices of veal as above directed; lay on each a slice of ham and a smooth layer of mashed potatoes; sprinkle on a little sifted sage and cayenne pepper, roll them up and confine them with skewers; lard them handsomely with slips of bacon, and roast them till done, pinning white paper over them to preseve the bacon. In the mean time prepare a rich gravy of boiling water, butter, chopped parsley, salt, pepper and mace; boil it up, put in the collops with some minced oysters, and boil them together for six or eight minutes; then stir in gradually a glass of sweet cream, with the yolk of an egg, and serve all together in a dish. If you have not got the oysters, you may substitute little forcemeat balls.

CHOPSA-LA-MANTA OF VEAL

Cut small pieces from a rack of veal, which is the best end of the neck; divide it so as to have a bone in each, the end of which should be left bare one inch. Beat them flat with a roller, season them with salt, pepper and grated nutmeg, put over them beaten yolk of egg, and roll them in bread crumbs; wrap them up in pieces of white paper, and broil them on a gridiron over clear coals till they are thoroughly done, basting them occasionally with butter; then take them carefully out of the envelopes, lest the crumbs should fall off; wrap strips of curled white paper round the end of each bare bone, and lay them in a dish with the wrapped ends towards the edge. Send them warm to table, with a boat of onion, tomato or parsley sauce. They are eaten at breakfast.

STEWED CHOPS OF VEAL.

Prepare them as before directed, only you need not leave any of the bones bare. Make a batter of milk and eggs, thickened with equal proportions of flour and mashed potatoes. Have ready a frying-pan of boiling lard; dip each chop in the batter, and fry them a nice brown on both sides in the lard; then pour out a part of it, stir into the remainder a lump of butter, rolled in flour, a cup of boiling water, some pepper, salt, sifted sage, sweet marjoram and a tea-spoonful of curry powder. Put in the chops, and stew them a few minutes, add the juice of an orange or half a lemon; serve them up hot with the gravy poured round, and garnish with sprigs of curled parsley. They are fine for breakfast.

A FRICANDO OF VEAL.

Cut as large slices as you can get from a fillet of fresh veal, beat them lightly with a rolling-pin, and season them with salt and pepper; lard them in rows or diamonds with slips of bacon, dust them lightly with flour, and fry them a nice brown in boiling lard or butter. Transfer them to a warm dish by the fire, and having cut some bacon into small slices, and skewered the ends together, fry them brown also, and garnish the dish with them, first withdrawing the skewers. Mince very fine some onions or ripe tomatoes, after peeling them, and stir them into the butter with a spoonful of brown flour and two of lemon catchup; give it a boil up, pour it at once over the fricando, and send it up warm. They may be eaten at breakfast or supper.

FRIED STEAKS OF VEAL.

Cut them from the fillet or leg, having them tolerably small and about half an inch thick; beat them evenly, not tearing them in the least, lay them for a minute or two in a pan of fresh water or milk, which will improve them greatly; then squeeze them a little, spread them out smoothly, sprinkle them with salt and black pepper, and dust them with flour. Have ready a frying-pan of boiling lard, place it over a bed of clear coals, and put in your steaks side by side, not crowding them too much, a fault that is often practised. As soon as they are a nice brown on both sides, put them into a warm steak-dish by the fire, thicken the gravy with a little flour, cream and chopped parsley, or minced onion, give it a boil, stir in gradually the juice of half a lemon; pour it over the steaks and send them up warm. Or, you may omit the cream, and flavor the gravy with mushroom, tomato or any kind of catchup you choose.

BROILED VEAL STEAKS.

Prepare them as above directed, only do not season them. Have ready a clean hot gridiron, placed over a bed of clear coals, rub the bars with suet to prevent the steaks sticking to them, and broil them hastily on it, turning them over once or twice; then put them into a warm steak-dish, sprinkle them immediately with salt and pepper, pour on some melted butter with chopped parsley, and send them to table as warm as possible. These dishes are also nice for breakfast and supper.

STEAKS WITH JELLY.

Broil and season them as directed, and stack them with slices of currant, quince or tomato jelly; garnish the dish with small lumps of jelly, and send them up hot with a small boat of wine sauce.

A VEAL PIE.

Cut some small steaks from the leg, fillet or loin of a fresh veal, beat them tender, and season them with salt, pepper and nutmeg; stew the bones and trimmings of the veal in a small quantity of water, to extract the gravy; strain it into a sauce-pan, and stew the steaks in it till nearly done, adding a large lump of butter, rolled in flour. Line the bottom and sides of a deep dish with lard or dripping paste, and roll out another sheet for the top or lid, and also one for dumplings, which should be cut into small squares and sprinkled with flour. Cut some small slices of boiled ham, and put them with the squares of paste and steaks in the dish, in alternate layers; pour in the liquor or gravy, and if it is not sufficiently rich, put in some bits of butter; put on the lid of paste, notching or girdling it neatly round the edge, stick a bunch of paste leaves and flowers in the centre of the pie, and bake it in a moderate oven till a light brown.

A SWEET-BREAD PIE.

Slice the sweet-breads thin, and stew them till nearly done in a rich highly seasoned gravy. Boil three or four eggs, peel them, and cut each in two. Take as many oysters as you have sweet-breads, rinse them clean, trim off the hard part of them, and stew them a few minutes with the sweet-breads. Have ready a deep dish, lined with a sheet of puff paste; put in your prepared materials, stratifying them, add a large lump of butter, rolled in flour and broken up, a grated nutmeg and the gravy in which the sweet-breads and oysters were boiled; put a lid of paste over the top, ornamenting it handsomely with scolloped or crimped leaves of the paste, and bake it till a nice brown in a moderate oven.

MINCED VEAL.

Take a piece of cold roasted or baked veal; mince it fine from the bones, fat and lean together; put it into a pan with some nice gravy, which has been drawn from the trimmings and coarse pieces of fresh meat; add a lump of butter, rolled in flour, a glass of red wine, and a few spoonfuls of mushroom, walnut or tomato catchup; just let it come to the boiling point, stirring it all the time, and serve it up with the gravy. Lay small buttered toasts or very small shells around it on the edge of the dish, and send it to table warm. In helping round fill the shells with the mince and the gravy.

HASHED VEAL.

Take cold boiled or stewed veal, and mince it as before directed. Put it into a pan with a little water, or what is better, some of the gravy, or liquor in which it was boiled or stewed; add a large spoonful of butter, one of flour, one or two minced onions, some pepper, salt and two or three cold biscuits, sliced thin; let it come to a boil, stir in a glass of sweet cream, and serve it up with the gravy about it.

VEAL FRITTERS.

Shred some cold boiled or roasted veal as fine as possible, and season it with salt, pepper, grated nutmeg and lemon. Make a common fritter batter of milk, eggs and flour, and stir the mince into it. Have ready a frying-pan of boiling lard, placed over a bed of coals; drop the batter into it by large spoonfuls, and fry them brown on both sides; then drain them, and send them up warm with a small boat of melted butter and wine. Beef fritters may be made in the same manner.

VEAL CAKES.

Take cold roast or boiled veal, cut the meat from the bones, and chop it fine with some onions and parsley;

add some pepper, salt, sifted sage, and enough catchup, or flavored vinegar, to make it sufficiently moist. Work it well, make it into small cakes, dip them in yolk of egg, roll them in bread crumbs, and fry them brown in boiling lard. Drain them, transfer them to a warm dish, pour over a few spoonfuls of melted butter and white wine, and send them up warm. Beef cakes may be made in the same manner. These dishes are chiefly introduced at breakfast.

VEAL PATTIES.

Mince some cold roast or boiled veal very fine, and season it with nutmeg, lemon, mace and cloves. Have ready some very small shells of paste, fill them with the mince, fill them up with a rich gravy, and a few spoonfuls of white wine to each, grate some stale bread thickly over the top, put on some broken bits of butter, and brown them delicately with a salamander, or hot shovel. Or you may substitute mashed potatoes for the bread crumbs, put on some bits of butter, and brown them in a Dutch oven. Cold roast beef may be warmed in the same manner.

A VEAL PUDDING.

Remove the fat and gristle from a piece of cold boiled veal, and pound the lean part of it to a paste, moistening it with oiled butter, and seasoning it with pepper, mace, and nutmeg. Mince an equal portion of fresh hard lumps of suet, sprinkle it lightly with salt, and mix it with the veal paste. Mix with it an equal proportion of preserved cherries and raisins, and stir it into a common batter, made of milk, eggs and flour, having no more of the batter than is necessary to bind the other ingredients together; add the juice of an orange or lemon, with the grated peel, beat it well, pour it in a buttered dish, and bake it in a moderate oven. Serve it warm, with a boat of melted butter, sugar and wine.

VARIEGATED VEAL.

Boil very tender two smoked tongues, peel them, cut them up, and pound them to a paste, moistening it with oiled butter as you proceed. Having seasoned with salt, and boiled tender an equal proportion of the lean tender part of a fresh veal, pound it to a paste also, moistening it with oiled butter. Keep them separately, season them with cayenne pepper, nutmeg, mace, cloves, and grated lemon; add the juice of one lemon, and a small glass of white wine to each parcel of the meat, work them till well incorporated, and put them together in small potting cans, stratifying them, that they may look nubilated or variegated when sliced. Press it down hard, and finish by pouring a little oiled butter, and a few spoonfuls of brandy on the top; cover the cans, and keep them in a cool, dry place. It is introduced at the tea-table, and should be sliced before it is served.

TO STEW A CALF'S HEART.

Trim the heart neatly, enlarge the cavities, and fill them with a rich force-meat; lard it handsomely on the outside, dust it with flour, and stew it in a small quantity of water, with some force-meat balls and slices of bacon. When it is done, enrich the gravy with butter, flour and cream, and serve the heart up right in the dish, with the balls laid round it.

TO BROIL A CALF'S HEART

Cut it into thin, smooth slices, beat them lightly, and broil them hastily on a gridiron, first rubbing the bars with a lump of suet, to prevent the slices sticking to them. When they are done, put them in a warm dish, sprinkle them immediately with salt and pepper, and pour over them a few spoonfuls of melted butter, with chopped parsley. It is fine for breakfast or supper. Calf's heart may be fried, baked or roasted, as directed for beef's heart.

TO BROIL CALF'S LIVER.

Take a nice piece of liver, rub it with salt, and let it lie for at least twenty-four hours; otherwise it will have a strong, disagreeable taste. Slice it tolerably thin, rinse them in several cold waters, and wipe them dry with a cloth. Have your gridiron hot and well greased, and broil them rather slowly on it, till thoroughly done, turning them over once or twice. Then put them in a warm dish, sprinkle them immediately with pepper and salt, and pour on some melted butter, with a few spoonfuls of lemon, walnut, or onion pickle. It is excellent when done in a proper manner.

TO FRY CALF'S LIVER.

Prepare it as before; season them with salt and pepper, dredge them with flour, and fry them brown in boiling lard. Dish them, and set them by the fire, pour out a part of the lard, add to the remainder a lump of butter, a spoonful of browned flour, a small cup of boiling water, and one or two minced onions; give it a boil, and pour it over the fry.

LARDED CALF'S LIVER.

Take a nice piece of calf's liver, after lying in salt a day or two, wash it clean, and lard it handsomely with slips of fat bacon. Put some slices of bacon in a stew-pan, put in the liver, with two or three minced onions, cover it with water, and stew it gently for several hours. Then take it out, sprinkle on some grated bread and broken bits of butter, and brown it before a brisk fire, moistening it occasionally with a little wine. Garnish it with sprigs of parsley, and send with it a boat of rich, highly seasoned gravy. It may be stuffed and roasted to look very nice.

TO STEW SWEET-BREADS.

Split your sweet-breads, season them with salt and pepper, and stew them till nearly done. Have ready an equal quantity of fresh oysters, trim off the hard part, rinse them clean, and put them in with the sweet-breads, add a large lump of butter, rolled in flour, some salt, pepper, grated nutmeg and mace. Stew them gently together till all are done, then stir in a glass of sweet cream, and the juice of half a lemon very gradually, and serve it up immediately, lest it curdle. Lay round it, on the edge of the dish, some small toasts, and send it up warm.

BROILED SWEET-BREADS.

Parboil them, having first salted them well, then season them with pepper, nutmeg and grated lemon; dip them in yolk of egg, and then in bread crumbs, making as many adhere to them as possible; wrap them up in pieces of paper, giving each end a twist, to envelop them entirely, and broil them till thoroughly done, basting them occasionally with a little butter. Then take them out of the papers, lay them in a dish, garnish with force-meat balls, fried in butter, and pour over them a small portion of melted butter and wine.

CALF'S TRIPE.

Calf's tripe should be prepared in every respect like beef's, only it does not require so much cooking.

TO STEW A CALF'S HEAD.

Having cleaned the head neatly, take out the brains and tongue, season the head with salt, and boil it till nearly done. Then cut the meat from the bones in tolerably small pieces, put them in a pan with a quart of rich gravy, drawn from coarse pieces of meat; add a large lump of butter, rolled in flour, some force-meat balls, pepper and nutmeg; stew them till very tender, and just before you take it from the fire, stir in a glass of madeira, and the juice of a lemon. In the meantime, pick and wash the brains clean, parboil them, and pound them fine, with an equal proportion of boiled eggs; season it with salt, pepper, sage and nutmeg, make it into small cakes, put over them some beaten yolk of egg, flour it, and fry them a nice brown, and lay them round the stew when served.

TO BAKE A CALF'S HEAD.

Clean it neatly, rub it with salt, and boil it till nearly done. Then rub it over with yolk of egg, sprinkle on some bread crumbs and bits of butter, and brown it in a Dutch-oven. Garnish with force-meat balls, fried in butter, and serve with it a boat of highly seasoned gravy, flavored with wine and lemon juice. You may stuff a calf's head with sausage meat, boil it, and brown it before a brisk fire, putting on some bread crumbs and bits of butter.

TO HASH A CALF'S HEAD.

Having boiled it tender, cut it into mouthfuls from the bone; put it in a pan, with some rich gravy, cut up some slices of boiled ham, and mix with it, add some butter, flour, a gill of white wine, a grated nutmeg, and two or three spoonfuls of anchovy catchup; give it a boil, and lay round it some small toasts when served.

TO DRESS CALVES' TONGUES.

After lying in salt or pickle for several days, wash them very clean, and boil them tender with a small piece of bacon. Then peel them, and lay them side by side, in a small dish. Melt a little butter, stir into it a little brown sugar, pepper and nutmeg; pour it over the tongues, and lay round them sprigs of curled parsley.

SMOKED TONGUES.

Having salted and smoked the tongues, parboil them, peel them, and cut them across in tolerably thin slices.

Broil them hastily, but superficially, on a well greased gridiron, over a bed of clear coals.   Serve them hot, with a little melted butter and pepper poured over them.   They are excellent for the tea-table.

TO FRY CALVES' FEET.

Clean them nicely, soak them for a day and night in water, with a handful of salt, and boil them very tender, in a good quantity of water.   Then split them, take out the large bones, season the meat with pepper, dip them in a thin flour batter, and fry them brown in lard or butter, which should be boiling when they are put in.   Season the gravy with a little brown flour, minced onion and vinegar; pour it over the fry when served, and garnish with crisped parsley.

A FRICASSEE OF CALVES' FEET.

Having boiled them tender, season them with salt, pepper and nutmeg; put over them the beaten yolk of egg, and grated bread, and let them stand to dry a little.   Put some clear beef's drippings, or lard, in a frying-pan, and when it boils, put in the feet; fry them a nice brown on both sides, dish them, and set them by the fire.   Pour out a part of the lard, and stir into the remainder a lump of butter, a small handful of bread crumbs, a glass of wine, a minced onion, and the juice and grated peel of half a lemon; give it a boil, and pour it over the feet.   Lay round them some sprigs of parsley, and send them up warm.

TO HASH CALVES' FEET.

Boil them till they are so tender that the bones will drop out; mince the meat tolerably fine, and put it in a pan with enough of the liquor in which they were boiled to nearly cover the mince, add a lump of butter, enough flour to make it a little thick, two minced onions, and salt and pepper to your taste.   Just let it come to a boil, stir in gradually enough flavored vinegar to slightly acidulate it, serve it with the gravy, and lay round it, on the edge of the dish, some small toasts.

A CALF'S RENNET.

A calf that has been fed entirely on milk, is said to have much more gastric juice in its stomach than when fed on any thing else. Take the rennet from the calf as soon as it is killed, empty it of its contents, and hang it in a cool, dry place for four or five days. Then turn the inside out, slip off the curd with your hand, fill the rennet with salt, having mixed with it a very little saltpetre, and lay it in a stone pot. Sprinkle over it a tea-spoonful of vinegar and a handful of salt, cover it, and set it in a cool, dry place for several weeks. Then hang it up, dry it thoroughly, and it will keep good a year or two. When you wish to make use of it, cut a piece the size you wish, put it in a cup, pour on a few spoonfuls of wine or brandy, cover it well with lukewarm water, and next day the liquid will be fit for use. It is an excellent plan to keep rennet ready prepared; being always in readiness, it will be found a great convenience. Cut off a piece six or eight inches square, put it in a small jar, or wide-mouthed bottle, pour on a pint of water, half a pint of brandy, and stop it securely. Shake it up each time before you use it; a table-spoonful of the liquid will be sufficient to turn a quart of milk, if the rennet is good. Beef's rennet may be saved in the same manner. The weather must be quite cool, or they will not keep well. They must be handled neatly, and not washed with water from the beginning to the ending, as it would weaken the gastric juice, and spoil the rennet.

MUTTON AND LAMB.

REMARKS.

Mutton is said to be in the height of perfection from the latter part of the summer until the early part of the winter, after which time it begins to decline in goodness. In buying mutton, if it is young, fat, and recently killed, you may pinch or cut the meat easily with your nails; it will rise, and be quite elastic when dented or pressed down with your finger, and the lean will easily part with the fat; on the contrary, if it is old, and been long killed, it will be tough, remain in dents when pressed, and the fat and lean cling together by small stringy fibres. It is best if practicable, to let mutton lie in salt for a day or two, and it greatly improves roasting pieces to lie in sweet milk for an hour or two previous to roasting; then wipe the meat dry, wrap it up in buttered paper, and roast it on a spit before a clear, and rather a brisk fire, basting it till well seasoned, with salt-water and pepper, and then with its own drippings, adding a little lard, till it is nearly done. Then take off the paper, dust the meat lightly with flour, and baste it bountifully with butter till a rich froth is raised, turning the spit very fast, and making the fire rather brisker than before. Serve it up with such sauces and accompaniments as will hereafter be directed. Mutton for boiling, like all other butcher's meat, should be rubbed well with salt and pepper, sprinkled with flour, and put on in cold water; then the heat will strike gradually through the meat, and it will cook much more evenly than if put on when the water is boiling. For frying, the lard, drippings and butter in which it, and all other kinds of meats are to be fried, should be boiling hot when the meat is put in; otherwise it will soak up the fat, and become completely saturated. Great care should be taken, too, to prevent the fat burning, as it would spoil both the looks and taste of the meat. The leg, loin and chump, as it is frequently called, compose the hind quarter of mutton; the fore quarter comprises the breast, shoulder, and neck, the thick end of which is called the scrag, and the thin ribby part behind the shoulders, which is the best end, is called the rack; both racks, or both loins, with the chump, are called the saddle of mutton. Mutton, like beef, is sometimes preferred a little rare; in that case, be your own judge, but if you wish it thoroughly done, try it by piercing a fork or a sharp pointed knife through a thick part that will not be exposed when dished, and if the essence that exudes from it is clear and white, it is surely done, but if the essence looks a little bloody, you must cook it longer. You may also tell when it is as tender as you wish by plucking it with a fork. Lamb is generally divided into hind and fore quarters, without any other names. In whatever way lamb is cooked, it should be thoroughly done, as the least rawness renders it unpalatable and disgusting. It should be roasted, boiled and fried, as directed for mutton, taking care to keep it wrapped in paper whilst it is roasting, to preserve the fat and color, as it is considered nicest to remain perfectly white. The eyes of lamb that is recently killed will look lively and plump, while those of a stale one will look sunk and shriveled.

A BOILED LEG OF MUTTON.

Wash it very clean, cut off the shank, skewer the flap, and if entirely fresh, rub it well with salt and pepper, dust it with flour, and put it in a pot with a piece of bacon, and enough cold water to cook it tender. After skimming it, cover the pot, and boil it gently till the meat is about half done; then put under it some turnips, or carrots, that have been neatly scraped and rinsed, and boil them with the meat till all are done. You may mash the vegetable, season the pulp with butter, salt and pepper, and serve it under the meat, or serve them whole in a separate dish, putting on a little butter and pepper. Spot the mutton over at intervals with black pepper, and send to table with it a boat of nasturtian, or caper sauce; either is very much liked with boiled mutton. A neck, breast or shoulder may be boiled in the same manner.

TO BOIL A BREAST OF MUTTON.

Divide the bone in several places, for the convenience of carving at table; wash it clean, rub it with salt and pepper, dredge it with flour, and boil it in a small quantity of water, with a piece of bacon, or salt pork, removing every particle of scum, as it rises. Thicken the gravy with minced onion, flour, butter and pepper, and pour it over the breast when served. Accompany it with onion or celery sauce, and a dish of mashed turnips or carrots. A leg or shoulder may be boiled in the same manner.

TO BOIL A SHOULDER OF MUTTON.

Make numerous incisions through the fleshy parts of the shoulder, and fill them up with slips of ham, highly seasoned with salt, pepper and sage; season, dredge, and boil it in a small quantity of water, skimming it well. When it gets nearly done, put in some small slices of ham, having skewered the ends together, and dusted them with flour; add two or three minced onions, some butter, rolled in flour, and rather stew than boil it till done very tender. Spot the shoulder at intervals with black or red pepper, garnish with the curled bacon, pour over the gravy, and send with it celery sauce, and mashed turnips, parsnips, carrots or potatoes. A leg or breast may be boiled in the same manner.

A ROASTED LEG OF MUTTON.

Cut off the end of the shank bone, skewer up the flap, and roast it as directed. Season the drippings with tomato catchup and browned flour. Garnish the leg with slices of pickled beet, and serve with it mashed turnips, boiled rice, slaugh, or raw tomatoes, and currant jelly.

A BAKED LEG OF MUTTON.

Trim the leg neatly, take out the bone, and fill the space with slices of ham, highly seasoned with pepper and sage.

Rub it over with salt and pepper, and then with lard; put it in a pan, on some slices of bacon, pour in a pint of water, a gill of wine, and one of tomato catchup; add two or three minced onions, a head of celery, cut small, and bake it with moderate heat, raising the lid, and basting it with butter occasionally, to prevent its getting too hard. Thicken the gravy with butter and brown flour, and accompany it with stewed beets, fruit, rice and cucumbers.

ANOTHER MODE.—Prepare it as before, lard it handsomely with slips of bacon, drawn through the outside with a larding needle, and baked as before directed, omitting the wine and catchup, and adding in their place half a pint more of water. When it gets about half done, put under it some sweet potatoes, neatly scraped and rinsed, or white potatoes or tomatoes, with the skins taken off. Bake it till thoroughly done, and thicken the gravy with butter and browned flour. A breast of mutton may be baked in either of these ways.

TO STEW A LEG OF MUTTON.

Cut off the shank and trim off the fat flap, make deep incisions in the leg, fill them up with grated ham, and lard it handsomely over the outside with slips of bacon; season, dredge and stew it with a bit of bacon or salt pork, in just enough water to cook it well. Remove the strings, &c. from some hard lumps of suet, shred them as fine as possible, and rub them in double their quantity of flour; add a little salt and enough cold water to make it into good paste, knead it well, roll it into a sheet an inch thick, cut it out with the edge of a wine glass or small tumbler, and dust them with flour to prevent them sticking together. About twenty-five or thirty minutes before you take the meat from the fire, drop in the dumplings, and stew them together till all are done. Thicken the gravy with butter, flour, cream and pepper. A shoulder or breast may be stewed in the same manner.

TO STEW A SHOULDER OF MUTTON.

Prepare the shoulder neatly, season it well with salt
and pepper, if it has not lain in salt, rub it over with lard
and sifted sage, and put it into a pot with a small piece
of bacon, and just enough water to cook it tender. After it has stewed some time, put in some turnips, carrots,
a head of celery cut small, and a little salt. When the
whole is done very tender, serve the meat and vegetables in separate dishes, cutting the bacon into narrow
slips and laying them round the shoulder; strain the
gravy into a sauce-pan, thicken it with butter, flour, tomato catchup, powdered sweet marjoram and pepper,
and pour it hot into a gravy boat.

A leg or breast may be stewed in the same manner.

TO STEW A BREAST OF MUTTON.

Separate the joints, trim it, season it, and rub it over
with lard and powdered sage; put it into a stew-pan
with enough water and gravy, which has been drawn
from trimmings and coarse pieces of meat, to cover it
well, and after stewing it for some time, put in some
white potatoes that have been scraped and rinsed, and
some force-meat balls that have been rolled in yolk of
egg, floured and dried a little; cover the pan, and stew
them gently till the meat and vegetables are done very
tender. Garnish the breast with the balls, mash the
potatoes with a little butter and pepper; serve them in a
separate dish, and thicken the gravy with butter, flour,
chopped parsley and pepper, adding a small portion of
nasturtian pickle.

A leg or shoulder may be stewed in the same way.

A BAKED BREAST OF MUTTON.

Separate the joints, score the top deeply, and fill them
up with a mixture of grated ham, grated bread, butter,
powdered sage, sweet marjoram, pepper and salt; rub
some of the stuffing over the top, and put it into a pan

with a pint of water, half a pint of wine and a gill of tomato catchup; put round it some force-meat balls, lay on some slices of bacon, and bake it in a moderate oven till thoroughly done. Garnish with the balls, thicken the gravy with browned flour and pickled nasturtians, capers, or a minced green pickle, and serve it in a boat. Have mashed potatoes and raw vegetables to eat with it.

A GRILLADE OF A BREAST OF MUTTON.

Prepare the breast neatly, and roast it before a brisk fire till nearly done and a nice brown color; then put it into a pan with enough rich gravy to cover it, which has been drawn from coarse pieces of fresh meat; add half a pint of madeira, a gill of mushroom, walnut, or tomato catchup, two minced onions, a handful of shred parsley, and one of bread crumbs. Simmer it a few minutes, pour over the gravy when served, and garnish with small slices of bacon, curled and fried brown.

TO ROAST A BREAST OF MUTTON.

Separate the joints, &c., saw off the sharp ends of the bones, make numerous small, but deep incisions in it, fill them up with minced oysters or grated ham highly seasoned, and roast it as directed before a clear and rather brisk fire, basting with butter, and frothing it richly at the last. Season the drippings with brown flour, catchup and minced pickle, or wine, jelly and bread crumbs. Garnish the breast with lumps of fruit jelly, and send with it rice, potatoes and raw vegetables.

TO ROAST A LOIN OF MUTTON.

After soaking the loin in sweet milk, bind it up in paper, and roast it before a brisk fire: at the last, take off the paper, loose the thin skin and draw it off, spinkle on a handful of grated bread, with some broken bits of butter, and let it remain on the spit a few minutes longer.

In the mean time scrape very fine some pickled red beets, and make it into balls to lay round the breast when served. Season the drippings with any thing you choose, and accompany the loin with currant jelly, rice, or potatoes, and raw vegetables.

A TOASTED LEG OF MUTTON.

Cut off the shank bone, roll up the flap, and confine it with skewers; season, dredge and boil it with a piece of bacon or salt pork, and some turnips, carrots, celery and onions. When it is done, score the top, rub it over with butter, sprinkle on some pepper, mace and a large handful of grated bread; put on some bits of butter, and brown it delicately before a brisk fire. Garnish with slices of lemon, and send with it a boat of melted butter, flavored with wine and currant jelly; also have boiled rice, baked sweet potatoes and sliced cucumbers, tomatoes or slaugh.

TO GRILL A LOIN OF MUTTON.

Soak it for an hour or two in sweet milk; then divide it into four pieces, season them well with salt and pepper, make numerous incisions in them, and fill them up with minced oysters or grated ham, seasoned with pepper and nutmeg; rub over them the beaten yolk of egg, strew bread crumbs thickly on, with some small bits of butter, wrap them up separately in white paper, and roast them till thoroughly done on a bird spit before a brisk fire; then take off the envelopements, garnish the mutton with sliced ripe fruit, or lumps of fruit jelly, and serve with it a boat of rich gravy and a dish of sweet or white potato rolls.

MUTTON HARICO.

Divide the rack into small pieces, all of equal size; beat them flat, season them with salt, pepper, and grated lemon, dust them with flour, and fry them a light brown in butter, lard or drippings. Stir into the gravy a small handful of bread crumbs and a minced pickle. Pour it round the harico, and squeeze over them a little lemon juice.

MUTTON CHOPS.

Prepare the rack as for the harico, leaving a bone in each, beat them flat, season them with salt, pepper, mace and grated lemon; put over them the beaten yolk of eggs, roll them in bread crumbs, and wrap each one separately in white paper, giving the ends a twist, that the meat may be entirely covered. Broil them on a gridiron, over a bed of clear coals, turning them over occasionally, and basting them with butter as they may require. When done, take them carefully from the paper in which they are enveloped, (being generally soiled,) and lay them on separate pieces of clean white paper, the corners of which having been neatly fringed, give each one a twist and send them up warm, with a boat of rich gravy.

STEWED MUTTON CHOPS.

Cut them as before directed, and beat them flat, draw narrow strips of fat bacon all through the outer edge of each piece, with a larding needle, leaving the ends about one inch long, season them well with salt, pepper, grated nutmeg and sifted sage, and stew them in a very little water or veal gravy, keeping the vessel closely covered. When nearly done, put in two minced onions, two spoonfuls of butter, and one of flour; stew them a few minutes longer, and add a handful of chopped parsley and a glass of sweet cream. Having a dish of neatly scolloped toast, each of which being a little larger than a chop, place them on the toasts, pour the gravy round, and send them to table warm.

MUTTON ALLAMENTA.

Cut the neck in small pieces, leaving a bone in each, the ends of which should be bare one inch. Beat them flat, season them with salt, pepper and grated nutmeg; dip them in batter, and fry them a handsome brown, in boiling lard; after which drain them, wipe the ends of the bare bones dry with a cloth; wrap a strip of curled white paper round each of them, place them in a dish, with the wrapped ends toward the outer edge, lay on each piece a slice of fruit jelly, and send them up warm, with a boat of rich gravy.

MUTTON CASSEROLLES.

Take small scolloped pans, butter them well, and put over each a smooth paste of mashed potatoes, which have been highly seasoned with salt, pepper, butter and sweet cream. Peel, slice and season some fine, ripe tomotoes; put a layer of them on the bottom of each pan, then put on a layer of cold boiled mutton, shred as fine as possible, and one of grated ham, sprinkle on some grated lemon, pepper and nutmeg. Add a few spoonfuls of rich gravy, and as much wine; put a paste of the potatoes over the tops, and bake them a delicate brown, in a brisk oven. When done, turn them out smoothly in a dish, spread over them a heated napkin, and send them to table immediately, with a boat of melted butter and wine.

MUTTON CUTLASS.

Cut long, thin slices from the leg of mutton, beat them evenly and smoothly, with a roller, season them with salt, pepper and powdered mace; spread them out smoothly on a board, and put over each a layer of fresh sausage meat, chopped suet, onions and parsley; roll them up tightly, confine them with skewers, and roast them till done, on a bird spit, before a clear fire, basting them with butter occasionally. Garnish them with slices of pickled beets, pour over a little melted butter and wine, and accompany them with fruit sauce, and a dish of sweet potato rolls.

STEAKS OF MUTTON.

Cut thin smooth slices from the leg of a fresh mutton, beat them tender, season them with salt, pepper and grated nutmeg, broil them on a gridiron, over clear coals, turning and basting them with butter occasionally, till done. Serve them hot, with melted butter, seasoned with mushroom or tomato catchup.

FRIED CAKES OF MUTTON.

Take equal quantities of ripe tomatoes, boiled white potatoes, and onions, which have been peeled and mashed fine; beat them all together till they form one mass, beat to a paste cold boiled mutton and ham, in equal quantities, mix it with the vegetables in equal proportions, work them thoroughly together, seasoning it with salt, pepper and nutmeg, and moisten it with gravy or butter; make it into cakes as large round as the top of a tea-cup, and about half an inch thick. Put over them the beaten yolk of an egg, flour them, and fry them a light brown in lard or drippings. Serve them warm, with melted butter and shred parsley.

MUTTON HASH.

Take the fat and lean of cold boiled mutton, and mince it fine; extract the gravy from the bones by stewing them in a little water; strain the liquid into a clean pan, put the mince into it, and if you have any cold potatoes, or any other nice vegetable, which have been boiled with the mutton, mince them fine, and put them in with the hash; it is an excellent way to save vegetables and small pieces of meat, that might otherwise be thrown away. Add one or two minced onions, a spoonful of flour, a little salt and pepper, if needed, and a glass of sweet cream; simmer it a few minutes, stirring it all the time, and serve it with the gravy, upon toast or sliced biscuit.

TO WARM COLD MUTTON.

Cut smooth, thin slices from a roasted leg of mutton, season them with pepper, nutmeg and lemon; dip them in flour batter, and fry them a light brown, in lard or drippings; drain them, and serve them warm, with alternate layers of fruit jelly. The liver of mutton may be dressed like beef's liver.

LAMB.

TO ROAST A HIND QUARTER OF LAMB.

Having soaked the hind quarter in milk and water for one or two hours, wipe it dry with a cloth, cover it with paper, and roast it upon a spit before a clear, brisk fire, basting it till sufficiently seasoned with salt-water and pepper, and then with cold lard, which will make the meat more crisp than if basted with that of the dripping-pan. See that the spit is turned regularly, that the meat may roast evenly, and every part get done as near the same time as possible; it should be done through, but not too brown and hard, as the flavor will be much impaired. As soon as it is done, remove the paper, dust a little flour over it, and baste it with butter, till you have raised a handsome froth. Then remove it from the fire, separate the joints smoothly, squeeze a little lemon juice over it, and garnish with slices of lemon. For gravy, season the drippings with chopped parsley, sweet basil, a little raspberry, or cherry shrub, and brown flour. Cold slaugh, lettuce, raw cucumbers, raw tomatoes, green peas, asparagus, boiled rice, and baked potatoes are all nice accompaniments to roasted or baked lamb.

TO ROAST A FORE QUARTER OF LAMB.

Roast it in every respect as directed for the hind quarter, and when it is done, remove the paper, and baste it with sweet cream, made a little thick with mashed sweet potatoes. Let it remain on the spit for a few minutes, for the basting to get a little brown; then separate the joints, for the convenience of carving, and squeeze on them a little lemon juice, or a spoonful or two of some nice kind of shrub, garnish with broken bits of jelly. Have upon the table a boat of made gravy, one of mint, or parsley sauce, and some suitable vegetable.

BAKED LAMB.

Take either the hind or fore quarter, trim it nicely, and separate the joints; season it with salt and pepper, and put it in a pan, with some suitable vegetable, such as ripe tomatoes, white or sweet potatoes. The vegetable should be neatly prepared and laid under the meat. Pour in a pint and a half of water, cover it with white paper, and bake it in rather a brisk oven, raising the lid, and basting it with butter occasionally. When it is thoroughly done, remove the paper, and put over the meat a little brown flour and broken bits of butter, which will give it a rich appearance. Enrich the gravy with a little brown flour and pepper.

STEWED LAMB.

Cut it in small pieces, sprinkle a little salt and pepper over it, and stew it in a small quantity of water, with a few sliced onions, and enough butter to season it well. Season the gravy with a few leaves of mint, chopped fine, flour, pepper and sweet cream.

LAMB CRAMPOES.

Divide the loin, or some other nice part of the lamb, into small pieces, all of equal size; beat them flat, season them with salt, pepper and nutmeg, rub over them the beaten yolk of egg, cover them with bread crumbs, envelop them in white paper, and broil them hastily, upon a bird spit, basting them with butter, as they may require. When they are well done, take them carefully out of the papers, lay them in a dish of curled parsley, or tongue-grass, so arranging them as for the parsley to extend up between each piece of the lamb, and have a boat of drawn butter, flavored with lemon, to eat with them. Lamb is very nice when fried or broiled like veal steaks.

A LAMB FRY.

Cut the liver, heart and sweet-breads into smooth, thin slices, season them with salt and pepper, dredge them with flour, and fry them a light brown. Having the head and feet boiled tender, minced fine, and heaped in the centre of a dish, lay the fry around it, and pour over the gravy, which should be seasoned with butter, brown flour, and chopped parsley.

VENISON.

TO ROAST A HAUNCH OF VENISON.

The haunch of a venison for roasting should be quite fresh and fat; wash it in warm water, wipe it dry with a cloth, and rub it over with lard, wrap it up in white paper, and roast it precisely as you would beef or mutton, only do not season it quite so much. Baste it with lard till it gets nearly done, then remove the paper, dredge it lightly with flour, and baste it with butter till it is well done, which you may tell by running a knife along the bone, through the under part of it, and if there is no appearance of bloody water, and the meat is tender, you may be sure it is done. Serve it with a strip of curled white paper, wrapped round the end of the shank bone; lay over it a heated napkin, neatly folded; as venison chills very soon, keep it by the fire till the moment before your guest sits down to table, and if the weather is cold, keep your plates on heaters. For gravy, have melted butter and wine, made rich with currant jelly, or for a change, season the drippings (after skimming them well) with claret, mace, brown flour, and currant jelly. And as currant jelly is generally much liked with venison, have some on the table; also boiled rice, and a dish of sliced cucumbers or tomatoes, if in season, and if not, have a dish of cold slaugh.

TO BOIL A HAUNCH OF VENISON.

Cut off the shank bone, season the ham with salt and pepper, dredge it with flour, lard the back part, or outside of it with narrow strips of fat bacon, drawn through the flesh, in regular form, with a larding needle. Boil it in as small a quantity of water as will be barely sufficient to cook it tender; after removing the scum, keep the pot covered till the meat is done, and the gravy sufficiently low; then season it with two ounces of butter, two minced onions, a glass of sweet cream, and a little flour, mace, and pepper. Serve with it stewed fruit and boiled rice. In whatever way venison is cooked, it should be accompanied with boiled rice and boiled ham.

A BAKED HAUNCH OF VENISON.

Trim the haunch nicely, and season it well. Make deep incisions on each side of the bone, and fill them with fresh sausage meat, chopped parsley and bread crumbs; put it in a pan, with a pint and a half of water, and half a pint of claret, lay slices of bacon over it, and bake it with moderate heat. When it is done, lay aside the bacon, dredge the ham lightly with flour, and put on some broken bits of butter. Enrich the gravy with butter, brown flour, chopped parsley, mace, and tomato catchup.

STEWED VENISON.

Take some of the fore quarter of a fresh venison, with the ribs, chop them into small pieces, rinse, and season them, stew them in a small quantity of water, with a few slices of pork or bacon. Stew it till very tender, season the gravy with butter, flour, onions, pepper and sweet cream; simmer a few minutes, and serve it on toast.

FRIED VENISON STEAKS.

Cut your steaks from the haunch, as it affords better slices than any other part of the venison; season them with salt, pepper, and sifted sage, dust a little flour over them, and fry them a light brown, in lard. They will not require as much frying as pork or beef steaks. When they are done, transfer them to a warm covered dish, and set them by the fire, where they will keep warm. Turn out a part of the lard if there is too much; it will answer for frying again. Pour into the remainder a few spoonfuls of boiling water, add two minced onions, a spoonful of brown flour, one of butter, and a glass of sweet cream; stir it till it raises the boil, and then pour it round the steaks.

BROILED VENISON STEAKS.

Cut very thin slices from the haunch, and beat them a little, but be sure you do not beat them to rags. Broil them hastily on a gridiron, having it cleaned, greased, and placed over a bed of clear coals. The moment they are done, place them in a warm dish, and pour over them a few spoonfuls of boiling salt and water, with a little pepper, and send them perfectly hot to table, with a boat of melted butter, seasoned with wine and currant jelly. In whatever way venison is dressed, it should be sent to the table as warm as possible, for a great deal of its excellence will be lost, if served cold.

VENISON CRAMPOES.

Take the thin ribby part of a fresh venison; cut it into pieces about four inches square, beat them till flat, lard them handsomely round the edges with narrow strips of bacon, season them with salt, pepper and mace, put over them the beaten yolks of eggs, cover them with grated bread, wrap them up in white paper, and broil them hastily on a gridiron. If you find yourself at a loss to know when they are done, take one from the fire, run a sharp knife through the centre of it, and if bloody water will ooze out, return it again to the grid-iron. When they are done, take them carefully out of their envelopes, lay them in a warm dish on toasts of the same size, and pour over some melted butter, seasoned with currant jelly and lemon juice.

VENISON PASTRY.

Take cold venison that has been boiled, and as much boiled ham or fresh suet; mince them fine together, stew the bones in a very little water till the gravy is extract-ed: mix with the mince its weight of preserved cher-ries and currants. Having a deep dish lined with fine paste, put in your mince, &c. with half a pint of the gravy, half a pint of sweet cider, one ounce of butter, rolled in flour and broken up, a grated nutmeg and a tea-spoonful of powdered mace; then put a crust of paste over the top, ornament it around the edge with scol loped or crimped leaves of the same, and bake it in a moderate oven till the crust is a delicate brown. The crust should be at least one fourth of an inch thick, as the most of people, who are fond of meat pies, prefer a thick crust. The meat having been previously boiled tender, a very short time will be sufficient to bake it.

A VENISON PUDDING.

Take one pound of cold boiled venison, half a pound of boiled ham, and mince them fine together; mix with them a pint of currants, which have been picked, washed and dried, a pint of baked apples, having them mashed fine, six beaten eggs, a grated nutmeg, a tea-spoonful of powdered cloves, six table-spoonfuls of flour and half a pound of sugar: make it into good pudding batter, with sweet milk, pour it into a buttered mould, and bake it in a moderate oven. When done grate loaf sugar over the top, and eat it warm with melted butter, wine and sugar. This pudding is very nice baked in small moulds, turned out smoothly into a dish, and melted butter, sugar and wine poured over.

SAVORY VENISON.

Cut the meat from a haunch of fresh venison, mix with it one fourth of its weight of the leaf fat of pork, chop them very fine together, and season it with nutmeg, cloves, salt, pepper, sage, thyme, parsley, summer savory, sweet marjoram and sweet basil, all made fine and rubbed through a sieve; work it with your hands till it is well incorporated, moistening it with claret as you proceed; put it into small potting cans, pour a little oiled butter over the tops, cover them securely, and set them in a cool place. In extreme cold weather it will keep good for some weeks, and will be found very nice for breakfast or supper. When you wish to make use of it, make it into small cakes, put over them the beaten yolks of eggs, flour and fry them a light brown in lard.

TO HASH COLD VENISON.

For making hash, the venison should be quite fresh, as stale venison will not make good hash. Season and boil it very tender; then mince the meat fine from the bones, and put it into a pan with enough of the liquor in which it was boiled to make plenty of gravy; add a few sliced onions, a cup of sweet cream, a grated nutmeg, and enough butter, rolled in flour, to season it well. Just let it raise the boil, stirring it all the time, and serve it warm upon toasts or sliced biscuit.

VENISON HAMS.

Take the hams of large fat venison, (no other sort being fit for the purpose); cut out the bones smoothly, rub on the meat a sufficient quantity of salt to keep it well, having first rubbed on each ham a small handful of brown sugar. Pack them away in a tub, cover it securely to keep out trash or dirt of any kind, and set it in a cool place. When the salt has sufficiently struck through the hams, raise them, brush them off clean with a cloth, hang them in as cool and dark a place as possible, to keep them secure from flies, and smoke them till dry with corn-cobs or some sweet kind of bark; then rub them over slightly with hickory ashes, and pack them away in layers of wheat bran. It is said that it is an excellent plan to salt fresh venison and barbecue it immediately, and pack it away as before directed. Dried venison makes excellent chip for the table, but never attempt to dry it with the bones in it, for they will never fail to impart a very unpleasant taste to the meat in a short time, and if suffered to remain long, will render it uneatable.

TO DRESS A KID.

The only nice way of dressing a kid, is to roast it. It should be from three to four months old and very fat, having been fed entirely on milk. As soon as it is killed, clean it nicely and soak it in milk and water for one hour; then wipe it dry with a cloth, rub a very little salt on the inside, and fill it with a stuffing made of light bread, butter, salt, pepper, sifted sage, sweet marjoram, nutmeg and mace, and made sufficiently moist with the yolks of eggs. Skewer the legs to the body, rub it over with lard, pin white paper over it, and roast it before rather a brisk fire; baste it with salt water and a very little pepper till it is sufficiently seasoned; then remove the paper and baste it with rich sweet cream till it is done. Season the drippings with butter rolled in flour, the juice and grated rind of a lemon, and a handful of chopped parsley. Garnish with broken bits of fruit jelly, and have boiled rice and baked apples, or some other kind of fruit sauce to eat with it.

PORK, DRIED HAMS, &c.

—◦✦◦—

GENERAL REMARKS.

In choosing pork, either for present use or bacon, select that which is firm and hard, the lean of a lively red, and the fat quite white. Meat that is soft and flabby, the lean of which is dark and the fat yellow, is never good, and no doubt but it is generally diseased.

Small pork, if nice and fat, is much finer for present use than that of a large size; but for bacon, never object to its weighing two hundred pounds; for the hams of large pork are much superior to those of a small size.

Hogs that are fattened on mast, should be fed for a few weeks, before they are killed, on corn, to harden the meat. If it is entirely fattened on mast, the lard will be oily, and the meat will drip a good deal when dried, and will shrink very much when cooked.

In cutting up meat, be careful to cut it smoothly: to have it rough and haggled does not only spoil the looks of it, but flies are much more apt to get into it than when cut smooth. Cut off the head and feet, take out the back bone or chine, ribs and leaf fat, and separate the shoulders and hams from the sides or middlings. For salting, use such tubs as are directed for salting beef, and sprinkle the bottoms with salt. When the meat gets entirely cold, if the hams are large, rub a tea-spoonful of saltpetre on the inside of each of them; rub it into the meat with your hand, and if you wish them very fine, rub well on each ham a small tea-cupful of brown sugar, with a tea-spoonful of cayenne pepper; then put on as much common salt as will be sufficient to keep them well. Never let meat spoil for want of salt; for if it will not imbibe all that is put on, it need not be wasted: boil and skim it well, and it will be just as good for stock as for any other, or it will answer for salting meat again.

You need not put quite so much saltpetre on the shoulders and middlings, but salt them well with common salt, and put them into the tubs with the skin downwards, placing the joints at the bottom. Separate the jowls from the heads, and salt them likewise; cut the ears from the heads, and reserve them for souse. The heads should be cooked in a few days after the hogs are killed, or they will not be fit to eat: they may be made into souse; but as they make very dark souse, and greatly inferior to that which may be made of the feet and ears, it is not generally liked.

The best time to kill hogs for bacon is about Christmas; and the meat should lie in salt from three to four weeks, according to the size of the hogs and the temperature of the weather. When you raise it, brush it a little, or wipe off the brine with a cloth; hang it up with the small end of the joints downwards: it is thought that it prevents them dripping in a great measure. Smoke your meat till it is well dried, avoiding a blaze as much as possible, and even then, in wet weather, it will be well to make a smoke under it occasionally. Let it hang in the smoke house till spring; then take it down, examine it carefully, and pack it away in layers of hickory ashes: it is said to be far superior to wheat bran to keep out the bugs, &c., and may be very readily cleaned with warm soap suds. Hams will keep very well put up in little sacks, and dipped in lime batter; but, for a large quantity of hams, it will be found troublesome, and no advantage over putting them in ashes.

TO MAKE SOUSE.

As soon as your hogs are cut up, clean the feet and ears nicely, by scalding and scraping them. Never put them into the fire to loosen the hoofs, as the manner of some indolent cooks is: it is apt to scorch the meat, make it dark, and it is then unfit for souse. Soak them in water, made tolerably thick with white corn meal, for at least twenty-four hours; then boil them very tender in a good quantity of water, replenishing the pot with more water as it may require. When they become very soft, pick all the meat from the bones, and season it well with salt, pepper and mace. Put it into a hoop of proper size, while warm, and press it lightly till it gets cold; then put it into a can, and keep it covered with weak vinegar for use. When you wish to make use of it, cut it into smooth, thin slices. Pigs' feet are very nice, boiled tender, and split, and put into vinegar, without mincing.

TO ROAST A PIG.

A pig for roasting should be recently killed, very fat, and not too large to lie in a dish. Having it neatly prepared, rub a little salt on the inside of it, cut off the feet close to the joints, skewer the legs to the body, and fill it with a stuffing, made of bread crumbs, fresh suet, or butter, pepper, sifted sage, grated nutmeg, and lemon, and made sufficiently moist with the yolks of eggs. Then rub it over with lard, truss it for the spit, pin white paper over it, and roast it before a clear, brisk fire, basting it with salt-water and pepper, till well seasoned, and then with cold lard till it is done. While the pig is roasting, boil the feet, heart and liver, mince them fine, and reserve them for the gravy. When the pig is done, dust a little flour very evenly over it, having removed the paper, and baste it well with butter; let it remain a few minutes on the spit, and if it is small, serve it whole, garnished with slices of lemon; but if it is rather large to serve whole, take off the head, separate the chop from the face, split the pig lengthwise, from one end of the chine to the other, press it open, and lay it in a dish with a part of the stuffing laid round it, and the head and chop placed one on each side. Having skimmed the drippings, put the mince into it, with a lump of butter, rolled in flour, a handful of shred parsley, and a glass of madeira; serve it in a gravy boat, and also have a boat of bread sauce, as it is generally liked with roasted pig, and a dish of stewed cranberries, peaches, or some other kind of fruit sauce.

TO BAKE A PIG.

Take a small, fat pig, that is well cleaned, cut off the feet above the joints, skewer the legs to the body, season it sufficiently with salt and pepper, rub it over with two spoonfuls of butter, and fill the body with a stuffing made of light bread, butter, pepper, sage, grated lemon, chopped parsley, and onions; all chopped fine, and worked well together, having moistened it with yolk of eggs, or sweet milk. Then put it in an oven of suitable size, make a part of the stuffing into small balls, and lay them round it, pour in a pint and a half of water, lay a piece of paper over the top, to prevent its getting too brown, and bake it with moderate heat, raising the lid occasionally, and basting it with butter till done. In the meantime, boil the feet, heart and liver, mince them fine, put them in a sauce-pan, with enough of the liquor in which they were boiled to make the gravy; add a small lump of butter, rolled in flour, a spoonful of sifted sage, a teaspoonful of pepper, a grated nutmeg, a handful of chopped parsley, and a glass of sweet cream; give it one boil up, and serve it. Split the pig lengthwise, and serve it with the balls of stuffing laid round it. Have stewed fruit and green peas to eat with it.

TO CORN SHOAT.

This name has been given to very small, young hogs, for no other purpose than to distinguish their size, from pigs, or pork of a large size, they being of an intermediate size. When you merely wish to corn shoat, rub a very little saltpetre over it, with enough common salt to keep it from spoiling. Put it in a tub, cover it securely from flies, and keep it in as cool a place as possible. In extreme cold weather, it should be in salt for at least ten days, but in very warm weather, forty-eight hours will be long enough. Corned shoat should always be boiled with whatever vegetable it is to accompany.

TO BARBECUE SHOAT.

Take either a hind or fore quarter, rub it well with salt, pepper, and a small portion of molasses, and if practicable, let it lie for a few hours; then rinse it clean, and wipe it dry with a cloth, and place it on a large gridiron, over a bed of clear coals. Do not barbecue it hastily, but let it cook slowly for several hours, turning it over occasionally, and basting it with nothing but a little salt-water and pepper, merely to season and moisten it a little. When it is well done, serve it without a garnish, and having the skin taken off, which should be done before it is put down to roast, squeeze over it a little lemon juice, and accompany it with melted butter and wine, bread sauce, raw sallad, slaugh, or cucumbers, and stewed fruit. Beef may be barbecued in the same manner.

TO ROAST A HIND QUARTER OF SHOAT.

The usual manner of cutting up shoat is to split it lengthwise, and cut each half across, at equaldistance, making four equal parts. Take the leaf fat and kidney from a hind quarter, cut off the feet above the joint, roll up the flank, and confine it with skewers, confine it on a spit, before a clear, brisk fire, and baste it in the usual manner for roasting meats, till it is done. While the meat is roasting, boil the feet and kidney tender, mince them fine, and put them in the drippings, with a few small toasts, a little of the liquor in which they were boiled, a large spoonful of butter, rolled in flour, and a cup of sweet cream. When the meat is well done, draw the skin off smoothly, and cover the meat with very fine grated bread, shaken on through a dredging box; add some broken bits of butter; let it remain on the spit for a few minutes, and serve it up, garnish with slices of pickled beets, cut in regular form. Be very careful to have shoat, or pork, perfectly done, as the least rawness renders it disgusting.

TO ROAST A FORE QUARTER OF SHOAT.

Take off the head and feet, boil it tender, and mince it for the gravy. Grate a stale loaf of bread, and mix with it butter, pepper, sifted sage, and grated nutmeg, add a little sweet milk, and work it with your hand till well intermixed. Make several deep incisions in the thick part of the meat, and fill them with the stuffing. Tie a pack-thread, or buttered twine, round the meat in several places, to prevent the stuffing from coming out, and roast it as directed for other fresh meats. When it is done, draw off the skin, and dredge and froth it handsomely. Make a rich gravy of the mince and drippings. Roasted shoat should always be accompanied with stewed fruit and raw vegetables.

TO BAKE A HIND QUARTER OF SHOAT.

Prepare it as for roasting, score the skin transversely about half an inch apart, rub it over with salt, pepper, and sifted sage, brush it with lard, or sweet oil, and put it in a pan. on some sweet, or white potatoes, having them scraped and rinsed clean; add a pint and a half of water, and bake it with moderate heat. During the time it is baking, raise the lid several times, and baste the meat with butter, lard, or sweet oil. When it is well done, and of a light brown color, thicken the gravy with butter, flour, cream and parsley. A fore quarter may be baked in the same manner.

SHOAT CUTLASS.

Shoat cutlasses are very fine; take them from the hind quarter, as it affords the best slices, cut them in long, smooth slices, about half an inch thick, beat them evenly, and season them with salt, pepper, and mace; dredge them with flour, and fry them a light brown, in lard, which should be boiling when the cutlasses are put in. Make a rich gravy of the skins and trimmings of meat, two ounces of butter, rolled in flour, two minced onions, the grated rind and juice of a lemon, and two spoonfuls of tomato catchup; pour it round the cutlasses when served, and garnish with crisped parsley.

STEWED SHOAT.

For stewing, the fore quarter is preferable. Take out the middle ribs, chop them into small pieces, and stew them with a few sweet potatoes, having them neatly scraped and rinsed. Put in just enough water to cover them well, and after skimming them, keep the pot closely covered till all are done. Having seasoned the meat, enrich the gravy with butter, flour and cream.

HASHED SHOAT.

Take a piece of cold shoat that has been boiled tender; mince it fine from the bones, and put it into a pan with a small portion of water, or what is better, veal or poultry gravy. Slice two or three biscuits, and put them in also, with two minced onions, butter, pepper, flour and cream. As soon as it begins to boil, serve it all together in a deep dish, and lay round it some bunches of curled parsley. The meat, having been boiled tender, should not be cooked more than just enough to heat it through, or it will be insipid.

A SHOAT PIE.

Having taken out the chine or ribs, chop them fine, wash and season them, and stew them for half an hour in a small quantity of water. Line the bottom and sides of a deep dish with a thick crust of standing paste, as people who are fond of meat pies, generally pefer a thick crust. Roll out another sheet, and cut it into small squares; put them into the dish with the meat, interspersing them all through it; pour in the gravy in which the meat was boiled, with two ounces of butter, rolled in flour and broken up: put a thick crust of the paste over the top, ornament it round the edge with scolloped leaves of the same, cut out with little tin cutters and handsomely notched; put a bunch of leaves in the centre of the pie, and bake it in a moderate oven.

SHOAT CHEESE.

Having cleaned the head and feet, soak them for at least twenty-four hours in water, with a little white corn meal, which will draw out the blood in a great measure, and make them look white; after which boil them very tender in a good quantity of water, carefully removing the scum as it rises. When they are perfectly soft, pick the meat fine from the bones, season it with salt, pepper, grated nutmeg and sifted sage. Make it a little soft with some of the liquor in which it was boiled; put it into small cheese-hoops while warm, and press them with a light weight on the tops till they get cold. Send them to table with vinegar, mustard and scraped horseradish. They are generally eaten at breakfast.

Shoat's head and feet make excellent hash when boiled tender, minced, and seasoned with butter, cream, flour and onions.

TO FRY SHOAT'S LIVER AND HEART.

Cut them into thin smooth slices, season, dredge and fry them brown in lard. Fry them slowly, lest you scorch them; for the liver of any thing is much easier scorched than any other part of the meat. Transfer them to a warm dish, pour into the gravy a few spoonfuls of boiling water, two minced onions, a spoonful of brown flour, and two of vinegar: just stir it up, and pour it over the liver.

SHOAT STEAKS.

Cut as large steaks from the hind quarter as you can get, having first removed the skin; beat them very smooth, and broil them on a gridiron over a bed of clear coals. Turn them over occasionally till they are well done. They require a longer time to broil than beef steaks. As soon as they are done, place them in a dish, and season them immediately with salt and pepper, and pour over them a rich gravy, made of the skins and trimmings of meat, butter, flour and grated horseradish.

TO DRESS SHOATS' BRAINS.

Take them from the heads as soon as the shoats are killed; pick all the strings and fibres from them, rinse them clean, mix them with an equal portion of eggs, season them with salt, pepper and grated nutmeg; beat them together till they are well intermingled, and pour them into a pan of hot butter: stir them all the time they are cooking. A few minutes will be quite enough to cook them sufficiently. Serve them in a deep dish with small buttered toasts laid round the edge.

ON ROASTING, BAKING, BOILING AND FRYING PORK.

Pork, for roasting or baking, should be entirely fresh, fat, and not of the largest size. It should be roasted upon a spit turned by a jack, before a clear brisk fire. Do not rub dry salt on it, but baste it with salt water and a little pepper till it is well seasoned, and then baste with cold lard, tied up in a small piece of linen, till it is well done. Notice the meat particularly while it is roasting, and see that it roasts evenly, and have the fire so arranged that every part of the meat will be done at the same time. Avoid having a blaze or smoke, which would cause a disagreeable smell on the meat. When you think it is done, try it, by running a fork or knife into the centre of it, beginning on the under side, so as not to spoil the looks of it; and if the bloody water will ooze out, you must roast it longer; but if there is no appearance of blood, and white gravy exudes from it, you may be sure it is done.

Pork, in whatever way it is cooked, should be perfectly done throughout, as the appearance of bloody water in the dish renders the meat disgusting, and also a discredit to the cook. When it is perfectly done through, draw off the skin smoothly, dust the meat with flour, and baste it well with butter; turn the spit fast, and continue to baste with butter till you have raised a rich froth on the meat, and it drops white gravy; then serve it up.

Roasted pork should never be served with the skin on,

without having it well scored at a small distance apart. You should be very careful in baking pork, not to have the skin hard and tough: this may be avoided by keeping paper over it till it is nearly done, and basting it frequently with sweet oil, lard or butter. For boiling, it should be corned or salted, dusted with flour, and put on when the water is cold. Have your lard or butter for frying, boiling hot; otherwise the dredging will become saturated with the fat, and be spoiled.

TO ROAST A LOIN OF PORK.

Pork in every respect should be roasted like shoat, only the former being larger, of course it is not so tender, and will require a long time to cook.

Wash and scrape it nicely, make several deep incisions in it, at equal distances apart, and fill them with stuffing prepared thus: Take equal portions of boiled onions and mashed potatoes, season them with butter, salt, pepper and chopped parsley, and make it sufficiently moist with yolks of eggs, and work it with your hand till it is well incorporated. Place it upon a spit before a clear fire, and roast it by the directions previously given. When it is done, draw off the skin smoothly, and dredge it with brown flour or grated bread, and baste well with butter. When you have a fine rich froth, serve it up, garnished with small heaps of grated bread. For gravy, skim the drippings, add to them butter, brown flour, pepper and two spoonfuls of grated horseradish, having boiled it in a small cup of sweet milk. Have upon the table apple sauce, cold slaugh, and turnips or potatoes.

A ROASTED LEG OF PORK

Make deep incisions on each side of the bone, and fill them with mashed sweet potatoes, which have been highly seasoned with butter, cream and pepper. Bind it up with buttered twine or pack-thread, and roast it as directed for roasting pork; then skin, dredge and froth it.

Garnish with pickled beets, which have been scraped fine and made into small balls. Season the drippings for gravy, and have upon the table cold slaugh or sliced cucumbers and mashed turnips.

———◦◦◦———

TO ROAST A SPARERIB OF PORK.

Saw the ribs across in several places, for the convenience of carving. Roast it before a clear brisk fire, but be careful not to roast it too brown and hard. Make a rich gravy for the rib, of scraps or trimmings of the fresh meat, butter, flour, parsley, pepper, cream and any kind of catchup you choose. Serve with it apple jelly, a dish of baked sweet potatoes, and one of raw tomatoes, which have been peeled, sliced, and highly seasoned with salt pepper and vinegar.

———◦◦◦———

TO BOIL PORK.

The leg, shoulder and middling of pork, may either be boiled, and should always be corned or salted before it is boiled. Boil it in plenty of water and skim it well. When it gets about half done, put with it some suitable vegetable, such as turnips, parsnips, carrots, cabbage, dried beans or peas. When the meat is put on, the water should be cold; but it should be boiling when the vegetables are put in, and there should be plenty to cook them tender without having to replenish it. If, however, water should be absolutely necessary, replenish the pot from a boiling kettle. The meat should be skinned, trimmed, neatly spotted over at equal distance with black or red pepper, and served in the same dish, on the vegetable with which it was cooked. Turnips and parsnips should be mashed fine, and seasoned with butter and pepper. Beans and peas should also be mashed fine, and seasoned with butter, cream and pepper.

TO BAKE PORK.

Take a leg, shoulder, or a part of the middling, rinse it clean, and score the skin crosswise, so as to form diamonds, season it with salt, pepper, and sifted sage; brush it over with sweet oil, lard, or butter, and put it in an oven with a small quantity of water, having placed in the bottom some suitable vegetable, such as squash, tomatoes, sweet, or white potatoes. Bake it with moderate heat, till it is thoroughly done. If the meat is large, it would be best to bake it till about half done, before the vegetable is put in. Thicken the gravy with brown flour, and flavor it with any kind of catchup you choose.

A BAKED CHINE.

Take the neck part of a fresh chine, chop through the bone in several places, but do not cut through the meat on one side, that it may remain whole, sprinkle a little salt on it, and lay it aside, till you prepare some sweet potatoes to cook with it, by scraping and rinsing them; place them in the bottom of a pan, and lay the meat on them, pour in a pint of water, and bake it with moderate heat, till it is done. Then sprinkle a handful of bread crumbs over it, with some broken bits of butter; let it remain in the oven for a few minutes, and serve it up. Enrich the gravy with brown flour, butter, cream and pepper.

A ROASTED CHINE.

Take the neck chine, and roast it before a clear fire, on a bird spit, basting it with salt-water and pepper, till it is well seasoned, and then with butter, till done. At the last, sprinkle over it a handful of bread crumbs, with some broken bits of butter; let it remain on the spit a few minutes longer, and serve it up, garnished with slices of lemon. For gravy, add to the drippings a handful of bread crumbs, some butter, and a glass of madeira.

TO GRILL A CHINE.

Separate the neck chine into small pieces; season them with salt, pepper, nutmeg and lemon. Mix together equal portions of bread crumbs and minced onions; moisten them with yolks of eggs, and put a coat of it over each piece of the chine, pressing it on hard with a knife; let them stand to dry a little; then wrap them up separately in white paper, and broil them on a gridiron over clear coals, turning them over once or twice and basting them with butter. When done, take them out of the envelopements carefully, lest the dressing slips off. Arrange them neatly in a dish, and squeeze over them a little lemon juice.

A STEWED CHINE.

The small part of a chine answers very well for stewing. Chop it small, rinse, season and put them into a stew-pan, with just enough water to cover them well. When it boils hard, skim it, and then cover the pan. While it is stewing, make up a little standing paste, roll it out a quarter of an inch thick, cut it into small squares, and when the meat gets about half done, put them in with it, having first sprinkled them with flour, to prevent them sticking together. When it is done, and the gravy sufficiently low, stir in a little butter, flour, cream and pepper. Fresh chine is also nice stewed with sweet or white potatoes.

A FRICANDO OF PORK.

Cut as long slices from a leg of fresh pork as you can get, having them all of a size and about half an inch thick; beat them very evenly, so as not to have them ragged. Rinse them, squeeze the water from them, and season them with salt and pepper; spread them out smoothly, and sprinkle them over with sifted sage and flour. Put some lard into a frying-pan, set it over the fire; and when it boils up, and then becomes still, it is in good order for frying. Lay the slices in smoothly, and fry them a light brown, turning them over once. Be particular that you do not scorch the gravy, for it would spoil both the looks and taste of the meat. Serve them in a warm, covered dish. Enrich the gravy with two minced onions, a large spoonful of brown flour, the beaten yolks of two eggs, and a cup of sweet milk; keep constantly stirring it, lest it curdles, and as soon as it comes to a boil, pour it over the fricando. This is an excellent dish, chiefly used for breakfast.

TO MAKE SAUSAGE.

Remove the skin, sinews, &c. from a tender part of fresh pork; chop it very fine, with one-fourth its weight of leaf fat, beat it till it becomes thoroughly intermingled, and one perfect mass. Then season it well with salt, cayenne, and sifted sage; put it away in stone, or earthen jars; and when you wish to make use of it, make it into small round cakes, put over them the yolks of eggs and flour, and fry them brown in lard.

VERY FINE SAUSAGE.

Having removed the skin, &c. from a nice, tender part of fresh pork, beat it exceedingly fine, with one-fourth its weight of the leaf fat. Prepare some sage leaves, by drying and rubbing them through a sifter, season the meat highly with the sage, salt, cayenne, mace, powdered rosemary, grated nutmeg, and lemon. Work it with your hand till it is very well incorporated, making it a little moist with water. Stuff it into skins, which have been neatly prepared, and soaked in vinegar and water for a few hours; hang them up, and smoke them, and when you make use of them, cut them into links, and stew, fry or broil them. Serve them up on small toast, and pour a few spoonfuls of melted butter around them.

BOLOGNA SAUSAGE.

Take eight pounds of tender, fresh beef; mix with it two pounds of the tender parts of pork, and two pounds of fresh, hard lumps of suet; chop them fine, and beat them to one perfect mass. Mix with it a small portion of grated bread, and season it with salt, pepper, sifted sage, grated nutmeg and minced onions. Work it very well together, make it a little moist with water, and having some skins neatly prepared, fill them with the sausage. Confine the ends with twine, to prevent the sausage coming out; pierce them with a fork in several places, and boil them slowly for half an hour, then rub them over with sweet oil and a very little cayenne pepper, and hang them up to dry. You may eat them cold, or broil, and serve them on toast. To prepare the skins, take the small entrails from a hog as soon as it is killed, empty them of their contents, wash and scrape them nicely, soak them in water, with a little salt, for forty-eight hours, shifting them once or twice, into fresh water, and lastly, soak them for a few hours in very weak vinegar, and scrape them well.

TO PICKLE PORK.

Get a tight tub, that will not leak one drop, put into it eight gallons of water, eight pounds of salt, eight ounces of saltpetre, six pints of molasses, and two spoonfuls of capsicum; cover the tub, and let it stand for four days, then boil it for a short time, skim it well, and when it gets perfectly cold, put it in the tub again; this brine will be sufficient for one hundred weight of pork; having it cut up in the usual manner, place it in the brine in such a way as for it to rise over the top of the meat, and sprinkling between each layer a small portion of salt. Cover the tub securely with a piece of carpet and boards, so as to keep out every particle of dirt, and set it in a cool, dry place. Pickled pork should be soaked in fresh water for at least twelve hours before it is cooked, to draw out a part of the salt; otherwise it would be uneatable, and should always be boiled in plenty of water, with some suitable vegetable, such as cabbage, green beans, dried beans, or peas.

TO BOIL A HAM.

Smoked hams should be soaked in fresh water for twelve hours before they are boiled, and if very dry, twenty-four hours will still be better. Put the ham in a large pot of cold water, and boil it slowly till it is done, which will take several hours, carefully removing the scum as it rises to the top. When it is sufficiently tender, (which you may tell by trying it with a fork,) draw off the skin carefully and smoothly, so as to preserve the skin whole, and not tear the ham, to make it look ragged. Trim it nicely, and spot it over at intervals with red pepper; wrap a bunch of curled parsley round the shank bone, which should be sawed short, and garnish with small bunches of asparagus, which have been neatly prepared, and served upon buttered toasts. Accompany it with stewed fruit and green vegetables. After dinner skewer on the skin again, to prevent its getting dry.

·A TOASTED HAM.

Soak the ham for twelve hours in lukewarm water, after which simmer it in a kettle, with plenty of water, till it is done, which will take several hours; however, try it with a fork, and when it is sufficiently tender, draw off the skin smoothly, sprinkle over the ham a handful of grated bread, with some broken bits of butter, and brown it a little on a spit, before a clear, brisk fire. Wrap fringed white paper round the end of the shank bone, which should be sawed short, and garnish with little heaps of raspings of bread. Ham, whatever way it is cooked, except to broil or fry, should always be accompanied with stewed fruit, green vegetables, vinegar and mustard.

A BAKED HAM.

Having a fine smoked ham well soaked, trim it nicely, make several incisions in it, fill them up with chopped parsley and minced onions, and boil it very slowly, in plenty of water, till nearly done. Then remove the skin, place the ham in an oven, dredge it well with raspings of bread, shaken on through a dredging box, put over it, at intervals, some broken bits of butter, put in a pint of the liquor in which it was boiled, with a pint of madeira; sprinkling a part of it over the meat, and bake it for fifteen or twenty minutes, or till the ham becomes a little brown. Thicken the gravy with butter and brown flour. After dinner, skewer on the skin again, cover it with a napkin, set it in a cool place, where it will be secure from flies, and it will keep good for several days. Ham, like beef, is frequently preferred a little rare.

TO FRY HAM PLAIN.

When hams are new and sweet, they are considered nicest to fry without washing. Remove the skin, cut the meat across the grain in thin smooth slices, and fry them a nice brown on both sides, but do not fry them too hard. Serve them with or without eggs as you choose, thicken the gravy with flour and sweet milk, stir it constantly till it comes to a boil, and becomes a little thick, and pour it immediately round the fry. Garnish with bunches of curled parsley.

FRIED HAM ANOTHER WAY.—When you cut a ham to fry or broil, begin near the centre, and cut it crosswise: it affords better slices, and is nicer in every respect; you then have a part of the lean and a part of the fat together, and being cut across the grain, it is more tender than when cut in any other way. Cut the slices smooth and thin, pour boiling water on, and let them stand for a few minutes, which will draw out the superfluous salt, and much ameliorate the taste of the meat. If it is very old and hard, put some lard that is perfectly clear of sediments into a frying-pan, set it over some coals, and as soon as it gets hot, put in your slices of ham, turn them over once, and serve them up. They should not be fried but a few minutes. Have ready some eggs, crack the shells, turn out the eggs without breaking them, carefully examining them, as you proceed, to see if they are good. Put them into the frying-pan while the gravy is hot:

do not turn them over, but supersede the necessity by throwing some of the hot gravy over them with a spoon. If this is done dexterously, the whites of the eggs will be so transparent that you may see the yolk through them in their full size and shape. Two or three minutes will be sufficient to fry them hard enough. Serve them upon the meat, having it placed smoothly in the dish; stir into the gravy a large spoonful of flour, and a cup of rich sweet cream. Stir it up and pour it round the fry.

BROILED HAM.

Clean your gridiron, grease the bars to prevent the meat from sticking to them, place it over some clear coals, and having some slices of ham prepared as for trying, wipe them a little dry with a cloth, and lay them upon it; turn them over once: a very few minutes will be sufficient to broil them enough. Serve them up in a dish, put over them immediately some pepper, a few spoonfuls of butter, and lay on each slice a poached egg, having them trimmed round the edges.

HAM PODDAGE.

Fry the ham and eggs as before directed; make some mashed potatoes into cakes the same size of the slices of ham; fry them brown, lay them in a dish with a slice of the ham on each toast, and an egg on each slice of ham. Stir into the gravy a little brown flour and sweet cream; pour it round them, garnish with small bunches of tongue-grass, and eat them warm. This is a dish chiefly used for breakfast.

HAM SANDWICKS.

Cut smooth thin slices from a cold boiled ham; season them with pepper, nutmeg and lemon, dip them into flour batter, and fry them a yellowish brown in lard.

Stir into the gravy two minced onions, a small handful of chopped parsley, a large spoonful of flour, a teaspoonful of pepper and a glass of sweet cream. Just let it come to a boil, and pour it over the fry. This is also a breakfast dish, and is very fine.

A HAM PIE.

Having a fine young fowl cleaned and cut up in the usual manner, season it with salt and pepper, and stew it till nearly done in a small quantity of water. Cut some thin small slices from a boiled ham, and season them with pepper and mace. Roll out a thick crust of standing or dripping paste; line the bottom and sides of a deep dish with it; roll out another sheet of the paste, cut it into small squares, and fill the dish with the slices of ham, fowl and dumplings, put in alternately; then put in the liquor in which the fowl was stewed, with four ounces of butter rolled in flour and broken up. Put a paste over the top, ornament it round the edge with scolloped or crimped leaves of the same, and bake it in a moderate oven: it will not require but a short time to bake.

HAM TRUFFLE.

Cut some slices of bread from a fine loaf, having them all of equal size; spread them over with butter, and grate some cold boiled ham thickly on each of them. They are chiefly eaten at supper or luncheon. Sides and shoulders of bacon should always be boiled in plenty of water with some suitable vegetable.

POULTRY, GAME, &c.

In buying poultry, choose those that are fully grown, fat and young. The lower end of the breast bone of young poultry is soft, the skin thin and tender, so that you may easily rip it with a pin; the legs are smooth, the feet light and limber, the breast round and flat, the body thick, and will admit your finger into the flesh, under the wings, without much forcible pressure; the bills are of a light color, and comparatively smooth and soft.

Poultry should always be scalded, that the feathers may be drawn or picked off easily without tearing or breaking the skin. When they are picked clean, hold them over a blaze of fire for a few moments, to singe off the little down or hairs that adhere to the skin, and then wash them clean in cold water before they are cut up.

It is best to salt poultry before it is cooked in any way, and for boiling it should be dredged well with flour, and put on while the water is cold: when the salt is thrown into the water, the gravy is always more highly seasoned than the fowls; and when they are put in to cook in boiling water, the skins are apt to break, and the outsides become done and ragged, while the sides are tough. Pierce them with a fork to the bone in several places, to ascertain when they are done.

TO BOIL A TURKEY.

Begin your preparation by making the stuffing. Boil a fine smoked beef's tongue till very tender; peel off the skin, mince the tongue fine with an equal proportion of boiled ham; add a large handful of grated bread, with enough butter, pepper, nutmeg and sifted sage, to season it well; make it sufficiently moist with yolks of eggs, and work it with your hands till the whole is very well incorporated. Having the turkey ready prepared and seasoned with salt and pepper, skewer the liver and gizzard to the sides under the wings, and the legs to the body; dredge it with flour, and fill it with the miscellaneous mass; then put it into a kettle of cold water, heat it gradually till it comes to a boil, skim it, cover the pot and boil it slowly, till it is nearly done; then take it off set it by the fire, keep it closely covered, that the steam may finish cooking it. For the gravy, take enough of the liquor in which it was boiled, put it into a sauce-pan, with four ounces of butter rolled in flour, a handful of small toasts, a grated nutmeg, a tea-spoonful of pepper, a small cup of cream and the beaten yolk of egg: just let it raise the simmer, and stir it all the time, lest it curdle; serve it in a boat, and send with the turkey stewed fruit, baked potatoes and boiled rice.

TO BOIL A TURKEY WITH OYSTERS,

This is an old fashioned way of dressing a turkey, but a very good one, to those who are fond of oysters. Clean and season your turkey as before directed, and fill it with a stuffing made in the following manner: Chop fine twenty large fresh oysters, mix with them a large handful of grated bread, four ounces of butter, a small handful of chopped parsley, a grated nutmeg, enough of the yolks of eggs and sweet cream to make it sufficiently moist, and work it with your hands till it is well mixed. Skewer the liver and gizzard to the sides, the legs to the body, dust and boil it as before directed. Serve it with a boat of oyster sauce, and have stewed fruit and boiled ham to eat with it.

TO ROAST A TURKEY.

Make a stuffing of equal portions of bread crumbs and chopped suet; season it with salt, pepper, sifted sage, grated nutmeg and lemon, and moisten it with yolks of eggs. Prepare the turkey as directed, skewer the legs to the body, rub a little salt on the inside as well as the out, and having the stuffing well intermingled, fill the turkey with it. Pin white paper over it, spit it and roast it before a clear, but not too hot a fire. Baste it for a time with cold lard, having it tied up in a piece of linen, for the convenience of basting. When it gets nearly done, remove the paper, dust the turkey lightly with flour, and baste with butter till the skin rises and looks quite rich, and is of a light brown color. Having the liver, neck and gizzard boiled tender, mince them fine, put them into the drippings with the liquor in which they were boiled, a few spoonfuls of grated tongue or ham, one or two sliced biscuits and a little butter, cream and pepper. Garnish the turkey with slices of lemon, and accompany it with fruit, boiled rice and ham.

ANOTHER WAY TO ROAST A TURKEY.—Prepare it as before, and fill it with a stuffing made of equal portions of fresh sausage meat and light bread, seasoned with sweet marjoram, nutmeg and lemon, moistened with yolk of eggs, and well commingled together. Pin white paper over it, to prevent its getting too brown, and roast it before a clear fire, basting it as before directed. In the mean time boil the heart, liver, neck and gizzard, and mince them fine for the gravy. Pour the liquor in which the liver, &c. were boiled, on some slices of light bread, and let it stand till it becomes completely saturated; then put it into the drippings with the mince, and enough butter, cream, sage and pepper, to season it well. Make a part of the stuffing into small balls, brown them a little, and when the turkey is well done, and looks sufficiently brown and rich, serve it; garnish with the balls, and send with it smoked tongue, fruit and rice.

Never pour the gravy round a turkey, but serve it in a boat. There is one great mistake which is often made by those who give recipes for cooking poultry and game, that is, directing the craw to be stuffed, which is only a ventricle, or the digestive apparatus, which should always be taken out of the fowl and thrown away, being eqally as unfit to eat as any other part belonging to the fowl.

TO BONE A TURKEY.

Begin at the top of the wings with a very sharp knife, and scrape the flesh loose from the bones without cutting or dividing it into pieces; and when every part is thus loosed, you may draw out the frame or skeleton, leaving the flesh entire. But it requires practice to perform this dexterously: in fact this art was taught in schools some years ago.

Having every particle of bone taken out, fill the turkey with a light, highly seasoned force-meat. Every part should be completely filled with the stuffing, that it may resume its former shape. A boned turkey may be roasted or baked; it is generally sent to table cold, handsomely ornamented with broken bits of jelly, or some delicious kind of fruit, accompanying it with any kind of warm sauce you choose. Any kind of poultry or game may be boned in the same manner; but as it is a troublesome process, it is seldom done.

Turkeys may be larded on the breast with narrow strips of bacon, by means of a larding-needle. to look very pretty.

A NICE DISH OF COLD TURKEY.

Take a boned turkey, cut smooth slices the whole length of it, stack them in a dish with broken bits of fruit jelly, laid between each slice, and garnish with slices of jelly or ripe fruit.

TO HASH COLD TURKEY.

Take cold broiled turkey, mince it fine from the bones, put it into a pan with just enough water to cover it well, add some of the stuffing, a large spoonful of butter, two minced onions, a little salt, pepper, nutmeg, lemon and a glass of sweet cream. Let it get perfectly hot, but do not suffer it to boil hard, lest the cream curdles: stir it frequently, and serve it warm in a deep dish. This is a breakfast dish, and thought by many people to be better than when the turkey is first cooked.

TO ROAST A GOOSE.

A goose for roasting should be young and very fat, otherwise it is not good; and if practicable, let it lie in salt for a few hours, before it is cooked; then rinse it clean, and wipe it dry with a cloth. Make a stuffing of equal portions of minced onions, bread crumbs and grated ham; season it with butter, salt, pepper, and sage; make it moist with sweet milk, and work it together till it is well incorporated. Then fill the body of the goose with the mixed mass; skewer the legs to the body, rub it over with lard, pin white paper over the breast, and roast it on a spit, before a good fire, basting it occasionally with lard or butter. When you think it is done, try it, by piercing it with a fork in several places to the bone, and if it is very tender, and will admit the fork to the bone with ease, you may be sure it is done; but if it will not, roast it longer. At the last, take off the paper, dredge and froth the goose handsomely, and see that every part of it is of a light brown. Having boiled the heart and liver, mince them fine, and put them in the drippings, with a large spoonful of brown flour, and a few minced sage leaves; do not pour it round the goose, but serve it in a boat, and have upon the table apple sauce, or stewed peaches, and green peas or mashed potatoes.

ANOTHER WAY TO ROAST A GOOSE.—Prepare the goose as before directed, fill it with white potatoes, which have been boiled tender, mashed fine, and highly seasoned with salt, pepper, butter and cream. Pin white paper over it, to prevent its getting too brown, roast it before a good fire, taking care to have every part of it done as near the same time as possible, and basting it with lard or butter, as it may require. In the mean time, take some scraps or trimmings of fresh beef, or veal, stew them in a small quantity of water, till the gravy is extracted, strain the liquid into a clean sauce-pan, add to it two spoonfuls of butter, one of flour, two minced onions, a few minced sage leaves, a tea-spoonful of pepper, a grated nutmeg, a glass of port wine, and the giblets, which should be previously boiled, and minced fine. When the goose is well done, having laid aside the paper, dredge, froth, and brown it nicely, and serve it with apple-sauce and smoked tongue.

A GOOSE PIE.

Having a young, fat goose nicely cleaned, cut it into small pieces, rinse them in cold water, season them with salt and pepper, and stew them in a small quantity of water, with four ounces of butter, rolled in flour. Line a deep dish with a thick crust of standing or dripping paste. Peel and slice a fine smoked tongue, which has been boiled tender, and put it in the dish, in alternate layers, with the goose; add the gravy, and then put a paste over the top, ornamenting it handsomely round the edge with scolloped or crimped leaves of the paste, and bake it in an oven with moderate heat. A similar pie may be made of ducks.

Another way to make goose pie is to cut up, season and boil the goose as before directed; mix with it slices of cold boiled ham and boiled eggs, having them peeled, and each one cut in four, and baked in an oven, which is lined with a thick crust of lard, or dripping paste. Baked in this manner, you may have a greater quantity of gravy than you could possibly have if baked in a dish, of which the most of pie eaters are very fond.

TO BOIL A PAIR OF FOWLS.

Clean, season and dredge your fowls, put them on in a pot of cold water, heat it gradually, till it comes to a boil, then skim, cover the pot, and boil them slowly, till they are nearly done; then take the pot off the fire, set it over a few coals, to stew slowly till the fowls are well done, and the gravy sufficiently low. Season the gravy with two ounces of butter, rolled in flour, a tea-spoonful of black pepper, a handful of chopped parsley, and a cup of sweet cream. Garnish the fowls with boiled eggs, having them peeled smoothly, put over them a few spoonfuls of the gravy, and serve the rest in a boat. Large fowls are very often stuffed with a light force-meat, and boiled in the same manner; whatever way they are boiled, they should be accompanied with fruit sauce, and smoked tongue, or ham.

TO ROAST A PAIR OF FOWLS.

Make a stuffing of light bread, butter, sifted sage, salt, pepper, nutmeg, lemon and yolks of eggs. Having your fowls neatly prepared and seasoned, fill them with the mixture, having it well incorporated, and roast them before a good fire, basting them occasionally with lard or butter. Boil the livers and gizzards, strain the liquid in which they were boiled into the drippings, mince the livers and gizzards, and put them in also, with a spoonful of flour, one of butter, four minced eggs, which have been boiled and divested of the shells, and a glass of sweet cream. Have upon the table stewed fruit, boiled rice, and asparagus.

TO BAKE A PAIR OF FOWLS.

Having scalded and cleaned them well, rinse them clean in cold water, skewer the legs to the bodies, and fill them with a stuffing made of equal portions of light bread and grated ham, seasoned with butter, pepper, and sifted sage, and moistened with yolks of eggs. Lard the breasts handsomely with narrow strips of fat bacon, put them in a pan with a pint and a half of water, two ounces of butter, and the livers and gizzards, chopped fine; put a piece of white paper over the top, and bake them in an oven, with moderate heat. When done, thicken the gravy with brown flour, garnish with curled parsley, and have stewed fruit, boiled rice, and cucumbers, to eat with the fowls.

TO BOIL SMALL CHICKENS.

When you scald young chickens, be very careful in drawing or picking them, lest you tear the skin, and spoil the looks of them. Make a stuffing of light bread, boiled eggs, butter, pepper, and sage, and enough sweet milk to make it sufficiently moist. When they are ready prepared, fill them with the stuffing, skewer down the legs, dust them with flour, put them in a pot of cold water, hang it over the fire, and as soon as it boils hard, skim it; then set the pot by the fire, cover it, and let it boil very slow-ly, till the chickens are done, which will take but a short time. Season the gravy with butter, flour, chopped pars-ley, pepper, and sweet cream. If you choose, ornament the breasts with narrow strips of boiled venison, veal, or smoked beef's tongue; draw them through with a larding needle, arranging them in diamonds; they look very pret-ty, dressed in this manner.

TO ROAST YOUNG CHICKENS.

If your chickens are very small, take four, cut off the feet and heads, skewer up the legs to the bodies, and the livers and gizzards to the sides, under the wings, having turned up the pinions. Make a force-meat of grated tongue, light bread, butter, pepper, chopped sweet herbs, and yolk of eggs; fill them with this stuffing, roast them before a clear fire, baste with lard, or butter, and dredge and froth them handsomely; a short time will be sufficient to roast them well. Serve them up with drawn butter and chopped parsley, in a boat, and garnish with slices of lemon. This is a delicious way to prepare young chick-ens.

TO STEW YOUNG CHICKENS.

Chickens for this purpose should be about half grown. Split them open on the backs, season, dredge and put them in a stew-pan, with half a dozen onions, some butter roll-ed in flour, and just enough water to cover them well. Cover the pan, and stew them slowly till done. Then stir in a glass of rich sweet cream, and serve them with the onions and gravy poured round.

TO SMOTHER YOUNG CHICKENS.

Take two half grown chickens, split them open on the backs, season them with salt, pepper, nutmeg and lemon, dredge them with flour, and put them in a pan, with four ounces of butter, and enough water to cover them; cover the pan, and stew them slowly till they are very tender; then add a handful of chopped parsley, four boiled eggs, minced, and a glass of port wine. Serve up the chickens with the gravy poured round.

TO SMOTHER CHICKENS BROWN.

Take two half grown chickens, split them open on the backs, and beat them flat with a roller. Season them with salt, pepper, mace, lemon, and sifted sage, and fry them a light brown in lard. Stew some trimmings of beef, veal, or poultry, in a very little water, till the gravy is extracted; then strain the liquid into a sauce-pan, add to it two ounces of butter, two spoonfuls of flour, two minced onions, a small handful of mint, chopped fine, a tea-spoonful of pepper, and a glass of sweet cream; put in your chickens, simmer them a few minutes, and serve up all together.

FRIED CHICKENS.

Chickens are nicest for frying when they are about half grown. Cut off the wings and legs, separate the back from the breast, cut it across, and split each piece, divide the breast, clean the giblets, and rinse them all in cold water; season them with salt and pepper, dip them in batter, and fry them a yellowish brown in lard, which should be boiling when the chicken is put in. Thicken the gravy with brown flour, chopped parsley, pepper and cream; serve up the chicken, and pour the gravy round.

TO GRILL CHICKENS.

Having two half grown chickens, neatly cleaned, split them open on the back, beat them flat, season them with salt, pepper, nutmeg and lemon, dust them with flour, and stew them in a small quantity of water, with four ounces of butter, till they get about half done; then take them out, drain them, and broil them on a clean gridiron, over clear coals, till they are done, and a light brown.   After which, serve them up, squeeze over them the juice of an orange; stir into the gravy a handful of grated bread, and pour it round them.   Another mode is to boil them first, and then stew them in a rich gravy.

TO FRICASSEE CHICKENS WHITE.

Cut them up as for the fry, soak them for an hour or two in warm milk and water, to draw out the blood, and make them look white.   Season them with salt, pepper, and nutmeg, put them in a pan, with two ounces of butter to each chicken, and one spoonful of flour; put in as much water as will cover them well, cover the pan, and stew them slowly till they are done very tender, and the gravy sufficiently low; then stir in a handful of chopped parsley, and a glass of rich sweet cream, having the yolks of two eggs beat well into it; take it from the fire immediately, lest it curdle, and stir very gently into it a wine glass of white wine.   Serve it up with the gravy poured round.

TO FRICASSEE CHICKENS BROWN.

Cut them up as before, season them with salt, pepper, and nutmeg, dredge them with flour, and fry them a light brown in butter.   After which, serve them up, squeeze over them the juice of a lemon, and set them by the fire till the gravy is prepared.   If you have two chickens, add to the butter in which they were fried, half a pint of sweet cream, a spoonful of flour, a spoonful of sage, and a handful of chopped parsley; squeeze in the juice of half a lemon, stir it up, and pour it immediately over the fry.

TO BROIL YOUNG CHICKENS.

Chickens for broiling should be of a small size; large ones will not be tender, and should always be cooked in some other way. Place a clean, hot gridiron over some clear coals, grease the bars, and wipe them with a cloth, to prevent the grease from dropping on the coals, which would cause a disagreeable smell on the chickens. Having them neatly prepared, split open on the back, pressed flat, and seasoned with salt and pepper, lay them on the gridiron, and broil them slowly till they are done, turning and basting them with butter, as they may require. Serve them up warm, and put a few spoonfuls of drawn butter with chopped parsley, over them.

A CURRY OF CHICKENS.

Take a pair of fat young fowls, clean them nicely, cut them up, season them with salt and pepper, dust a little flour over them, and fry them a yellowish brown. Having beat to a smooth paste six large sweet onions, mix with it one spoonful of turmeric, one of curry powder, two of powdered ginger, a tea-spoonful of mace, one of salt, half a one of cayenne pepper, and a grated nutmeg. When the whole is well incorporated, put the miscellaneous mass into a pan, with just enough water to cover it; as soon as the paste is completely dissolved, put in your chickens, simmer them for fifteen minutes; serve all together in a large dish, and accompany it with boiled rice. See receipt for boiling rice.

A CHICKEN PILAU.

Take a fat young fowl, that has been nicely cleaned, skewer the legs to the body, chop the liver and gizzard small, with two onions and two boiled eggs; season them with salt, pepper and mace, and put them into the fowl, having moistened them with butter. Skewer some thin slices of ham to the breast, put it in a pan, with just enough water to cover it well, and boil it for half an hour, carefully removing the scum as it rises. Then put in a pint of rice, which has been picked and washed clean; boil them together till all are done; then serve it up, covering the fowl entirely with the rice, and send with it to table a boat of drawn butter, seasoned with pepper and nutmeg.

A CHICKEN PIE.

Take two small chickens, (no other sort being fit for a dish pie) cut them up in small pieces, and season them with salt and pepper. Line a deep dish with puff paste, roll out another sheet tolerably thin, and cut it into small squares; put the chickens and dumplings in the dish, in alternate layers; put in a pint of water and four ounces of butter, that has been rolled in flour, and broken up, put a paste over the top, ornament it handsomely round the edge with scolloped or crimped leaves of the paste, and bake it in a moderate oven.

A NICE CHICKEN PIE.

Line the bottom and sides of a deep dish with fine paste, and roll out a sheet of the paste, and cut it into small squares. Cut up two small chickens in the usual manner, season them with salt, pepper and nutmeg, and boil them till nearly tender, in a small quantity of water, and four ounces of butter, rolled in flour. Having taken twenty fine fresh oysters from the shells, wash them in their own liquor, trim off the hard part, season them with a little nutmeg, and put them into the dish with the chickens in alternate layers, interspersing between each layer some of the squares of paste; pour in the liquor in which the chickens were boiled, with half a pint of the oyster liquor, having it strained through a cloth; put a paste over the top, ornament it handsomely round the edge, and bake it in rather a brisk oven. When it is nearly done, raise the paste a little, and pour in a glass of rich sweet cream. A very short time will be sufficient to bake it well.

A CHICKEN POT-PIE.

Take two fat young fowls, not fully grown; cut them into joints, rinse them clean in cold water, and season them with salt and pepper. Have ready a porridge-pot, or oven, rub the bottom and sides with lard, then with flour, and line it with a thick crust of suet or dripping paste. Lay in the bottom a few slices of ham. Having a sheet of paste rolled out thin, cut it into squares and put them into the oven with the chickens, in alternate layers, interspersing between each layer some raw eggs, carefully dropping them from the shells, lest you break them. When they are all put in, lay a few slices of ham on the top, pour in three pints of water, or what is better, veal gravy: and four ounces of butter, rolled in flour and broken up; then put on the top a crust of paste, and bake it with moderate heat. When it is done, turn the crust bottom upwards on the dish; put the other ingredients on it, pour the gravy round, and eat it warm. Just before you take it from the fire, raise the top-crust; and if it looks too dry, add a little water, in which a spoonful of flour and a tea-spoonful of pepper have been stirred, or a cup of sweet milk, prepared in the same manner, as people who are fond of pot-pies universally prefer a good deal of gravy. A similar pie may be made of almost any kind of poultry or game.

CHICKENS ALLAMENTA.

Take a couple of half grown chickens, season them well inside and out with salt, pepper, nutmeg and lemon; roast them before a clear brisk fire till they are thoroughly done, basting them occasionally with butter; then cut them into joints, having first taken off the skin; place them evenly in a dish, sprinkle on a spoonful of rum catchup, and cover them with broken bits of savoury jelly.

CHICKEN SALLAD.

Take a fine young fowl, season it well, and either boil or roast it till it is very tender; set it by to cool; then take off the skin and mince the meat fine from the bones. Wash two large heads of celery, cut the white part into small pieces, mix them with the minced fowl, put the mixture into a covered dish, and set it by till the dressing is prepared, which should not be put on till a few minutes before it is sent to table, as it has a tendency to harden both the chicken and sallad, and make them tough. For the dressing, take the yolks of six hard boiled eggs; mash them to a smooth paste with a spoon, add to it half a tea-spoonful of fine salt, half a tea-spoonful of cayenne pepper, half a gill of made mustard, a gill of vinegar and one of sweet oil. Mix all these ingredients well together, mashing and stirring them till they become very smooth; then pour it over the chicken and sallad, and mix them thoroughly together. Send it to table in a deep dish, accompanied with slices of light bread neatly spread with butter, also crackers, grated tongue, oysters, &c.

A CHICKEN PUDDING.

Having two small chickens cleaned, cut up in small pieces and rinsed in cold water, season them with salt and pepper, and stew them in a very little water, two ounces of butter, and a small bundle of sweet herbs. Make a batter of eight beaten eggs, a quart of rich sweet milk, two ounces of butter, a little salt and enough flour to make it into good pudding batter, and when the chickens are nearly done, stir them into it; put the whole into a buttered dish, and bake it in an oven with moderate heat. Thicken the gravy or liquor in which the chickens were boiled with flour, season it with pepper, nutmeg, the juice of half a lemon and a part of the rind, finely grated. Serve it warm to eat with the pudding; or for a change, send with it a boat of drawn butter and white wine.

CHICKEN CROQUETS.

Take the skin from a cold boiled chicken: mince the meat fine from the bones, mix it with an equal portion of grated tongue or ham, add a handful of grated bread, a tea-spoonful of pepper, a grated nutmeg, a tea-spoonful of grated lemon and enough yolks of eggs to make it sufficiently moist to make into balls; pound it in a mortar till it becomes a smooth mass; then make it into small balls, flour and fry them a light brown in butter.

CHICKEN SU-PEER.

Take the skin from a cold boiled chicken, mince the meat fine from the bones, put it in a mortar with an equal portion of ripe tomatoes, having been peeled; add salt, pepper and nutmeg to your taste, and beat it till it is a perfect mass, adding as you proceed two spoonfuls of flavored vinegar and a little grated bread, to make it of a proper consistence: then make it into cakes about as large as the top of a tea-cup; flour and fry them a delicate brown in butter, which should be boiling when the cakes are put in.

A CHICKEN OLLO.

Take a fine fat young fowl; clean it nicely, cut it into four equal parts, put them into a pot with an equal portion of fresh veal, sprinkle over them enough salt and pepper to season them well, and add as much water as will be sufficient to cook them tender. When they get about half done, put in a dozen white potatoes, six onions and a large handful of noodles. Boil it slowly till all are done and the gravy quite low; then add two ounces of butter, two spoonfuls of flour, a small handful of mint, chopped fine, half a dozen boiled eggs, which have been divested of the shells, and a glass of rich sweet cream.

TO ROAST DUCKS.

Having drawn your ducks, rinse them in cold water, wipe them dry with a cloth, rub a little salt on the inside, and lay them by till you prepare the stuffing. Mix together boiled onions and grated beef's tongue in equal proportions; season them with salt, pepper and sage, moisten them with cream, and work them well together: fill the bodies of the ducks with this stuffing, skewer up the legs, truss and roast them before a brisk fire, taking care not to let them burn, and basting them with salt and water till they are well seasoned. Chop the livers and gizzards small, stew them in a very little water, stir in a spoonful of flour, one of butter, a tea-spoonful of pepper, one blade of mace and the juice of half a lemon. At the last, baste the ducks well with butter, dredge them lightly with flour, and serve them with stewed fruit, boiled rice and green peas or asparagus.

STEWED DUCKS.

Take one large fat duck, or two small ones; split each one into two, season them with salt and pepper, and stew them in a very little water with a few slices of ham, keeping the pan closely covered. At the last, add two or three minced onions, some flour, butter, cream and pepper. Serve the ducks warm, and pour the gravy round.

BOILED DUCKS.

Scald and draw your ducks, rinse them clean in cold water, and wipe them dry with a cloth; rub them inside and out with salt and pepper, dredge them with flour, skewer up the legs, and fill them with slices of bread and butter, having pepper and sage sprinkled over them; put them on to boil while the water is cold: as soon as it boils hard, skim it, and then cover the pan and boil them slowly till they get nearly done; then put in a quart of green peas, and continue to boil them till done. Enrich the gravy with butter, flour, cream and pepper, and serve all together in a dish.

HASHED DUCKS.

Ducks should always be boiled before they are hashed. Cut them up into small pieces, put them into a pan with a very little water, two or three minced onions, some butter, flour salt and pepper. It should only boil a few minutes just before you take it from the fire. Stir in half a pint of sweet milk, in which the yolk of one egg has been stirred; squeeze in the juice of half a lemon, and serve it up immediately.

TO BAKE DUCKS.

Having drawn your ducks, skewer the legs to the bodies, season them, and rub them well with lard; fill them with equal portions of mashed sweet potatoes and bread crumbs, seasoning them with butter, pepper and sage; put them into a pan with a pint of water and two ounces of butter, lay slices of bacon on them, and bake them in rather a brisk oven. When done, serve them up, squeeze the juice of an orange over them, and lay round them slices of orange; thicken the gravy with brown flour, add a glass of madeira, and serve it in a boat. Have stewed cranberries or peaches and boiled rice on the table.

TO ROAST WILD DUCKS.

After your ducks are cleaned, lay them in milk and water for at least three hours before they are cooked, which will in a great measure draw out the strong taste. Wipe them dry with a cloth, season them sufficiently with salt and pepper, and put into each a minced onion, with two or three minced sage leaves, a very little mace and a spoonful of red wine. Roast them before a brisk fire, basting them occasionally with lard. When nearly done, dredge them lightly with flour, and continue to baste them till done. Serve them up with slices of lemon or some other nice fruit, laid round. Make gravy of the giblets, a little butter, flour, cayenne pepper, nutmeg and lemon pickle; put a few spoonfuls over the ducks, and serve the rest in a boat.

Accompany them with stewed cranberries, cherries or peaches and rice.

STEWED WILD DUCKS.

Split them open on the backs, and let them lie in milk
and water for two or three hours; then wipe them dry,
season them with salt, pepper and mace, stew them in a
small quantity of water, with a few slices of bacon and
two minced onions.   When they become quite tender, enrich the gravy with butter, flour, chopped parsley, and
sweet cream; pour it over the ducks when served, garnish
with raspings of bread, and send with them green peas
and stewed fruit.

TO BAKE WILD DUCKS.

Prepare them as for boiling, put in each a baked apple,
which has been pared and cored; lard them on the breast
with strips of bacon, drawn through with a larding needle; put them in a pan with a pint of water, lay a piece
of paper over them, and bake them in rather a brisk oven.
Garnish with bunches of asparagus, add to the gravy butter, brown flour, pepper, bread crumbs and wine.

TO ROAST PHEASANTS.

Draw and clean them immediately after they are killed,
and let them lie in salt for two or three hours; then wipe
them dry, stuff them with grated ham, mixed with bread
crumbs, butter, yolks of eggs and pepper; brush them over
with lard, cover them with bread crumbs, wrap them up
separately in white paper, and roast them before a brisk
fire, basting them occasionally with lard or butter.   Make
a rich gravy of fresh meat, having it stewed in a little
water, till the gravy is extracted, strain the liquid into a
sauce-pan, add brown flour, butter, and a glass of claret.
When they are done, take the envelopes carefully off,
serve up the birds, squeeze over them the juice of an orange, or some other ripe fruit, garnish with slices of ripe
fruit, and send with them stewed cranberries or peaches.

TO ROAST PHEASANTS WITH ORANGES.

Prepare them as directed, fill them with slices of ripe oranges, lard the breasts handsomely with slips of bacon, drawn through the flesh with a larding needle, and roast them before a clear, brisk fire, basting them with butter. Having moistened a plate of small toasts with a few spoonfuls of wine, set them under the drippings, and serve them with the birds. Garnish with slices of orange, and have drawn butter, seasoned with orange juice; also have cranberry, or peach sauce. Quails and grouse may be dressed by either of these receipts.

TO ROAST PHEASANTS WITH OYSTERS.

Having them neatly prepared, fill them with fresh oysters, which have been trimmed, chopped fine, and seasoned with salt, pepper, and grated nutmeg. Brush them with lard, roll them in bread crumbs, wrap them separately in white paper, and roast them upon a bird spit, before a clear, brisk fire, basting them with butter, as they may require. When they are done, take off the envelopments carefully; serve the birds with drawn butter and chopped asparagus; also send with them a boat of oyster sauce, stewed fruit and rice.

TO ROAST PARTRIDGES.

Make a stuffing of equal portions of light bread, butter, grated tongue, or ham, and preserved cranberries or peaches, and season it with grated nutmeg and lemon. When the birds are prepared, fill them with the mixture, rub them over with lard, and roll them in bread crumbs. Wrap them separately in white paper, and roast them on a bird spit, before a clear, brisk fire, basting them occasionally with butter. In a very short time they will be done; then take off the papers in which they are enveloped, place the birds in a dish of suitable size, and pour over them a little drawn butter, with chopped parsley. Partridges may also be dressed by either of the receipts for pheasants.

STEWED PARTRIDGES AND PHEASANTS.

Having them prepared, season, dredge and stew them, in a small quantity of water, with a few slices of ham, and three or four minced onions. Stew them slowly, keeping the pan closely covered till they are done; then stir in butter, flour, cream, and pepper, and serve them with the gravy in the dish, and garnish with raspings of bread.

TO BROIL PHEASANTS AND PARTRIDGES.

Pick and draw them carefully as soon as they are killed. Split them open on the back, and rinse them in cold water. Season them with salt and pepper, and broil them hastily on a clean and greased gridiron, over clear coals, turning them occasionally, and basting with a very little butter. When they are done, which will be in a very few minutes, serve them up immediately, sprinkle over them a handful of grated bread, and pour on a few spoonfuls of melted butter, seasoned with lemon juice and pepper.

TO ROAST WOODCOCKS, FEELARKS OR SNIPES.

Pluck them carefully, touch a slip of writing paper to a blaze of fire, and hold them immediately over it to singe off the little hairs that adhere to the skin; wash them very clean in cold water, and if practicable, let them lie in sweet milk and water for at least one hour before they are cooked. Season them inside and out with salt, put in each a lump of butter, rolled in bread crumbs, and seasoned with a little pepper; rub them over with butter, and roast them before a brisk fire, which will cook them in a few minutes; then serve them up, garnish with little mouns of ripe, soft peaches, having them mashed fine; add to the drippings, or trail, some drawn butter, chopped asparagus, or parsley and pepper, and serve it in a boat, to eat with the birds.

TO DRESS RED-BIRDS, OR ANY SORT OF SMALL BIRDS.

Rub the birds inside with a little salt, and put into each a spoonful of grated ham, a minced oyster or a lump of butter rolled in bread crumbs and seasoned with pepper and nutmeg: rub a little lard or butter over them, and roast them before a brisk fire: ten or fifteen minutes will be quite long enough to roast them well. Serve them upon small buttered toasts, the edges of which having been neatly scolloped; pour over them the trail, with a few spoonfuls of drawn butter, and lay on the top of each bird a broken bit of orange jelly or a slice of ripe fruit.

TO ROAST PIGEONS.

Scald, draw and wash them very clean, rub a little salt and pepper on them, stuff them with a little grated ham, bread crumbs, butter, chopped parsley, salt and pepper; spit, dredge and roast them before a brisk fire; then serve them up, put over them a handful of grated bread, with a few spoonfuls of butter, in which the juice of an orange or half a lemon has been stirred, and accompany them with stewed peaches or cranberries, and green peas or asparagus.

TO BROIL PIGEONS.

Prepare them as before; turn up the pinions, skewer up the legs to the bodies, and stuff them with chopped parsley, bread crumbs, butter and grated tongue or ham, seasoned with salt and pepper; dust them with flour, and put them into a stew-pan with a few slices of ham and a sufficiency of water to cover them: cover the pan, and boil them slowly till they are done. While they are boiling, cut up some asparagus about four inches long, tie it up in little bundles, and boil it in the nicest manner. [See Recipe for boiling asparagus.] When the pigeons are done, serve them up; place the bunches of asparagus on little buttered toasts, and lay round them. Season the gravy with butter, flour, chopped parsley, pepper and sweet cream, and serve it in a boat. Have stewed fruit to eat with them.

Pigeons make a very good pie prepared like a chicken-pie, when they are young and fat; otherwise they are not good.

—◦✦◦—

TO ROAST A PEA-FOWL.

These fowls have generally been admired more for their gay, plumagerous appearance than for diet; yet where they are raised in abundance, they are often cooked in various ways, and are thought by many people to be much better than a turkey.

Prepare the fowl precisely as directed for a turkey, and fill it with force-meat, prepared thus: Chop some hard lumps of fresh suet very fine, mix with it an equal portion of beef's tongue, which has been smoked dry, boiled tender and grated fine; season it with salt, pepper, sifted sage and powdered mace; moisten it with butter, bind it with yolk of eggs, and work it together till the whole is well incorporated. Bind up the breast in white paper, roast it upon a spit before a clear, but moderate fire, baste it with butter, and at the last dredge it lightly with flour. Let it remain on the spit till the skin rises or froths, so as to look very rich and is browned all over regularly and handsomely; after which serve it up and garnish with slices of ripe orange, lemon, or some broken bits of fruit jelly. For gravy, skim the drippings; and having the liver, heart and gizzard boiled tender, mince them fine and put them into it, with a handful of grated bread and a glass of port wine; serve it in a boat, and accompany the fowl with boiled ham, stewed fruit, mashed potatoes and rice.

—◦✦◦—

TO BOIL A PEA-FOWL.

Having prepared your fowl, rub a little salt and pepper on the inside and out; skewer the liver and gizzard to the sides under the wings, and the legs to the body; stuff it with a force-meat made of equal portions of fresh oysters, eggs, bread crumbs and butter, and seasoned with salt, pepper and nutmeg; rub it over with lard or butter, dredge it well with flour, and put it into a pot with a good quantity of cold water; heat it gradually lest the skin cracks. As soon as it boils hard, skim it; then cover the pot and boil it slowly till it is done. Serve with it a boat of oyster or egg sauce; also have boiled tongue, stewed fruit, mashed potatoes and green peas or asparagus.

TO ROAST A HARE.

A hare, for roasting, should be young and very fat, no other sort being fit for this purpose. Clean it and wash it in two or three waters; season it, skewer up the legs, and stuff it with a force-meat, made of fresh sausage meat, bread crumbs, butter, and enough red wine to make it sufficiently moist; brush it over with butter, and roast it before a clear and rather a brisk fire, basting it with butter, to keep it sufficiently moist. When it is done, let it remain on the spit for a few minutes, and baste it two or three times with rich sweet cream, shaking on it some bread crumbs through a dredging-box; then serve it and garnish with broken bits of fruit jelly, or slices of ripe fruit, laid round on the edge of the dish. For gravy, season the drippings with a glass of rich sweet cream and the juice of half a lemon, which should be stirred in very slowly, lest it curdle; add a handful of bread crumbs, and serve it in a boat: or, if wine is prepared, stir a glassful of it into the drippings, with a handful of chopped parsley or two or three sliced crackers: either of these sauces will be found very fine. Accompany the hare with mashed potatoes, sliced cucumbers and fruit sauce.

TO BOIL RABBITS.

Having cased and cleaned a couple of young fat rabbits, skewer up the legs, season, dredge and boil them in a small quantity of water with a few slices of ham till they are about half done; then put in half a dozen onions, and boil them till they are very tender; add two ounces of butter, a large spoonful of flour, a tea-spoonful of pepper and a glass of sweet cream. Serve the onions in a deep dish without breaking them, put over them a few spoonfuls of the gravy, and pour the rest round the rabbits. When you season gravy with cream, be sure it is quite sweet, and do not let it boil hard, or it will be sure to curdle and spoil the looks of the gravy. When cream is scarce, sweet milk and yolks of eggs make a very good substitute, allowing one yolk to half a pint of milk; but if it boils hard, it will curdle as easily as cream.

TO STEW RABBITS

Cut into joints, rinse, season and stew them in a very little water, keeping the vessel covered. When they are done quite tender, add four ounces of butter, a large spoonful of flour, a tea-spoonful of pepper, a handful of chopped parsley, two or three sliced biscuits and a glass of sweet cream. Just let it raise the simmer, stirring it all the time, and serve it up with the gravy.

TO GRILL RABBITS.

Take two fat young rabbits; case, clean and split them open on the backs, beat them flat with a roller, season them with salt, pepper, nutmeg and mace, and broil them on a gridiron till they are done and of a light brown, turning and basting them with butter as they may require. Have ready in a pan four ounces of drawn butter, to which add a glass of sweet cream, two minced onions, two ripe tomatoes which have been peeled and sliced, a tea-spoonful of pepper and a small handful of grated bread; lay the rabbits in, let them simmer a minute or two, and serve up all together in a dish.

TO ROAST RABBITS.

Prepare a stuffing of light bread, butter, parsley and onions; chop them fine, and commingle them together, seasoning with salt, pepper and nutmeg, and moistening with yolks of eggs. Put a little salt and pepper in your rabbits, rub it on with your hand, put two spoonfuls of sweet cream in each, skewer up the legs, and fill them with the stuffing. Sprinkle a little salt on them, brush them over with lard, pin paper over them, and roast them before a brisk fire. For the first half hour baste with lard, and after that with butter. When they are done, take off the paper, and dredge them with bread crumbs, shaken on through a dredging box, serve them up, and lay round them slices of ripe fruit. Season the drippings with half a pint of sweet cream, a spoonful of flour, and a handful of chopped parsley; put a few spoonfuls of it over the rabbits, and send the rest in a boat. Have lettuce, rice, and mashed potatoes, to eat with them.

TO FRICASSEE RABBITS.

Cut them into joints, rinse them clean, season them with salt, pepper and nutmeg, dredge them with flour, and fry them brown in butter. Then serve them in a warm dish, place them by the fire, stir into the butter two minced onions, a spoonful of tomato catchup, a handful of bread crumbs, half a pint of rich sweet cream, and the juice of half a lemon; do not let it boil, but stir it up, and pour it immediately over the rabbits.

TO SMOTHER RABBITS.

Having two fine young rabbits nicely cased and cleaned, rinse them in cold water, beat them flat, and season them with salt, pepper, mace and lemon; put over them the beaten yolks of eggs, cover them with bread crumbs, wrap them separately in white paper, and broil them on a gridiron over clear coals, turning and basting them occasionally with a little butter. They should be broiled till thoroughly done, and of a light brown color. While they are broiling, peel a dozen large sweet onions, boil them in a very little water, till they are perfectly soft, mash them fine, season them with salt, pepper, and nutmeg; add half a pint of rich, sweet cream, with four ounces of drawn butter, and pour it over the rabbits as soon as they are served.

TO FRY RABBITS.

Disjoint or cut them into small pieces, rinse them in cold water, season them with salt, pepper and grated nutmeg, dip them in a thin flour batter, and fry them brown in boiling lard; transfer them to a warm dish by the fire, stir into the gravy a handful of chopped parsley, a spoonful of flour, and a glass of sweet cream. Just stir it up, and pour it at once over the rabbits.

RABBIT SALLAD.

Having a fine young rabbit boiled very tender, mince it fine from the bones. Mince an equal portion of lettuce, which should be of the loaf lettuce, that heads up, and is quite white and frangible; mix them together, and set them by till the dressing is prepared. Mash very fine the yolks of six boiled eggs, add to it a tea-spoonful of salt, a tea-spoonful of pepper, half a gill of vinegar, half a gill of made mustard, and four .. table-spoonfuls of sweet oil. Mash and stir it together till it becomes very smooth; then put it over the rabbit and lettuce, stir it up lightly together with a fork, put it in a dish of suitable size, and send with it to table plates of bread and butter, crackers, grated cheese, &c. It is a supper dish, and seldom eaten at any other meal. Do not prepare it till just before you sit down to table, that it may be as fresh as possible. Rabbits make a very good pie, prepared like a chicken pie.

STEWED SQUIRRELS.

Take a couple of fat young squirrels, case and cut them into small pieces, rinse them very clean in cold water, sprinkle on enough salt and pepper to season them well; stew them in a small quantity of water, with a few slices of bacon, till nearly done. Make a thick batter with eggs, milk and flour; drop it by spoonfuls in with the squirrels, add a large spoonful of butter, rolled in flour, stew it fifteen or twenty minutes longer, then pour in a cup of sweet cream, and serve it up. Or you may omit the dumplings, and serve with the squirrels a handful of chopped parsley, having it stirred in the gravy.

FRIED SQUIRRELS.

Prepare them as for the stew, season them with salt, pepper, and nutmeg, dredge them with flour, and fry them a handsome brown, in lard or butter. Stir into the gravy a spoonful of flour, one of tomato catchup, and a glass of sweet cream, and serve the squirrels with the gravy poured round.

BROILED SQUIRRELS.

Case and clean two fat young squirrels, (old ones will not do;) split them open on the back, rinse them very clean in cold water, season them with salt, pepper, and grated lemon; broil them on a gridiron, over clear coals, turning and basting them two or three times with butter. When they are well done, place them in a warm dish, sprinkle on them a handful of grated bread, and pour over them two ounces of drawn butter.

FISH.

REMARKS.

When fish are entirely fresh and fat, they are thick and firm, the fins stiff and horny, the gills red, and eyes bright, full and prominent. A fresh lobster may be told by raising with your finger the spawn or purses which surround the end of them. If they resist and pull backward, it is a sign that the lobster is fresh; but if, to the contrary, they move slowly and flabbily, you may be sure it is not good. Pinch the soft part of mackerel with your finger: if it feels soft, or like it might be half filled with wind, it is a bad omen; but if it feels hard and firm, it is good. Codfish and haddoc may be told apart by the stripes, codfish having white stripes, while the haddoc is striped with black. The scales on a lean herring will adhere very closely to it, when to the contrary the scales on a fat one will be quite loose. All fish that have scales may be cleaned very easily by scraping them with a knife, and keeping them wet with cold water. Such fish as have to be skinned, should be dipped into boiling water: then run a knife under the thin skin, and you may draw it off easily. All fish should be cleaned immediately after they are killed; then wash them in cold water, salt them well, and keep them in a cool place, secure from flies. In very warm weather they will not keep good more than two or three days at farthest. To keep them a longer time would render them unwholesome and disgusting, as they naturally tend more to decomposition or putrefaction than any other kind of meat. Fish may be eaten at any meal. For dinner, they are generally preferred at the commencement, and are introduced with nothing more than bread, potatoes and sallad, except the seasonings or sauces, which are served up with them; and at many fashionable tables they are eaten with bread only.

—◦◦◦—

TO BOIL A FRESH CODFISH.

Having your fish cleaned, rub a little salt on the inside of it, place it on the strainer of a large fish kettle, fill it up with water, throw in a handful of salt, and boil it slowly till it is done, carefully removing the scum as it rises. The precise length of time that is required to cook it tender depends greatly on the size of the fish and the quantity of heat that is applied to it while cooking; there-

fore, experience and good judgment must determine for
the cook. All fish, in whatever way they are cooked,
should be perfectly done, as no diet is more disgusting
than fish when raw. Try it with a fork, and whenever
it is tender clear through, it is done. Then raise the
strainer carefully, and let it drain, place it on a dish of
suitable size, garnish with the roe and liver, which should
be cut up and fried nicely, and send with it a boat of
oyster sauce, also mustard and vinegar.

TO BOIL A SALT CODFISH.

Soak your fish all night in water that is a little warm,
having mixed with it a glass of vinegar, which will assist
in extracting the exuberant salt, and impart a pleasant
taste to the fish. Next morning rinse it very clean, put
it in a kettle of cold water, on a slice, or strainer, and boil
it very slowly till done, as boiling fast will make it hard
and stringy. As soon as it is done, drain it, cut it in large
smooth pieces, lay them neatly in the folds of a napkin,
place it on a large dish, garnish the edge with hard boiled eggs, whites and yolks cut separately, and thrown pro-
miscuously round, and send it up warm, with a boat of
egg sauce, and a dish of mashed potatoes. Have upon
the table mustard, vinegar and sweet oil.

ANOTHER MODE OF DRESSING SALT CODFISH.—Having
it boiled as directed, mince it fine, pick out all the bones,
put it in a pan, with enough drawn butter and vinegar to
make it rich and moist; serve it up perfectly hot, as it
chills very easily, and decorate it over the top with hard
boiled eggs, whites and yolks cut separately, in fanciful
figures. Have mustard and vinegar on the table.

TO BOIL FRESH SALMON.

Scale and clean your fish, place it on a slice or strainer
of a fish kettle, fill it up with cold water, throw in a handful of salt, and boil it slowly till it is done, removing the
scum as it rises. When it has boiled enough, which you

may tell by trying it with a fork, raise it carefully lest you break it; drain the water from it; place it on a hot dish, and send it to table immediately with a boat of lobster sauce and one of horseradish; also have mustard and vinegar.

TO BAKE SALMON.

Take a fresh salmon of common size, rub it over with salt, pepper and nutmeg, putting a little on the inside of it; rub it over with butter, sprinkle on it a handful of bread crumbs, lay it in a pan with a glass of wine, and bake it in a moderate oven, raising the lid and basting it occasionally with butter. When it is done and served, thicken the gravy with a little brown flour and tomato catchup; pour it over the fish, garnish with crisped parsley, and send with it a boat of horseradish and one of lobster sauce.

ANOTHER MODE OF DRESSING SALMON.—Having taken out the bones, cut the flesh into small slices, season them with salt, pepper and mace; put them into a deep dish with a pint of water, four ounces of butter rolled in flour and broken up, and a spoonful of catchup. Lay a piece of buttered paper ever the dish, and bake it in a moderate oven. When it is nearly done, add a glass of rich sweet cream; let it remain in the oven a few minutes longer, and serve it up, garnished with curled parsley.

SALMON CUTLASS.

Cut smooth slices from a fresh salmon, all of equal size and not too thick; wash them in cold water, wipe them dry, and season them with salt, pepper and mace; wrap them separately in white paper, and broil them on a gridiron over clear coals. When they are done, take them out of the papers, place them in a warm dish by the fire, spread over it a heated napkin, neatly folded; garnish with curled parsley, and send it warm to table with a boat of drawn butter, in which a glass of claret has been stirred. Have mustard and vinegar on the table.

TO PICKLE SALMON.

Take a fine fresh salmon; clean it nicely, and cut it into several pieces; place them on a slice in a kettle of cold water, into which throw a handful of salt; boil them slowly till they are done; then drain them and set them by to cool. Take three quarts of very pale weak vinegar, put it into a pan with a small handful of horseradish, one of parsley, one ounce of whole black pepper, half a dozen blades of mace, two powdered nutmegs, and two tea-spoonfuls of lemon pickle; cover the pan, and boil it slowly till the flavor of the spices is extracted; then strain it, add to it a gill of sweet oil, and when it gets cold, pour it over the fish, which should be placed in an earthen jar. There should be a plenty of the pickle to cover the fish well. If this quantity should not be enough to cover the fish you wish to pickle, make more in the same proportions, for it must be kept entirely under the pickle. Cover the jar, and keep it in a cool place. It will keep good for several months, and is a handsome and ready dish for any meal. When you wish to make use of it, garnish with curled parsley.

STURGEON CUTLASS

Having skinned the sturgeon, cut large smooth slices from the tail piece, about half an inch thick; rinse them clean, wipe them dry with a cloth; sprinkle them over with salt, cayenne pepper, nutmeg and a little flour. Place a clean hot gridiron over a bed of clear coals, grease the bars and wipe them with a cloth, and rub them with a little flour, to prevent the fish sticking to them; lay slices on the fish, and broil them carefully without scorching, turning them over once or twice: then place them in a warm dish by the fire, squeeze over a little lemon juice, sprinkle over each piece some minced boiled eggs, and arrange them carefully and handsomely in the folds of a fine napkin, which should be heated. Garnish with slices of lemon, and send them warm to table with a boat of prawn or lobster sauce.

GRILLADE STURGEON.

Prepare your sturgeon as before directed and broil them in the same manner. Put them into a pint of gravy, made of equal portions of drawn butter and wine, and seasoned with two spoonfuls of lemon pickle, one of brown flour, a tea-spoonful of pepper and a handful of chopped parsley. Simmer them a minute or two, and serve them with the gravy.

STURGEON STEAKS.

Prepare them as before for cutlass, season them in the same manner, and wrap them in separate pieces of white paper. Place a hot gridiron over clear coals, rub the bars clean with a cloth, to prevent them soiling the paper, broil them on the gridiron carefully, till thoroughly done, and send them warm to table with a boat of drawn butter and chopped parsley, flavored with lemon juice.

BOILED SHAD.

Get a fine fresh shad; clean, season and dust it with flour; put it on a slice in a kettle of cold water, throw in a handful of salt, and boil it slowly till it is done: then serve it carefully, lest you break it; sqeeze over it the juice of a lemon, dust on it a little cayenne pepper, garnish it with minced lobster, and send it to table warm, with a boat of parsley sauce, mustard and vinegar.

A BAKED SHAD.

Stuff the shad with grated ham, bread crumbs and mashed potatoes, seasoned with butter, pepper, mace and chopped parsley; rub the outside of it with the beaten yolk of eggs; cover it with grated bread, put it into a pa of suitable size, with a little water, a gill and a half o. wine, and a few spoonfuls of horseradish vinegar. Roll four ounces of butter in a little flour, break it into small bits, and put them over the fish: lay on it a piece of paper, and bake it with moderate heat, raising the lid and basting it occasionally with the gravy. Serve it up warm, garnish with small force-meat balls, and pour over the gravy.

BROILED SHAD.

Having cleaned the shad, split it lengthwise, press it open, but do not cut it into two. Season it with salt and pepper, and place it on a clean gridiron over clear coals: broil it very carefully, turning and basting it occasionally with a little butter till it is done; then serve it up, and pour over it melted butter, pepper and chopped parsley.

TO BOIL ROCK-FISH.

Clean the rock fish nicely, put it into a fish kettle, with enough cold water to cover it well, having dissolved in it a handful of salt. Boil it gently and skim it well. When done, drain it, sprinkle over it a handful of grated bread, with some broken bits of butter; place it before the fire, and brown it a little: then serve it up warm, garnish with slices of lemon, and accompany the rock with parsley and egg sauce, a dish of mashed potatoes and a plate of sallad.

TO WARM COLD ROCK-FISH

Take a piece of cold boiled rock-fish; mince it very fine from the bones, mix with it an equal portion of mashed potatoes, season it with a little pepper and cayenne, work it together till it resembles sausage meat, moistening it with a little lemon pickle; make it into small cakes, put over them the yolks of eggs, dust them with flour, and fry them a light brown in hot lard.

MANTELOPE OF ROCK-FISH.

Having seasoned and boiled a fine rock-fish tender, cut it up into large pieces, removing the bones smoothly.

When they get perfectly cold, place them in an earthen jar, and prepare the liquor. Take half as much of the liquor in which the fish was boiled as will be sufficient to cover the pieces; put it into a pan with enough whole black pepper, cloves, mace and horseradish, to flavor it well; cover the pan, and boil it slowly till the flavor of the spices is extracted; then take it from the fire, and when it gets cold, mix with it an equal portion of vinegar, strain it over the fish, cover it, keep it in a cool place, and it will keep good for a week or two, and is a ready dish for any meal. When you wish to make use of it, take a piece of suitable size, trim it neatly, wipe it dry with a cloth, place it in a dish, garnish with hard boiled eggs, cut in circular form, and have suet, oil, mustard and vinegar on the table.

SEA-BASS, OR BLACK-FISH.

Having cleaned your fish, put it into a kettle of cold water, with a handful of salt and a bunch of parsley; when it boils up, skim it, and then boil it slowly till it is done. Then drain it, brush it over with yolks of eggs, shake on it some finely grated bread, through a dredging box, put a few small lumps of butter on it, and brown it a little. Serve it warm, garnish with hard boiled eggs, having been divested of the shells, the whites cut in ringlets, leaving the yolks whole, and placing them alternately round the fish, on the edge of the dish. Have a boat of drawn butter, flavored with lemon, to eat with it.

FRIED SEA-BASS.

Score the thick parts of the fish, that the heat may penetrate them easily. Season them with salt, pepper, and nutmeg, put over them the beaten yolks of eggs, roll them in bread crumbs, and fry them a nice brown in hot lard. Be very particular in turning them, lest you break them. When done, transfer them to a warm dish by the fire; stir into the gravy two minced onions, a small lump of butter, a spoonful of brown flour, and a small glass of pepper vinegar; stew them a few minutes till the onions become soft, then pour it over the fish, and garnish with sprigs of parsley.

TO BOIL TROUT.

Trout should be boiled like sea-bass; a very short time is sufficient to cook them well. Garnish with scraped horseradish, and send with them a boat of drawn butter, to mix with the different catchups and vinegars, as taste may desire.

TO FRY TROUT, CARP OR FLOUNDERS.

Having neatly cleaned your fish, season them with salt, pepper and mace, dredge them with flour, and fry them a light brown in boiling lard. Stir into the gravy a large spoonful of brown flour, and a cup of rich sweet cream; then stir in gradually the juice of half a lemon, pour it over the fish, and garnish with sprigs of parsley.

TO STEW CARP.

Prepare them neatly for cooking, season them with salt, pepper and mace, put them in a stew-pan, with just enough water to cover them well; cover the pan, and stew them slowly till they are nearly done, put in a good lump of butter, rolled in flour, and continue to stew them till they are done; then stir in a handful of powdered crackers, one of chopped parsley, and a cup of sweet cream. Do not break the fish, but serve them whole with the gravy.

BOILED HALIBUT.

As halibut is seldom cooked whole, cut a piece from one the size you wish place it on the strainer of a fish kettle, fill it up with water, throw in a handful of salt, and boil it gently till it is done, skimming it well; then tak it out carefully, score the back part, or outside of th piece, brush it with the yolk of egg, strew over some bread crumbs, with some broken bits of butter, place it on a trivet, before a brisk fire, and when it gets a little brown, serve it up, garnish with slices of lemon, and accompany it with a boat of drawn butter, a plate of lettuce, and a dish of mashed potatoes. Haddoc may be dressed in the same manner. If there should be any of the halibut left from dinner, mince it fine from the bones, and set it by for breakfast; then put it in a stew-pan, with a little water, a good lump of butter, rolled in flour, a little salt and pepper, the juice of half a lemon, and two or three spoonfuls of lemon pickle. Let it get perfectly hot, and serve it up.

TO BOIL FRESH MACKEREL.

Having the mackerel nicely cleaned, put them in a fish kettle, throw in a handful of salt, and boil them gently till they are done; it will take but a very short time to cook them tender. Raise them carefully, lest you break them. Garnish with small lumps of boiled lobster, or bunches of curled parsley, and send with them to table a boat of parsley sauce, also mustard and vinegar.

TO BROIL FRESH MACKEREL

Clean your mackerel, split them open on the back, rinse them clean in cold water, wipe them dry with a cloth, rub a little salt on both sides of them, and broil them over a bed of clear coals, on a clean gridiron, the bars of which, having been greased, wiped with a cloth, and rubbed with a little chalk, or flour, to prevent the fish from sticking to them. As soon as they are done, put over them pepper, butter and chopped parsley. Salted mackerel may be broiled and served in a similar manner, after soaking them for several hours in fresh water.

TO BOIL SALTED MACKEREL.

Salted mackerel should be soaked all night in fresh water before it is boiled; then put them in a pan with plenty of water to cover them well. Set them by the fire, on a few coals, and merely let them simmer a few minutes, as boiling fast makes the meat comparatively hard and stringy, and the fish is much more apt to break in serving. When they are quite tender, serve them up, and pour over them a few spoonfuls of melted butter, with a small portion of black pepper.

TO TOAST MACKEREL.

Having boiled them tender, raise them carefully from the kettle, and drain the water from them, sprinkle on some finely grated bread, and broken bits of butter, and brown them delicately before a brisk fire. Have melted butter and chopped parsley to eat with them.

TO ROAST MACKEREL.

Wash them very clean, wrap them up in paper, wet it to prevent its burning, and roast them in wood ashes on a clean hearth. Then take off the envelops, and serve the fish with melted butter and chopped parsley, or melted butter, made a little thick with grated horseradish.

TO BROIL ANY KIND OF SALTED FISH.

Soak your fish for at least twelve hours before they are broiled; then wash them clean, and wipe them dry with a cloth. Place a clean, hot gridiron over a bed of clear coals, having greased the bars, wipe them with a cloth, put on your fish, and broil them till thoroughly done, turning them over as they may require; then place them in a dish, pour over them enough hot water to cover them, and let them set a few minutes. This process not only cleanses the fish from the strong superfluous salt that exudes from them in broiling, but imparts to them moisture, and a pleasant taste. Turn off the water, sprinkle on a little pepper, and send with them to table a boat of melted butter, to mix with the different catchups and vinegars, as may be preferred.

TO WARM ANY KIND OF SALTED FISH.

When salt fish are cooked for dinner, there are many times broken pieces left, which are not sufficiently nice to return to the table without some further preparation. Mince the meat fine from the bones, and set it by till next morning; then mix with it an equal portion of mashed potatoes, or parsnips if preferred, season it with butter, pepper, nutmeg and lemon, moistening it with sweet cream; work it very well till it resembles sausage meat; then make it into small balls, put over the beaten yolk of egg, flour, and fry them a delicate brown in hot butter, and serve them warm. By many people this is thought to be the nicest way of preparing salt fish.

TO WARM ANY KIND OF FIRM FRESH FISH.

Having any kind of firm fresh fish, boiled tender, mince the meat fine from the bones, put it in a covered dish, and set it in a cool place till next morning; then put it in a stew-pan, with a little water, some butter, rolled in flour, vinegar, lemon juice, and pepper; the seasonings must be proportioned to the quantity of fish. Simmer it a few minutes, serve it warm, and lay round it, on the edge of the dish, some small buttered toasts; or for a change, omit the vinegar, and pour in a cup of rich sweet cream, stirring in the lemon juice slowly and gradually, to prevent it curdling; either way is very nice, and thought by many people to be better than when first cooked. Cold pieces that are left from dinner will be found very fine warmed up in this manner for breakfast.

A NICE WAY OF PREPARING FISH FOR SUPPER.

Take any kind of firm fresh fish, that has been boiled tender, mince it fine, pick out every particle of bone, and put it in a deep china dish. Make a plentiful dressing of boiled yolks of eggs, sweet oil, vinegar, pepper, and a very little salt; mash and mix them together with a spoon till they are perfectly smooth, then pour it over the minced fish, and stir it up lightly with a fork.

CHOWDER.

Take any kind of firm fresh fish; cod or haddoc is gene rally preferred. Cut it into large, smooth slices, sprinkle salt and pepper on them, cut as many slices of the same size from a piece of salt pork, which has been boiled about half done; lay some of them in the bottom of a porridge-pot or oven, strew over some minced onions and sliced crackers, then put in a layer of fresh fish. Repeat this, putting them in, in alternate layers till your chowder is as large as you wish it: then pour in a pint and a half of water, or a sufficient quantity to cook it tender, and bake it with moderate heat. When it is well done, serve it up; thicken the gravy with butter, flour, pepper, chopped parsley and sweet cream; simmer it a minute or two, then stir in the juice of half a lemon, and pour it at once over the chowder.

TO FRY PERCH.

Small perch should be fried whole. Scale and clean them immediately after they are killed; rinse them clean in two or three waters, wipe them dry with a cloth, season them with salt and pepper, and sprinkle on them a little flour or fine Indian meal. Put some lard into a frying-pan, set it on the fire, and when it boils up, and then becomes still, put in your fish; turn them over once, but do not break them. As soon as they are a light brown and crisp on both sides, serve them up. Send with them to table a boat of plain melted butter, to be seasoned with catchup, &c., as may be preferred. Large black perch may be fried in this manner, having them first split in two.

TO BAKE LARGE BLACK PERCH

Having them neatly scaled and cleaned, rinse them in several waters. Season them with salt, pepper and nutmeg, dip them into yolks of eggs, and roll them in bread crumbs; put them into a pan with a very little cold water, some butter, rolled in flour, and a few minced onions: lay slices of bacon over the top, and bake them in rather a brisk oven. They should be baked till thoroughly done. Serve them very warm: add to the gravy a spoonful of lemon pickle, one of pepper vinegar, and pour it over the fish. Any kind of small fresh water fish may be dressed in the same manner.

TO BOIL BUFFALO.

The buffalo-fish is a very coarse meat and rather soft: it should be cooked soon after it is killed. Scale and clean it, cut off the head, rinse it in cold water, season it well with salt and pepper, inside and out, and dust it with flour; put it into a fish kettle on a slice, fill it up with cold water, and boil it gently till it is done, carefully removing the scum as it rises: then drain it, brush it with yolks of eggs, cover it with finely grated bread and small lumps of butter, and place it before a brisk fire till it is a light brown: then serve it up, lay round it some small force-meat balls, and have on the table parsley sauce, mustard and vinegar.

TO BOIL EELS.

Eels have a very strong, oily taste, and are not admired by many people. The best way to cook them is to boil them. As soon as they are killed, dip them into boiling water, loosen the skin about the head with a sharp knife, and draw it off without tearing it. Take off the heads, clean and rinse them well in cold water, fill the bodies with grated ham that is highly seasoned with salt and pepper; rub them over with salt, lard and flour, put them into a kettle with a small quantity of water, and boil them gently till they are done. Serve them without breaking, squeeze on them the juice of a lemon, pour over a good quantity of melted butter, chopped parsley and pepper, and accompany them at table with mustard, vinegar and a dish of mashed potatoes.

STEWED CAT-FISH.

There are two kinds of cat-fish, the yellow and the blue. The latter is considered the finest, though they should both be cooked in the same manner. As soon as they are killed, dip them into boiling water; then run a knife under the thin skin, and draw it off smoothly. Cut the fish into large thick slices, rinse them clean in cold water, put them into a stew-pan, with some salt and pepper, a good lump of butter, rolled in flour, and enough water to cover them; cover the pan, and stew them gently till they are done quite tender: then add a handful of chopped parsley, a glass of rich sweet cream and the juice of half a lemon. Serve up the fish, and pour the gravy round. Any kind of nice fresh fish may be stewed in the same manner.

TO BOIL CAT-FISH.

Take a cat-fish of a proper size, (as some of them are remarkably large;) clean it as directed, fill it with a force-meat, made of grated ham, bread crumbs, chopped parsley, butter and pepper. Put it on a slice in a fish kettle, pour in water enough to cover it, throw in a handful of salt, and boil it gently, skimming it well. When it is done very tender, raise it carefully, lest you break it, drain it and rub over it the beaten yolks of eggs; dredge it well with finely grated bread, put over some broken bits of butter, and brown it lightly before a brisk fire. Take a pint of the liquor in which it was boiled, put it into a stew-pan with two ounces of butter, a large spoonful of flour, half a gill of pepper vinegar; boil it a few minutes, and serve it in a boat. Serve up the fish very warm, squeeze over it the juice of a lemon, garnish with chopped parsley and butter, mixed together and made into little balls or bats, and send with it to table a plate of sallad and a dish of baked potatoes.

CAT-FISH CUTLASS.

Having a fine fresh cat-fish neatly cleaned, cut from it some smooth slices, about six inches long and half an inch thick. Rinse them in cold water, wipe them with a cloth, pressing it on the fish with your hand, so as to absorb as much of the moisture as possible: season them with salt, pepper and nutmeg, dusting them lightly and evenly with flour. Place a clean hot gridiron over a bed of clear coals, the bars of which having been greased and wiped with a cloth; lay on your cutlasses and broil them till they are thoroughly done, and of a light brown color; then take them from the fire, lay them immediately in the folds of a heated napkin, garnish with slices of lemon, and accompany them with parsley sauce, mustard and vineger.

STEAKS OF CAT-FISH.

Cut and season them as for the cutlass; dredge them with flour and fry them a handsome brown in boiling lard. Serve them up warm, stir into the gravy a handful of chopped parsley, a spoonful of flour, a tea-spoonful of cayenne pepper and a glass of sweet cream; shake it up, and pour it at once over the steaks.

TO GRILL CAT-FISH.

Prepare the fish as for cutlass, having seasoned them with salt, pepper and grated lemon; put over them the beaten yolks of eggs, roll them in bread crumbs, wrap them separately in buttered white paper, and broil them on a gridiron over clear coals. When they are thoroughly done, take off the envelopements carefully, lest you throw off a part of the bread crumbs. Serve them in a warm dish, put over them two spoonfuls of lemon pickle, two of pepper vinegar, and a good quantity of melted butter and chopped parsley.

TO CAVEACH CAT-FISH.

Having cleaned a fine fresh cat-fish, boil it as for eating, throwing in a handful of salt, and removing the scum as it rises. As soon as it is done, drain it, and set it by to cool: then cut it into pieces about twice as large as your hand, and put them into a stone jar, having first taken out every particle of bone. Take half as much of the liquid, in which it was boiled, as will be sufficient to cover it; put it into a stew-pan with the following quantity of seasoning to each quart: One ounce of whole black pepper, half an ounce of cloves, half an ounce of mace, two grated nutmegs, two spoonfuls of whole mustard and a small handful of horseradish. Cover the pan, and boil it a few minutes: after which, strain it, cool it, add to it an equal portion of good vinegar, and pour it over the fish. There should be plenty of pickle to cover the fish entirely. Lastly, pour on the top a gill of sweet oil; cover the jar securely, and keep it in a cool place. It will keep good for several days, and may be eaten at any meal. Garnish with bunches of parsley, fennel or pickled eggs, cut into ringlets. Large cat-fish may be dried—broiled as directed for salt fish, preparing it in the same manner.

TO BOIL A LOBSTER.

Take a fresh lobster, brush it, tie the claws together, and put it into a pot of boiling water, with a handful of salt. Let it boil till it is perfectly done, but no longer, as it would make the meat hard and stringy: then drain and cool it. Having taken off the head, split the body and tail, cut off the claws, lay them round it, and garnish with curled parsley.

TO WARM COLD LOBSTER.

Boil a fine fresh lobster as before directed; drain it, wrap it up in a cloth, and set it by till next day: then extract the meat from the shell, cut it into very little pieces, and put them into a stew-pan, with enough vinegar or white wine to cover them: add four ounces of butter, rolled in flour and broken up, and a little pepper, mace and lemon. Stew it a few minutes, and as soon as it gets perfectly hot, serve it up.

LOBSTER SALLAD.

Take a common sized lobster, boil it in plenty of water, with a handful of salt, till it is very tender; then drain it, and when it gets cold, mince it fine from the bones. Take an equal portion of lettuce, that is white and frangible, mince it fine also, and mix it with the lobster. Make a dressing of the yolks of four boiled eggs, a gill of vinegar, a gill of sweet oil, half a gill of made mustard, a tea-spoon-ful of cayenne pepper, and one of fine salt; mix the whole together in a deep plate, mashing and stirring it with a spoon till it is well incorporated and quite smooth; and having put the lobster and sallad in a deep china dish, pour over the dressings; stir it up lightly with a fork, and send it to table immediately, as lying in the dressing but a short time has a tendency to make both the meat and sallad hard and tough.

MINCED LOBSTER.

Having boiled a common sized lobster very tender, extract the meat from the shell and claws, and mince it fine. Mash fine the coral, moistening it with a very lit-tle water, and seasoning it with a salt-spoonful of salt and a tea-spoonful of pepper. When it is well intermingled, add three table-spoonfuls of vinegar, two of sweet oil, one of lemon pickle, and half a one of made mustard. When the whole is well incorporated and perfectly smooth, mix it with the minced lobster, and send it immediately to ta-ble in a deep china dish, handsomely garnished with the claws of the lobster, or curled parsley; or you may send the dressing and mince separately to table, to be handed round, and mixed by the company as their tastes may prefer.

TO FRICASSEE LOBSTER.

Boil a fine fresh lobster in plenty of water, with a hand-ful of salt, till it is nearly done; then extract the meat from the shell and claws, and cut it in small pieces. Sea-son them with pepper and nutmeg, or mace, and if they are not sufficiently salt, add a little more. Put them in a stew-pan, with enough milk, which is perfectly sweet, to cover them well, and stew them gently till they are done; then beat well into a gill of rich sweet cream the yolk of an egg, stir it gradually into the fricassee, lest it curdle. Serve it up warm, with the gravy, and lay about it some small bunches of curled parsley.

TO FRY OYSTERS.

Take large fresh oysters from the shells, rinse them in their own liquor, trim off the hard part, wipe them dry with a cloth, and season them with salt, pepper and nutmeg. Beat the yolks of two or three eggs very well, dip the oysters in it, and roll them in finely grated bread, taking care to make as much of the bread adhere to them as possible. Put a good quantity of fresh butter in a frying-pan, set it over a bed of clear coals, and when it boils up, and becomes still, put in your oysters, fry them of a delicate brown on both sides, and serve them warm.

STEWED OYSTERS.

Take the oysters from the shells, trim off the hard part, and put them in a stew-pan, seasoning them with a little salt, pepper and mace. Strain over them enough of their own liquor to cover them, add a small lump of butter, and stew them gently till they are done, which will only take a few minutes, (as much cooking will make them insipid and corrugated,) then stir in a small handful of grated bread and a gill of rich sweet cream. Simmer them a minute; serve them warm with the gravy, and lay round them, on the edge of the dish, some small buttered toasts.

SCOLLOPED OYSTERS.

Having taken the oysters from the shells, trim off the hard part, and season them with pepper and mace. Put a layer of them in the bottom of large scollop shells, strew over some bread crumbs, and lay on each a slice of butter; having put in a second layer of oysters, bread crumbs, and butter, strain over them enough of the liquor to nearly fill the shells, and brown them in a Dutch-oven. Serve them warm in the shells, arranging them neatly in a large dish. Scolloped tin shells may be substituted for real shells, if preferred. Butter them well before you put in the oysters, &c.

OYSTER FRITTERS.

Take large fresh oysters, trim them, and season them with salt, pepper, and nutmeg. Prepare a thick batter with flour, milk and eggs; having a frying-pan placed over a bed of clear coals, put in a good quantity of fresh butter, and when it gets hot, drop in your batter by spoonfuls, dropping on each an oyster, and then another spoonful of batter. When they are ready, turn them over, and as soon as both sides are of a light brown, serve them up, drain them, and send them to table hot.

AN OYSTER PIE.

Butter a deep dish, and line the bottom and sides of it with puff paste. Take large fresh oysters, (no other sort being nice for a pie,) trim them, and season them with salt, pepper and nutmeg. Put a layer of them in the dish, strew over a handful of grated bread, with some broken bits of butter, and then some yolks of boiled eggs, which have been minced fine. Repeat this till the dish is full, putting on the top some broken bits of butter. Pour in a glass of rich sweet cream, and fill up the dish with their own liquor. Then put over the top a thin sheet of paste, and having it neatly serated or scolloped. Bake it in a brisk oven; a few minutes will be sufficient to bake it well. As soon as the crust is done, remove it instantly from the fire, or the oysters will get hard and shriveled, and a part of their fine flavor will be destroyed. If this is done dexterously and carefully, it is much the nicest way to bake an oyster pie.

PICKLED OYSTERS.

For this purpose, select the finest and largest oysters, trim off the hard part, put them in a stew-pan, with a very little salt, strain over them their liquor, set the pan over some coals, and merely let them scald, till they get hot through; then put them in a jar, and set them by to cool. The pickle must be proportioned to the quantity of oysters, there should be plenty to cover them well. Add to the oyster liquor a sufficient quantity of vinegar, with as much pepper and mace as will season it to your taste; boil it up, pour it over the oysters, cover the jar, and keep it in a cool place for use.

CRABS.

Boil the crabs, extract the meat from the shell, mince it fine, and make a dressing as directed for minced lobster; or if they are preferred warm, season the mince with salt, pepper and nutmeg; fill the back shells of the crabs with it, pour over them enough vinegar or white wine to make them sufficiently moist, put on some broken bits of butter, and make them a little brown by holding over them a salamander. When they get warm, arrange them neatly in a dish, and lay on the top of each a buttered toast, or a slice of bread and butter.

CLAMS.

Boil the clams in their own liquor, no other being needed, except the bottom shells should look like scorching, then add a little water to prevent it. As soon as the shells start open, take the clams from them immediately, rinsing them in their own liquor. Put them in a stew-pan, strain the liquor, and put that in also, with a little butter rolled in flour, pepper, a few spoonfuls of vinegar, and if they look like being too dry, add a very little water. Let them stew for eight or ten minutes. Serve them warm, and lay round them some small buttered toasts or sliced crackers.

PRAWNS.

Put your prawns in a kettle of boiling water, throw in a handful of salt, and boil them for fifteen or twenty minutes; then drain and set them by to cool. Make a plentiful dressing of vinegar, mustard, sweet oil, salt and pepper, preparing it in the same manner as for minced lobster. When the prawns are cold, arrange them neatly in a dish, lay round them small toasts, sliced crackers, or slices of bread and butter, and send with them to table the dressing, to be handed round to the company, and mixed by them in their plates, as their tastes may desire.

SEPARATE RECEIPTS.

LARDING.

For larding, take the fat of bacon, and for common fresh meats, cut it in slips, about half an inch wide, two inches in length, and nearly half an inch thick. For poultry, game, &c., it should not be more than one quarter of an inch thick, and if they are to be larded after they are cooked, the bacon should first be boiled, and set by till it gets cold, before it is used; this, however, is not common for coarse meats. The instrument used for larding is termed a larding needle, or pin; this instrument is quite a common article, and may be readily obtained at the hardware stores. Put the ends of the bacon one at a time in the cleft end of the needle, giving it a little twist, and pressing it in the needle with your finger, so as to confine it. Introduce the needle in the surface of the flesh, and when you draw it out, the ends of the bacon will be confined in the flesh. Poultry or game are seldom larded any where else than on the breast. The great beauty of larding is to arrange it in regular forms or figures, cutting the bacon all of the same size, making the hoop or middle part of it stand up right. This requires practice. Small boiled poultry and game look very pretty ornamented in the same manner with boiled beef's tongue or venison that has been dried thoroughly.

FORCE-MEAT BALLS.

This force-meat makes very good stuffing for poultry, especially when mixed with bread crumbs and yolks of eggs. When it is used for a garnish, it is made into balls or cakes, and fried or boiled, as the case may require.

Take a pound of fresh veal, a pound of fresh beef's suet, and a few oysters, if you choose; chop them fine together, seasoning it with salt, pepper, mace, lemon and sifted sage. If it is to be used immediately, moisten it with yolks of eggs; but if not, moisten with water. Beat it thoroughly together till the whole is well amalgamated, and forms one glutinous mass: then, if to garnish roasted meats, make it into small balls or cakes; flour and fry them brown in lard: but if it is to garnish boiled meats, or to put into gravy, or sauce for boiled poultry, &c., they should not be fried, but boiled for a few minutes in a very little water, with enough salt, pepper and sage to season the water, lest it draws out a part of the seasonings of the meat. After making it into balls, they should be rolled in yolk of eggs, floured well, and dropped into boiling water: this in a great measure prevents them coming to pieces.

VERMICELLI AND NOODLES.

Beat fresh eggs till light, add a very little salt, and make it into good paste with flour: work it well with your hands, roll it out till it is about as thin as common pie-crust; then cut it into little squares with tin cutters, sprinkle flour over them, and spread them out on a cloth for an hour or two to dry. Noodles are made in the same manner, only cut them in the slips about half an inch wide and as long as your hand, and giving each end a twist, form them into a curl; then flour and dry them as the vermicelli. These are German cookeries, principally used for thickening soups and sauces.

CURRY POWDERS.

Coriander seeds thirteen ounces, black pepper two ounces, cayenne pepper one ounce, tumeric, and cumin seeds each three ounces, and trigonella seeds four drachms; all to be pulverized and mixed together.

SECOND MODE.—Spice, ginger and curcumæ root each one pound, cloves one ounce, cayenne pepper and coriander seeds each half a pound; to be ground and mixed together.

THIRD.—Coriander seeds thirteen ounces, black pepper five ounces, cayenne pepper one ounce, trigonella seeds and cumin seeds each three ounces, and six ounces curcumæ root: pulverize and mix.

FOURTH.—Coriander seeds one pound, curcumæ root half a pound, ginger six ounces, cumin seeds, red pepper, each four ounces, black pepper three ounces, cinnamon and lesser cardamon seeds each one ounce, and tamarinds two pounds. Grind and mix.

FIFTH.—Rice nine pounds, curcumæ root four pounds and a half, coriander seeds four pounds, two pounds and four ounces of cumin seeds, three and a half pounds of mustard seeds, black pepper seven pounds, and cayenne one pound. Grind fine and mix.

SIXTH.—Coriander seeds and curcumæ root each four pounds, ginger, spice, cayenne and capsicum pepper each one pound, lesser cardamon seeds four ounces, mace, cloves and cinnamon each one ounce. These ingredients must all be ground fine, sifted, mixed and corked up securely in dry bottles, tying leather over the corks to prevent the flavor from evaporating. A small portion of these powders gives an agreeable taste to fresh meats, gravies, soups, &c.

HAM PATTIES.

Grate some cold boiled ham, mix with it an equal portion of boiled veal or smoked tongue, having it also grated fine; chop with them two or three boiled eggs, according to the quantity of meat; season it with salt, pepper and nutmeg, and make it tolerably liquid with white wine. Have ready some puff paste, roll it out rather thin, line some small pattie pans with it, put in your mince, lay a lid of paste over the tops, crimp them handsomely round the edges, and bake them crisp in a brisk oven.

HAM OLLO.

Having grated some cold boiled ham, peel some ripe tomatoes, mince them fine, and mix them with the ham in equal portions, seasoning it with salt and pepper, and making it sufficiently moist to drop from a spoon, with a little weak vinegar. Have ready a frying-pan of boiling lard; drop the ollo by spoonfuls into it, fry them a light brown on both sides; then drain them and eat them warm.

WEST INDIA GUMBO.

Take two quarts of young tender pods of ochra, wash them clean, slice them and put them into a pan with a very little water, salt and pepper: stew them gently till they are tender, stirring them occasionally. Serve them up with melted butter.

SPANISH MANGOES.

Get fine ripe tomatoes and green cucumbers, that are not too large; peel and slice them thin. Peel some large sweet onions, and slice them also. Stack them in a deep dish in alternate layers, strewing between each layer a little salt and pepper; then fill up the dish with good vinegar, having stirred into it a small portion of made mustard.

KITCHEN PEPPER.

Take an ounce of black paper, one of white pepper, one of cinnamon, one and a half of ginger, half an ounce of red pepper, half a one of nutmegs, one dozen blades of mace and two dozen cloves. Mix them all together, and grind or pound them till they are very fine. Bottle and cork it securely. It will keep its strength, and will be found a very convenient article—nice for flavoring fresh meat gravies, &c.

CAYENNE PEPPER.

Take ripe chillis, and dry them perfectly in the sun, or before a slow fire, taking care not to scorch them, which would in a great degree spoil their flavor. Grind or pound them to a perfect powder, mixing with them one eighth of their quantity of fine salt. Put it up in small dry bottles, securing the corks with leather. It will keep its strength, and a very small portion of it will give a fine flavor to gravies, soups, &c.

ANOTHER WAY NO MAKE CAYENNE PEPPER.—Take ripe capsicum, bury it in flour, and bake till they are dry enough to powder; then, holding them by a pair of pincers, cut them into small pieces. To each ounce add one pound of flour and a sufficient quantity of water and yeast to make it into stiff paste: make it into small cakes, bake them over again, powder them, and sift and bottle it.

MADE MUSTARD.

Grind and sift three pounds of black mustard seed; mix with it one pound of salt, and liquefy it sufficiently with currant wine, adding four spoonfuls of sugar to each pint.

COMMON MUSTARD.

The most common way of preparing mustard for the table is to add to the best flour of mustard a very little salt and a sufficient quantity of boiling water to dilute it to the proper consistence, mashing and stirring it with a spoon till it becomes quite smooth. Some people make use of vinegar instead of water, and others, preferring it very mild, substitute for the water and salt, sweet milk and sugar.

FRENCH MUSTARD.

Take a quarter of a pound of the best flour of mustard, mix with it two salt-spoonfuls of salt, two of grated horse-radish and two spring eschalots, having them minced fine. Pour as much tarragan vinegar as will be sufficient to dilute it to the proper consistence. Mix it very well, mashing it and stirring it with a spoon till it becomes quite smooth. Put it up in wide mouthed bottles, (for convenience.) stop it closely, and use it as common mustard.

HORSERADISH MUSTARD.

Mix together equal portions of the best powdered mustard and grated horseradish. Have ready enough boiling sweet milk to liquefy the whole sufficiently; pour it on the mixture, gradually, mashing and stirring it with a spoon till it is very well incorporated: then put it up in small jars or wide mouthed bottles, cork them securely, and use it as other mustard.

TO BROWN FLOUR.

Brown flour should be used in all brown gravies to thicken them. Put it into an oven that is moderately heated, set it over a few coals, and keep stirring it as you would coffee to brown it evenly and prevent its burning. As soon as the whole is of a light brown, take it up, cool it, put it up in dry bottles, and cork them tight. It will be found a very convenient article, being always in readiness.

TO MELT BUTTER.

To melt or draw butter in the best manner, it should be weighed, and to each ounce allow a table-spoonful of water and a small tea-spoonful of flour. Rub the flour into the butter till it is completely saturated; then put it into a covered sauce-pan with water; set it in an oven of hot water, which should be placed over a bed of coals; stir it slowly and constantly till it melts; and as soon as it begins to boil, it is enough; then remove it from the fire.

With great precaution, butter may be melted over embers, but it requires double the care and attention to prevent its oiling as when melted in hot water.

Melted or drawn butter is the basis of a great many delicious sauces. In preparing your sauces, if you wish to add a very thick condiment or seasoning to melted butter, such as chopped herbs, fish, &c., you had best omit half of the flour and double the quantity of water: but if it is to be seasoned with wine, &c., melt it as first directed.

PLAIN SAUCES, CATCHUPS, &c.

BROWN GRAVIES.

Brown gravies are seldom served with any thing else than roasted or baked meats. In such cases the drippings are preferable. Boil and skim them, add boiling water and brown flour in such proportions as will dilute and make them of a proper richness and thickness, flavoring them with such seasonings as may suit your own taste. It is the practice of some cooks to fry coarse pieces of meat for the purpose of making brown gravies. This is only a superfluous waste; for in the former you have the essence of the meat as well as in the latter, and as the choice pieces of meat are generally used for roasting, the drippings are certainly the nicest.

WHITE OR DRAWN GRAVY.

This kind of gravy, to avoid expense and trouble, should be made of the liquor in which fresh meat, poultry or game has been boiled. Put it away in a covered vessel, and in cold weather it will keep good for several days: then, by adding the different catchups, &c., with a little butter, flour and cream to thicken it, you can have nice gravy at a few minutes' warning; and besides that, it is saving what otherwise might be thrown away.

OYSTER SAUCE.

Wash a pint of fresh oysters, trim off the hard part of them, and put them into a stew-pan, strain over them their liquor, and add eight ounces of butter, rolled in flour: simmer them eight or ten minutes; then add a little mace, nutmeg and the juice of half a lemon. Stir it up with a spoon and serve it in a boat. It is generally served with boiled fish or poultry.

Another way is to mince the oysters, put them into a pan with half their own liquor, and all other seasonings above named, and simmer them five or six minutes.

LOBSTER SAUCE

Put a glass of water into a stew-pan with half a dozen blades of mace, a tea-spoonful of cayenne pepper and a powdered nutmeg; boil it a few minutes till the flavor of the spices is extracted; then strain it, return the liquid to the pan with three quarters of a pound of butter, rolled in flour and broken up. Having boiled a lobster tender, extract the meat from the shell and claws; mash the coral to a smooth paste, moistening it with a little butter from the pan; cut the white part of the meat into small pieces, and stir it with the coral into the butter, &c. Just let it boil up, shaking it together in the pan, and serve it in a sauce-boat. It is a very excellent sauce for fish.

SHRIMP SAUCE.

Having washed half a pint of shrimps, mince them fine and put them into three quarters of a pound of melted butter, with a spoonful of pepper vinegar and one of lemon pickle. Put it into a stew-pan, set it over the fire, simmer it five or six minutes, stirring it with a spoon, and serve it up. It is also a nice sauce for fish.

ANCHOVY SAUCE.

Soak half a dozen anchovies in fresh water for two or three hours; then put them into a stew-pan with a quart of water, and simmer them till they are completely dissolved and the liquor reduced to half a pint: then strain it, return it to the pan, with half a pint of red wine and eight ounces of butter rolled in flour and broken up. Place the pan over a bed of clear coals; just let it raise the simmer, stirring it all the time, and serve it up. It is to accompany fresh fish.

PRAWN SAUCE.

Having boiled your prawns, mince half a pint of them, put them into a stew-pan with three quarters of a pound of butter rolled in flour and broken up, a few spoonfuls of vinegar and a tea-spoonful of pepper. Melt the butter slowly, stirring it all the time, and when it begins to boil, serve it up.

CRAB SAUCE.

Having boiled your crabs, extract the meat from the shells, mince it fine, season it with salt, pepper and nutmeg; put half a pint of it into a stew-pan with three quarters of a pound of melted butter and a glass of white wine. Just let it raise the simmer, and serve it in a boat. All these sauces are very good for fish.

EGG SAUCE.

Boil six eggs till they become hard, drop them immediately into cold water, which will make the shells slip off smoothly, without tearing or breaking the eggs. Chop very small the whites of four, and cut the yolks in two. Stir them in six ounces of melted butter, add a tea-spoonful of pepper, and serve it in a boat.

ANOTHER EGG SAUCE.—Mash to a paste the yolks of four eggs with four table-spoonfuls of vinegar, a tea-spoonful of pepper, and one of salt. Chop small the yolks of four more boiled eggs, and the whites of two, and having ready a pint of drawn butter, stir them gradually into it. Both of these sauces are excellent for poultry or fish.

WHITE SAUCE FOR FOWLS.

Beat well into half a pint of rich sweet cream the yolks of two eggs, half a grated nutmeg, a tea-spoonful of pepper, and two minced onions. Stir them in half a pint of melted butter, set it over a bed of coals, and keep constantly stirring it till it raises the simmer; then serve it up.

ANOTHER WHITE SAUCE FOR FOWLS.—Put in a saucepan half a pint of veal or poultry gravy; add to it two ounces of butter, rolled in flour, and a tea-spoonful of pepper. Stir in a gill of rich sweet cream, with a small handful of chopped parsley. As soon as it begins to boil, remove it from the fire, and stir slowly and gradually into it the juice of half a lemon and a teaspoonful of curry powders.

AN EXCELLENT SAUCE FOR POULTRY, GAME, &c.

Put half a pint of nice poultry or veal gravy in a saucepan, with four ounces of butter, and a spoonful of flour; add a small handful of grated bread, a tea-spoonful of pepper, one of grated lemon, and half a grated nutmeg. As soon as it comes to a boil, remove it from the fire, and stir in the juice of two fine ripe oranges.

PARSLEY SAUCE.

Pick a bunch of fresh green parsley; rinse it clean in cold water, and boil it for five minutes, in a pan of water, with a handful of salt; after which drain it, pick the leaves from the stalks, chop them fine, and stir four table-spoonfuls of them into a pint of drawn butter; add a tea-spoonful of black pepper, two spoonfuls of vinegar, and serve it warm. This sauce may be eaten with any kind of fresh meats.

NASTURTIAN SAUCE.

Having drawn your butter in the usual manner, make it as thick as you desire it with pickled nasturtian seeds, add a little of the vinegar in which they were pickled, a small portion of pepper, and serve it warm. It is a fine sauce for boiled mutton.

CAPER SAUCE.

Caper sauce may be very readily made by stirring capers and vinegar into melted butter, in the proportions of four large spoonfuls of capers and four of vinegar, to a pint of drawn butter. Green pickle sauce may be made in the same manner, and both are nice for boiled mutton.

HORSERADISH SAUCE.

Boil half a pint of sweet milk for three or four minutes with four table-spoonfuls of grated horse-radish, a desert-spoonful of flour, a tea-spoonful of black pepper, and half a one of salt. Mix with it half a pint of drawn butter, and stir slowly and gradually into it four table-spoonfuls of vinegar. Serve it up immediately, and eat it with poultry, mutton or fish. It will be found very good.

FORCE-MEAT SAUCE.

Force-meat sauce will be found very fine for boiled poultry or fish. Stir half a pint of sweet cream with half a tea-spoonful of pepper, into half a pint of melted butter. Make your force-meat into small balls, about the size of a partridge egg; roll them in yolk of egg, then in flour, and put them in a stew-pan, with the butter, &c. Stew them for five or six minutes, add a tea-spoonful of curry powder, and serve them in a boat. See receipt for making force-meat.

NOODLE SAUCE FOR BOILED FOWLS.

Take a small handful of noodles after they are dried, chop them small, (see receipt for making noodles.) Put them in a stew-pan, with a tea-spoonful of pepper, one of flour, half a one of salt, and enough sweet milk to cover them. Boil them for ten or fifteen minutes; then put in six ounces of butter, boil it up again, and serve it.

TOMATO SAUCE.

Roll a pound of fresh butter in flour, break it up, and put it in a sauce-pan, with eight table-spoonfuls of vinegar. Take fine ripe tomatoes, peel them, chop them small, season them with salt and pepper, and stir enough of them into the butter to make it as thick as you desire it. Just let it boil up, and serve it in a boat. It will be found very fine for beef, veal or mutton.

BREAD SAUCE FOR A PIG.

Cut several slices from a fine loaf of bread, put them in a sauce-pan, and having skimmed the drippings from a roasted pig, pour it over the bread. Let it set for a few minutes, till the bread is completely saturated with the drippings; then add a table-spoonful of powdered sage, a tea-spoonful of kitchen pepper, one of grated lemon, four ounces of butter, and enough sweet cream or madeira wine to liquify it sufficiently; boil it up, and serve it in a boat

---

BREAD SAUCE FOR POULTRY AND GAME.

Roll a pound of butter in flour, break it up, and melt it in a sauce-pan, with eight spoonfuls of water. Stir in a small handful of bread crumbs, and one of currants, shred raisins, or cherries. Boil it up, add the juice of one lemon, or two fine oranges. Shake it in the pan a minute or two, and serve it in a boat. It is a delicious sauce for poultry, &c.

MINT SAUCE FOR LAMB.

Get a handful of young, tender mint, and put it in fresh water, with a lump of ice, for one hour before you wish to make use of it; this makes it tender. Then pick the leaves from the stalks, chop them very fine, mix with them an equal portion of powdered sugar, and make it moist or rather liquid, with vinegar.

WARM MINT SAUCE FOR MUTTON AND LAMB.

Take equal portions of drawn butter and vinegar; put them in a sauce pan, with a very little pepper, and when it begins to boil, make it tolerably thick, with equal portions of mint and boiled yolks of eggs, having picked the tender leaves of mint from the stalks, and chopped them fine, and cut each yolk in four.

CELERY SAUCE.

Having washed and pared your celery, cut it in small pieces, put it in a stew-pan, with a very little water, and a small portion of salt. Boil it slowly till it is quite tender, and nearly dry; then add a little pepper, mace, a good lump of butter, rolled in flour, and enough sweet cream to make it sufficiently liquid. Boil it up again, and serve it in a boat. This sauce is eaten with poultry, game, and boiled mutton.

MUSHROOM SAUCE.

In gathering mushrooms, select those that are of a pearl color on the top, and the under side of a pale pink. Having removed the stems and outside skin from a pint of mushrooms, mince them, season them with a little salt, pepper and mace, and put them in a stew-pan, with enough sweet milk to cook them tender. Stew them gently till they are done, and the liquor quite low; then add one ounce of butter, rolled in flour, and a cup of sweet cream. Boil it up, and serve it. This is a suitable sauce for boiled poultry, also beef and veal steaks.

ONION SAUCE.

Peel half a dozen large sweet onions, cut each one in four, and boil them till very tender, in a small quantity of sweet milk. Then mash them fine, season them with salt, pepper and butter; add a small spoonful of flour and a cup of rich sweet cream; boil it up again, and it is ready for use. Onion sauce may be used with any kind of boiled poultry, game, beef, veal and mutton.

ASPARAGUS SAUCE.

Take the white tender stalks of asparagus, wash and scrape them neatly, tie them in little bundles, and boil them in water, with a little salt, till they are tender; then chop them small, season them with pepper, and put them into a sauce-pan, with equal portions of butter and cream; add a very little flour, boil it up, and serve it in a boat. There should be plenty of butter and cream, to make the sauce sufficiently liquid; a small handful of asparagus to a pint of the butter and cream, will be well proportioned. This is a delicious sauce for poultry and game.

WINE SAUCE FOR MEATS.

Mix together half a pint of melted butter, half a pint of red wine, four spoonfuls of grated tongue, two of currant jelly, and a tea-spoonful of pepper. Having put it in a pan over a bed of coals, just let it raise the boil, and it will be ready for use. It is eaten with venison, roasted beef and pork.

OYSTER CATCHUP.

Having taken the oysters from the shells, wash them in their own liquor, trim off the hard part, and pound them to a paste in a mortar, seasoning them to your taste with salt, cayenne pepper and mace. Put the paste or pounded oysters in a stew-pan, with a pint of white wine to each pint of the paste. Set it over the fire, and as soon as it boils, skim it; then cover the pan, and let it boil for ten minutes, after which cool it, and put it up in small bottles, securing the corks with leather. Catchups are principally designed to flavor sauces and gravies, at a time when the fresh materials cannot be procured.

LEMON CATCHUP OR PICKLE.

Mix together two ounces of grated horseradish, two of mustard seed, half an ounce of nutmegs, half an ounce of mace, half an ounce of black pepper, a quarter of an ounce of cayenne pepper, and a quarter of an ounce of cloves. Beat them very fine in a mortar, and put it in a stew-pan with one dozen lemons, which have been sliced and divested of the seeds, a large handful of salt, and three pints of good vinegar. Cover the pan, and boil it for fifteen or twenty minutes; then put it in a jar, cover it, and let it stand for four weeks, stirring it up occasionally; after which strain it, put it in small bottles, and cork them tight. A very little of this catchup (or pickle, as it is sometimes called,) gives quite an agreeable flavor to fish and other sauces.

RUM CATCHUP.

Chop fine a small handful of thyme, parsley, sweet basil, sweet marjoram, the peel of two fresh oranges, and one lemon, half an ounce of mace, half an ounce of black pepper, a quarter of an ounce of cayenne pepper, and a quarter of an ounce of cloves. Put them all in a pan with a quart of good vinegar, cover it, and boil it a few minutes till the flavor of the spices, &c. is extracted. Then strain it, throw in a handful of salt, and set it by till it gets cold; after which stir into it half a pint of madeira wine and half a pint of rum. Put it up in small bottles, filling them quite full, and securing the corks with leather. This, like other catchups, is designed to flavor sauces and gravies; they are sometimes sent to table in castors, and sometimes sent in the small bottles in which they are put up.

TOMATO CATCHUP.

Gather your tomatoes when fine and ripe, peel them and crush them to pieces; put them in a stew-pan, without water, season them with salt, as for table use, and boil them gently for two hours, stirring them frequently; then strain them through a seive, pressing them with a large spoon or ladle, to get as much of the juice as you can. Season it to your taste with pepper, mace, cinnamon, nutmegs and ginger; put it again in the pan, and simmer it till tolerably thick, then cool it, put it in small bottles, and cork them tightly, securing them with melted rosin. You may flavor it with onions, or salt and pepper only.

LOBSTER CATCHUP.

Having boiled a common sized lobster very tender, extract all the meat from the shell and claws, season it to your taste with salt, cayenne pepper, and mace, and beat it to a perfect paste, adding as you proceed, a little of the best vinegar to moisten it; then mix with it a bottle of muscat or sherry wine. Stir it well together, and put it up in small wide-mouthed bottles, stopping them closely, and securing the corks with leather.

MUSHROOM CATCHUP.

Having selected the proper mushrooms, remove the stems, brush them, pack them away in an earthen or stone jar, strewing between each layer a small handful of salt; cover them, and set them by till next day. Then crush them with your hands, press them through a fine sieve, put the liquid in a pan, allowing to each quart half an ounce of whole black pepper, half an ounce of cayenne pepper, half an ounce of ginger, a quarter of an ounce of cloves, and a quarter of an ounce of mace. Cover the pan to prevent the flavor of the spices evaporating, and boil it gently till reduced to half its original quantity; then cool it, strain it through a cloth, and put it in small bottles, securing the corks with melted rosin. To secure it against all possibility of spoiling, give it a boil up once a month. Skim it, and bottle it again, as directed.

ANCHOVY CATCHUP.

Mix together a quart of white wine, a quart of red wine, a pint of anchovy liquor, and a pint of vinegar.

Having boned three dozen anchovies, chop them small, mix with them two lemons, cut in slices, one dozen spring eschalots, minced fine, half an ounce of black pepper, a quarter of an ounce of mace, and two powdered nutmegs. Put the mixture in a sauce-pan with the liquid; cover it, and boil it gently till reduced to one half the original. Then strain it, and when perfectly cold, put it in small bottles for use, securing the corks with rosin or leather. Two spoonfuls of this preparation will give an agreeable flavor to a pint of sauce or gravy, and if made as directed, will keep good a year or more.

FISH CATCHUP.

Take two quarts of the proper mushrooms, chop them small, and sprinkle them with salt. Mix with them a pound and a quarter of anchovies, chopped small, one pound of chopped onions, sprinkling them with salt, half an ounce of allspice, half an ounce of mace, a quarter of an ounce of whole black pepper, a quarter of an ounce of red pepper, and a quarter of an ounce of sliced ginger. Put the whole into a pan or kettle, with two quarts of good vinegar, two quarts of strong beer and one pint of the anchovy liquor or pickle. Cover the vessel, and boil it till the liquor is reduced two quarts: then strain, cool and bottle it securely. It will be found fine for flavoring fish sauces, gravies, &c., and if made as directed, will be good for any length of time.

WALNUT CATCHUP.

The walnuts should be gathered while very young and tender, so that you may pierce them through with a needle. Put them into a stone jar, pour enough boiling water on them, that is strongly impregnated with salt, to cover them well; tie a cloth over them, and set them by for four days: then take them from the liquor, mash them fine, put them into a jar, and pour over enough good vinegar to cover them entirely. Close the jar, and let them stand for two days, stirring them well once a day: after which put them with the vinegar into a linen bag; press through all the juice you can, mix it with the other liquor, and to each quart add one ounce of black pepper, one ounce of pounded ginger, half an ounce of allspice, half an ounce of mace and a quarter of an ounce of cloves. Boil it in a closely covered vessel for twenty minutes, skimming it well, and when cold bottle it for use.

KITCHEN CATCHUP.

Chop fine two quarts of ripe tomatoes, sprinkle them with salt and put them into a pan with one dozen minced onions, a handful of scraped horseradish, and boil them gently for one hour, adding no water, but stirring them frequently: then strain them, put the liquid into a pan with an equal portion of red wine; add half an ounce of black pepper, half an ounce of nutmegs and half an ounce of cloves. Cover the pan and boil it gently till reduced to half the original quantity: then cool and bottle it.

FRUIT SAUCES, OR ACCOMPANIMENTS TO FRESH MEATS.

PEACH SAUCE.

Take fine ripe plum peaches, pare and slice them from the stones, put them into a stew-pan with enough water to cover them, cover the pan and stew them till very tender, raising the lid and stirring them occasionally: then stir in a small lump of butter, rolled in flour, a little nutmeg and a small portion of sugar; simmer it a few minutes longer, mashing and stirring it well, and send it to table with poultry or game.

RAW PEACH SAUCE.

This sauce makes a very fine desert eaten with cream, nutmeg and powdered white sugar, and is also nice with game. Take ripe soft peaches, taking care to select those that are as dry and farinaceous as possible. Peel them, mash them very fine, seasoning them lightly with nutmeg and powdered sugar. Put the mass into a glass or china dish, and make it smooth.

DRIED PEACH SAUCE.

Peaches that are dried with the peelings, are not so nice for sauce, being comparatively coarse and rough, though for common purposes they answer very well.

Take fine cling-stone peaches, that have been nicely pared and dried in the sun; wash them very clean; but if you wish the full flavor of the peach, do not soak them. Put them into a pan with plenty of water to cover them well, cover the pan and stew them gently till they become soft and the syrup quite low: then mash them to a pulp, and season it with sugar and nutmeg, cloves or mace. It is nice with poultry or game.

STEWED PEACHES.

Take peaches that are nicely dried, wash them clean in two hot waters, put them into a preserving kettle with enough water to cover them well, cover and stew them gently till very tender and the syrup low; but do not mash them, as they are prettier to remain in whole pieces. Serve them in a glass dish with the syrup about them, and introduce them at the dinner table with fresh meat.

APPLE SAUCE.

Take ripe acid apples, pare and slice them, put them into a pan with a little water, cover them and stew them till soft; add enough sugar to make them as sweet as you desire, mashing and stirring them till they become a smooth pulp and nearly dry. It is eaten with poultry, game and roasted pork.

GREEN APPLE SAUCE.

Take good cooking apples before they get half grown; wash them clean, cut off the stems and blossom ends, and chop them small; put them into a stew-pan with a very little water, cover them and stew them till quite soft; then stir in a small lump of butter, a little grated lemon and a good quantity of sugar. Mash and stir them till they become nearly dry and quite smooth; then serve it in a glass or china dish. It is to accompauy roasted poultry or game of any kind, and also pork.

BAKED APPLES.

Baked apples are a very common desert, eaten with boiled custard or sugar, cream and nutmeg, and they may also be eaten with game. Pare and core some fine ripe apples; put them into a pan, grate a little lemon over them, sprinkle on a handful of brown sugar, and bake them in an oven of moderate heat. As soon as they are perfectly done, serve them carefully, and eat them warm or cold.

DRIED APPLE SAUCE.

In drying apples, be careful to select fine ripe ones that will cook perfectly soft, no other sort being fit for this purpose. Having them pared, cored and nicely dried, pour boiling water on and wash them in two waters: stew them till they are very soft and the syrup low; mash them fine, seasoning it with sugar and cloves, or nutmeg, and if for present use, a little sweet cream will make it better.

CRANBERRY SAUCE.

Take ripe cranberries, wash and stew them with a little water till they are soft and become a gelatinous mass, stirring it constantly at the last. To a quart of the pulp allow three quarters of a pound of loaf sugar; mix them well, put it into a mould, and when it gets cold, turn it smoothly into a glass or china dish. Send it to table with any kind of roasted or baked poultry or game.

CHERRY SAUCE.

Select large cherries that are ripe; break them over a pan to catch the juice, and pick out all the seeds: put them into a pan with a little water, a small lump of butter rolled in flour, and half a pound of sugar to each quart of the cherries. Stew them gently till they are a thick smooth pulp, stirring them frequently. Mould it in teacups; and when they get cold, turn them out smoothly into a glass dish; grate loaf sugar and nutmeg over them, and eat them with poultry and game.

PEAR SAUCE.

Take the large bell-pears, peel them and extract the cores without cutting the pears into pieces. Put them into a deep dish, pour over enough white wine to prevent them burning, lay a piece of white paper over the top, and bake them in rather a slow oven. When they are done quite soft, place them side by side in a glass dish, squeeze on them a little lemon juice, grate on some nutmeg and enough loaf sugar to dulcify them sufficiently, and eat them with the nicest of roasted poultry and game. They are often eaten as a desert, accompanied with rich sweet cream and powdered sugar or boiled custard. Common pears may be prepared for sauce by peeling, slicing and stewing them in a very little water till soft and nearly dry, sweetening them with sugar and mashing them very fine. They are sometimes eaten at tea with sweet cream and powdered sugar.

STEWED PEARS.

Take pears that have been neatly dried in the sun, wash them clean, put them into a porcelain skillet or preserving kettle, with enough water to cover them, and stew them gently till tender, leaving but very little syrup: serve them in a glass or china dish, pour over them the syrup, and send them to the dinner table with poultry or game.

GOOSEBERRY SAUCE.

Gather gooseberries when ripe, take off the stems and blossom ends, pour boiling water on them, and stew them in a covered pan till done and the liquor low: then add half a pound of sugar to each pound of berries, and a small lump of butter, rolled in flour; stew them a few minutes longer and serve them. They are a nice concomitant to roasted poultry and game, and are also nice at tea with powdered sugar and cream. Red currants may also be prepared in the same manner, and are also nice.

GRAPE SAUCE.

Take large white grapes, pick them, weigh them, and to each pound allow half a pound of sugar, but do not mix it till the grapes are done, as it makes the syrup scorch more easily. Put them into a stew-pan with a very little water, cover them and stew them gently till they are soft and the syrup or liquor quite low: then stir in the sugar, and continue to stew them, stirring them all the time till they become a smooth pulp, and so thick that it will glutinate in the moulds. Then put it into tea-cups, and when they get perfectly cold, turn them out into a glass dish; grate loaf sugar over them, and lay on the top of each a spoonful of whipped cream. It is a fine sauce for birds, and is also nice with powdered sugar and sweet cream. Plum sauce may be prepared in the same manner.

FLAVORED VINEGARS.

ESCHALOT VINEGAR.

Flavored vinegars are particularly useful to flavor gravies, soups and sauces. Take the large spring eschalot; peel, wash, chop them small, and put them into a jar: sprinkle on a handful of salt, cover them with the best vinegar, close the jar and set it by for one week: then strain it, empty the jar, fill it up again with eschalots, prepared in the same manner; pour over the vinegar, close the jar and set it by for another week; after which strain and bottle it for use. Onion vinegar may be made in the same manner.

TARRAGON VINEGAR.

Pick the leaves of the tarragon from the stalks just before it blooms; spread them out on a cloth, and let them lie for two or three days to dry a little; then put them into a jar, close it and set it by for one week; then strain and bottle it. If you wish it very strongly flavored with the tarragon, fill it up the second time with fresh leaves and soak them in the same manner. Any kind of nice sweet herbs may be soaked in the same manner for the purpose of seasoning.

PEPPER VINEGAR.

Chop a good quantity of ripe red peppers very small, put them into a stone or earthen jar, close it and let it set for several days: then boil it for a few minutes in a covered vessel, and strain and bottle it for use.

HORSERADISH VINEGAR.

Wash your horseradish very clean, scrape it fine, put it into a jar and cover it with the best vinegar; stop it closely, and let it stand to infuse for several days: then strain it, pour the vinegar on a fresh supply of horseradish, and let it stand again for several days; after which strain and bottle it.

CELERY VINEGAR.

To make celery vinegar, use the seeds. pound them fine, put them into a jar or wide mouthed bottle; pour on enough good vinegar to cover them, stop it closely and let it stand to infuse for a week or two; then strain and bottle it. Black mustard vinegar is made in the same manner.

PICKLING.

—◦✦◦—

TO PICKLE CUCUMBERS,

The nicest cucumbers for pickling are the long green ones. Gather them while they are young and small, leaving a short bit of the stem on. Be very careful in gathering them, lest you bruise them, which would cause them to rot. Make a brine of cold water and salt, which should be so strongly impregnated with the salt as to bear up an egg upon its surface. Put it in a very tight tub, put in your cucumbers, cover it to keep out the dirt, set it in a cool dry place, and if they are well covered with the brine, they will keep good a year or two. If you wish to keep them through the second summer, and the brine begins to smell a little old, take them out, wash them in clean water with your hand, taking care not to bruise them, and put them in a fresh brine. When you wish to make use of them, soak them in fresh water for two or three days, changing the water two or three times. Then put them in a porcelain or block tin kettle, cover them with good vinegar, throw in a little mace, cloves, whole mustard seed, and a good quantity of red pepper; all tied up in a muslin rag. Put a thick layer of green vine leaves over the top, and simmer them for a few minutes; then put them in a stone or earthen jar, and tie a bit of oil-cloth over the top. When you take them from the brine, if you discover they are getting a little soft, throw a small lump of alum in the vinegar with them, which will have a tendency to make them hard and brittle.

—◦✦◦—

GHERKIN.

The gherkin is a species of cucumber, though very different in shape to the common cucumber, being small, thick, and of an oval shape, with a rough and horny surface; wholly cultivated for pickling, and are not fit to eat in any other way. Gather them carefully, leaving a part of the stem on, and put them away in brine, as directed for cucumbers. When you wish to make use of them, soak them for two or three days in fresh water, changing them into fresh water every day. Then put them in a kettle that is lined with green vine leaves, (a porcelain kettle is best,) add enough sliced ginger, mace and cayenne pepper, to flavor them sufficiently, put a thick layer of green vine leaves on the top, and pour in enough strong vinegar to cover them well. If they are not very firm, put in a small lump of alum, which will make them hard and frangible. Simmer them a very few minutes over a slow fire, and put them up in jars. Look to those in the brine occasionally, and if the brine leaks or dries up, so that the pickles are not covered, make more, and pour over them, for they will not keep well if they are not kept entirely under the brine.

⟶◇◆◯⟵

PARSLEY.

Pickled parsley is quite a convenient article; it answers for seasoning gravies at a time when fresh parsley cannot be obtained. Gather a good quantity of very green double or curled parsley, wash it clean, but do not bruise it. Make a plentiful brine of salt and water, strong enough to bear up an egg. Having tied your parsley in little bunches, put them in a tight tub; pour over them the brine, cover them, and let them stand for ten days. Then take them out, and soak them in fresh water two or three days, changing them into fresh water several times. Boil a sufficient quantity of vinegar to cover them well, for five or six minutes, with a little pepper, mace, cloves and a small lump of alum, and having put the bundles of parsley in a jar, pour the pickle over them, scalding hot. Tie a cloth over the top, first securing it with a cork, and set it by for use.

⟶◇◆◯⟵

ASPARAGUS.

Gather your asparagus while young and tender; cut it in equal lengths. tie it up in small bundles with bits of tape, put them in a jar, pour boiling salt and water on, cover the jar, and let them stand till next day; then take them out, dry them on a cloth, and let them soak in weak vinegar for three days, stirring them occasionally. Prepare enough vinegar to cover them well, by adding to it red pepper, sliced ginger, scraped horseradish, whole mustard seed, powdered mace, and nutmegs; these seasonings must be proportioned to suit yonr own taste. Having it all prepared, put your asparagus in a stone or earthen jar, pour over the vinegar with the spices, and secure the jar with a cork or piece of leather.

NASTURTIANS.

It is the seeds of nasturtians that are used for pickling; gather them when full grown, before they get hard, put them in a jar of plain, cold vinegar, close it with a cork, and set it in a cool, dry place; it is not necessary to add salt or spices, as they keep well without.

CHERRIES.

Take any kind of fine, large cherries, that are full grown, but not soft. Be very careful in gathering them that you do not bruise them, remove the stones, and put the cherries in a glass jar. Mix a pound of sugar with three quarts of good vinegar; boil it in a covered vessel till reduced to two quarts, set it by till it gets perfectly cold, and then pour it over the cherries. Plums may be pickled in the same manner, and either of them makes a pretty garnish for fresh meats.

RADISH PODS.

Radish pods for pickling should be full grown, but young and fragile. Cut them in little bunches, as they make a prettier garnish than when separated; pour boiling salt and water over them, cover them to keep in the steam, and when cold, repeat it again and again, till you have them a fine green. Then put them in a jar, disseminating between each layer some whole mustard seed, pepper corns, and sliced ginger; add a very little powdered alum, and a little turmeric, mixed with a small portion of sweet oil, which will impart to the pickles rather a resplendent appearance, that they otherwise would not have.

Then pour over them enough strong vinegar to cover them; close the jar with a cork or leather, and keep it in a cool, dry place.

BARBERRIES.

Gather your barberries when ripe, but firm; put them in bunches into a jar; sprinkle on them a large handful of sugar, and cover them with the best vinegar; close the jar, and set it in a cool, dry place. Grapes may be pickled in the same manner, and both are very nice for garnishing dishes.

ONIONS.

Take small white onions, cut off the roots and top ends smoothly, removing the outer skin. Put them in a jar, pour over them boiling water, strongly impregnated with salt, cover them securely, and set them by for ten days, stirring them at least once a day. Then take them from the brine, wipe them dry with a cloth, put them in a jar, strewing among them a little powdered nutmeg and whole mustard seeds. Pour over as much distilled white wine vinegar as will cover them well, and close the jar with a cork or leather. For common purposes, inferior vinegar will answer, but the pickles will not be so white.

TOMATOES.

Take ripe tomatoes that are firm; pierce them through in several places with a needle; put them in a suitable vessel, disseminating between them a little salt, cover them, and let them remain in it for two days; then take them out, wipe them dry, and put them in a jar of plain cold vinegar, with a little black pepper, whole mustard seeds, and enough eschalot vinegar to give them a sufficient flavor. Cover the jar securely.

GREEN TOMATOES.

Gather your tomatoes when full grown, but before they begin to turn red. Put them in a tub of brine that will bear up an egg; cover them with a piece of carpet, set them in a cool, dry place, and they will keep good for years. Examine them occasionally, and if there are any that are likely to rot from being bruised, throw them out, or if the tub should leak, replenish it with fresh brine. When you wish to make use of them, soak them two or three days in fresh water, to draw out the salt, changing the water every day. Then put them in a preserving kettle, that is lined with green vine leaves, put in a small bit of powdered alum, some pepper, cloves, mustard and ginger. Pour in enough good vinegar to cover them well, put on the top a thick layer of the vine leaves, and scald them for a few minutes. Then put them up in jars, stopping them closely.

HORSERADISH.

Get young, tender roots of horseradish; wash them clean, and scrape them remarkably fine with a sharp knife. Put it in a jar, with enough plain cold vinegar to cover it well; add no seasonings. Cover the jar securely with a piece of leather. Horseradish thus prepared will be found an excellent condiment for fresh meats.

PEACHES.

For pickling, select large plum peaches that are ripe, but not the least soft. Wipe off the fuzz with a cloth, put them in strong salt and water, and let them stand for ten days; then soak them in fresh water two or three days, to draw out the salt, shifting the water every day. Put them in a jar, strewing between each layer a small handful of sugar, a few cloves, and a little powdered cinnamon, and cover them with the best vinegar. Firm clingstone peaches may be kept a year or two in strong brine, as directed for cucumbers, and pickled in the same manner. They look very pretty when pared, and colored pink with beet juice or cochineal.

PEACH MANGOES.

Take fine large freestone peaches, that are ripe, and rather farinaceous; split them open, extract the stones, and fill them with equal portions of cloves, cinnamon and whole mustard seeds. Tie them together again with a twine, put them in a jar, disseminating between each layer some sugar, whole mustard seeds, slips of lemon peel, and cloves; cover them with good vinegar that is colored pink with cochineal, and cork the jar securely.

NECTARINES AND APRICOTS.

Gather them while the shells are soft; put them in a suitable vessel, and pour boiling salt and water on once a day till you have them a good green, keeping the vessel covered with a cloth; then soak them in plain cold vinegar for ten or twelve days, to draw out the salt; then put them in a jar, strewing amongst them scraped horseradish, sliced ginger, pepper, mace and whole mustard seeds; pour over enough good vinegar to cover them well, and cork the jar securely.

WALNUTS, BLACK.

Gather them while so young that you can pierce them through with a needle; pour boiling salt and water on, and let them stand for twelve days, repeating the process every third day, and keeping them covered with a cloth; then take them out of the brine, wipe them with a cloth, lay them on dishes in the sun for a few minutes, turning them over once; put them in a jar, interspersing between each layer cloves, allspice, mace, pepper, whole mustard seed, and scraped horseradish. Pour over enough strong vinegar to cover them, and secure the cork with leather. Put up in this manner, they keep better than to boil the vinegar.

WALNUTS, GREEN.

Gather them as before directed, wrap them separately in green vine or mustard leaves, put them in a jar, pour over enough scalding vinegar to cover them, having been strongly impregnated with salt; tie a cloth over them, and set them by for two weeks. Then repeat the same pro-

cess, having fresh vine leaves, vinegar and salt; set them
by again for two weeks, after which put them in a jar,
with a thick layer of vine leaves between each layer of
walnuts.   Having boiled a sufficient quantity of the best
vinegar a few minutes with a little nutmeg, pepper, mustard seeds, and mace, pour it boiling hot on the walnuts,
&c., and cork the jar securely.

RED CABBAGE.

Select large, firm heads of red cabbage, cut each one
in four, and slice them as for slaugh; put them in a vessel of strong salt-water, and let them lie in it for twenty-
four hours; this will make them more brittle than to sprinkle dry salt on them; take them from the brine, and put
them in a stone or earthen jar.   Boil for a few minutes a
sufficient quantity of the best vinegar to cover them well,
with cloves, mustard seeds, and mace, proportioning them
to suit your own taste; strain it, color it a fine pink with
cochineal, and when it gets perfectly cold, pour it over
the cabbage, stopping the jar closely with cork or leather.

WHITE CABBAGE.

Take hard, white heads of cabbage, that are very tender and frangible; cut off the stalks, trim off the outer
leaves, cut each head in four, and slice them thin.   Put
them in strong salt and water for a day or two; prepare
a pickle by boiling the best white wine vinegar for a few
minutes, with a little mustard seed, scraped horseradish,
white onions, mace, and pepper; all these to be proportioned to suit your own taste; strain it, and when it gets
cold, having placed the cabbage in a jar, pour the pickle
over them, and cover them securely.

MUSHROOMS.

Be careful to select the esculent mushrooms, as some
of them are very poisonous.   Take small button mushrooms as soon as they are gathered, peel them, remove
the stems, and boil them hastily for five or six minutes in
a covered vessel.   Then take them out, drain the water

from them, but do not break them to pieces, and sprinkle them immediately with salt. Put them into jars, interspersing between each layer a very little pepper, mace and ginger, and cover them with good vinegar.

BEETS.

There are three species of the beet, the white, red and yellow, though the difference is more in color than taste, and should all be prepared alike. Trim off the tops, but do not break the roots nor outer skin, which would cause them to fade or lose their color in boiling. Put them into a kettle of cold water, and boil them gently till you can pierce them through with a fork: then scrape off the skin, (this may be done nicer by throwing them into cold water as soon as you take them from the boil,) slice them roundwise, if large; sprinkle on them immediately while warm, a very little salt and pepper, and cover them with plain cold vinegar. They make excellent pickle, and a pretty garnish for roasted meats, particularly when scraped and made into balls. When they are very young and small, they look nice to remain whole.

PICKLED EGGS.

Boil them till they are hard; throw them into cold water immediately while hot, which will make the shells slip off smoothly without breaking the eggs. Boil some red beets till very soft; peel and mash them fine, and put enough of the juice into some plain cold vinegar to color it a fine pink; add a very little salt, pepper, nutmeg and cloves; put the eggs into a jar, and transfuse the vinegar, &c. over them. They make a delightful garnish to remain whole, for poultry, game and fish, and still more beautiful when cut in ringlets.

MUSKMELONS.

Muskmelons may be gathered when as small as a walnut, and pickled whole like cucumbers; but the usual way of pickling them is to gather them a size larger, and make them into mangoes.

Select those that are of a regular and handsome figure; put them into a small tub or jar, and cover them with boiling water, having it strongly impregnated with salt; cover them and set them by till next day: then cut a narrow slip out of one side of each, remove the seeds carefully without cutting the melon; put them again into the brine, cover them, and let them remain in it for one week: then drain the brine from them, wrap them separately in green leaves from the melon vines, put them into a kettle that is lined with the leaves, put in a small lump of alum, which will tend to make them hard and firm, pour in enough vinegar to cover them well, put a thick layer of the leaves on the top, and merely scald them till they are a good green. If they should look like not being sufficiently green, take them out, put a fresh supply of the leaves into the same vinegar, return the melons, and let them scald again for a few minutes. Make a stuffing for them of finely scraped horseradish, white ginger, sliced thin, whole mustard seeds, very small onion cloves, whole black pepper, cloves, broken blades of mace, powdered nutmegs and turmeric. Mix the whole together, moistening it with a little sweet oil, and fill the melons with the miscellaneous mass, fitting to each the piece that was taken out, and confining them together with pack-thread: then put them into jars, strewing between each layer a small portion of the stuffing; cover them with good vinegar, and close the jars.

⌗

WATERMELON.

Take a fine ripe watermelon, cut out the soft part of it, leaving all the white part of the meat that is firm: cut them into any fanciful figure you please; put them into strong salt and water, and let them remain in it for ten days; then soak them in fresh water three days, changing the water once a day, and put them into a jar of strong vinegar, with a little pepper, mace and cloves. They may be colored green with vine leaves, or red with beet juice, and either makes a pretty garnish for meats.

PEPPERS.

Get the large bell pepper while young and green, leave the stems on, cut a slit in one side, and carefully extract the seeds and cores, pour boiling salt and water on them, cover them, and keep them in a warm place for one week, repeating the process every day, and stirring them occasionally; then if they are not a good green, keep them still longer in the brine, repeating the same process every day till they are; after which fill them up with a stuffing made as for muskmelon mangoes, tie a pack thread round them, to prevent the stuffing from coming out, and put them in a jar of plain cold vinegar; add a small lump of alum to keep them firm, and close the jar.

GREEN BEANS.

Take green beans that are young and tender, string them, put them into strong salt and water, and let them lie in it for one week; then take them out, put them in a kettle in alternate layers of green leaves from the bean vines; put in a small lump of alum, fill it up with weak vinegar, and scald them for a short time; this will make them green. Then put them in a jar, and prepare the vinegar. Boil in a covered vessel, for a few minutes, a sufficient quantity of good vinegar to cover them well, with a little pepper, nutmeg and mace; transfuse it over the beans while boiling; when it gets cold, stir into it a small portion of turmeric, having it made into a paste with sweet oil, which will give the pickles a glossy appearance, and make them a deeper green; then stop the jar closely, and set it by for use.

MARTINOES.

Put the martinoes in salt and water, cover them, and let them remain in it for three days; then put them in a kettle lined with porcelain, pour in enough good vinegar to cover them well, add a few cloves, allspice, and cinnamon; cover the kettle closely, scald them for a few minutes, pour the whole into a jar, and cover it securely.

INDIA PICKLE.

Begin your pickle by preparing the vinegar; to every gallon of good vinegar add a quarter of a pound of mustard seeds, a quarter of a pound of scraped horseradish, a quarter of a pound of sliced ginger, a quarter of a pound of white onions, two ounces of red pepper, two of black pepper, half an ounce of mace, half an ounce of cloves, and two ounces of turmeric.   Put the whole into a jar, cork it securely, and set it by for one month, shaking it up every few days; then strain it, put it in a clean jar, and prepare the pickles.   Take a firm head of white cabbage; trim it, cut it in four, and slice it; prepare a fine head of red cabbage in the same manner: string some young, tender green beans, take the stems from green tomatoes, peel some large white onions, get some small cucumbers, small muskmelons, gherkins, and radish pods. Put them in strong salt and water, and let them remain in it for twenty-four hours; then take out the cabbage, drain them, put them into the vinegar, and let the other vegetables remain in the brine for one week.   After which take them out, soak them in fresh water for two days, shifting them once into fresh water; put them into the vinegar with the other pickles, add a small portion of powdered alum, and cork the jar securely.   As they come in season, add ripe tomatoes, nasturtian seeds, parsley, peppers, plums, peaches, apricots, nectarines and barberries, taking care to prepare each article by the preceding receipts, and adding, as may be required, fresh strong vinegar, preparing it as before directed.   If, by adding fresh articles, the vinegar should become weak, and the pickle likely to get soft, empty out the whole of the vinegar, and fill up the jar with fresh vinegar, prepared in the same manner with the spices, adding a small lump of alum to make the pickles firm.   The liquor of this mixed variety will be found fine for seasoning gravies, &c.   The pickles are also good, being always in readiness, and by proper management may be kept for years; but they are used more for the novelty of the thing than the reality or nicety.

VEGETABLES.

BOILED CABBAGE.

The most usual way of boiling cabbage is with bacon.
Wash your bacon very clean in warm water, put it into
a pot with a good quantity of water, and boil it till about
half done. Having picked your cabbage very carefully,
halve and quarter it, rinse it clean and put it in to boil
with the meat. As soon as it is tender, which you may
tell by taking out a small piece, and mashing it with a
spoon, serve it, drain the water from it, place it smoothly
in a dish, skin and trim the bacon, and lay it on the cabbage, spotting it over at intervals with black or red pepper.

NICE BOILED CABBAGE.

Take a large firm head of cabbage, cut off the stalk,
trim off the outer leaves, cut it in four, and rinse them in
clean water. Put a good quantity of water into a stew-
pan, throw in a handful of salt, and when it boils hard,
skim it. There must be plenty of water to boil the cabbage tender without replenishing it except from a boiling
kettle, as putting in cold water after the cabbage is put
in, will make it tough and stringy. Put in your cabbages, boil them briskly till they are done; then take
them up in a deep dish, drain the water from them, but
be sure you do not break them. They should look very
white, and stand upright in the dish. Send them hot to
the table, as they chill soon. They are eaten with boiled ham, drawn butter, pepper and vinegar.

In preparing inferior cabbage for boiling, be careful to
examine the leaves, as they often have insects lurking
about them, they should be washed in at least two waters.

FRIED CABBAGE.

Get a firm white head, trim off the outer leaves, and
cut the cabbage fine from the stalk; rinse it in cold water,

put it into a pan with a very little water, salt, pepper, and enough lard or butter to season it well: cover the pan and fry it till it is done, raising the lid and stirring it frequently.

STEWED CABBAGE.

Prepare them as for frying; put them into a stew-pan with just enough water to cover them well, add a sufficient quantity of salt to season them, cover the pan, and stew them gently till they are very tender; then take them out, drain them, put them into a sauce-pan with a small lump of butter rolled in flour, a little pepper and a glass of rich sweet cream; mash them fine together, stirring them till they become nearly dry; serve them warm, and make them smooth in the dish. None but the nicest white heads of cabbage are fit to stew.

CABBAGE WITH ONIONS.

Boil them separately till they are very soft; then mix them in equal proportions, mash them very fine, season the pulp with salt and pepper, moistening it with sweet cream; make it into small cakes, dust them with flour, and fry them a light brown in butter; serve them warm, stir into the butter a spoonful of flour and a glass of sweet cream, boil it up and pour it over the cakes.

COLD SLAUGH.

Select firm, fragile heads of cabbage, (no other sort being fit for slaugh); having stripped off the outer leaves, cleave the top part of the head into four equal parts, leaving the lower part whole, so that they may not be separated till shaved or cut fine from the stalk. Take a very sharp knife, shave off the cabbage roundwise, cutting it very smoothly and evenly, and at no rate more than a quarter of an inch in width. Put the shavings or slaugh in a deep china dish, pile it high, and make it smooth; mix with enough good vinegar to nearly fill the dish, a sufficient quantity of salt and pepper to season the slaugh; add a spoonful of whole white mustard seeds, and pour it over the slaugh, garnish it round on the edge of the dish

with pickled eggs, cut in ringlets. Never put butter on
cabbage that is to be eaten cold, as it is by no means pleasant to the taste or sight.

WARM SLAUGH.

Cut them as for cold slaugh; having put in a skillet
enough butter, salt, pepper, and vinegar to season the
slaugh very well, put it into the seasonings; stir it fast,
that it all may warm equally, and as soon as it gets hot,
serve it in a deep china dish; make it smooth, and disseminate over it hard boiled yolks of eggs, that are
minced fine.

CROUT.

This receipt for crout is taken from the British Ency-
clopedia. As crout prepared in this manner is said to
be both food and medicine, I have taken it down ver-
batim, though I have often seen it prepared in nearly
the same manner. It is as follows:

As this preparation of cabbage has been found of sovereign efficacy as a preservative in long voyages from
the sea scurvy, it may not be unacceptable to give a
concise account of the process for making it, according
to the information communicated by an ingenious German gentleman. The soundest and most solid cabbages
are selected for this use, and cut very small, commonly
with an instrument made for this purpose, not unlike
the plane which is used in this country for slicing cucumbers. A knife is used when the preparation is made
with great nicety. The cabbages thus minced are put
into a barrel in layers, hand high, and over each is strew-
ed a handful of salt and carroway seeds; in this manner
it is rammed down with a rammer, stratum super stratum, till the barrel be full, when a cover is put over it and
pressed down with a heavy weight. After standing some
time in this state, it begins to ferment, and it is not till
the fermentation has entirely subsided, that the head is
fitted to the barrel, and it finally shut up, and the cabbage
preserved for use. The most usual way of making crout

in America is to omit the carroway seeds, and sprinkle on it salt only. Crout may be boiled with pork, or fried like common cabbage.

TO BOIL IRISH, OR WHITE POTATOES.

When potatoes are very young, they should not be boiled, but should be cooked in some other way; they are then more watery than when full grown, and to boil them in clear water makes them insipid. Take the full grown potatoes as near one size as possible, wash them clean, and put them in a kettle, with just enough water to cover them well; boil them briskly till they are done, so that you may pierce them through easily with a fork. Then turn off the remaining water, throw a folded cloth over them to absorb the exuberant moisture, and set them by the fire for a few minutes. After which peel them smoothly, and send them warm to table, with salt, pepper, and a boat of drawn butter. They are good with any kind of meat.

ANOTHER WAY OF BOILING POTATOES.—Select fine large potatoes, that have no blemish; wash them clean, and boil them as before directed. Make a sauce or gravy for them in a pan, by putting a lump of butter in it, and when it gets hot, stirring into the butter a little salt, pepper, flour, and a glass of sweet cream. Having your potatoes peeled, put them in the pan, stir them round without breaking them, and serve them with the gravy; this is quite a common way of dressing potatoes, and to most of people's taste a very good one. In the latter part of the winter and spring, when the potatoes are old, they are very apt to have blemished spots, or rotten specks; they should therefore be examined carefully before they are boiled, and all the bad looking parts cut off, or they will impart their imperfections to the potatoes, and of course render them unfit to eat.

MASHED POTATOES.

In the spring, when the potatoes are old and strong, they are much nicer mashed than when served whole, though mashed potatoes are fine at any season. Boil them till they are very tender; if old, in a good quantity of water, but if young, in barely enough to cook them tender. Peel them, mash them fine, press them through a sieve, to get out all the lumps, season the pulp with salt, pepper and butter, moistening it with sweet cream or milk; stir it with a spoon till the seasonings are well intermingled with the mass, and serve it warm, making it smooth in the dish. They are nice with any kind of meat, particularly poultry.

BAKED POTATOES.

Take the pulp of mashed potatoes, make it a little more moist or rather liquid, with sweet cream, stir in one or two beaten eggs, put it in a deep dish, make the top smooth, and bake it a delicate brown in a brisk oven; it will be found very fine.

ANOTHER WAY OF BAKING POTATOES.—Having boiled your potatoes till done, peel and mash them to a pulp while they are warm. Season it with salt, pepper and butter, add a few spoonfuls of sweet cream, but by no means enough to make it liquid, or too soft to retain its shape when made into rolls. Make it into rolls, so as for three to fill a plate; having placed them smoothly in it, set them in an oven, and bake them a light brown with a brisk fire. They are frequently eaten for breakfast.

FRIED POTATOES.

Take the pulp of common mashed potatoes, make it in small balls or cakes, dip them in the beaten yolks of eggs, flour, and fry them brown in lard or butter; the fat or butter should be boiling when they are put in, or they will soak it up, and become soft, and break to pieces. These are also often eaten for breakfast. Potatoes may be boiled till about half done, then peeled, sliced, seasoned with salt and pepper, floured, and fried brown in lard or butter.

STEWED POTATOES.

Take young potatoes; you need not peel them, but wash and scrape off the thin peeling or skin with a knife; put them in a stew-pan, with a very little water, cover them, and stew them gently till done. Season the gravy with a lump of butter, rolled in flour, some salt, pepper, and a glass of rich sweet cream; stir them up without breaking, and serve them with the gravy. Young potatoes are much nicer prepared in this manner, than to boil them in clear water. They are also fine when scraped, and stewed with young chickens. In making gravy of any kind, in which flour is to be used, be careful not to use it too lavishly, as very thick gravy is not nice; a common sized desert-spoonful is plenty for a pint of gravy.

TO STEAM POTATOES.

Select very white round potatoes, all of equal size, wash and peel them, put them in a pan, cover them closely, and set them over a steam on a stove, till they become sufficiently cooked; then serve them up whole, with melted butter in a boat. Those who have eaten them say they are very fine indeed, quite white and farinaceous, much resembling balls of snow. It is the nicest way to prepare potatoes for snow, but many families, not having a stove, are not prepared for the process.

POTATO SNOW.

Very old potatoes or very young ones are not fit for snow, the former being heavy and sodden, while preparing the latter for snow renders them insipid. Select large white, full grown potatoes, which are quite dry and farinaceous. Wash them clean, put them in a kettle with enough cold water to cover them little over an inch, as when boiled in too little water, they will not be so white. Boil them rather briskly till done, which you may tell by trying them with a fork, or by taking one out, and mashing it. Then turn off the remaining water immediately, set the kettle by the fire for a few minutes, throwing over it a folded napkin or flannel, to absorb the superfluous moisture; after which peel them, rub them through a coarse wire sieve, letting the snow fall into a dish, forming a pyramidal heap: do not disturb it in any way, but send it immediately to table with salt, pepper and a boat of drawn butter, to be handed round with it to the company, that they may season it to suit their own tastes. Potato snow is very pretty when properly made, but if sent to table without the seasonings, it is quite an insipid dish.

ROASTED POTATOES.

Take smooth white potatoes, no other sort being nice to send to table with the skins on. Wash them clean, wipe them dry, and roast them before rather a brisk fire in a tin toaster. When they are done clear through, send them warm to table with salt and a plate of firm butter. They are generally eaten at supper with cold meat, &c.

POTATOES WITH MEAT.

To stew potatoes with meat, take fresh beef, pork or poultry; stew it by its proper receipt till it gets about half done; then, having pared, sliced and washed your potatoes, put them with the meat, and stew them till done. Thicken the gravy with butter, flour, pepper and cream.

To bake potatoes under meat, peel and wash them clean, but do not cut them. When the meat gets about half baked, put the potatoes under it, and bake them till done. The gravy that exudes from the meat while baking, will keep the potatoes sufficiently moist. Thicken the gravy with brown flour and any kind of catchup you choose. Irish potatoes keep well through the winter and till late in the spring, buried in heaps in the garden or in a cellar, by covering them with matting or carpeting, to secure them from the frost.

BAKED SWEET POTATOES.

The Spanish potatoes are considered the finest, and next to them the red permadus, the white and yellow potatoes, are not so much admired. Select those that are as near the same size as possib'e, that they may all get done nearly at the same time. If, however, there should be any difference, put the smallest into the middle of the pan or oven. As there must necessarily be a fire on it and under it, those nearest the top and bottom will be done a little before the middle ones, if they are all of the same size. Trim off the roots, and wash them very clean, but do not peel or scrape them; put them into a pan or oven with a very little water, merely enough to keep them from burning; put a good fire of coals on and under the oven, and bake them till they are done through and of a light brown, raising the lid only to see when they are done, as it not only retards the baking very much, but makes them sodden to raise the lid often while they are baking. Send them warm to table. They are generally eaten at supper, and carried in with firm butter, cold meat, &c.

ROASTED SWEET POTATOES.

Get them as nearly the same size as possible, wash them clean, trim off the sharp ends, but do not break the skins, wipe them with a cloth, lay them on a clean hearth before the fire to dry, and then roast them in clean wood ashes. When they are done perfectly soft, draw them out carefully, lest you break them; brush them nicely with a flannel, and send them to table warm. They are also nice for supper with butter, &c.

BOILED SWEEET POTATOES.

Wash them clean, trim off the roots, but do not peel them; put them into a pan with a little water, and boil them till they are done, which you may tell by trying them with a fork; then drain off the water, throw a flannel or folded napkin over them, and set them by the fire for a few minutes to dry; after which peel them, but do not break them, and send them up warm with a boat of melted butter. They are very nice with most kinds of fresh meats.

STEWED SWEET POTATOES.

Scrape and wash them clean, trim off the sharp ends, and cut each one into four: put them into a stew-pan with a little water, only enough to cook them tender, and have a small portion left for the gravy; cover the pan and stew them till they are done: then enrich the gravy with butter, flour and cream. Do not mash them, but serve them without breaking, and pour the gravy round. Sweet potatoes are fine prepared in the same manner and stewed with nice fresh meat.

SWEET POTATO BALLS.

Get fine large potatoes, boil them, peel and mash them fine and rub them through a cullender; add to the pulp a little butter, sugar, nutmeg and cinnamon; work it well together, make it into small balls, lay them on buttered tin sheets, and bake them a light brown in a brisk oven. Send them to the tea-table very warm. They are also nice for breakfast.

SWEET POTATO ROLLS.

Boil and mash your potatoes as directed for the balls, and if the pulp is not sufficiently moist to make into rolls, add a little rich sweet cream: make it into small rolls, six or eight inches long, and bake them a light brown on buttered tin sheets in a brisk oven. Eat them warm either for breakfast or supper.

BROILED SWEET POTATOES.

Take a fine large Spanish potato, boil it till half done, then cut it across in slices about half an inch thick, broil them on a gridiron over clear coals, the bars of which having been greased to prevent the potatoes sticking to them; turn them over once, and when both sides are of a light brown: serve them up, pour over a little melted butter, and eat them at breakfast or supper. Sweet potatoes may be half boiled, sliced, floured and tried in butter.

SWEET POTATOES WITH MEAT.

Sweet potatoes, like Irish potatoes, may be stewed or baked with meat. They should be scraped and rinsed very clean, and not put with the meat till it is about half done. Thicken the gravy with butter, flour and cream, and serve the meat and potatoes in separate dishes.

BOILED TURNIPS.

Take a thick paring from your turnips, rinse them clean, and boil them tender in a good quantity of water with a handful of salt. When you think they are done, try them with a fork, and if you can pierce it through them easily, they are done; if not, boil them longer. Serve them whole in a deep dish, sprinkle on a little black pepper, and send them to table very warm with a boat of melted butter. They are to accompany beef, mutton and pork.

MASHED TURNIPS.

Boil them as before directed, mash them fine, put the pulp into a pan with a small lump of butter, some pepper and salt, stir it till it is well mixed with the seasonings, and serve it up; make it smooth in the dish, and spot it over at intervals with black pepper.

TO BOIL TURNIPS WITH MEAT.

Boil some fresh beef, or corned or salted pork, till about half done, skimming it well. Peel some turnips, slice and rinse them clean, and put them in to boil with the meat, taking care to have plenty of water. When they are done, drain them, mash them fine and serve them in the dish under the meat. If the turnips are young and very small, do not peel, but scrape them; let them remain whole, leaving on them a short bit of the tops; boil them with the meat as before directed. Serve them whole in a deep dish, sprinkle on some pepper, and pour over them a few spoonfuls of melted butter.

TO STEW TURNIPS WITH MEAT.

Having prepared some fresh beef or pork, stew it in a small quantity of water till at least half done, carefully removing the scum as it rises. Peel some turnips, slice them tolerably thin, rinse and stew them with the meat till done soft: then dish the meat, add to the turnips a small portion of pepper, and a cup of sweet cream, mash them fine, stirring them till they get nearly dry, and is a smooth pulp, then put it in a deep dish, and make it smooth. Turnips will keep well through the winter, buried in heaps in the garden.

PARSNIPS, BOILED.

Get them as nearly the same size as possible; wash, trim, and scrape them neatly, boil them in a small quantity of water, with a handful of salt, till they are done very tender; to have them in perfection, they should boil for some time after you can pierce them through with a fork. Serve them whole, with a little pepper and melted butter, and as they are a vegetable that requires a good deal of seasoning, send with them to table a boat of drawn butter. They may accompany boiled beef, mutton, pork and salt codfish; send them up warm, as they are easily chilled, and are not so good when cold.

MASHED PARSNIPS.

Boil them as before directed, till very soft; then drain them, put them in a sauce-pan, with a large lump of butter, and a small portion of pepper; mash and stir them till fine and dry, and serve it up warm, making it smooth in the dish. It may be brought in with boiled meat of any kind.

STEWED PARSNIPS.

Scrape, wash and split your parsnips; stew them in a small quantity of water, with sufficient salt to season them, keeping the pan closely covered. When they are done very well, and the liquor quite low, stir in a good lump of butter, rolled in flour, pepper, and a glass of sweet cream; boil them once, and serve them warm, with the gravy.

PARSNIPS WITH MEAT.

Many people think this is the most delicious way of cooking parsnips. Wash and scrape them clean, and if large, split them; put them on to boil with a piece of tolerably fat beef or pork, the latter being preferable. There should be plenty of water to cover the whole very well, and if the meat has not been corned or salted, throw in a handful of salt. Cover the pot, and boil or rather stew them till they are well done, and the gravy low; then serve up the meat, mash the parsnips fine and smooth together, adding a little pepper, and place it under the meat in the same dish. If you boil the parsnips in a large quantity of water, take them out when done, drain and put them in a sauce-pan, with a small lump of butter and a little pepper; mash them fine, stirring it till it gets nearly dry, then make it smooth in the dish, and lay the meat on it; if it is pork, skin it, and spot it over at intervals with black or red pepper. Parsnips should not be drawn, and buried like turnips, but should remain in the same ridge in which they grew; they will keep perfectly through the winter, and until they begin to grow, and put forth leaves in the spring.

CARROTS.

Carrots may be cooked in every respect like parsnips, and will also keep well in the ridges in which they grew; in very hard, cold weather, scatter a little straw over them, to assist in preserving them through the winter.

TURNIP SALLAD.

Cut the young, tender tops that shoot forth from the turnips in the spring, pick them carefully, as the under leaves are apt to have little roots and dry leaves sticking to them. Wash them clean in at least two waters, and if they have been gathered more than a few hours, soak them for an hour or two in fresh water, which will make them fresh and lively, and boil tender with greater facility. They should always be boiled with bacon, it being the only good way they can be prepared. Let your bacon be more than half done; have a good quantity of water; if they are boiled in a small quantity, they will be tough and yellow, and to put them in the water when it is cold, has the same effect. Having skimmed the pot, raise the bacon with a fork, put in the tops, lay the bacon on, and boil them till they will mash easily; then drain off the liquor, make them smooth in the dish, skin the bacon, lay it on the sallad, and send it up warm. Have salt, pepper and vinegar to season it at table. It is a plain dish, but when well prepared, it is a very good one.

SPROUTS AND OTHER YOUNG GREENS,

Should be boiled in every respect like turnip sallad, served warm with the bacon, and seasoned at table with salt, pepper and vinegar. All kinds of sallad should be thoroughly washed in two waters, otherwise it will be gritty.

ASPARAGUS.

Asparagus is a nice vegetable, and requires equally as much nicety in preparing it. Gather them when fully grown, but very tender, taking care to have them as near the same size as possible, that they may all get done at the same time. Scrape the stalks nicely, cutting them of an equal length, and throwing them into a pan of cold water as you proceed: let them remain in it for an hour or two, which will make them more tender and fragile. Tie them up in small bundles with tape, and having ready a pot of boiling water, throw in a handful of salt, skim it, put in the bundles of asparagus, and boil them rather briskly till they are tender, which you may tell by taking out a stalk and mashing it: then take them out of the liquor immediately, as if suffered to remain in it a longer time, it would give them a yellow, sodden appearance, and injure the taste very much. Having in the mean time prepared a fine large toast, equal in circumference to the dish in which you intend to serve it, dip it first into the asparagus liquor, then into melted butter, and lay it immediately on the dish. Having divested the bunches of asparagus of the tape with which they were tied, arrange them handsomely upon the toast, the edge of which suffered to project beyond the asparagus, and send them warm to table with a boat of melted butter.

If you serve asparagus without a toast, chop it small and pour melted butter over it.

SEA-KALE

Should be dressed in every respect like asparagus, and served warm with melted butter, with or without toast, as you choose.

POKE ASPARAGUS.

Poke, when gathered at a proper season and nicely dressed, is considered by many people to be as fine as asparagus. It is called poke asparagus, and as such frequently cultivated in gardens: it is the young tender stalks of the common pokeberry plant that shoots forth in the spring, and should be gathered when about the size of asparagus of the largest size. Scrape and cut the stalks of equal lengths, soak them in fresh water for an hour or two, and then boil them as directed for asparagus. Serve them warm, lay round them on the edge of the dish some small buttered toasts, and send with them a boat of melted butter, seasoned with pepper

---

POKE TOPS

Poke tops, or sprouts that put forth in the spring of the year, are considered fine sallad by many people. Gather them when very young and tender, pick them carefully, pour boiling water on, and let them stand for an hour or two, to draw out the strong taste. Having ready a pot of boiling water, in which a piece of bacon has been boiled till nearly done, put the poke into it, and let it boil with the meat till it is tender. It will take but a short time to boil it sufficiently, as it is not good when boiled very soft. Serve it with the meat, drain it well, and have salt, pepper and vinegar to season it at table.

BOILED SALSIFY.

Having washed and scraped the roots, put them in a pot of boiling water, with a handful of salt. When they are done, serve them whole, drain them, and pour over a few spoonfuls of melted butter. Do not expose your salsify to the air while you are preparing it, more than is really necessary, as it has a tendency to darken it.

STEWED SALSIFY.

Scrape and rinse them clean, put them in a pot of boiling water, with a handful of salt, boil them till nearly half done, then cut them in small pieces, put them in a pan with a very little water and a small lump of butter. Stew them till dry, and serve them up with melted butter in a boat.

FRIED SALSIFY.

Having parboiled the salsify, grate them fine, make it into small cakes, and fry them in butter; or for a change, parboil them, cut them in pieces, and fry them.

SPINACH.

After picking the spinach very carefully, wash it in several waters, drain it, throw it in a pot of boiling water, and boil it briskly for a few minutes; when it is tender, take it up, drain and squeeze out the liquor, put it in a sauce-pan, with a lump of butter, some salt and pepper; set it on coals, and chop and stir it constantly till nearly dry. Serve it warm, and make it smooth.

SPINACH WITH EGGS.

Having boiled the spinach by the preceding receipt, drain and press it well, put it in a sauce-pan, with sufficient butter, pepper and salt, to season it. Stir it till it becomes dry, or nearly so, and serve it up. In the meantime, having poached some eggs in the nicest manner, lay them over the top of the spinach, sprinkle over them a spoonful of hot vinegar, with a little black pepper, and send them up warm.

18

SORREL.

Sorrel should be dressed like spinach, and many people think when they are mixed together in equal proportions, the taste of both is much ameliorated.

CAULIFLOWER.

Select those that are of a common or middle size, and very close and white; trim off the outside leaves and stalk, split the flower, or white part in four, and let them lie in water for an hour or two before they are boiled; tie the head together again, to prevent its coming to pieces, put it in a pot of boiling water, with a handful of salt, and boil it gently till done, skimming it well; then take it up immediately, as, if suffered to remain in the water a few minutes longer would spoil it, drain it well, and send it to table with a boat of melted butter.

BROCOLI.

Trim off the loose leaves, peel the end of the stalk, that should be suffered to remain on it, split the head in two, and soak them in water for an hour or two; then tie them together to prevent them coming to pieces in boiling, put it in a pot of hot water, with a handful of salt, and merely let it simmer till the stalk is tender; then drain, and send it up warm with a boat of melted butter.

ANOTHER KIND OF BROCOLI.—This kind of brocoli does not head as the other, but grows up in stalks, bearing flowers round the joints; cut them of an equal length, scraping them nicely, tie them up in bundles with tape, put them in boiling water, throwing in a handful of salt, and boil them briskly till tender, skimming them well, then drain and chop them small, pour over melted butter, and send them to table warm.

STEWED EGG-PLANT.

The purple egg-plants are generally preferred. Scrape and parboil them, split them on one side, take out the seeds, fill them with the common force-meat, directed for balls, and stew them in some nice fresh meat gravy. When done enrich the gravy with bread crumbs, cream and pepper, and circumfuse it round the plants when served.

FRIED EGG-PLANT.

Having parboiled them to take out the bitter taste, cut them into thick slices, season them with salt, pepper and nutmeg; dip them into the beaten yolks of eggs, cover them with bread-crumbs, and fry them brown in butter; add a cup of sweet cream to the butter, boil it up, and pour it over the fry. This is a breakfast dish, and thought by many people to be very fine.

BAKED EGG-PLANT.

Prepare them as for the stew, boiling them nearly tender; fill them with a rich force-meat, brown them in a Dutch oven, and serve them up with a rich gravy. Or, for a change, scrape and boil them tender, drain and mash them fine, and season them with salt, pepper, nutmeg and a large piece of butter; make it smooth in a deep dish, cover the top with finely grated bread, lay on some broken bits of butter, and brown it in a Dutch oven. It may be eaten at breakfast or dinner.

STEWED MUSHROOMS.

There are many varieties of mushrooms, some of which are very poisonous; therefore you should be careful in selecting them, that you do not mistake the poisonous for the esculent ones. Those that are proper for food are only found in open ground, where the air is pure. They may be found in abundance during the months of August and September, more particularly after a misty night or heavy morning dew. The esculent mushrooms may be told by the color, if carefully examined before or soon after they are gathered. They are then of a dull pearl-colored white on the outside or top, while the under part is tinged with pink. Reject all other colors, and even the white ones, if they grow in low marshy ground, where the air is much confined. The color of all will change very soon after they are gathered.

Take either the large mushrooms that are young and tender, or the small button ones, which you choose; wash them clean, removing the skins and stalks, put them into a stew-pan, with a little salt, but no water, cover the pan, and stew them slowly till tender; then season them with a small piece of butter rolled in flour, a very little sweet cream, and serve them with the gravy.

BROILED MUSHROOMS.

Take large mushrooms soon after they are gathered; wash them clean, removing the skins and stems, score them on the under side, wipe them dry, and broil them on a gridiron over a bed of clear coals, having first greased the bars to prevent them sticking; turn them over as they may require till they are done; then serve them up, and put on them immediately some salt, pepper and melted butter.

COMMON SNAP OR BUNCH BEANS.

Bunch beans should be young and tender, otherwise they are not good. Gather them in the morning while the dew is on, cut or break off a small bit of each end, merely to draw off the strings, break them in two, and let them lie in a pan of fresh water for an hour or two, which will make them tender, and facilitate the boiling in some degree. Put them into a pot of cold water with a small piece of bacon, throwing in a small handful of salt; cover the pot and boil or rather stew them till they are done very tender and the liquor quite low; then draw the skin from the bacon, strew on a little finely grated bread, and set it before the fire to toast a little. Serve the beans in a dish of suitable size, drain off the liquor, make them smooth, and lay the bacon on them. Field beans, when young and green, should be cooked in every respect like these, only they require a longer time to boil, as, to have them in perfection, they should boil for several hours slowly and steadily.

STEWED GREEN BEANS.

Prepare them as before directed; put them into a pot with enough cold water to cover them well, throw in a handful of salt, cover the pot, and stew them gently till they are done and nearly dry; then stir in a large slice of butter rolled in flour, some pepper and a cup of rich sweet cream; stir them till nearly dry again, and serve them warm. They are finer prepared in this manner than any other way they can be dressed.

FRENCH BEANS.

These beans, like all others, should be young and tender. Gather them in the morning, string them as the bunch beans, cut them small, and let them lie in fresh water till time to put on your dinner; then put them into a pot of boiling water, and boil them slowly till very tender, which you may tell by taking one out and mashing it. Have ready a pan of rich highly seasoned gravy, drawn from pork, ham or beef, and seasoned with butter, salt, pepper and cream; drain the beans without mashing them, put them into the gravy, and simmer them till nearly dry, stirring them frequently but lightly, lest you mash them. They are generally brought in with ham or bacon.

LIMA BEANS.

These beans are very fine, and should be full grown, but quite tender. Having shelled them, rinse them in cold water and boil them till soft, throwing in a small handful of salt; drain and serve them, and put over them pepper and melted butter.

BUTTER BEANS STEWED.

Butter beans should be full grown, but by no means hard. Gather them early, divest them of the hulls, throw them into a pan of fresh water, and let them lie for a short time; stew them in a small quantity of water till very soft and the liquor low; then add enough butter, rolled in flour, salt, pepper and cream, to season them well, boil them up again, and serve them in a deep dish with the gravy. These beans are very fine, and are by many people considered superior to all others.

BOILED BUTTER BEANS.

Prepare them as above; boil them gently till done quite soft; then drain and mash them fine, seasoning them with salt and pepper and a large slice of butter. When the pulp is smooth and the seasonings well intermixed with it, serve it up. It is really fine, and should accompany the nicest of meats.

DRIED BUTTER BEANS.

They should be full grown and the pods turned yellow on the vines before they are gathered; then hull or shell them out, and dry them perfectly in the shade. They will keep well through the year tied in a cloth and hung up in the garret or some other convenient place, where they will be a little exposed to the air; and when properly managed, they are very near as good as when green.

DRIED BUTTER BEANS BOILED.

Parboil them to draw out the yellowish color and make them look white; then boil, season and serve them in every respect as directed for them when green. After parboiling them, they may also be stewed like green butter beans, and are very near as good.

COMMON DRIED BEANS.

The common field beans may be gathered when full grown, before the pods get hard and dry, and shelled and dried in the shade on a cloth like butter beans. They are much easier cooked than when dried perfectly on the vines before they are gathered. There are many varieties of this species of bean, some of which are very dark, and are not nice even when green. The white ones are the finest for drying. Parboil them till nearly half done, which will make them look white, and much ameliorate the taste: then rinse them well, put them into a pot of clean water, with a handful of salt, and boil them till soft; after which put them into a pan with a large slice of butter, some pepper, and a glass of rich sweet cream; mash them to a pulp, stir it till nearly dry, and serve it up. It is generally eaten with corned or salted pork.

BAKED DRIED BEANS.

Prepare them as before, make the pulp smooth in a deep dish, score the top, put over it some small broken bits of butter, and brown it a little in a Dutch oven. They may also be made into small cakes, floured and fried after mashing and seasoning them well. Be careful in turning them over, or they will break, being quite a friable vegetable.

BEANS WITH PORK.

Having parboiled them, rinse and put them to boil in plenty of water, with a piece of corned or salted pork. When they are done very tender, drain and mash them fine, seasoning the pulp with pepper and cream, and make it smooth in the dish. Having drawn the skin from the pork, dredge the meat with finely grated bread, brown it a little before the fire or in a Dutch oven, and serve it on the beans.

GREEN OR ENGLISH PEAS.

They should be nearly full grown, but green and tender. After they begin to turn yellow, they are not good. Gather them in the morning, shell them, and throw them into a pan of cold water. Boil them in a small quantity of water, with a very little salt. [An iron vessel is not good to cook them in; it is apt to turn them dark: porcelain, tin, or even a brass kettle, when well cleaned, is much better than iron.] Boil them gently till soft and the liquor low; then stir in a small lump of butter, rolled in flour, pepper and a cup of rich sweet cream, simmer them a minute or two, and serve them with the gravy. This is the most delicious way of seasoning them; but if you wish them to look very green, omit the flour and cream. They are generally served with poultry and game, but sometimes with coarse meats. The English way of dressing peas is, after boiling them tender, to add a few tender sprigs of mint and a small portion of loaf sugar.

FIELD PEAS.

Field peas, like field beans, have many varieties of size and color, the nicest and most delicate of which are small and white, much resembliug the English pea when dried; they should all, however, be dressed in the same manner. They should be gathered when full grown, and the pods just beginning to turn yellow; then they have their full flavor, are perfectly tender, and may be shelled without difficulty. Let them lie for a time in cold water; then you may cook them by every receipt given for beans; they are very good cooked with a small bit of bacon, and seasoned with butter, flour, pepper and cream. They may be dried and kept through the winter, and then parboiled and cooked like dried beans. They are generally eaten with boiled or baked pork.

PEAS PUDDING.

Boil them with a small leg of pork till very soft; then mash them fine, press them through a sieve, season the pulp with pepper and cream, and put it in a mould; draw the skin from the pork, toast it a little before the fire, dredging it lightly with flour, or finely grated bread, and serve it up. Turn the pudding carefully into another dish, and send with it the pork, and a boat of melted butter, to season it at table.

ARTICHOKES.

Having removed the stalks and coarse outer leaves, rinse the artichokes clean, put them into boiling water, with a handful of salt, cover them, and boil them gently till tender, taking care to have them well covered with the water. The best way to try when they are done, is to take out a leaf and mash it, and as soon as you find they are very tender, drain them well, and send with them melted butter in a boat.

JERUSALEM ARTICHOKES, BOILED.—Boil them till very tender, which you may tell by trying them with a fork; peel them, put them into a rich, highly seasoned gravy, and serve them up.

JERUSALEM ARTICHOKES, MASHED, &c.—Having boiled them till tender, mash them fine, pressing them through a cullender, and season them highly with butter and cream.

JERUSALEM ARTICHOKES, BAKED.—Take the pulp of mashed Jerusalem artichokes, make it into small rolls, bake them a light brown in a Dutch-oven, and serve them with a rich, highly seasoned gravy, poured over them. This is the most delicious way of preparing them.

BEETS, BOILED.

Draw them while young and sweet; if very old and strong, they should be reserved for pickles. Trim off the tops, but do not break the roots; wash them clean, and boil them till very tender, which you may tell by trying them with a fork. Then throw them while boiling hot into a pan of cold water, which will make the skin slip off smoothly and easily. Slice them quick, sprinkle on a little salt and pepper, pour over them some melted butter, and eat them warm. They generally accompany roast meats.

BEETS, STEWED.

Having boiled them till nearly tender, scrape off the skin, cut the beets in thick slices, put them in a stew-pan with a little salt, pepper, vinegar, and a good slice of butter, rolled in flour; stew them a few minutes, and serve them up with the gravy. Beets keep well through the winter, buried in heaps in the garden.

CYMBLINGS.

There is only one nice way of preparing summer squash or cymblings. Gather them when very young and soft, so that you can nip the peeling or rind with your nail; then they have their full flavor; the seeds are nothing more than blisters, and the whole of the cymblings are good to eat; do not cut them to pieces before they are boiled, as, to boil them in clear water after they are cut up, makes them insipid. Rinse them clean, put them in a pot of boiling water, with a handful of salt, and boil them gently till they are done very tender; then drain and mash them fine, pressing the pulp through a cullender, put it in a sauce-pan, with a good lump of butter, rolled in flour, some pepper, and a glass of rich sweet cream; set it over a few coals, and stir it constantly till it absorbs the seasonings, and becomes nearly dry. It is generally served with roast meats. There are various colors and sizes of the summer squash, but all should be dressed alike, except when they get very large, and rather old; of course they should be split, and the seeds taken out before they are boiled, though at such an age they are not good.

WINTER SQUASH, BAKED.

There are different colors and shapes of the winter squash, but all should be cooked alike. The neck of this squash is the nicest part, being thick, and containing no seeds. Pare it, split it open, put them in a pan with a little water, merely enough to keep them from burning, and bake them till very soft, in a moderate oven. Serve them up warm or cold, with a boat of melted butter. They are fine with any kind of fresh meat, particularly roast pork.

STEWED SQUASH.

Take the large part of the squash that contains the seeds, split it, peel it, and cut it in small pieces. Stew them in plenty of water till they get soft, and then stew and mash them to a pulp, stirring them frequently; add a large slice of butter, some salt, pepper and cream; continue to stir it till nearly dry, and serve it up; it will be found very nice with meat.

A STUFFED SQUASH.

Select a fine ripe squash, split it open smoothly, take out the seeds, scrape them nicely, and fill them with fresh sausage meat, and fit them together again, put it in a deep dish, and bake it in a moderate oven till done very soft. Send it to the table in the same dish in which it is baked.

SQUASH WITH MEAT.

Peel the neck of a squash, and split it in two; put them in a pan under a nice piece of pork, and bake them till thoroughly done. The essence of the meat, that exudes from it while baking, will season the squash sufficiently.

This kind of squash may be kept very easily through the winter, by keeping them in a shuck or fodder house, secure from the frosts.

POTATO PUMPKIN.

Potato pumpkin when large and ripe, is very good, tasting much like the sweet potato, and can be kept well through the winter, put up in a dry place, and covered securely with fodder or shucks. They may be dressed by the various receipts I have just given for winter squash.

PUMPKIN.

Select a large, deep colored pumpkin, as such are generally sweetest. Split it in two, take out the seeds and stringy fibres, but do not scrape off any of the firm part of the pumpkin, as that which is next to the seeds is much the sweetest part. Cut the pumpkin in slices of convenient thickness, peel them, cut them up small, and boil them in a large quantity of water till quite soft; then do not drain them from the liquor, but stew them gently in it, till they form a thick pulp, stirring it frequently at the last, to prevent its scorching. This is much the best way of cooking pumpkin, as by stewing down the liquor, you retain all its sweetness, and take off the raw taste that the pumpkin otherwise would have. To prepare it for table, put it in a pan, with some rich, highly seasoned gravy, or salt, pepper and butter; the former is preferable. Fry it a few minutes over hot coals, stirring it all the time; when it gets nearly dry, serve it up; it is eaten with fresh beef or pork. Pumpkin is sometimes stewed with pork, but the receipt I have just given is far superior to any other way it can be dressed; it requires so long a time to cook it well, that it would not be more than half boiled, when the meat would be perfectly tender, and to cook them separately, and then put the pumpkin in the gravy, you would have the flavor and essence of the meat as much as when cooked with it. They will keep well through the winter, put up as directed for squash and potato pumpkin; they are sweetest after taking a few light frosts in the fall of the year, which will not injure their preservation through the winter.

DRIED PUMPKIN.

When they are fully ripe, split them open, take out
the seeds, cut the pumpkins up in long slices about half
an inch thick, put them on a string, and hang them in a
dry place, where the air can have full admittance to them,
which will dry them in a short time, but let them still
hang through the winter, to secure them from all possibility of moulding.   Before you cook them, pour boiling
water on, and let them remain in it a few hours, to soften
them; then cut them in small pieces, parboil them, and
afterwards stew them till very soft, with a piece of tolerably fat pork; then mash them fine, and serve it with
the pork.   This is a homely dish, but to most tastes a
very good one.

STEWED TOMATOES.

Get fine ripe tomatoes, peel them, cut each one in two,
and put them in a stew-pan, with a few spoonfuls of water, barely enough to keep them from scorching, till the
juice begins to exude from them; sprinkle over them some
salt and pepper, add a large slice of butter, and stew them
gently till done, and nearly dry.   Serve them with any
kind of fresh meat.

BAKED TOMATOES.

Peel and slice them, put them in a deep dish in alternate layers, with finely grated bread and broken bits of
butter, strewing between each layer a sufficient quantity
of salt and pepper, to season the tomatoes well, which for
this purpose should be very ripe; let the top be thickly
covered with bread crumbs and a few broken bits of butter, and bake it a nice brown.

BROILED TOMATOES.

Take large ripe tomatoes, split them in two, and broil
them on a clean, hot gridiron, the bars of which have been
greased, to prevent the tomatoes sticking to them.   Turn
them over once, and when both sides are a little brown,
serve them up, put over them immediately some salt, pepper, melted butter, and a few spoonfuls of vinegar.

TO DRESS TOMATOES RAW.

Take ripe tomatoes, that are large and fine, peel and slice them tolerably thick, put them in a deep dish, and season them highly with salt, pepper and vinegar. This is a delicious breakfast dish, and is also a fine accompaniment to roast meats, for a dinner.

———◦✦◦———

FRIED TOMATOES.

Select them large and ripe, take off the peelings, cut them in thick slices, and season them with salt and pepper. Have ready a plate of finely grated bread, dip each side of the sliced tomatoes in it, taking care to make as much of the bread adhere to them as possible, and fry them brown in butter, which should be hot when they are put in. Serve them warm; mince very fine an onion or two, fry them in the gravy, and transfuse the whole over the tomatoes.

———◦✦◦———

TO KEEP TOMATOES THROUGH THE WINTER.

Select those that are large and ripe, but firm, and perfectly free from blemish. Wipe them clean with a cloth, taking care not to bruise them in the least; put them in a jar of the best vinegar, with a large handful of salt, adding no spices, as the design is to retain the pure flavor of the tomatoes as much as possible. They will be found fine for soups and gravies, and may be dressed in any way that fresh ones can, except for preserves or jellies. The jar should be closed securely.

———◦✦◦———

TOMATO JUMBLES.

Tomatoes for this purpose should be full grown, but quite green; remove the stems, wash and wipe them dry, chop them small, and stew them till soft, with a large proportion of salt and minced onions; then add pepper, cloves and ginger, all powdered fine, and continue to stew them slowly till they form a thick pulp; put it up in jars, stopping them closely; it will be found good for seasonings, gravies, &c.

TOMATO SOY.

Tomatoes for soy should be very ripe. Take off the stems, wipe the tomatoes clean and chop them small. Put them into a clean tub, in layers of two or three inches deep, strewing between each a large handful of salt and some minced onions; cover them and set them by till next day: then put them into a kettle sufficiently large, and boil them slowly and steadily for ten or twelve hours, and then set it by to cool; after which strain it through a sieve, pressing it with a spoon to obtain all the juice you can; put the liquid into a clean kettle, with a sufficient quantity of cloves, mace, ginger, black and red pepper, to season it well; boil it gently again for twelve hours, and cool and bottle it for use, securing the corks with leather or melted rosin. It will keep well in a cool dry place, and is an excellent condiment in soups, gravies, &c. There is no vegetable superior to the tomatoes, being very mild in taste, healthy, easily cultivated and yielding an abundant crop.

STEWED CUCUMBERS.

Gather them when green and young, peel and slice them about half an inch thick, put them into a stew-pan, with as much vinegar and water, mixed in equal proportions, as will cover them well; cover the pan and stew them for a few minutes, then put in a little salt, pepper, butter and flour; stew them a minute or two longer, and serve them with the gravy.

FRIED CUCUMBERS.

Peel and cut them across in slices about half an inch thick, sprinkle them with salt, pepper and flour, and fry them a light brown in boiling butter; then drain them, pour over them immediately some good vinegar, flavored with onions, and send them up warm.

TO DRESS CUCUMBERS RAW.

This is the most delicious way of dressing cucumbers. They should be quite green and not too large. Lay them for a short time in cold water, peel and cut them across in very thin smooth slices, put them into a deep dish, season them highly with salt, pepper and vinegar, and if you like the flavor, disseminate among them some minced onions. They are eaten for breakfast, and are also a nice concomitant to roast meats at the dinner table. People who raise them in the country, seldom pluck them from the vines till wanted for immediate use: those who live in cities and have them to buy, cannot always have them fresh from the vines, but may keep them well in an ice-house for two or three days.

TO BOIL ONIONS.

Take large white onions, which are much the finest, peel them, boil them in a small quantity of water, throwing in a little salt; boil them till you can pierce them easily with a fork, and then serve them up with melted butter, putting on them a little pepper. They may be eaten with any kind of fresh meat, but are commonly introduced with poultry and game.

TO BOIL ONIONS WITH POULTRY.

Having neatly prepared a fine young fowl, boil it till about half done: then peel and rinse some large sweet onions, and boil them with the fowl till they are done very soft, but by no means break them, as they look much nicer to remain whole. Serve up the fowl and onions in separate dishes, enrich the gravy with butter, flour, cream and pepper, give it one boil up, pour a part of it round the fowl, and the remainder over the onions. This is thought to be the best way of preparing them for table.

TO FRY ONIONS.

Peel and slice your onions, put them into a pan with some lard or drippings, and a very little water; cover the pan and fry them till they are done and a little brown, raising the lid and stirring them occasionally; then stir in a little brown flour, salt, pepper and cream.

TO STEW ONIONS.

Peel, rinse and cut each one in four, stew them till very tender in a small quantity of water; then add a large slice of butter, rolled in flour, some salt, pepper, a little powdered mace, and a cup of sweet cream; boil it up once, and serve it. Onions, when very young and tender, may be stewed in the same manner, leaving on a part of the green tops. They can be kept well through the winter by keeping them in a dry place, covered with a piece of carpeting, to shield them from the cold.

TO STEW ESCHALOTS.

There are the spring and fall eschalots. The former is much the finest every way, being larger, milder and sweeter than the others. Peel them, cut off the roots and a part of the green tops, rinse them clean, and cut them small; put them into a pan with some nice drippings or lard, a little water and salt, cover the pan, and stew them till they are done very tender, raising the lid and stirring them frequently; then stir in a little flour, pepper and a cup of sweet milk or cream; boil it up again and serve it.

TO DRESS LETTUCE.

Take a fine white head of loaf lettuce, cut off the stalks, and trim off the outer leaves, split the head in two, put them into a pan of cold water, with a lump of ice, and let them remain till your dinner is nearly ready: then take two pickled eggs, separate the whites from the yolks, mash the yolks smooth with two table-spoonfuls of sallad oil and one of vinegar, add a salt-spoonful of salt, a tea-spoonful of made mustard, and a tea-spoonful of powdered loaf sugar; mash and stir them till the whole are smoothly mixed, then superadd three more spoonfuls of vinegar, and having cut fine the lettuce, and placed it in a sallad dish, mix it well with the dressing; cut the whites of the eggs into ringlets, and scatter them over the lettuce in an immethodical manner, and send it very soon to table.

RAW SALLAD.

Gather your lettuce, tongue-grass, cress, &c., in the morning, while the dew is on; pick them nicely, and let them lie in a pan of cold water till dinner is nearly ready; then rinse them clean, drain them, put them in a plate, lay on the top a bunch of fine spring eschalots, having been nicely cleaned and the green ends split and curled; lay round them on the edge of the plate, some very small lumps of ice, and send it up immediately.

CELERY.

Celery is sometimes chopped small and mixed with a dressing made as directed for lettuce; but the usual way of preparing them is to scrape and wash them clean, and let them lie in cold water till just before they are to be sent to the table; then wipe them dry, split the ends of the stalks, leaving on a few of the green leaves, and send them to table in celery glasses. Celery should be kept in a cellar, aud the roots covered with tan to keep them from wilting.

RADISH.

Radish should be eaten fresh, as the taste is not only impaired by lying a day or two after they are drawn, but tough and heavy, which makes them hard of digestion, and of course renders them unhealthy. Trim off the roots, cut off the tops, leaving on about one inch of the green part; wash them, lay them in a pan of cold water with a lump of ice till shortly before they are sent to table, which will make them more tender and fragile: then take off a thin paring, cleave the large end of each in four, arrange them handsomely in a glass dish, with the large ends pointing out from the centre of the dish, and send them to table to be eaten with salt only. The round turnip radish has much the mildest taste, but it is not so nice to look upon.

HOMINY.

Hominy is a very convenient article, as, in cold weather it will keep good for several days, and is always in readiness. Wash it clean in two or three waters, and boil it in a vessel sufficiently large, with a good quantity of water. It must boil till it is very tender and soft, keeping it well covered with water, which will make it look white. If it should be likely to get too dry, replenish the kettle with more cold water, as, to add it will not hurt the hominy in the least. To prepare it for table, drain, mix with it a little salt and butter, and send it up warm. The small hominy should be boiled in the same manner, and is generally eaten with butter and sugar.

TO FRY HOMINY.

Having boiled your hominy very tender, drain it, and put it into a pan with some rich highly seasoned gravy, mash it fine, stirring it till it gets nearly dry, and serve it up warm. It is eaten with any kind of nice meat.

INDIAN CORN.

Get the large white corn, when nearly full grown, but very tender and full of milk; strip off the shucks in which the ears are enveloped, pick off the silks carefully, and boil them in plenty of water till they are done; then drain the water from them, cut off the grains close to the cobs, season them with salt, pepper and butter, and serve them in a deep dish. The sugar or rare-ripe corn is sufficiently small and nice to send to table whole; therefore it should not be cut from the cobs, but trimmed nicely and sent to the table, to be handed round with butter, pepper and salt.

FRIED CORN.

The corn should be nearly grown, but the grains tender and full of milk; shuck and silk them nicely, cut about half of the grains from the cobs with a sharp knife, and with it scrape off the remaining part of the corn; put it into a frying-pan with a very little water and enough salt, pepper and butter, or nice gravy, to season it well; cover the pan and fry it over a slow fire till done, raising the lid and stirring it occasionally. It is fine for breakfast, and is sometimes introduced as a side dish at dinner.

CORN FRITTERS.

Having removed the shucks and silks from a dozen young tender ears of corn, grate or scrape the grains fine from the cobs, mix with it the beaten yolks of four eggs, two spoonfuls of flour, a salt-spoonful of salt, and a tea-spoonful of pepper; mix the whole together, stirring it till it is well intermingled; then drop it by spoonfuls into a pan of boiling butter or lard, making them all as nearly the same shape and size as possible; turn them over once, and when both sides are of a light brown, serve them up. It is a breakfast dish, and is quite an agreeable relish.

VEGETABLE OYSTER.

This vegetable has some resemblance to a parsnip; it is planted and cultivated in the same manner, and requires about the same length of time to boil. In preparing them for table, first boil them till nearly tender, then cut them in smooth slices, season them with a little salt and pepper, dip them in flour batter, and fry them brown in butter. It is said to be very fine, tasting much like oysters.

TO BOIL RICE.

Having picked the rice very carefully, rinse it in several waters; put it in a stew-pan with a plenty of water to cover it well, and boil it briskly till it is done, which you may tell by taking out a few grains, and mashing them on a plate. No salt should be added while boiling, as the gravies and sauces with which it should be accompanied will be sufficient to season it. As soon as you find it is done, take it immediately from the fire, turn off the water, set the pan by the fire, for the superfluous moisture to evaporate, and the rice keep warm while you are dishing your dinner; do not stir it more than to shake the pan a little while it is drying, as the design is to keep the grains as whole as possible. It may be introduced with any kind of nice fresh meat at dinner, and is a nice concomitant, particularly for roast meats.

TO DRESS MACCARONI.

Boil a pound of the best maccaroni in milk and water, till it is quite tender, stirring it in by degrees, and stirring occasionally after it is all in; the water should be boiling when you commence stirring in the maccaroni. As soon as it is done, drain it, by raising it with a perforated skimmer, spread it out on a sieve, and sprinkle it with a very little salt. Grate half a pound of the best cheese, break up half a pound of butter, and mix them together, put them in a deep dish in alternate layers with the maccaroni. Having filled the dish in this manner, lay on the top some small bits of butter, and bake it in a brisk oven for about twenty-five minutes, raising the lid once or twice, for fear of its getting too brown.

EGGS.

TO CHOOSE EGGS.

There are many rules for trying the soundness and freshness of eggs, one of which is to put them in a pan of fresh water; all that will sink readily to the bottom of the pan are good, and all that rise or float on the top, are certainly rotten. It is said that in proportion to the freshness of the egg its progress to the bottom of the pan will be. There is another very good rule, though a singular one, that is, having washed and wiped the eggs clean, touch the large end with your tongue, and if, by holding it there a second or two, it feels warm to your tongue, it is good, but if it feels cold, it is a certain sign it is not good.

TO KEEP EGGS.

Eggs will keep good for some time, buried in charcoal or wheat bran, after greasing them a little with mutton tallow; but I believe the general opinion of those who have tried it is, that to keep them in lime-water is the best way they can be preserved. To half a bushel of water add little over a pint of unslaked lime, and as much coarse salt, and when the whole is dissolved, put in the eggs; be very particular that you do not put in one that is cracked, as it will spoil the whole; there should be plenty of water to cover them well; if the brine is too strong with the lime, it will eat the shells; this of course can be easily detected; if the eggs are fresh and whole, and water of the proper strength, it is said they will keep good for years.

TO BOIL EGGS.

When you use a tin egg-boiler that is sent to table with the eggs, scald it well in the water before you put in the eggs, which will make it keep warm the longer; the water should be boiling when they are put in; then with a very little experience, you can ascertain the exact time it will take to boil them to suit your taste. If you prefer them rare, send them to table on the tin boiler, to be eaten from egg-cups or glasses, each guest seasoning them in their cups, with butter, salt and pepper. If they are preferred hard, drop them while hot in a pan of cold water, which will make the shells slip off smoothly, and prevent the eggs from turning blue. After peeling them, put them in a dish, sprinkle on some salt and pepper, and pour over them some melted butter. Eggs for sallad dressing, &c., should universally be boiled hard, and peeled as above directed.

TO FRICASSEE EGGS.

Boil the eggs till tolerably hard, drop them in a pan of cold water, and peel them smoothly; put over them the beaten yolks of eggs, roll them in finely grated bread, that is highly seasoned with salt, pepper and nutmeg; let the dredging get a little dry, and fry them a delicate brown in butter. Transfer the eggs to a warm dish by the fire, sprinkle into the butter a small handful of grated bread, add a few spoonfuls of vinegar, pour it over the eggs, and lay round them, on the edge of the dish, some small sprigs of crisped parsley. They are generally eaten at breakfast.

EGGS IN CROQUETS.

Having boiled and peeled the eggs according to the above receipt, cut them in slices, season them with salt, pepper and nutmeg, and put them in a deep dish. Put a little nice veal or poultry gravy in a sauce-pan; add a small lump of butter, rolled in flour, a cup of **rich sweet** cream, a little pepper and mace, and a small handful of green tops of asparagus, having first been boiled and chopped fine. Boil it up once, then take it from the fire, stir into it slowly and gradually the juice of half a lemon, and pour it over the eggs.

EGGS ILLI CREAM.

Boil and peel one dozen eggs, cut each one in two, separating the whites from the yolks, put them in a deep dish, and sprinkle on some salt and pepper. Meanwhile, put in a sauce-pan a pint of sweet milk, two ounces of butter, rolled in flour, some powdered nutmeg, and enough fresh oysters, minced fine, or minced fowl, to make the gravy sufficiently thick; boil it for six or eight minutes, stirring it all the time; transfuse it boiling over the eggs, and send it to table immediately.

NICE WAY TO SERVE BOILED EGGS.

Wash and drain some fine bunches of curled parsley, and place it over the bottom and round the sides of a small dish. Boil a dozen eggs hard enough to peel, drop them in a pan of cold water, and peel them smoothly; then place them side by side in the dish, letting the parsley form a hedge round them, as though it was a nest, and send them to table warm, accompanied with a boat of melted butter, seasoned with pepper and nutmeg, and acidulated lightly with lemon juice. The eggs and sauce should be handed round together, that each guest may season them on their plates. It is introduced as a side dish at dinner, to accompany poultry and game.

BAKED EGGS.

Cut some small slices from a loaf of light bread, toast them lightly, and put them in the bottom and round the sides of a small, deep dish. Grate fine some of the crust of the loaf, and mix with it four ounces of butter, broken up. Boil one dozen eggs till hard enough to slice, and peel and slice them. Put them in the dish on the toasts in alternate layers with the bread crumbs and butter, seasoning them with salt and pepper; pour in a cup of rich sweet cream, sprinkle on the top some grated bread and small bits of butter, and brown it in a Dutch oven.

FRIED EGGS.

Put some nice fresh lard into a frying-pan, and heat it over a bed of clear coals. Have ready the eggs, break one end of each to ascertain if they are good, and drop them from the shells into the fat separately and carefully, lest you break them; commence immediately throwing the hot fat over them with an iron spoon, that the tops of them may get done as soon as the bottoms, and if adroitly performed, the whites will be so transparent that you may see the full size, color and shape of the yolks through them. They are generally served upon fried ham, the gravy thickened with cream and flour, and poured round. They should be served carefully with an egg-slice, and the edges smoothly trimmed. They are eaten at breakfast.

TO POACH EGGS.

Place a broad stew-pan of clean water over the fire till it boils, and set it level before the fire. Break the eggs separately into a plate or saucer, to ascertain if they are good, dropping them as you examine them into the boiling water. They must not be too much crowded, and there must be plenty of water to cover them well. Having put them all into the pan in this manner, let them remain till the whites become set; then place the pan again on the fire, and cook them as hard as you desire: they probably will be sufficiently hard by the time the water begins to boil. Raise them carefully from the water with an egg-slice, trimming the edges smoothly, and lay them separately upon small buttered toasts or broiled ham, arranging them neatly in the dish; sprinkle on a very little salt and black pepper; put on each a spoonful of melted butter, and send them up warm. They are eaten at breakfast. When prepared for the dinner table, omit the toasts or ham; serve them in a small deep dish, sprinkle on some salt and pepper, and pour over the same melted butter. They are sent as a side dish to accompany poultry and game.

A PLAIN OMELET.

Break eight eggs into a pan, beat them a little, add a tea-spoonful of salt, a large spoonful of butter, two minced onions, and a small handful of the young tender sprigs of mint, chopped fine; stir it all together till they are smoothly incorporated, and having a pan of hot butter placed over a bed of hot coals, pour in the omelet, make it smooth in the pan, and as soon as it is sufficiently done, and the under side a little brown, serve it in a dish without breaking it, and stick very little bunches of green asparagus over the top.

ANOTHER OMELET.

Having boiled a smoked tongue till tender, peel it and grate it fine. Beat eight eggs as for the other omelet, stir into it a little salt and pepper, and make it thick with the grated tongue. Have ready a pan of hot butter, pour in the omelet, and fry it till done, and the under side brown; then serve it up, put over it a spoonful of powdered sugar, and fold it over, forming a half moon. It is a breakfast dish, and should be eaten warm.

HAM OMELET.

Beat eight eggs till light, stir in four ounces of grated ham and as much ripe tomatoes, that have been peeled and minced fine; add a little salt and pepper, stir it well, and fry it as directed in the preceding recipe.

CHICKEN OMELET.

Having boiled a fine young fowl, remove the skin, and mince the meat very fine from the bones. Rinse some fresh oysters, trim off the hard part, and mince them fine also. Beat eight eggs light, add a little salt, pepper and nutmeg, and make it thick with equal proportions of the minced fowl and oysters; commingle the whole very well together, and pour it immediately into a pan of hot lard or butter. As soon as it is done, and the under side a little brown, serve it up without breaking; stick some very small bunches of curled parsley over the top, and send it warm to the breakfast table.

A SOFT OMELET.

Beat twelve eggs till a little light, add salt, pepper and nutmeg, acidulate it a little with lemon juice or vinegar, and stir it till the seasonings are well intermingled with eggs. Put four ounces of butter into a frying-pan, set it over a bed of clear coals, and when it gets hot, stir in the omelet. Do not let it get hard, but stir it constantly till it is sufficiently cooked, and serve it in a small deep dish. Send it to table warm. to be helped with a spoon.

AN OMELET SOUFFLE.

An omelet souffle, when rightly prepared, will rise very high and be light and fine, but when badly prepared, it is quite sodden and indifferent; therefore it should be as dexterously performed as possible. Break eight eggs, separate the whites from the yolks, and commence beating them, just allowing yourself enough time to have it baked against the first remove, as it is a desert that soon falls and becomes heavy. Its great excellence lies in having it immediately from the oven. When the whites become a stiff froth, and the yolks are well beaten, stir into the yolks twelve ounces of pounded loaf sugar and a little orange-flour water to flavor it; then stir in lightly and gradually the whites, pour the whole hastily into a buttered dish, having it a little heated, and bake it in a brisk oven five or six minutes.

RIPE MELONS FOR A DESERT.

At many of the most fashionable tables in North America, ripe melons and fruits are sent to the dinner table after the first or second removal of the dishes, &c. To prepare them for table, select a fine ripe muskmelon, rinse it clean and wipe it dry with a cloth; split it in two, scrape out the seeds, &c., and lay the two halves on a waiter of suitable size; set by them a bowl of powdered white sugar, and a knife to slice them at table; spread over them a fine white napkin, garnish the edge of the waiter with ripe fruits, and send it to table, the melon to be sliced and handed round to the company.

To prepare watermelons, none of course are fit for this purpose but the finest quality. Having kept it in cold water for two or three hours, wipe it dry, split it open, cut it up in slices of suitable size, arrange them neatly in a dish, strewing between each slice a tea-spoonful of powdered white sugar, and a little pounded ice, which will make them cool and frangible; throw over a fine white napkin, and send them immediately to table. They should not be prepared till shortly before they are sent to table, as the ice will melt and run in the dish, and a part of the water will exude from the melon.

RIPE FRUITS FOR A DESERT.

The most of ripe fruits, when eaten as a desert, are cooked in some manner before they are sent to table, the manner of which you will find in their respective recipes I have given for fruit sauces, &c.; but the flavor of some fruits is so delicate, that they are much injured by the process of cooking; therefore they are preferred raw, particularly strawberries, raspberries and soft peaches.

STRAWBERRIES.

Select the finest ripe strawberries, (the English red ones are prettiest, but no better in taste than the white ones); they should be recently gathered, as when suffered to lie a few hours, they begin to lose their juices. Pick the leaves and stems from them very carefully, put them in a large glass bowl in layers about an inch thick, strewing between each a large spoonful of powdered loaf sugar; then pile whipped cream on the top very high, forming a pyramidic heap, and introduce it as a second or third course at the dinner table, with rich sweet cream, and different kinds of cake.

RASPBERRIES.

None but the large English raspberries are fit for this purpose. Gather them when fine and ripe, pick the leaves and stems from them, and put them in a glass bowl, as directed for strawberries. Mash some of the remaining berries to a pulp, press out the juice, strain it, and mix it with an equal portion of rich sweet cream, (the cream will be much improved by keeping it a while in an ice house) whip it to a froth, pile it tastily upon the berries, and accompany it with sweet cream and sliced cake.

———◇◆◇———

PEACHES.

Take ripe, soft peaches, that are perfectly free from blemish, and as dry and farinaceous as possible. Peel them, extract the stones, and scrape out the rough part that lies next to them. Mash the peaches to a pulp, pressing it through a wire sieve, make it very sweet with powdered loaf sugar, and make it smooth in a glass or china bowl. Flavor a pint of rich sweet cream with orange or lemon juice, tinge it yellow with yellow coloring, whip it to a froth with rods or wires, and put it on the peaches. Send it to table immediately, and eat it with cream and cake.

PUDDINGS, DUMPLINGS, &c.

———◇◆◇———

REMARKS.

Puddings should be made of the best materials, and each article prepared in the best manner. Butter should be entirely sweet and new, and washed in cold water, to free it from salt. Sugar powdered and sifted, and if to be mixed with the butter, put it in a pan, add the butter, broken up, and set it by the fire, where it will get warm enough to make it soft, and readily unite with the sugar, but by no means suffer it to get hot, or it will become oily, and not fit for the purpose; then beat them to a cream, and add such seasonings as you may think proper, before the eggs, flour, &c. are put in. Eggs should be fresh and new; examine them as you break them, for fear of a bad one, which would spoil the whole, and beat them to a froth, otherwise they will not rise so well. It is the opinion of some that eggs for a pudding need not be beat but very little, but if you wish your pudding fine and light, beat them thoroughly. When milk or cream is used in puddings, it must be perfectly sweet, otherwise when scalded or boiled, it will curdle, and be spoiled; after boiling, let it get cold, before the eggs are put in. Flour must be of the best quality, and always sifted. Raisins should be seeded, cut small, and sprinkled with flour, to prevent them sinking; Sultana raisins have no seeds, but they must be cut and floured. Currants should be picked very carefully, washed, dried and dredged with flour, and almonds put in hot water till the skins will slip off, and then pounded in a mortar to a smooth paste, (a marble one is best); add as you proceed a little orange flower, or rose water, to prevent them from oiling. Cherries should be seeded, cut in two, and sprinkled with flour. Rice must be boiled in sweet milk, or milk and water, till very soft, then drained, and mashed fine while warm. The preparation of such articles as are not described here, I will give in their respective receipts.

Dishes for baking pudding should be sufficiently deep, and provided with a broad, flat rim, on which to lay a paste, or garnish for the pudding. For boiled puddings, you should have very thick cloths, made of German sheeting, or a remarkably thick linen, as a thinner article will admit the water and spoil the pudding. The cloths should be dipped into boiling water and dusted with flour before the puddings are put in. Tie a string tightly round the cloth, to exclude every particle of water, leaving plenty of room in it for the pudding to swell. They should be boiled in a large quantity of water, which must he boiling when the pudding is put in. Add no water except from a boiling kettle.

I do not design naming in my recipes any precise length of time that puddings should bake or boil, as I have heard so much complaint on that particular; and I think myself, that it is a bad rule. So much depends on the heat that is applied to them, that it is impossible to give the time correctly in a recipe.

SWEET POTATO PUDDING.

Take the real Spanish potatoes, wash them clean, and bake them in an oven with moderate heat till they are done; then peel them, press them through a sieve, and weigh out three quarters of a pound of the pulp. Mix together half a pound of butter and half a pound of powdered sugar, and beat them smooth. Beat separately the whites and yolks of eight eggs, and mix them together. Prepare the seasonings by mixing together a grated nutmeg, a tea-spoonful of pounded cloves, the juice and grated rind of a lemon, a glass of rose brandy and a glass of wine. Stir them into the sugar and butter, and then stir in gradually and alternately the potatoes and eggs. Beat the whole together till smoothly incorporated, then pour into a buttered dish, and bake it in a moderate oven.

Sweet potatoes for a pudding may be parboiled, then peeled and grated, but they are more troublesome to prepare, and not by any means superior, if as good, as when baked and made by the above recipe.

ANOTHER SWEET POTATO PUDDING.—Beat eight eggs till very light, and mix with them a pint of rich sweet cream. Add half a pound of powdered sugar, a powdered nutmeg, a tea-spoonful of pounded cinnamon, one of cloves, the grated rind of a lemon, a wine glass of rose-water and a glass of brandy. Mix it very well, and make it into good pudding batter with sweet potatoes, having them baked and mashed into a pulp, or parboiled and grated fine. Beat it very well, pour it into a buttered dish, and bake it in an oven with moderate heat.

——◦◆◦——

WHITE POTATO PUDDING.

Get large white potatoes, wash them clean, and steam or boil them in the nicest manner; then peel, mash them through a sieve, and weigh them. Beat seven eggs till very light, and mix together half a pound of butter and ten ounces of sugar: stir into the butter and sugar a tea-spoonful of powdered cinnamon, one of cloves, one of mace, four table-spoonfuls of rose-water, the juice and grated rind of a lemon, a glass of wine and one of brandy; stir them till they are well intermingled, and then add alternately the eggs and three quarters of a pound of the potato pulp: stir it hard till the whole is well incorporated; then pour it into a buttered dish, and bake it in a moderate oven.

ANOTHER WHITE POTATO PUDDING.—Mix together three quarters of a pound of powdered sugar, six ounces of butter, and a pint of rich sweet cream. Beat them together till very smooth; then add a powdered nutmeg, a tea-spoonful of mace, one of cloves, one of lemon, a glass of brandy, and one of wine. When the whole is very well commingled, stir into it a sufficient quantity of white potato pulp, (made as before directed,) to make it into good pudding batter; stir it very hard, and bake it as before directed.

ORANGE PUDDING.

Beat to a cream half a pound of fresh butter, mix with it half a pound of powdered loaf sugar, the juice of three fine oranges, the grated rind of two, a tea-spoonful of powdered cinnamon, a small wine-glassful of brandy, and one of wine. Grate fine a Naples biscuit, and beat very well six fresh eggs. Then stir alternately into the mixed variety the beaten eggs, and enough of the grated biscuit to make the whole into good pudding batter. Beat it well, put it in a buttered dish, lay round it, on the edge of the dish, a small rim of puff paste, handsomely serated, bake it in a moderate oven, and when done, and cold, grate loaf sugar thickly over it.

LEMON PUDDING.

Beat to a powder half a pound of loaf sugar, and pass it through a fine sieve; weigh half a pound of fresh butter, mix it with the sugar, and beat them to a cream; add a little rose brandy or wine, a teaspoonful of cinnamon, and the grated rind and juice of two fine lemons. Beat six eggs very light, grate or pound fine two or three crackers, stir the eggs and crackers alternately into the other ingredients, beat it hard for a few minutes, and bake it as directed for the orange pudding.

ANOTHER LEMON PUDDING.—Grate the yellow rind from three fresh lemons, and squeeze out the juice, mix with it half a pound of butter, half a pound of sugar, and a glass of mixed brandy and wine; then stir in the beaten yolks of twelve eggs, and the whites of four, which have been beaten to a stiff froth, and as much Naples biscuit, finely grated, as will make the pudding sufficiently thick. Beat the whole till well incorporated, pour it into a buttered dish, which should have a broad rim, lay round it on the edge of the dish, a small rim of puff paste, neatly serated, or crimped, and bake it in a moderate oven. Be sure you do not have it too brown, as a very short time is sufficient to bake it well. Grate loaf sugar into it when cold.

A CURD PUDDING.

Make two quarts of sweet milk lukewarm, by holding it over embers; then stir into it two large spoonfuls of the preparation of rennet, or a small piece of dried rennet, sufficient to turn the milk to a curd. When the curd is fully set, break it up, turn off the whey, pound the curd in a mortar, with six ounces of butter, eight of sugar, a grated nutmeg, and the juice and grated rind of a lemon. Then mix with it six well beaten eggs, and enough rice flour or pounded crackers, to thicken it. Beat it very well, bake it in a buttered dish, and when done, turn it smoothly out; ornament it over the top with thin slices of citron, and eat it with butter, sugar and wine. See pudding sauces.

ALMOND PUDDING.

Take three quarters of a pound of shelled sweet almonds, and two ounces of bitter ones, or peach kernels; scald and peel them, and throw them into a pan of cold water as you proceed. Then pound them in a marble morter, adding a little orange flour, or rose water, to prevent them oiling or getting heavy; pound them to a perfect paste, removing them as you beat them. Mix together three quarters of a pound of powdered sugar, half a pound of fresh butter, and beat it to a cream, adding a wine-glass of wine; then stir into it alternately and lightly the pounded almonds, and eight well beaten eggs. Put the whole into a buttered dish, which has a broad, flat rim, lay round it, on the edge of the dish, a thin, narrow slip of puff paste, having one edge neatly serated, notched or crimped; bake it in a moderate oven, and when cold, grate loaf sugar over it.

ANOTHER ALMOND PUDDING.—Put a pint of sweet cream into a pan, set it over some coals till it gets scalding hot, and pour it over four small rusk, cover them, and let them set till they become saturated with the cream, and perfectly soft; then beat them smooth, add to it ten ounces of butter, twelve of powdered loaf sugar, a tea-spoonful of pounded mace, and a glass of wine. When they are very well mixed, stir in three quarters of a pound of sweet almonds, and two ounces of bitter ones, having prepared them by the above receipt, stirring in at the same time alternately with the almonds, the yolks of six eggs, and the whites of twelve, having beaten them to a stiff froth. When the whole is well mixed, pour it in a buttered dish, and bake it in an oven with moderate heat. Grate loaf sugar over the top, and eat it cold.

RICE PUDDING.

Having picked and washed a pint of rice, boil it tender, drain it, and set it by to cool; then mix with it six ounces of sugar, four of butter, a tea-spoonful of pounded cloves, and one of grated lemon; mix them very well, and stir the whole into a quart of rich sweet milk. Beat six eggs very light, stir them into the other ingredients, and bake it in a buttered dish, with moderate heat.

ANOTHER RICE PUDDING.—Boil half a pound of rice in sweet milk till it is quite soft; then mash it fine, and when it gets cold, add half a pint of sweet cream, half a pound of sugar, half a pound of butter, a grated nutmeg, and a tea-spoonful of pounded cloves. Beat them with a wooden spoon till the whole is smoothly mixed together; then stir in gradually six well beaten eggs, and pour it in a buttered dish, that has a broad, flat rim. Roll out a sheet of puff paste, cut it into small scolloped leaves, with little tin cutters; concatenate them together, so as to form a wreath, lay it round the pudding, on the edge of the dish, and bake it in a moderate oven. Grate loaf sugar over it when cold.

A GROUND RICE PUDDING.

Take a pint of rich sweet milk, stir into it four ounces of ground rice, and beat it till it is a smooth batter. Boil three pints of sweet milk, and while it is boiling, stir gradually into it the rice batter. The milk must be entirely sweet and new, or by boiling it will curdle. Stir it hard till it is very smooth, adding six ounces of butter; then take it from the fire, superadd half a pound of powdered white sugar, and set it by to cool, stirring it frequently while cooling, to make it light. When it gets perfectly cold, stir in the juice and grated rind of a lemon and eight well beaten eggs; stir it again very hard, pour it into a buttered dish, lay round it on the edge of the dish a small rim of serated puff paste, and bake it in a moderate oven. When done and quite cold, grate loaf sugar thickly over it.

A BOILED RICE PUDDING.

Boil half a pound of rice in sweet milk till it is very soft, then drain and mash it fine; mix with it half a pound of butter and half a pound of powdered sugar; beat them well together, and set it by to cool: then add the juice and grated rind of a lemon, a grated nutmeg, a wine glass of wine, one of brandy, and eight eggs that have been beaten to a froth. Beat the whole together till well incorporated and quite smooth; then put it into a pudding-mould. Have ready a thick pudding cloth; dip it into boiling water, and dust it with a little flour, tie it tightly over the pudding, put it into a pot of boiling water, and boil it gently till thoroughly done; then turn it out smoothly in a dish of suitable size, stick narrow slips of citron over it, and eat it warm with sauce. See pudding sauces.

A RICE PUDDING WITHOUT EGGS.

Pick and wash half a pound of rice, and boil it till nearly done in three pints of milk; then add six ounces of powdered sugar, four of butter, and a grated nutmeg; stir it till it is well mixed, pour it into a buttered dish, and bake it in a moderate oven.

RICE FOR A DESERT.

Boil it in milk and water, or in sweet milk alone, till very tender: then drain it and put it into a bowl, and set it by to cool. When it has completely glutinated, turn it out smoothly, pile whipped cream on the top, and send it to table with a bowl of powdered sugar and rich sweet cream, flavored with lemon.

RICE MILK FOR A DESERT.

Pick, wash and boil half a pint of rice: when it is very tender, drain it, put it into a quart of entire sweet milk, add three beaten eggs, a grated nutmeg and four ounces of sugar: set it over hot coals, and simmer it a few minutes, stirring it all the time, but be sure you do not let it boil hard, lest the eggs curdle. It is eaten with cake, &c.

YAM PUDDING.

Press through a cullender three quarters of a pound of roasted yam; mix with the pulp half a pound of butter, half a pound of sugar, half a pint of cream, a grated nutmeg, a tea-spoonful of mace, a wine glass of wine and one of brandy. Beat them together till smoothly united, and then stir in six well beaten eggs. When the whole is well incorporated, put it into a buttered dish, and bake it in a moderate oven.

PUMPKIN PUDDING.

Take a pound of stewed pumpkin, press it through a sieve, to take out all the lumps; stir the pulp into a quart of rich sweet milk, set it over the fire, and when it boils, add eight ounces of powdered sugar and six of butter. Boil it up again, stirring it all the time, and then take it from the fire. When it gets cold, add a grated nutmeg, a tea-spoonful of cinnamon, one of cloves, a wine glass of brandy and one of white wine: then stir in very hard eight well beaten eggs; bake it in a buttered dish with moderate heat, and when done and cold, grate loaf sugar thickly over it.

SQUASH PUDDING.

Take three quarters of a pound of stewed squash, pass it through a cullender, and stir it into a quart of rich sweet milk: put it into a pan and set it over the fire till it boils; then stir in six ounces of powdered sugar and four of butter; boil it up again, and set it by to cool; then stir in a glass of white wine, a tea-spoonful of grated lemon, one of mace and half a grated nutmeg. Stir it till it is well intermingled, and then stir in very hard eight beaten eggs; pour it into a buttered dish, lay a rim of puff paste round it, and bake it in a moderate oven. Grate loaf sugar over it when cold.

COCOANUT PUDDING.

Cut up half a pound of butter, mix it with half a pound of powdered white sugar, put them into a pan, set them by the fire till they get a little warm, and beat them smooth, adding a wine glass of rose brandy and one of white wine. Pare off the brown skin of a cocoanut: wash, wipe and weigh three quarters of a pound, and grate it fine. Having beaten the whites of twelve eggs to a stiff froth, stir them into the batter, &c., alternately with the grated cocoanut. As it is made entirely of the whites of eggs, they should be stirred into the other ingredients very slowly and gradually, which will make it rise the better, and pour it immediately into a buttered dish. Having rolled out a sheet of puff paste of the common thickness, cut it into three long strips, about three quarters of an inch wide; roll them on the paste-board till they become round; plat them together, and lay it round the pudding on the edge of the dish. Bake it in a moderate oven, and grate sugar on it when cold.

ANOTHER COCOANUT PUDDING.—Having taken a cocoanut from the shell, pare it, wash it, weigh one pound, and grate it fine. Beat to a cream half a pound of butter and ten ounces of powdered white sugar, adding a wine glass of rosewate nd one of white wine. Beat eight eggs very light, and stir them alternately with the grated cocoanut into the butter and sugar. Beat it very hard at the last, put it into a buttered dish, lay round it on the edge of the dish a handsome ornament of paste leaves, and bake it with a moderate heat.

A VERY GOOD COCOANUT PUDDING.—Make it in every respect by the above recipe, only stir in at the last, in turn with the cocoanut and eggs, a Naples biscuit, finely grated: then bake it as before directed, and grate loaf sugar over it when cold.

AN ENGLISH PLUM PUDDING.

Beat ten eggs till light, and to them add a pound of powdered brown sugar, a quart of rich sweet milk and a pound of fresh suet: superadd a powdered nutmeg, a teaspoonful of powdered cinnamon, one of mace, the juice and grated rind of two oranges and one lemon. Having prepared a pound of raisins, by seeding, cutting and flouring them, and a pound of currants, by washing and dredging them with flour, stir them also into the eggs, &c., in turn with enough flour to make it of the consistence of common pudding batter. Beat all together with a wooden spaddle till very well mixed, and put it into a pudding-cloth, which should first be dipped into boiling water and sprinkled with flour. Tie a string firmly round the cloth, leaving plenty of room for the pudding to expand, and dusting the tying place with dry flour, to prevent the admission of the water to the pudding while boiling. Put it on in a good quantity of boiling water, as it will require several hours to cook it sufficiently. Boil it gently, and when it is well done, turn it smoothly into a dish. Stick blanched almonds, split lengthwise, thickly over it, and send it warm to table with wine sauce. Do not let it stop boiling from the time you put it into the pot till it is done, and turn it over several times during the process.

A BOILED PLUM PUDDING.

Beat six eggs light, stir into them a pint of cream, three quarters of a pound of brown sugar, the same of raisins and currants, (first preparing them by the preceding recipe,) half a pound of finely chopped suet, glass of brandy, one of wine and two powdered nutmegs. Beat the whole together till well amalgamated, stirring in gradually as much finely grated bread as will make it sufficiently thick; then put it into a cloth, and boil it as directed in the above recipe. It should boil slowly and steadily for several hours. When it is done, turn it into a dish without breaking it: ornament it with strips of preserved citron, and eat it warm with sweet sauce.

A BAKED PLUM PUDDING.

Boil a quart of sweet milk, and stir into it while boiling half a pound of fresh butter, broken up, half a pound of brown sugar and a large spoonful of finely grated bread; stir it very well, and set it by to cool. Seed, cut and dust with flour half a pound of raisins, pick, wash, dry and dredge half a pound of currants, to prevent them sinking, carefully avoiding the flour sticking to them in lumps. Mix together a glass of brandy, one of wine, a powdered nutmeg, a tea-spoonful of cinnamon, the juice and grated rind of a lemon, and stir it into the milk, &c. Cut four ounces of preserved citron into large slips, and beat to a froth eight fresh eggs. When the boiled mixture is entirely cold, stir into it alternately and gradually the prepared fruit and eggs. Beat it with a wooden spaddle till quite smooth, put it into a butter dish, incrustate the top with a little finely grated sponge-cake or Naples biscuit, and bake it in rather a slow oven. Eat it warm with wine sauce, or cold white wine and powdered sugar.

A PLAIN PLUM PUDDING.

Pick, wash and boil half a pint of rice in a quart of sweet milk. When it is tender, stir in two ounces of butter and four of sugar; pass it through a sieve, and set it by to cool, adding a wine glass of white wine, one of brandy, a powdered nutmeg and a tea-spoonful of cinnamon. Having picked, washed and dried a pound of currants, dredge them lightly with flour, and beat to a froth six fresh eggs; stir them alternately and very gradually into the mixture, giving it a hard stirring at the last. Put it into a buttered dish, bake it in a moderate oven, and grate loaf sugar over it when cold.

A RAISIN PUDDING.

Beat six eggs very light, and stir them into a quart of sweet milk, with a large spoonful of mixed mace and cinnamon, a grated nutmeg and a glass of white wine, adding by degrees enough flour to make it into a common pudding batter. Seed, cut and dust with flour a pound and a half of raisins; (Sultana raisins are preferable, having

no seed;) stir them gradually into the other ingredients,
giving all a hard stirring at the last. Put it into a pudding cloth, having first dipped it into boiling water, and
dusted it with flour; tie a string firmly round the end of
the cloth, leaving plenty of room for the pudding to
swell, and dusting the tying place with a little dry flour,
to secure it against the admission of the water, which
would spoil the pudding, if suffered to approach it. Put
it in a large pot of boiling water, and boil it gently and
steadily for several hours, turning it over several times,
and replenishing the pot with water from a boiling kettle.
When it is done, turn it smoothly into a dish, sprinkle
over it some preserved raisins, finely shred; grate on some
loaf sugar, and eat it warm, with wine sauce, or white
wine and sugar.

A BAKED RAISIN PUDDING.

Make a good pudding batter, with six beaten eggs, a
quart of sweet milk, and finely grated bread. Add a wine
glass of rose water, one of white wine, two powdered nutmegs, and the juice and grated rind of a lemon. Having
beat to a cream four ounces of butter, and four of sugar,
stir them in also. Seed a pound and a half of raisins, or
take as many Sultana raisins, which have no seeds; sprinkle them with a little flour, rubbing them with your hands,
to make a small portion of the flour adhere to them, without having any lumps; shred them as fine as possible, and
stir them, a few at a time, into the batter. When all are
in, beat the mixture very hard with a wooden spaddle;
then pour it in a buttered dish, and bake it in a moderate
oven. Eat it warm, with wine or cold sweet sauce.

A BIRD'S NEST PUDDING.

Pare as many fine ripe pears as will fill your pudding
dish, placing them side by side, and with a sharp penknife
extract the cores, without cutting the pears in two. Fill
the space whence the cores were taken with thin slips of
fresh lemon peel, put them in the dish, strew over a little
powdered cinnamon, and a handful of brown sugar; add a
few spoonfuls of water, merely to keep them from burn
ing, and bake them about half done, in a moderate oven.

Beat six eggs very light, stir them into a quart of sweet milk, with four ounces of powdered sugar, and pour it over the pears. Lay a puff paste round the pudding, on the edge of the dish, and bake it in a moderate oven. When done, grate loaf sugar over it, and eat it cold, or eat it warm with cream sauce. A similar pudding may be made of pippen apples.

A BAKED APPLE PUDDING.

Pare, core and bake some fine cooking apples, press them through a sieve, weigh a pound of the pulp, mix with it while hot, eight ounces of sugar, six ounces of butter, and set it by to cool. Beat six eggs light, and when the apples, &c. are cold, stir them into it, adding a pint of sweet cream, a wine glass of brandy, two grated nutmegs, a tea-spoonful of powdered cinnamon, and one of pounded cloves. Commingle the whole very well together, with a wooden spoon, or spaddle; put it in a buttered dish, laying round it, on the edge of the dish, a small rim of neatly serated puff paste, and bake it in a moderate oven. Eat it warm with cream sauce, or grate loaf sugar over it, and eat it cold, which you choose.

A SLICED APPLE PUDDING.

Beat six eggs till light, and stir them into a quart of sweet milk, with enough flour to make it a good batter, four ounces of butter, four of sugar, a glass of brandy, and two powdered nutmegs. Pare and slice very thin from the cores half a dozen well flavored apples, and put them in the batter, stirring and mixing them evenly through it. Put it in a buttered dish, or pan, and bake it in a moderate oven. Eat it warm, with cold cream sauce, or butter and sugar, flavored with lemon. A peach pudding may be made in the same manner.

A BOILED APPLE PUDDING.

Pare and slice very thin from the cores one pound of fine pippen apples; pick, wash and dry half a pound of currants, and dredge them lightly with flour; make a batter of six beaten eggs, a quart of milk and flour, add eight ounces of sugar, four of melted butter, two powdered nutmegs, and the juice and rind of a lemon. Beat it with a spoon or spaddle for some minutes; then stir in alternately the apples and currants; having all well intermingled, put it in a pudding cloth, after dipping it in hot water, and dusting it with flour; tie it up securely, leaving plenty of room for the pudding to swell, and boil it for several hours in a good quantity of water, which should be boiling when the pudding is put in. When done, turn it smoothly out, and eat it warm with cream sauce.

A PLAIN APPLE PUDDING.

Make a paste of finely chopped suet, in the proportions of one pound of suet to two of flour, adding a little salt, and enough cold water to make it into good pie or dumpling paste; knead it well, and roll it out into a large sheet, about half an inch thick. Prepare as many fine cooking apples as you wish for your pudding, by peeling and slicing them from the cores; spread them on the sheet of paste in layers an inch thick, strewing between each a small handful of brown sugar, a little powdered nutmeg, and grated lemon. When you have got your pudding as large as you wish, fold up the corners of the paste, pressing them smoothly and closely together, in the form of a large dumpling. Dust it well with flour, tie it up securely in a pudding cloth, put it in a pot of boiling water, and boil it gently and steadily until it is done. Eat it warm with cream sauce. A similar pudding may be made of ripe clingstone peaches.

A SWEET-MEAT PUDDING.

Cut slices of bread about half an inch thick from a fine, light loaf; spread them over with butter, and then with peach, quince or pear marmalade. Put them in layers the thickness of a slice, into a pudding dish, strewing between each a few slips of preserved citron, or watermelon rind. When the dish is full, pour in a glass of white wine, with the juice and grated rind of a lemon. Beat four eggs very light, stir them into a quart of sweet milk, with four ounces of sugar, and pour it over the pudding. Incrustate the top with a little finely grated bread, and a few broken bits of butter, and lay round it, on the rim of the dish, a festoon of paste leaves, cut and scolloped with little tin cutters. Bake it in a moderate oven; a short time will be sufficient to bake it well. Grate loaf sugar over it when cold.

CHERRY PUDDING.

Mix together six well beaten eggs, six ounces of grated bread, six of sugar, and half a pound of chopped suet, rubbing in it a very little salt, add a grated nutmeg, a glass of wine, and a pound of cherries, having first extracted the seeds; then stir in enough cream or sweet milk, to make the whole the consistence of good pudding batter, and put it in a buttered dish, lay round it a small rim of puff paste, lay a few small pieces of twisted paste over the top, and bake it with moderate heat. Eat it warm, with melted butter, sugar and wine.

ANOTHER CHERRY PUDDING.—Make a good batter of six eggs, a quart of sweet milk, and flour. Stir into it a pound of preserved cherries, four ounces of melted butter, a spoonful of mixed spice, and a wine glass of brandy. Beat it till very well incorporated, put it in a dish, and bake it in a moderate oven. Eat it warm with cream sauce, or butter and powdered sugar, mixed together, and flavored with nutmeg. This pudding may be boiled, and eaten warm, with wine, or cream sauce.

A BOILED CHERRY PUDDING.

Make a paste of flour and butter, as for common pies, or make it of finely chopped suet and flour, in the proportions of a pound of suet to two of flour, sprinkling the suet lightly with salt, and adding enough cold water to make it into good paste, knead it well, and roll it out into a large sheet, about half an inch thick. Extract the seeds from as many ripe cherries as will make your pudding sufficiently large, put them over the paste in layers about an inch thick, strewing between each a small handful of grated bread, one of sugar, a few broken bits of butter, and a very little powdered nutmeg. When all are put in, fold up the corners of the paste, pressing them securely together, in the form of a large dumpling; dust it well with dry flour, tie it up in a cloth, and boil it as other puddings till done. Then turn it carefully into a dish, grate loaf sugar thickly over it, and eat it warm, with wine sauce.

A CRANBERRY PUDDING.

Beat six eggs very light, stir them into a quart of sweet milk, with as much finely grated bread as will make it into good batter. Add four ounces of melted butter, a grated nutmeg, a spoonful of mixed mace and cinnamon, and a glass of mixed brandy and wine; then stir in very hard a pound of preserved cranberries, continuing to stir it till well incorporated; after which put it in a buttered dish, lay round it a rim of puff paste, neatly serated or scolloped, and bake it in an oven with moderate heat. Grate loaf sugar over it when cold. A boiled cranberry pudding may be made as directed for a cherry pudding, and eaten warm with wine sauce.

WHORTLEBERRY PUDDING.

Having picked, washed and dried a quart of ripe whortleberries, sprinkle them lightly with flour. Make a batter of five eggs, a quart of sweet milk and flour, or finely grated bread. Add six ounces of sugar, a grated nutmeg and a glass of white wine; then add the whortleberries by degrees, stirring them in very hard. Pour the mixture in a buttered dish, lay over the top some narrow strips of twisted puff paste, and bake it with moderate heat. Eat it with cream, or cold sweet sauce.

A BOILED WHORTLEBERRY PUDDING.

Boil a quart of entire sweet milk, pour it while boiling on a small loaf of bread, cover it, and set it by to cool; when the bread is completely saturated with the milk, beat it to a pulp, adding two ounces of melted butter, four of sugar, a small cup of molasses, a wine glass of brandy, two powdered nutmegs, and six beaten eggs. Beat the mixture with a wooden spoon or spaddle, till smoothly united, and then stir in a quart of whortleberries, hard and a few at a time, having prepared them by the preceding recipe. Dip your pudding cloth into boiling water, sprinkling it with a little dry flour; put in the pudding, tie it securely, leaving plenty of room for the pudding to expand; and boil it as directed for other boiled puddings, turning it over in the pot several times. It is eaten warm with wine or cream sauce.

A BREAD PUDDING.

Remove the crust from a small loaf of bread, grate fine the soft part, mix with it four ounces of butter and six of sugar, pour a quart of boiling milk over the mixture, cover it, and set it by to cool; then add a glass of brandy, a grated nutmeg, a tea-spoonful of powdered cinnamon, and six well beaten eggs, giving it a hard stirring at the last. Bake it a short time in a buttered dish, and serve it cold.

A BOILED BREAD PUDDING.

Pare the crust from a small loaf of bread, and put the soft part into a pan of suitable size; pour over it a quart of boiling sweet milk, cover it and set it by for at least half an hour; then uncover and cool it. Beat six eggs light, stir them into the bread and milk, having first beaten them to a pulp; add two ounces of butter, four of sugar, a grated nutmeg and the juice and grated rind of a lemon. Beat it hard till well incorporated and very light; then dip your pudding cloth into boiling water, sprinkle it with flour, spread it over a deep dish or pan, and pour in your pudding. Tie a string firmly round the cloth, leaving plenty of room for the expansion of the pudding, dust a little dry flour round the tying place, to prevent the water from oozing in; put it into a pot with a large quantity of water, and boil it steadily till done, replenishing the pot if necessary from a boiling kettle. It is eaten warm with wine or cold sweet sauce.

A BREAD AND BUTTER PUDDING.

Pick nicely a pound of gooseberries, and stew them tender with half a pound of sugar. Cut slices of bread about half an inch thick from a stale loaf; lay on each a slice of butter, grating on a little nutmeg; put some of them on the bottom and round the sides of a deep dish, and fill it with alternate layers of the bread and butter and stewed gooseberries. Beat two eggs light, stir them well into a quart of rich sweet milk, and pour it over the pudding; incrustate the top with a little finely grated bread and broken bits of butter, and bake it with a moderate heat. A short time will be sufficient to bake it well. When done, squeeze over it the juice of a lemon, grate on a little loaf sugar, and eat it warm. A bread and butter pudding may be made in the same manner with any kind of nice stewed fruit.

A PLAIN BATTER PUDDING.

Beat eight eggs very light, and stir them into a quart of sweet milk; add a grated nutmeg, a wine glass of brandy, and make it into good pudding batter with flour, stirring it very hard; put it into a buttered pan or dish, and bake it in rather a brisk oven. When done, send it to table immediately, as it soon falls, and eat with it cream or cold sweet sauce, for which see recipe.

A FINE BATTER PUDDING.

Beat to a powder three quarters of a pound of sugar, mix with it half a pound of butter, and beat them to a cream; add a pint of sweet cream, a grated nutmeg, a spoonful of mixed cinnamon and mace and a glass of wine; then stir in eight well beaten eggs alternately with a pound of sifted flour. Beat it hard till it is quite smooth, and bake it in a buttered dish in rather a slow oven.

A CUSTARD PUDDING.

Nearly fill a pudding dish with slices of Naples biscuit or sponge-cake; stir well into a quart of milk six beaten eggs, four ounces of sugar and two of bitter almonds, having them blanched and pounded to a paste, and pour it into the dish over the slices of cake. Lay a fine puff paste round it on the edge of the dish, and bake it in rather a brisk oven. A few minutes will be quite enough to bake it well. Grate loaf sugar over it when cold.

HASTY PUDDING.

Boil a quart of entire sweet milk, and stir into it while boiling enough thin flour batter, made of milk and flour, to make the whole as thick as good pudding batter. Add a little powdered cloves and cinnamon, a large spoonful of butter and two ounces of sugar. A handful of seeded raisins or cherries would improve it. Stir it constantly till done, then serve it up in a bowl of suitable size, sprinkle a handful of brown sugar over the top, grating on a little nutmeg, and send it to table warm.

A BOILED INDIAN PUDDING.

Warm a quart of sweet milk, and add to it half a pint of molasses, four ounces of fresh suet, finely chopped, and sprinkled lightly with salt, four beaten eggs, a grated nutmeg, a glass of brandy, and enough sifted Indian meal to make it into a thick batter. Beat it very hard, and tie it up in a cloth that is scalded and dusted with flour, leaving a good deal of room, as Indian puddings expand very much in boiling. Put it into a good quantity of boiling water, and boil it steadily for several hours, turning it over several times in the pot, and replenishing it if necessary from a boiling kettle, as, to fill it up with cold water would spoil the pudding. When it is done, turn it carefully out and eat it warm with butter and molasses.

A BAKED INDIAN PUDDING.

Sift three gills of fine Indian meal, and stir it into a quart of warm milk, cover it and set it by for at least one hour: then add half a pint of molasses, four ounces of melted butter, or as much finely chopped suet, a grated nutmeg, a tea-spoonful of powdered cinnamon, a small glass of brandy and six beaten eggs. Stir all together till very well incorporated, and bake it in a buttered dish with moderate heat. It will require from two to three hours to bake it well. Send it warm to table, and eat it with butter and molasses or warm sweet sauce.

AN INDIAN PUDDING WITHOUT EGGS.

Stir half a pint of molasses into a quart of warm sweet milk, add a grated nutmeg, and make it into a thick bat-

ter with sifted Indian meal. Stir it very hard for some
minutes with a wooden spaddle, and tie it up securely in
a cloth, and boil it as directed for the other Indian pudding. Eat it warm with wine sauce, warm sweet sauce,
or molasses and butter.

A QUINCE PUDDING.

Pare and scrape fine a pound of ripe quinces, mix with
the pulp a pint of sweet cream, half a pound of powdered
sugar, four ounces of melted butter, two powdered nutmegs, the juice and grated rind of a lemon and a glass of
white wine. Beat very well the yolks of eight eggs and
the whites of two, and stir them hard into the mixture.
Pour it into a buttered dish, lay round it on the edge of
the dish a small rim of serated puff paste, and bake it in
rather a brisk oven. Grate loaf sugar on it when cold.

AN ARROW ROOT PUDDING.

Boil a quart of entire sweet milk, and make it into a
thick batter with arrow root. Beat to a cream half a
pound of powdered sugar and four ounces of butter, adding a little grated lemon and powdered mace, and mix it
with the batter; then stir in very hard six well beaten
eggs, pour it into a buttered dish, lay round it a handsome
rim of paste leaves, cut and scolloped with little tin cutters, and bake it nicely with moderate heat. When done
and cold, grate loaf sugar over it, and ornament the top
with bits of preserved lemon.

A SUET PUDDING

Grate the soft part of a small loaf of bread, and mix
with it three quarters of a pound of hard lumps of suet,
that have been finely shred and sprinkled with a little
salt, and two spoonfuls of flour. Boil a quart of sweet
milk, pour it over the bread crumbs and suet; cover them,
and set them by till they get cool. In the meantime, prepare a large spoonful of mixed mace and nutmeg, a glass
of mixed brandy and wine, and beat very light six fresh
eggs. When the suet, &c. are cold, beat them together,
stir in the spices and brandy, and then stir in the eggs.

When the whole are very well commingled, put it in a pudding cloth, tie it securely, and boil it in the usual manner for all boiled puddings. Send it to table very warm, and eat with it wine sauce or warm sweet sauce.

A CHEESE PUDDING

Cut slices of cold Indian mush about half an inch thick. Grate some nice kind of cheese thickly over them, and lay on each a thin slice of butter. Put them in a deep dish, stratifying them till the dish is full; then incrustate the top with a little finely grated bread, and broken bits of butter; bake it a few minutes in a moderate oven, and send it warm to table with white wine and sugar.

SAGO PUDDING.

Pick and wash very clean six table-spoonfuls of sago, boil it soft, in a quart of sweet milk, stir in six ounces of butter, eight of sugar, and set it by to cool. In the meantime, pick, wash, dry and dust with flour six ounces of currants, prepare a spoonful of mixed cinnamon and mace, a wine glass of wine, and beat six eggs to a froth. When the sago, &c. are cold, stir in the wine and spices, then the eggs, and lastly the currants. After stirring it very hard, put it in a buttered dish, lay round it a rim of puff paste; bake it nicely in a moderate oven, and send it to table cold.

PRUNE PUDDING.

Stew a pound of prunes in a very little water till the stones will slip out; then extract them, spread the prunes on a large dish, and sprinkle them lightly with flour. Stir into a quart of rich sweet milk eight table-spoonfuls of flour, having first made it into a smooth batter, with some of the quart of milk. Add a glass of white wine and six beaten eggs alternately with the prepared prunes, stirring them in very hard; dip your pudding cloth into boiling water, spread it over a deep dish or pan, and dust it well with dry flour; pour in your pudding, tie it up securely, leaving plenty of room for it to expand, and dusting the tying place with a little dry flour. Put it into a pot, with a large quantity of boiling water, and boil it steadily till done. Send it to table very warm, accompanied with cold cream sauce, or butter and powdered sugar, worked together, and flavored with grated nutmeg, or lemon juice.

APPLE DUMPLINGS.

Roll out a large sheet of suet, potato, or common pie paste tolerably thick, and cut it up in circular pieces, sufficiently large to cover an apple. Pare and core, without cutting to pieces, some well flavored cooking apples, fill the space whence you extract the cores with brown sugar, and squeeze on each a little lemon juice. Put one apple in each piece of paste, closing it securely and smoothly round the apple on one side; dust them thickly with flour, put them in a pot of boiling water, and boil them steadily till done, which you may tell by piercing one with a fork. When they are done, serve them warm, in a covered dish, and accompany them with cream or cold sweet sauce. If you are not well experienced in the matter, tie them up separately in little cloths, and boil them as directed for puddings. This will secure them from all possibility of coming to pieces, though by proper management there is but little danger without the cloths.

STRAWBERRY DUMPLINGS.

Get ripe strawberries, pick the stems and leaves carefully from them, put them into a dish, and strew over them a little sugar. Roll out a thick sheet of standing or common paste, cut out as many circular pieces as you wish to have dumplings, having them all of the same size, fill them up with the strawberries, making them about the size of a large apple, and closing them securely and neatly on one side. Having ready some little dumpling cloths, made of very thick linen, dip them into hot water and dredge them with flour; sprinkle the dumplings well with dry flour, put them separately in the cloths, and tie them up; put them into a pot of boiling water, and boil them steadily till done, which will only take a short time: then take them out of the cloths in which they are enveloped, put them into a covered dish, and send them warm to table with cream sauce. Blackberry and raspberry dumplings may be made in the same manner.

CHERRY DUMPLINGS.

Roll out a thick sheet of suet paste, cut it into pieces about eight inches long and four wide. Extract the seeds from some fine ripe cherries, sprinkle them lightly with sugar, and put three large spoonfuls on one end of each piece of paste; turn the other end of the paste over the cherries, press the edges securely together, and crimp them nicely; dust them very well with flour, to make them look white and prevent them sticking together and coming to pieces; put them into a pot of boiling water, and boil them gently and steadily till done: then lift them carefully from the water with a perforated ladle, put them into a covered dish, and send them warm to table with cream or cold sweet sauce.

CRANBERRY DUMPLINGS.

Stir four beaten eggs into a pint and a half of sweet milk, make it into good batter with flour, and stir into it a pint of cranberries. Beat it very well, put it into buttered tea-cups, tie a little cloth over each, and boil them as you would a pudding. When done, turn them out into a dish, sprinkle on them a large handful of brown sugar, and pour over a pint of rich sweet cream. Cranberry dumplings may also be made like apple dumplings.

RICE DUMPLINGS.

Peel some nice cooking apples, and with a sharp knife extract the cores, excavating with it at least half of the apples, and fill the cavities with boiled rice, first sweetening it with brown sugar and flavoring it with nutmeg or cloves. Take some suet or common pie paste, roll it out rather thick, and cut it into circular pieces sufficiently large for each to cover an apple; put your apples and rice into them, closing them firmly and smoothly on one side; sprinkle them well with flour, and tie them up separately in dumpling cloths, after dipping them into hot water and dredging them with flour. Boil them as other dumplings or puddings till done, and eat them warm with cream sauce or butter and sugar, worked together and flavored with lemon.

LIGHT DUMPLINGS.

Make up your dough exactly as for light bread, and let it set by the fire till it rises well: then flour your hands, make out the dough into balls the size of a goose's egg, dust them well with flour, tie them up in separate cloths, put them into boiling water, and boil them till done. Eat them warm with butter, powdered sugar and grated nutmeg, or cream or wine sauce.

SUET DUMPLINGS.

Mince very fine one pound of fresh hard lumps of suet, sprinkle it with a salt-spoonful of salt, rub it well into two pounds of sifted flour, and make it into good paste with cold water. After kneading it thoroughly, make it into balls the size of a goose's egg, sprinkle them well with dry flour, drop them into boiling water, and boil them briskly till done; then serve them up with a perforated ladle, letting the water drain from them; put them into a covered dish, and eat them warm with molasses or wine sauce. This kind of paste makes excellent dumplings to accompany fresh beef or mutton, for which purpose they should be rolled out about an inch thick and cut into small squares, or made into small round balls, very little larger than a hen's egg, and cooked with the meat which they are to accompany.

INDIAN DUMPLINGS.

Sift a quart of fine Indian meal, mix with it a salt-spoonful of salt, a spoonful of butter, or two of finely chopped suet, two well beaten eggs and enough sweet milk to make it into good bread dough. Work it well with your hands, make it into dumplings the size of a large biscuit, flour them well, drop them into a pot of boiling water, and boil them briskly till done. Be very careful in serving them, lest you break them. Eat them warm with molasses. Indian dumplings are sometimes eaten with corned pork or bacon. In such cases they should be boiled with the meat with which they are served.

BIRD DUMPLINGS.

Take any kind of nice small birds; pick and wash them clean and cut off their heads and feet, score the breasts, mash the joints, but do not cut them apart, fill them with a little grated bread and butter, seasoned with pepper and nutmeg, and moistened with white wine, and season them with salt and rub them over with butter. Roll out a thick sheet of suet or standing paste; cut it into pieces sufficiently large to cover the birds, and put one into each piece of paste, close them up securely, dust them with flour, tie them separately in pudding cloths, and boil them as other dumplings. Eat them warm with melted butter and wine or highly seasoned gravy.

APPLE BUTTER ROLLS.

Roll out a sheet of common pie paste, about one fourth of an inch thick, and put a thick smooth layer of apple butter over it, roll it up into a scroll, making the roll about as large in circumference as a large glass tumbler, and about eight inches long; close the paste very securely at both ends and the side that is open, making the paste as smooth as possible where the edges meet. Having made out three in this manner, dust them well with flour, tie them up separately in dumpling cloths, having first dipped them into boiling water and dusted them with flour, and boil them like puddings till they are done; then take them carefully out of the cloths, lay them side by side in a dish of suitable size, and eat them warm with cream sauce.

RAISIN ROLLS.

Make a paste of flour and fresh suet, minced fine, or butter, allowing one pound of flour to half a pound of the suet or butter; mix in as much cold water as will make it into good paste, knead it well, and roll it out into oblong sheets about one fourth of an inch thick. Having seeded and cut in half some raisins, stew them tender in a very little water; then mix in some brown sugar, and spread a smooth layer of them over each sheet of paste, roll them up evenly and closely into a scroll, close the side by pressing it together with your fingers, trim the ends smoothly, and close them also securely, by pressing them smoothly together; then sprinkle them thickly with flour, tie them up in separate cloths, taking care that you do not bend or spoil the shape of them, and boil them in a vessel sufficiently large to contain them at full length; there should be plenty of water to keep them well covered till done, which should be boiling when they are put in. Serve them up in a flat dish of suitable size, grate a little sugar over them, and eat them warm with cream sauce, or cold butter, powdered sugar, and nutmeg. Peaches, pears, quinces, apples, gooseberries, grapes, cherries and plums will all make nice rolls by first stewing them tender in a little water, and sweetening them with sugar.

PLAIN PANCAKES.

Beat four eggs light, stir them into a quart of sweet milk, add a salt-spoonful of salt, and make it into a thin batter, with flour; beat it till perfectly free from lumps, as lumps of dry flour through the cakes when fried, are disgusting. Have your frying-pan hot, clean it neatly, and grease it with a lump of cold lard or butter, (never grease your pan with gravy, or essence that has flown from roast meats, as the salt taste will be quite perceptible on your cakes,) put a large ladleful of the batter in the pan, which for this purpose must be very thin; make it even over the pan as large as a common desert plate, and as soon as the under side is a light brown, turn them over. Fry them all in the same manner, and as soon as you take them from the pan, sprinkle them with powdered sugar, roll them up separately, pile them in a plate, grate on a little nutmeg, and send them warm to table, with cold white wine, or cold sweet sauce.

FRUIT PANCAKES.

Make a batter as above directed, and fry them in the same manner. Spread over them immediately a thin layer of some nice kind of marmalade or preserves; roll them as before directed, grate on a little loaf sugar, and eat them warm with cold cream sauce.

COMMON FRITTERS.

Beat eight eggs very light, and stir them into 2 quarts of sweet milk, add a salt-spoonful of salt, and stir hard into it enough flour to make it a thick batter, as if made thin, they will soak the lard in which they are fried, and be greasy and heavy, and of course not good. Have ready a frying pan, with a good quantity of boiling lard, place it over a bed of clear coals, put in your batter, allowing a large spoonful to each fritter, and do not suffer them to touch each other, neither turn them, as there should be plenty of lard to cover them well. When they are of a light brown on both sides, drain them, and send them to table immediately, and eat them warm with cold sweet sauce, slightly acidulated with lemon juice or vinegar, or eat them with cold sweet milk and honey, or sugar, nutmeg and wine.

APPLE FRITTERS.

Pare, core, and chop very fine, some fine ripe cooking apples. Make a batter as above directed, only not so thick, and stir in the minced apples till it forms a thick batter. Fry them as before directed, drain them, and eat them warm with sweet milk and honey, or molasses, or powdered sugar, nutmeg and cold white wine.

SLICED APPLE FRITTERS.

Make a thick batter with six beaten eggs, a quart of milk, and flour, adding a little salt. Pare and slice thin some large pippins, and having ready a pan of boiling lard, lift up a small ladleful of the batter, drop in it a slice of apple, and pour it into the lard; fry them all in the same manner, drain them, squeeze on each a little lemon juice, and eat them with powdered sugar, nutmeg, and sweet milk.

INDIAN FRITTERS.

Make a thick batter of six beaten eggs, 3 pints of sweet milk and sifted Indian meal, stirring in a salt-spoonful of salt. Beat it very well, and fry it in boiling lard, allowing a small ladleful to each fritter. When a nice brown on both sides, drain them, and eat them warm with molasses.

PUDDING SAUCES.

WINE SAUCE.

Melt or draw half a pound of butter, and stir into it immediately, while warm, three gills of white wine, three table-spoonfuls of powdered sugar, and a grated nutmeg. Serve it up with any kind of boiled puddings that have in them flour, butter, or grated bread.

COLD SWEET SAUCE.

Take equal portions of fresh sweet butter and powdered loaf sugar; work them thoroughly together, and flavor it with grated nutmeg and a few drops of essence of lemon. This is an excellent sauce, and may be eaten with almost any kind of boiled puddings, also baked batter, plum and bread puddings, dumplings, rolls, fritters, pancakes, &c. It should be sent to table in a small glass plate, provided with a tea-spoon or butter knife.

COLD CREAM SAUCE.

Take a pint of rich sweet cream, and stir into it four ounces of powdered sugar; when the sugar is entirely dissolved, stir in gradually the juice of half a lemon, and grate nutmeg over the top. It may be eaten with plain batter puddings, or boiled puddings of almost any kind, also dumplings and rolls.

WARM CREAM SAUCE.

Melt four ounces of butter, and stir into it while warm four ounces of powdered sugar and a pint of sweet cream; flavor it with orange juice, grate nutmeg thickly over it, and eat it with any kind of boiled puddings, baked batter puddings, dumplings, rolls, fritters, pancakes and tarts.

A VERY CHEAP SAUCE.

Boil a pint of water, and stir into it while boiling a large spoonful of butter, one of flour, four of sugar, or enough molasses to make it sufficiently sweet, and a grated nutmeg. It is eaten with plain batter and Indian puddings. Molasses makes very good sauce for plain puddings, dumplings, fritters and pancakes, when lightly acidulated with lemon juice or plain cold vinegar.

PASTRY, ETC.

PLAIN PASTE.

All pastry should be made of the best materials: the flour should be superfine and quite new, and the butter fresh and sweet. For fine puff or sweet paste, every particle of salt should be washed from the butter; otherwise it will not rise well nor have a pleasant taste. For meat pies, dumplings, &c., the butter should be freely washed in cold water, to give it a sweet taste, but salt should be sprinkled in the flour, or the paste will have a flat unpleasant taste. Sift two quarts of flour, and weigh out a pound of butter; rub half of the butter into the flour, sprinkling in a little salt. Make it into a stiff paste with cold water, and roll it out into a thin sheet; divide the half pound of butter into two equal parts, break them up into small bits, and put one half over the sheet of paste, mashing it smooth with a knife; sprinkle on a little flour, roll up the paste into a scroll, and flatten it with a rolling-pin; roll it again into a sheet, put on the last portion of butter in the same manner, and springling on a little flour; fold it up, roll it into a sheet the third time, and it will be ready for use. Plain paste is generally used for pies, dumplings and breakfast cakes. By rolling in the butter in this manner, it makes the paste much lighter and more flaky than when the butter is all rubbed into the flour at first.

STANDING PASTE.

This paste is generally used for fruit pies, fruit dump and rolls. Sift three pints of flour, rub well into it one pound of fresh butter, a spoonful of salt, and make it a good paste with sweet milk; knead it well, and beat it with a rolling-pin till quite smooth.

RAISED PASTE.

Beat four eggs very light, and rub them into two quarts of flour, sprinkling in a little salt; make it a stiff paste with cold sweet milk, and roll it out into a thin sheet. Divide a pound of butter into four equal parts; break one portion up and spread it evenly over the paste, sprinkle on a little flour, fold up the paste, and roll it out again, put on a second portion, and in like manner the third and fourth, sprinkling on a little flour, folding it up and rolling it into a sheet each time. When this is done the paste is ready for use. It is generally used for meat pies and dumplings, and should be rolled tolerably thick.

SUET PASTE.

Take a pound of fresh hard lumps of suet, that is free from skins and stringy fibres; mince them as fine as possible, and divide it into two equal halves, sprinkling on it a very little salt. Sift two quarts of flour, rub well into it one portion of the suet, and make it into a stiff dough with cold water; then roll it out on your paste-board very thin, put evenly over it the remaining part of the suet, sprinkling on a little flour; fold it up, and roll it out again: after which roll it into a scroll, and cut it into as many pieces as you wish sheets of paste, and roll them out of a proper thickness: if for fruit dumplings, boiled puddings or pot-pies, roll it nearly half an inch thick; but if for dumplings, to accompany boiled beef or mutton, it should be at least one inch thick, and cut out with tin cutters or a small tumbler.

DRIPPING PASTE.

Boil and skim three quarters of a pound of fresh beef drippings, settle it, pass it through a fine sieve and rub it in three pints of flour till well intermingled; then make it into good paste with cold water, knead it well, and roll it out two or three times. This is an excellent paste for meat pies, and should be rolled out tolerably thick.

POTATO PASTE.

For this purpose take fine white mealy potatoes, boil them quite soft, and peel and press them through a cullender. Having sifted a quart of flour, rub well in it a pint and a half of the potato pulp, a spoonful of butter and a salt-spoonful of salt: when well incorporated, add as much cold water as will make it a good paste: knead it well, and roll it out half an inch thick. Make use of it for apple and meat dumplings and boiled puddings. It should always be boiled and eaten warm with rich sauce.

—◦◆◦—

LARD PASTE.

Make a quart of flour into a stiff dough with cream, adding a very little salt, and roll it thin on your paste-board. Divide half a pound of fresh sweet lard into four equal parts; put one portion evenly over the paste, dusting on a little flour; fold it up with your hands, roll it out again into a sheet with a rolling-pin, and put on a second portion; roll it again as before—do this till you have rolled in the last portion of the lard; then roll it into a scroll, cut off as many pieces of paste as you want sheets or crusts; roll them out tolerably thick, and they will be ready for use. Do not knead it in the least after the first portion of the lard is put in, or it will prevent it being flaky. This is a very good paste for meat pies, and also makes good cakes for breakfast, when rolled thin, cut into squares and baked hastily.

—◦◆◦—

SWEET PASTE.

Sift a pound and a half of the finest flour, rub well into it four ounces of powdered white sugar. two beaten eggs, and a wine glass of wine; make it into a stiff dough with sweet milk, knead it well, and roll it out thin on your paste-board with a rolling-pin. Divide three quarters of a pound of fresh butter into four equal parts, having first washed it in two or three cold waters; break up one portion of the butter, and spread it smoothly over the paste, sprinkling on a spoonful of flour; fold it up into a ball with your hands, roll it out again, put on the second portion, and in like manner the third and fourth: then it will be ready for use, as it should not be worked or kneaded at all. This paste is intended for shells and tarts of the finest quality. When shells are made of it, they should be baked empty and afterwards filled with the fruit. When made into covered tarts, they should be iced with tart icing, and baked in rather a brisk oven.

PUFF PASTE.

Take a pound of fresh butter, wash it well in two or three cold waters, beat out all the water, and divide the butter into six equal parts. Sift a quart of the finest flour, leave out a few spoonfuls for rolling, and make the remainder into a stiff dough with cold water; put it on your paste-board, roll it out thin with a rolling-pin, and with a knife spread one portion of the butter smoothly over it, sprinkling on a little of the flour; fold it up into a ball with your hands, but do not knead it in the least; roll it out thin, put on a second portion of the butter, sprinkling on a little flour, and fold it up and roll it out again; repeat this until you have rolled in all the butter, touching it as lightly with your hands as possible. When this is done, roll it up into a scroll, and set it in a cool place till you have your ovens hot in the proper manner. They should be heated very evenly and rather brisk, and carefully noticed while the paste is baking, as dexterity is never more in demand when cooking than when baking puff paste. Cut your paste into as many pieces as you wish sheets of paste. Having rolled it out of a proper thickness, cut it to fit your mould; notch, scollop, crimp or serate the edges handsomely with a small sharp-pointed knife, or cut them into scolloped or crimped leaves with little tin cutters; bake them in buttered patty-pans, plates or on tin sheets, laying a sheet of white paper over the tops to prevent them getting brown, and raising the lid no more than is necessary to ascertain how they are baking. If done precisely by this recipe, they will rise very high, be quite light, and look perfectly white when done.

SHELLS.

Shells are sometimes made of common pie paste, for the purpose of filling them with stewed fruit, &c. for tarts, but they are most commonly made of fine puff or sweet paste for nicer purposes, to fill with the finest of sweet meats. If you make them of pie paste, roll it out tolerably thick, and bake them in large scolloped patty-pans or deep plates, in a moderate oven, and when cold fill them with the fruit, having it prepared in a proper manner for tarts. If you make them of puff paste, make and bake them as before directed, in shallow pans or on buttered tin plates, and when they get cold, fill them with the nicest of sweet meats. Do not fill them till shortly before they go to table: the juice of the preserves will make them sodden and heavy. Sweet paste should be rolled out rather thick, cut out and baked in small scolloped moulds, the edges handsomely notched, crimped or serated, and baked in rather a brisk oven, laying over them a sheet of white paper, as the color should be quite delicate. When they are cool, put several on a plate, fill them with the finest of preserves, and send them to table very soon.

CHERRY TARTS.

Take fine ripe cherries, extract the seeds, saving all the juice, and sprinkle them thickly with brown sugar. Roll out as many sheets of plain paste as you want, rather thick, and allowing two to each tart. Butter some large scolloped patty-pans, spread over each a sheet of the paste, put in a thick layer of the cherries with some of the juice, sprinkle on each tart a small spoonful of flour, one of butter and a tea-cupful of water; then lay a paste over the tops, trim them smoothly round the edges, crimp them neatly with a sharp pen-knife, dipping the blade occasionally into dry flour, to prevent the paste sticking to it, and bake them in a moderate oven. They must be neatly iced with tart icing, and dried in the ovens, or have loaf sugar grated thickly over them. They are very fine, and should be eaten warm with cold sweet sauce or honey and sweet milk, boiled custard or some nice kind of cream.

CRANBERRY TARTS.

Prepare some plain paste as directed for the cherry tarts; butter some large scolloped pans, putting over each a sheet of paste, put in your cranberries, having first stewed them tender, and strew on at least half their weight in sugar, add to each a large spoonful of butter, rolled in one of flour and broken up, a wine glass of wine and a large tea-cupful of water, lay strips of twisted paste over the top, put round the edge a border of paste leaves, neatly notching and linking them together, and bake them in a moderate oven. Grate loaf sugar over them as soon as you take them from the oven, and eat them warm with rich sauce and boiled custard or cold cream.

WHORTLEBERRY TARTS.

Pick and wash your whortleberries, and stew them tender in a very little water, and one third their weight of brown sugar. Roll out sheets of plain paste tolerably thick, and put them over some large buttered patty-pans or deep plates; put in each a thick layer of the berries, with the juice, lay twisted slips of paste over the tops, and bake them in a moderate oven. Grate loaf sugar over them, and eat them warm or cold, with sweet milk or boiled custard. Common grape tarts may be made in the same manner.

CURRANT TARTS.

Roll out sheets of paste as for the other tarts, and put them over buttered patty-pans. Pick and wash very clean some currants, either green or ripe; the only difference in making them is, when green they require a little more sugar; put them in the pans, on the paste, strewing on each a handful of brown sugar, add a small tea-cupful of water, and a desert-spoonful of butter, rolled in one of flour, and broken up. Put a paste over the tops, cut them smooth round the edges, and crimp or scollop them neatly with a sharp penknife. Bake them in an oven with moderate heat, grate loaf sugar over them when done, and eat them warm with cold sweet sauce or honey, and cold sweet milk, boiled custard, or some kind of cream.

GOOSEBERRY TARTS.

Pick and wash your gooseberries, stew them tender in a small quantity of water, with half their weight in brown sugar, press them through a sieve, and set them by to cool; after which put a thick layer of the pulp in large scolloped shells of puff paste, make them very smooth, pile whipped cream high upon each, and introduce them with cold sweet milk or boiled custard. Gooseberry tarts may also be made as directed for currant tarts.

STRAWBERRY TARTS.

Pick the stems and leaves from fine ripe English strawberries, put them whole into large scolloped shells of puff paste, and grate loaf sugar thickly over them, mash to a pulp some of the remaining berries, pass them through a sieve, stir enough of the pulp into some rich sweet cream to make it tolerably thick, beat it to a froth, and set it for a time in ice, to get a little firm, and then pile it on the tarts, forming a pyramidal heap. The real English raspberries may be converted into tarts in the same manner, and both of them are very nice.

PEACH TARTS.

Select the finest flavored freestone peaches that are very soft and farinaceous; pare and slice them from the stones, and mash them to a smooth marmalade, pressing them through a sieve; add to the pulp half its weight of powdered loaf sugar; make it a little more moist with sweet cream, and put it smoothly into large scolloped shells of puff paste; grate on a little nutmeg, and crown them handsomely with whipped cream. They are fine with iced milk, boiled custard, &c.

GRAPE TARTS.

Take the white English grapes, pick them from the bunch; stew them till tender in a very little water, and half their weight of sugar, press them through a sieve, and set them by to cool. Then put a thick layer of the pulp in large shells of puff paste, make them very smooth, grate on a little nutmeg, and make them white with powdered loaf sugar. They are introduced with boiled custards, cold creams, &c. No fruit should be put in shells of puff paste till shortly before they are sent to table.

APPLE PUFFS.

All fruit puffs should be made of puff **or sweet** paste, either of which being much more delicate than what is denominated standing, raised or plain paste. Take well flavored cooking apples, pare and slice them from the cores, stew them in a small portion of water with half their weight of brown sugar, and press them through a sieve. Add to the pulp a little sweet cream, powdered nutmeg, and grated lemon, also a little rose water, if you are fond of the flavor. Having rolled out the paste of moderate thickness, cut it into small circular pieces, put the prepared apples on one half of each piece, and fold the other over them, forming a half moon; trim them smoothly round the edges, crimp or notch them neatly, having first pressed the edges firmly together, to prevent the fruit from coming out, and bake them in a moderate oven, that will permit them to rise. Grate loaf sugar over them when done.

STRAWBERRY AND RASPBERRY PUFFS

Should each be made of their respective jams, and made and baked in the same manner as apple puffs. Grate loaf sugar over them as soon as you take them from the oven. They should be small enough to put four in a plate, and should be baked on tin sheets.

BATTER PUFFS.

Cut up four ounces of butter, stir it into a pint of boiling sweet milk, and when it melts, set it by to cool; then stir in four beaten eggs alternately with four table-spoonfuls of flour; add a tea-spoonful of powdered cinnamon, a few drops of essence of lemon, and beat it till well incorporated, and very smooth. Butter some coarse tea-cups of common size, fill them about half full of the mixture, and bake them in a brisk oven. When done, turn them into a dish, and send them immediately to table, with cold cream sauce, or butter, wine, and sugar.

APPLE TARTS.

Pare, core and slice some fine cooking apples, and stew them quite soft in a very little water, seasoning them with brown sugar, powdered cloves, nutmeg, and a very little butter. Roll out sheets of plain or standing paste moderately thick, spread one over a large patty-pan, and fill it up with the prepared apples, put a paste over the top, trim the edges smoothly, pinch or press them together, crimp or notch it, and bake it in a moderate oven. When done, grate loaf sugar over it, and eat it warm or cold. This kind of pie is generally eaten with cold milk and honey, or sweet sauce. Peach pies may be made in the same manner, and are superior to apple pies; also dried apples and peaches, only they require a longer time to cook, and should be liquified with a little sweet cream, using no butter.

FRIED PIES.

Fried pies may be made of any kind of nice fruit, having prepared it in a proper manner, but dried fruit is preferable to green. Stew it tender, mash it fine, and season it to your taste with sugar and spices. Roll out a sheet of plain or standing paste, nearly one fourth of an inch thick, cut it in as many circular pieces as you wish pies, making them as large as a common sized patty-pan; put your fruit in one half of each piece, and turn the other half over, in the form of puffs, or half moons; cut them smoothly round the edges, closing the paste together, to keep in the fruit, and crimping or notching them handsomely; lay them in a pan of boiling butter, having plenty to cover the pies without having to turn them over, and fry them till they are a nice brown on both sides; then raise them carefully, drain them on an inverted sieve, grate loaf sugar over them, and send them to table warm. The butter in which they are fried may be used for seasoning brown gravies, &c.

AN APPLE POT-PIE.

Rub the bottom and sides of a porridge-pot, or small oven, with butter, and then with dry flour. Roll out some pieces of plain or standing paste about half an inch thick, line the sides of the pot or oven with the pieces of paste, letting them nearly touch in the bottom. Having pared and sliced from the cores some fine cooking apples, nearly fill the oven with them; pour in enough water to cook them tender, put pieces of paste on the top, or put a paste all over the top, and bake it with moderate heat, having a fire both on and under the oven. When the apples are very soft, the crust brown, and the liquor quite low, turn the crust bottom upwards in a large dish, put the apples evenly over it, strew on a large handful of brown sugar, and eat it warm or cold, with sweet milk. This is quite a homely pie, but a very good one.

A PEACH POT-PIE.

A peach pot-pie, or cobler, as it is often termed, should be made of clingstone peaches, that are very ripe, and then pared and sliced from the stones. Prepare a pot or oven with paste, as directed for the apple pot-pie, put in the prepared peaches, sprinkle on a large handful of brown sugar, pour in plenty of water to cook the peaches without burning them, though there should be but very little liquor or syrup when the pie is done. Put a paste over the top, and bake it with moderate heat, raising the lid occasionally, to see how it is baking. When the crust is brown, and the peaches very soft, invert the crust on a large dish, put the peaches evenly on, and grate loaf sugar thickly over it. Eat it warm or cold. Although it is not a fashionable pie for company, it is very excellent for family use, with cold sweet milk.

SWEET POTATO PIE.

Peel your potatoes, wash them clean, slice and stew them in a very little water till quite soft, and nearly dry; then mash them fine, season them with butter, sugar, cream, nutmeg and cinnamon, and when cold, add four beaten eggs, and press the pulp through a sieve. Roll out plain or standing paste as for other pies, put a sheet of it over a large buttered patty-pan, or deep plate, put in smoothly a thick layer of the potato pulp, and bake it in a moderate oven. Grate loaf sugar over it when done, and send it to table warm or cold, with cream sauce or boiled custard.

A SLICED POTATO PIE.

Boil your potatoes in a very little water till half done, then peel and slice them thin. Line a deep patty-pan that is well buttered, with a tolerably thick sheet of standing paste, put in a layer of the sliced potatoes, disseminate over them some grated nutmeg, powdered cinnamon, grated lemon, a small portion of butter, rolled in flour, and broken up, and a small handful of brown sugar; put in a second layer of the potatoes, and then the seasonings, stratifying them till the pan is full; pour in a glass of water. one of white wine, cover it with a sheet of paste, trim it smoothly round the edge, and bake it in a moderate oven. Grate sugar over it, and eat it warm.

WHITE POTATO PIES.

Boil some smooth white potatoes till very soft; then peel and mash them through a sieve while warm. Put the pulp into a sauce-pan, adding to each pint a large spoonful of butter, two ounces of sugar, half a grated nutmeg, half a tea-spoonful of cinnamon, and a gill of sweet cream; stir it till well incorporated, and set it by to cool; then stir in two well beaten eggs, and a glass of white wine; stir it again till well mixed, and bake them as directed for the sweet potato pies; sprinkle them thickly with powdered sugar, and eat them warm.

A SLICED WHITE POTATO PIE.

If your potatoes are young, you need not boil them, but peel and slice them very thin. If they are full grown, parboil them. Line a deep plate or patty-pan with paste as for other pies, and fill it with the sliced potatoes, interspersing among them some grated nutmeg, cinnamon and mace, a large handful of sugar, a large spoonful of butter, rolled in a small one of flour, and broken up, a wine glass of white wine, one of rose brandy, and a small cup of water. Put a paste over the top, notch, scollop, crimp, or serate it round the edge, and bake it in a moderate oven. To be good, there should be a good deal of syrup in it when done; therefore, it should not bake longer than is really necessary. It is best when warm. Yam pie may be made by this receipt, also carrot pies.

PUMPKIN PIES.

Line a buttered pie-pan with standing paste, and crimp it neatly round the edge. Having stewed a fine sweet pumpkin, mash it to a pulp, press it through a cullender, and put it in a sauce-pan, liquefying it with sweet milk. Put it on the fire, and when it begins to boil, add enough butter and sugar to make it sufficiently rich; stew it gently, stirring it all the time, till it is of the proper consistence for pies; then take it from the fire, and set it by to cool. After which, stir well into it two or three beaten eggs, a glass of brandy, some cinnamon, nutmeg, and cloves. Put a thick layer of it in your paste, bake it in a moderate oven, and grate sugar over it when done. Pumpkin pies when properly made, are very good. A salt-spoon of salt may be added to pumpkin and squash pies, which will assist in taking off the raw taste.

SQUASH PIES.

Boil a quart of milk, and make it a thin batter with stewed or baked squash; add two ounces of butter, four of sugar, and stew it slowly till it is a thick batter, stirring it all the time; if you choose, add a salt-spoonful of salt, which will assist in some degree in taking off the raw taste that belongs to pumpkin and squash. When it gets cold, stir in four beaten eggs, a glass of brandy, a powdered nutmeg, a tea-spoonful of mace, one of grated lemon, and one of cinnamon. Prepare a paste in a buttered pie-pan, neatly crimping it round the edge; put in a smooth, thick layer of prepared squash, and bake it in a moderate oven. When cold, grate loaf sugar thickly over it. It will be found very good.

CUSTARD PIES.

Beat eight eggs very light, stir them into a quart of sweet milk, and boil it till it is a thick custard, stirring it all the time. Add four ounces of sugar and a little grated lemon; put it in large shells of standing or sweet paste, set them in a moderate oven to brown a little, or brown them by holding a little above them a salamander, or red hot shovel. Grate a little nutmeg over them, and eat them cold. You may line a buttered patty-pan with plain or standing paste, and pour in the mixed custard before it is boiled, and bake it in the paste, though the crust will not be so light, except for the finest quality, which should be baked in puff paste.

MINCE PIES.

These pies should be baked in standing or plain paste, and should always be made with covers, handsomely ornamented with paste leaves, and eaten warm. In cold weather they are as good the second or third day after they are baked as the first, and may be kept a week, to eat very well, but should always be warmed on a stove, or in an oven, before they are eaten, as they are never sent to table cold. If by keeping them several days, they are likely to get too dry, raise the top crusts a little, put in a spoonful or two of white wine, sweet cider, or veal gravy to moisten them; then close the paste again as neatly as possible.

COARSE MINCE-MEAT.

Take two pounds of fresh venison, or beef, boil it very tender, and mince it fine from the bones; mix with it two pounds of fresh suet, finely minced, one pound of brown sugar, two pounds of currants that have been picked, washed and dried, and four pounds of juicy apples, that have been pared and sliced from the cores; add a large spoonful of cinnamon, one of cloves, two grated nutmegs, a large glass of brandy, and make it sufficiently liquid with sweet cider. Chop them very fine, commingle the whole well together, put it in a stone jar, and cover it with paper dipped in brandy. When you wish to make use of it, liquefy it a little with sweet cider, adding a very little salt and pepper, and bake it in plain paste.

ANOTHER PLAIN MINCE.—Take four and a half pounds of the tender parts of a fresh beef, two of which should be lean, and the rest fat; sprinkle it with salt, boil it very tender, and when it gets cold, mince it fine from the bones. Chop very fine three pounds of juicy apples, three of currants, two of raisins, that have been seeded, and mix them with the minced beef. Add a pound and a quarter of brown sugar, a spoonful of pounded cloves, one of mace, one of grated lemon, a large glass of brandy, and moisten it sufficiently with sweet cider. Mix the whole together till well incorporated, and put it up in stone jars; pour a few spoonfuls of brandy on the tops, and cover them with brandy paper. It will keep well a good part of the winter, by superadding a little brandy and sugar to the remaining mince every time you take any out of the jars.

———o◦o———

A VERY GOOD MINCE.

Take a beef's heart, with as much fresh veal that is entirely lean; sprinkle them with salt and pepper, boil them very tender, and set them by to cool. Then chop them exceedingly fine, with three pounds of fresh, hard lumps of suet, having first sprinkled them with a little salt, six pounds of Sultana or seeded raisins, six of pippin apples, after removing from them the peelings and cores, four of currants, having them picked, washed and dried, and one and a half of brown sugar. Add the grated peel and juice of two fine oranges, the grated rind and juice of one lemon, two powdered nutmegs, a dozen blades of mace, a spoonful of powdered cinnamon, one of cloves, a quart of madeira wine, and a pint of French brandy. Stir all together till well intermingled, put it in jars, cover them with several pieces of brandy paper, and keep them in a cool, dry place. When you wish to use it, after taking out what you want, put in the jars a little brandy and sugar, which will make the mince keep the better, and cover them up as before. Put a tolerably thick plain or puff paste in a buttered pie-pan; add to your mince a little sugar, broken bits of butter, and enough white wine to make it very moist, as, when too dry, it is not good; having blanched and sliced very thin some sweet and bitter almonds, intersperse them through the mince, stirring them in evenly, and allowing half as many bitter as sweet ones; put a thick layer of it in the pan, put a paste on the top, trim it smoothly round the edge, neatly notching or serating it, and bake it in a moderate oven.

ANOTHER GOOD MINCE.—Boil a fine salted tongue tender, then skin it, put it in a pan, pour over a pint of molasses, cover it and set it by till next day; then chop it very fine with an equal weight of beef suet, first picking the skins and stringy fibres from it, and sprinkling it lightly with salt; also six pounds of seeded raisins, five of the best flavored apples, two of cherries, two of currants and two of sugar: add the juice and grated peel of four oranges, two powdered nutmegs, one dozen blades of mace, a large spoonful of cinnamon, a quart of madeira wine and a pint of French brandy: work all together with your hands till intimately united, and put it up in jars, covering them with brandy papers.

Bake this mince in puff paste, moisten it with white wine, and strew amongst it some slips of preserved citron; add butter and sugar as you may think necessary, and put around it a handsome decorament of paste leaves and flowers, cut out in different forms with little tin cutters, and neatly concatenated together.

When you wish to make this mince, and cannot obtain all the fruits fresh, substitute preserves, which will do without adding any sugar.

—◦•◦—

THE FINEST MINCE.

Prepare beef's tongue and suet as before directed; mix with them five pounds of seeded raisins, four of best pippin apples, having divested them of the peelings and cores, three pounds of washed and dried currants; chop them very fine and commingle them together: then add two quarts of powdered loaf sugar one lb of preserved citron, cut into large slips, one pound of sweet almonds and two ounces of bitter ones, blanched and pounded to a paste with a little orange flower or rose water to prevent them oiling, the juice and grated peel of three oranges, two lemons, two powdered nutmegs, one dozen blades of mace, a spoonful of powdered cinnamon, a quart of madeira and a pint of French brandy. When the whole is very well mixed, put it up in stone or earthen jars, cover them with several folds of brandy paper, and keep them in a cool dry place. Be sure to add a little brandy and sugar to the mince in the jars each time you take out the smallest portion: cover them securely, and if the weather is cold when you make it, (which it may be by preserving your fruits,) you may keep it good through the greater part of winter.

This a very fine mince, and is too costly to be used for common purposes. When you make use of it, if you wish it any richer, add butter, sugar and wine. Bake it in the finest puff paste, handsomely ornamenting them round the edges with a wreath of paste leaves and flowers, cut out in various forms with cutters or a sharp pen-knife, and grate loaf sugar over them before you send them to table. The leaves and flowers should be very small, but quite conspicuous.

CAKES, &c.

—◦✦◦—

REMARKS.

In preparing for cake-baking, see that every article necessary for the purpose is in readiness, as it will not do to delay time after you have commenced. In the first place, having procured the proper utensils, have them in readiness. Scales and weights, measures, baking-pans of different sizes and shapes, coarse and fine graters, sieves and mortars, are all indispensable, as exactitude in proportioning the different articles must be attended to. None but the best materials are fit for cakes. The flour should be superfine, the eggs new, and the butter fresh and sweet. It is a good plan to prepare both fruits and seasonings the day previous to baking, as a good deal of time is required to prepare them in a proper manner. The best and least troublesome raisins are the Sultana, which have no seeds. Cut them in half and sprinkle them lightly with flour, to prevent them sinking to the bottom of the cake. Common raisins should be seeded, cut in half and floured, rubbing it on with your hands, to prevent its sticking to them in lumps. Almonds should be scalded in hot water till the skins will slip off, which is called blanching, then wiped dry and pounded one or two at a time in a marble mortar, with a little orange flour or rose water, to prevent them oiling and to make them white and light, removing them as you pound them. Citron should be preserved and cut into large slips; if cut too small, the taste of a small quantity, when mixed with other fruits, will scarcely be perceptible. Currants and cocoanuts should be prepared the same day they are used, but quite early. Pick and wash your currants, drain, dry and dredge them with flour, sprinkling on a little at a time, and stirring them with your hands to prevent the flour sticking to them in lumps. Cocoanuts should be peeled, washed, weighed and grated fine. To commence your cakes, have every article brought and laid before you. Having pounded very fine your seasonings, pass them through a fine sieve; weigh your sugar and break it up, spread it out on a cloth, crush it to a fine powder with a rolling-pin, pass it through a sieve and put it into a bread-pan. Weigh your butter, wash it in one or two cold waters, and work it with a wooden spaddle till firm, draining every particle of water from it: cut it up in small bits, commingle it with the sugar, set it before the fire, where it will get a little soft, but by no means suffer it to get hot, and beat it with the sugar till they are intimately united, and much the resemblance of rich cream. Next, weigh and sift your flour, and then beat your eggs; separate the whites from the yolks, carefully examining them as you proceed, to ascertain if they are good; beat the yolks very smooth, and beat the whites in an earthen dish to a stiff froth, using a broad-bladed knife, small hickory rods or a bunch of wire, bent in hoops or broken. In the mean time, butter your pans, heat your ovens in a proper manner to suit the cakes you are going to bake, which directions will be given in their respective receipts; and if oranges or lemons are to be used, grate off the yellow rind, squeeze out the juice, and mix the whole of the ingredients together, and bake them as will be directed in each receipt, that the process be not retarded, but that every thing may be done in the most expert and adroit manner.

If these directions, together with what I will hereafter give in each receipt, be carefully followed and dexterously performed, you may safely calculate on having the best of cake, besides relieving yourself of the expense and inconvenience of hiring a cook expressly for the purpose, or having them baked from home.

COMMON POUND CAKE.

Weigh a pound of fresh butter, wash it in cold water, cut it up, put it in a pan, and set it a short distance from the fire; weigh a pound of sugar, crush it to a powder, sift it, mix it with the butter, and beat them together till very soft and smooth. Mix together a wine glass of brandy, one of wine, a grated nutmeg, a little lemon juice, or a few drops of the essence of lemon, and stir it gradually into the butter and sugar. Weigh and sift a pound of flour, and beat to a stiff froth twelve fresh eggs; stir them alternately and gradually into the butter, &c., and beat the whole very hard till smoothly incorporated, put it in a deep buttered pan of circular form, not more than half filling it, that the cake may have plenty of room to rise, and set it in an oven a little warm, till it has well risen, and then allowing at the first but very little heat, and afterwards adding it gradually; do not raise the lid oftener than is really necessary, to ascertain how the cake is progressing. When you think it is done, run the blade of a knife down through the middle of it, and if upon drawing it out, you find it entirely clean, you may safely calculate it is done, but if to the contrary, there is batter or a little of the dough sticking to it, you may be sure it is not done, therefore, bake it longer. Another way to tell when it is done, is to take it from the oven, touch it to your face, and if it is thoroughly done, it will not burn in the least, but you must return it to the oven, withdraw the fire, and let it remain till it gets cool, otherwise it will be clammy. Then ice it handsomely with cake icing, for which see receipt.

BRIDE'S CAKE.

Prepare a pound of fresh butter and a pound of powdered loaf sugar, as before directed, mix them together, and beat them to a cream. Add to it a wine glass of white wine, one of rose brandy, a grated nutmeg, a tea-spoonful of powdered cinnamon, or a few drops of the essence, and the juice and grated rind of half a lemon. Sift a pound of the finest flour, and beat to a very stiff froth the whites only of twenty fresh eggs; then stir into the other ingredients alternately and gradually the flour and eggs, giving it a hard stirring at the last. Put it in a deep buttered pan, of circular form, having a straight, upright rim, and not filling it more than half full; let it stand to rise, and bake it in a moderate oven, very little warm at first, and gradually heating it, and putting rather more fire underneath than on the top. When it is thoroughly done, withdraw the fire, let it remain in the oven till it gets cool, and ice it smoothly with white cake icing, and when it gets about half dry, ornament it in the most elegant manner with devices and borders in white sugar, which you may obtain at the confectioner's. It should be considerably elevated upon the table, and stick firmly in the centre of it, a handsome assemblage of real or artificial leaves and white flowers.

LADY CAKE.

Crush with a rolling-pin one pound and a quarter of loaf sugar, wash the salt well from three quarters of a pound of butter, mix them together in a pan, warm them a little, and beat them to a cream. Add the juice and grated peel of an orange, half a lemon, and stir them with a wooden spaddle till very well mixed. Weigh and sift fourteen ounces of superfine flour, and beat to a stiff froth the whites of eighteen eggs; stir the flour into the other ingredients, in turn with the egg froth, stirring it very hard at the last. Pour it in a buttered square pan, put it in a slow oven, that it may have time to rise, and bake it with rather a brisk fire, adding it gradually; let it remain in the oven till it gets cold, then ice it very white, and when it gets about half dry, lay round it a handsome festoon of flowers.

QUEEN CAKE.

Sift into a pan a pound and a quarter of powdered loaf sugar, and cut into it one pound of fresh butter, having been washed thoroughly in cold water, to free it from salt; warm them a little by the fire, and beat them together till intimately united, and very smooth. Add to it a powdered nutmeg, a tea-spoonful of cinnamon, one of mace, one of grated lemon, a wine glass of brandy, one of white wine, and one of rose water. Then stir in alternately eighteen ounces of superfine flour, and the whites of twenty-four eggs, having beaten them to a very fine froth; beat it hard for some minutes, put it in a large buttered pan, and bake it in a moderate oven. When it is done, let it remain in the oven till it gets cold; then ice it very white, and when it gets about half dry, put around it a handsome decorament of tinsel leaves and flowers, put some small gilded leaves over the top, and elevate it considerably on the table. Cakes dressed in this manner are introduced only at large suppers, at which time, if you wish a splendid table, dress all your fine cakes in different attire, suitable to the names and materials of which they are made, and arrange them handsomely upon the table, that the company may see the different kinds of cake.

DANDY CAKES.

Mix a pound of fresh butter with a pound of powdered loaf sugar, beat them till smooth, and add to them two powdered nutmegs, a tea-spoonful of powdered cinnamon, the juice of an orange, and a glass of white wine. Then add alternately and gradually fourteen ounces of flour, and ten beaten eggs. Beat it very well, put it in small scolloped pans that are well buttered, and bake them in rather a brisk oven. When they are done, being made of so little flour, they will shrink a little from the sides of the pans; then turn them out, ice them very white, spot them over with red sugar sand, and stack them on a large plate, having at least three stacks, and every two inverted.

FRUIT CAKE.

Pick, wash and dry two pounds of currants, seed and cut in half two pounds of raisins, and sprinkle both lightly with flour, to prevent them sinking to the bottom of the cake, rubbing it on carefully with your hands, lest it should stick to them in lumps. Blanch and pound to a paste one pound of sweet almonds, and two ounces of bitter ones, adding a little orange flour, or rose water, to prevent them oiling, and being dark and heavy. Sift a pound and a half of powdered loaf sugar, and work it well into a pound of fresh butter, having washed it in cold water, to free it from salt. Add to it the juice and grated peel of an orange, a large table-spoonful of powdered cinnamon, one of mace, two powdered nutmegs, a large glass of brandy, and two of white wine. Beat as light as possible twelve fresh eggs, sift a pound of fine flour, and stir them in turn into the butter, sugar, &c.; beat it with a wooden spaddle till very smooth, and then add alternately and gradually the fruits; stir it again very hard, put it in a deep buttered pan, and bake it in a moderate oven; it will require several hours to bake it well. Let it remain in the oven till it gets cold, and then ice it very smoothly, putting it on with a broad bladed knife, and spot it over at short intervals with small spots of dark colored preserve juice.

A FINE FRUIT CAKE.

Prepare two pounds of raisins, and two of currants, as before directed. Cut up a pound of fresh butter, and work it well into two pounds of powdered loaf sugar, make it a little soft by holding it near the fire. Grate the peel, and squeeze the juice from a fine deep colored orange, and half a lemon; stir them into the butter and sugar with a large spoonful of powdered cinnamon, one of cloves, two powdered nutmegs, a glass of brandy, one of wine, and one of rose water. Cut up a pound of preserved citron in large slips. Beat to a froth fourteen eggs, weigh and sift eighteen ounces of fine flour, and stir them alternately into the other ingredients; stir it hard for some minutes, and then add in turn the currants, raisins and citron; beat it again very well, and bake it in a large, deep pan, with moderate heat. When it is quite cold, take it from the oven, scrape and brush it clean, ice it very white and smooth, using a broad bladed knife for the purpose, and decorate it with colored sugar sand, nonpareils, thick, dark colored preserve juice, or small leaves of citron, regularly cut out and notched, and placed round the edge, so as to form a wreath. It should be kept in mind that all large cakes, except sponge cake, should stand in the oven to rise, before they are put to bake.

A WEDDING FRUIT CAKE.

Blanch and pound to a paste one pound of sweet almonds and two of bitter ones, adding a little rose water, to

make them white and light. Cut in large slips a pound
of citron. Pick, wash and dry in the sun, or before the
fire, three pounds of currants, and dredge them lightly
with flour. Seed, cut and flour three pounds of raisins,
or cut in half and flour three pounds of Sultana raisins,
which have no seeds. Beat to a cream three pounds of
powdered loaf sugar, and three of fresh butter; grate the
yellow peel from an orange, and squeeze out the juice,
also one lemon, powder two nutmegs, a large spoonful of
cinnamon, one of mace; mix the seasonings together, and
stir them into the butter and sugar, with two large glasses of white wine, and one of brandy. Weigh three pounds
of superfine flour, sift it, and stir it into the mixture, in
turn with twenty-eight fresh eggs that are beaten to a
stiff froth; beat it with a wooden spaddle till well incorporated and very smooth, then stir in alternately the currants, raisins, almonds and citron; stir it till the whole
are evenly amalgamated; then put it in a large buttered
pan, and bake it in a moderate oven; it will require two
or three hours to bake it well. When it gets nearly
done, withdraw a part of the fire, that it may finish with
a slow heat. When it gets cold, if the outside is a little
too brown, scrape and brush it neatly, put a very thick
smooth coat of icing over it, having first colored it a fine
pink with cochineal, and flavored it with lemon. Ice it
with almond icing, putting it over nearly half an inch
thick and very smooth. It is best to prepare the fruits
for this cake the day previous to baking.

BLACK CAKE.

Pick and wash two pounds of whortleberries; spread
them out on a cloth, dry them and dredge them with
flour. Prepare two pounds of currants in the same way.
Seed, cut in half and flour two pounds of raisins. Wash
the salt from a pound of butter, and work it to a cream
with two pounds of sifted brown sugar; add half a pint
of molasses, two powdered nutmegs, a spoonful of powdered mace and a large glass of brandy. Sift a pound
of flour, beat a dozen eggs to a froth, and stir them in
turn into the butter, &c.; then stir in alternately the
fruits, beat it very hard at the last, bake it in a large
deep pan with moderate heat. Make an icing of pow-

dered white sugar and beaten white of eggs, in the proportion of four ounces of sugar to one white of egg; flavor it well with oil of lemon or extract of roses. Color it a little with some dark thick preserve juice, and put a thick coat of it over the cake.

A FRUIT POUND CAKE.

Blanch and slice very thin one pound of sweet almonds, and cut into large slips a pound of preserved citron, Prepare a pound of currants and a pound of raisins in the usual manner. Beat to a cream a pound of fresh butter and two pounds of powdered loaf sugar, and add to them two glasses of white wine, one of rose water, two powdered nutmegs, a spoonful of powdered cinnamon and one of mace. Sift a pound of flour, beat to a froth twelve eggs, and stir them into the mixture; then add the fruits alternately, and beat it hard, put it into a buttered pan, and bake it in a moderate oven, finishing with a slow heat. When cold, ice it very white, and decorate it with colored sugar sand or nonpareils.

A FRUIT QUEEN CAKE.

Beat together one pound of fresh butter and one and a half of powdered loaf sugar till it resembles thick cream: add the juice and grated rind of a lemon, the grated peel and juice of an orange, two glasses of white wine and two grated nutmegs: also add two ounces of sweet almonds, that have been blanched and pounded with a little rose water, twelve beaten eggs, a pound and two ounces of flour and the whites of twenty eggs that have been beaten to a stiff froth. Lastly, stir in one pound of currants, that have been properly prepared, and four ounces of preserved citron, cut into large slips; beat the whole very hard, and bake it in a moderate oven, finishing with a slow heat. When cold, ice it very white, and decorate it with devices and borders in white sugar, or lay round it a garland of flowers. Such dressings are only intended for fine suppers.

ALMOND CAKE.

Blanch and pound to a paste four ounces of shelled sweet almonds, and two ounces of bitter ones, moistening them with a little rose water as you proceed. Beat the whites of twenty-two eggs to a stiff froth, and stir the paste into it lightly and alternately with eight ounces of fine flour and one pound of powdered loaf sugar: add a grated nutmeg and a small glass of white wine; put in a square pan that is well buttered, and bake it in a brisk oven, withdrawing the fire when done, that it may remain in the oven till it gets cold: then ice it handsomely with almond icing.

ALMOND POUND CAKE.

Beat to a cream one pound of butter and one pound of powdered loaf sugar; add two glasses of white wine, a spoonful of powdered mace, and the juice and grated rind of a lemon. Blanch and pound to a paste with a little rose water, one pound of shelled sweet almonds: sift a pound of flour, beat to a froth twelve fresh eggs, and stir the almonds, flour and eggs alternately into the butter, &c., giving it a hard stirring at the last. Put it into a deep pan of circular form, that is well buttered, and bake it in a moderate oven. When cold, ice it neatly with almond icing.

PLUM CAKE.

Prepare two pounds of currants and two of raisins in the usual manner. Beat to a cream a pound of fresh butter and a pound of powdered brown sugar, and add to it a pint of molasses, a glass of brandy, one of wine, one of rose water, a spoonful of powdered cinnamon and three powdered nutmegs. Beat very light one dozen eggs, sift a pound and a half of flour, and stir them also into the butter, &c.; then add alternately the fruits, stirring them in very hard. Bake it in a deep pan with moderate heat. Do not remove it from the oven till it gets cold, and then ice it neatly, tinging the icing with preserve juice or cochineal.

LITTLE PLUM CAKES.

Beat to a cream three quarters of a pound of butter and a pound of sugar; add a glass of brandy, one of wine and two powdered nutmegs. Sift a pound of flour, beat ten eggs light, and stir them in turn into the butter, sugar, &c.; then stir in two pounds of currants, that have been prepared in the usual manner. Beat it very hard, and bake it in small scolloped pans with moderate heat. When cold, ice them very white and smooth, spot them over at intervals with thick dark colored preserve juice, and stack them, having three stacks in a place, and inverting every two.

RAISIN CAKE.

Seed three pounds of the best raisins, (Sultana raisins are preferable, having no seeds); shred or clip them very fine with sharp scissors, and dust them lightly with flour. Beat together a pound and a quarter of sugar and a pound of butter; add two glasses of white wine, one of brandy and three powdered nutmegs; also twelve beaten eggs and one pound of flour. Lastly, stir in the raisins and beat the whole till well intermingled; then put it into a large deep pan, of circular form, and bake it with moderate heat, having it rather slow at first, and gradually increasing it. Let it remain in the oven till it gets cold, and then brush it clean and ice it with pink icing, flavoring it with lemon juice or extract of roses.

LOAF CAKE.

Beat six eggs light, and rub them well into three pounds of flour; add one and a half pounds of powdered sugar, a gill of good yeast, a tea-spoonful of mace, one of cinnamon, one of cloves, and make it into a stiff batter with sweet milk, so that your spoon or spaddle will move with difficulty when stirring it. Cover it and set it by the fire, where it will keep a little warm till it rises well; then stir in one pound of butter, that is warmed a little and beaten to a cream. Stir it till very well incorporated, and bake it in a moderate oven. Do not remove it from the oven till it gets cold.

WHITE SPONGE CAKE.

Beat the whites of twenty eggs to a stiff froth, and stir very hard into it a pound of powdered loaf sugar, the juice and grated rind of a lemon, and the juice of two fine oranges. Beat them together till smoothly mixed, and then stir in very lightly and gradually three quarters of a pound of the finest flour. Do not beat it hard after the flour is stirred in, as it will make it tough and ruin the cake. Put it into a large square pan, that is well buttered, and put it immediately into a brisk oven, lessening the heat after the cake is well risen, that it may have time to soak thoroughly. Ice it very white and smooth; and if it is for a fine supper, place round the edge some very small gilded leaves, which is a common decorament on such occasions with some of the most fashionable people in America.

LITTLE SPONGE CAKES.

Take the weight of six eggs in loaf sugar, crush it with a rolling-pin, and pass it through a fine sieve. Take the weight of four eggs in flour, and sift it also. Separate the whites from the yolks of six fresh eggs, beat the yolks very smoothly, beat the whites to a stiff froth, and mix them together. Stir into them the sugar, the juice and grated rind of two lemons, and beat it very hard. Then add the flour, stirring it in slowly and lightly, lest you make it tough. Be sure you do not beat it or stir it in the least after the flour is well mixed with the other ingredients, but put it hastily into little scolloped pans, having them well buttered, and bake them as briskly as possible. When cold, ice them very white, set them in a warm room till they get dry, and then stack them in a plate, inverting every two.

YELLOW SPONGE CAKE.

Beat the yolks of twenty-four eggs very well, and stir hard into it the weight of twelve eggs in powdered loaf sugar; add a glass of white wine, the juice and grated rind of a lemon, and beat it till well incorporated; then stir in very lightly and slowly the weight of eight eggs in flour; put it into a buttered square pan, and bake it in a brisk oven. Rub some lumps of loaf sugar on a fine deep colored orange till they imbibe a fine flavor and a yellow color; then powder them, pass it through a fine sieve, mix it with whites of eggs, that are beaten to a stiff froth, in proportions of four ounces of sugar to one white of egg; mix it smoothly, and put a thick coat of it over the cake.

MORAVIAN CAKE.

Sift a quart of fine flour, sprinkle into it a small spoonful of salt, two powdered nutmegs, a spoonful of cinnamon, one of mace, and four ounces of powdered sugar. Rub in with your hands four ounces of butter and two beaten eggs; when they are completely saturated, add four table-spoonfuls of good yeast, and enough sweet milk to make it into a thick batter. Put it in a buttered pan, cover it, and set it by the fire to rise, but be sure you do not let it get hot, or the cake will be spoiled. When it looks quite light, superadd four ounces of sugar, and a handful of flour; sprinkle a handful of brown sugar over the top, and bake it in a moderate oven.

WASHINGTON'S CAKE.

Dissolve a tea-spoonful of saleratus in a small tea-cupful of boiling water, let it set by the fire a few minutes, and stir in three gills of butter-milk. Beat to a cream a pound of butter and a pound of powdered sugar, and mix them with the water. Add a glass of white wine and two powdered nutmegs; then stir in alternately six beaten eggs and eighteen ounces of flour. Stir it till well mixed and very smooth, put it in a buttered square pan, and bake it in a moderate oven.

SCOTCH CAKES.

Sift into a deep pan three pints of flour, sprinkle in a salt-spoon of salt, a spoonful of powdered cinnamon, one of mace, and three quarters of a pound of powdered sugar. Cut up three quarters of a pound of butter into small bits, and rub them into the flour, &c., with your hands, till it is completely saturated. Dissolve a tea-spoonful of saleratus in a large spoonful of boiling vinegar, pour in enough sour milk to make the whole into good paste. Mix it very well, and knead it a little. Put it on your paste board, roll it into a round or circular form, about an inch thick; cut it across into four equal

parts, crimp or notch them neatly round the edges; ice
them with tart icing, and bake them in rather a quick
oven.

A SCOTCH PLUM CAKE.

Sift two quarts of flour in a broad pan; rub well into it
one pound of butter, one of sugar, half a pound of raisins,
shred as fine as possible, half a pound of currants, that
have been picked, washed and dried, a spoonful of cinnamon, one of mace, a wine-glass of brandy, one of wine,
and six beaten eggs. When the whole of these are well
intermingled, make it into good paste with sweet cream;
sprinkle your paste board well with dry flour, roll the
paste again and again with a rolling-pin till it looks smooth
and light; then roll it into a circular form, about one inch
thick, cut it across in four equal parts, crimp the edges
neatly, pierce them through in several places with a fork,
lay them on tin sheets, and bake them in a brisk oven.
Grate loaf sugar thickly over them while warm.

AN EASTERN PLUM CAKE.

Pick, wash and dry a pound of currants, and dredge
them lightly with flour. Sift one pound of flour, and beat
to a cream one pound of fresh butter, and one of powdered loaf sugar. Beat twelve eggs very light, and commingle them with the butter and sugar, add the juice and grated rind of two lemons, and two glasses of white wine;
then stir in the flour and currants alternately, beat it very
well, put it in a large buttered pan, that has straight sides,
and bake it in a moderate oven. While it is baking, mash
to a smooth marmalade one pound of preserved plums, or
Sultana raisins; when the cake is done, and quite cold,
place the fruit smoothly and evenly over it, then put over
a good quantity of cake icing, dropping it on by large
spoonfuls, forming little conical figures, and brown them
delicately with a salamander, or red hot shovel, holding
it but a little above the icing.

MATRIMONIAL CAKES.

Sift two quarts of flour, sprinkle in the juice and grated
peel of two oranges, and two glasses of white wine. Rub

well into it with your hands a pound of butter, two of powdered sugar and two beaten eggs; dissolve a tea-spoonful of saleratus or pearlash in a small tea-cupful of boiling water; let it stand a few minutes; then mix it with enough sour cream or butter milk, to make the whole into good paste; mix it well, and roll it out on your paste board till it is very smooth, then roll it into a sheet about half an inch thick, cut it in long, narrow slips, and bake them in a brisk oven. When done, set them by to cool, after which ice them very white with cake icing, and when they get nearly dry, ornament them with little diversified spots of red sugar sand, and deep colored orange peel, that has been grated very fine and passed through a sieve. Stack them lengthwise in a large plate, round a solid figure of cake, resembling a cone.

CHEESE CAKE.

Boil two quarts of entire sweet milk, and pour into it while boiling, three gills of white wine; when it becomes a curd, strain the whey from it, pound it in a mortar with half a pound of butter, half a pound of powdered loaf sugar, six beaten eggs, and as much rice flour, or superfine wheat flour, as will make it of the consistence of poundcake batter. Add a grated nutmeg, and one spoonful of cinnamon; beat it very well, and bake it in small buttered pans, in a moderate oven. When done, turn them carefully out, and grate loaf sugar thickly over them. Half a pound of raisins or currants is sometimes added to cheese cake.

ANOTHER CHEESE CAKE.—Beat eight eggs light, stir them in a quart of sweet milk, and boil it till it becomes a thick custard, stirring it occasionally, to prevent its burning; then pour it in a clean sieve, drain off the whey, put the curd in a broad pan, mix with it a quarter of a pound of butter, six ounces of sugar, the beaten yolks of four eggs, four table-spoonfuls of sweet cream, a glass of lemon brandy, and two powdered nutmegs. Beat it thoroughly until it is well mixed and very smooth, adding enough rice flour to make it like common cake batter. Bake it in small buttered pans, in a brisk oven, and grate loaf sugar over them when cold.

ALMOND CHEESE CAKE

If you have the liquid preparation of rennet, turn your milk to a curd with some of that, allowing a large spoonful to a quart of milk; this is much more convenient than the dried rennet, being always in readiness. But if you have not got the preparation, cut a piece of dried rennet two or three inches square, according to the strength of it; put it in a cup, pour over it two or three spoonfuls of wine, and twice as much warm water, and set it by till next day. Then make a quart of sweet milk over lukewarm, pour in the rennet water, cover it, and set it by the fire, where it will keep warm, till the curd forms. When the curd is very firm, drain the whey from it, and put it in a pan, mix with it eight ounces of butter, eight of sugar, beat them well together, and set it by to cool. Blanch and pound to a paste four ounces of sweet almonds, and one ounce of bitter ones, adding a little rose water as you proceed. Beat very well the yolks of twelve fresh eggs and the whites of two; stir the almonds and eggs into the curd, &c. Add two glasses of white wine, two powdered nutmegs, and make it of the consistence of common poundcake batter with fine flour. Beat the whole very hard, and bake it in buttered square pans with moderate heat. You may make cheese cake without using any flour, and bake it in shells of puff paste; and you may also make it with half the quantity of butter, sugar and eggs to the same quantity of curd, and add half a pound of currants or raisins.

COCOANUT CAKE.

Having removed the hull and dark skin from a cocoanut, weigh a pound of it and grate it fine. Beat to a froth the whites of eighteen eggs and the yolks of twelve. Powder a pound of loaf sugar, and stir it into the eggs in turn with the cocoanut; add a handful of flour, beat it well, and bake it in a buttered square pan in rather a quick oven.

LITTLE COCOANUT CAKES.

Divest two cocoanuts of the shells and dark skins, break them up, wash, weigh and grate them fine. Mix them with an equal weight of powdered loaf sugar, add the juice and grated rind of two lemons and the milk of the cocoanuts: mix them very well, make it into small cakes, about the size in circumference of a half dollar, though some thicker; put them on buttered tin sheets, grate loaf sugar over them, and bake them a few minutes in a moderate oven. Be careful not to put them close enough to touch each other, lest they run together and spoil the shape.

COCOANUT MACCAROONS.

Beat the whites of eight eggs to a stiff froth, add the juice of two lemons, and stir into it as much powdered loaf sugar, with an equal quantity of grated cocoanut, as will make the whole into a stiff paste: then flour your hands, to prevent its sticking to them, make it up into small balls as near the size and shape of a nutmeg as possible. Put them on sheets of buttered white paper, grate a little loaf sugar over them, and bake them a few minutes in a brisk oven.

COCOANUT SNOW-BALLS.

Grate as fine as possible two decorticated cocoanuts, put it in an earthen pan, mix with it the milk of the cocoanuts, a few drops of essence of lemon, and enough powdered loaf sugar to make it into a stiff paste. Mix it well, make it into small balls, all of the same size and shape. Spread some sheets of fine white paper over the bottom of a large flat dish, put the balls on the paper, not suffering them to touch each other, grate loaf sugar over them, and set them in a warm room till next day, which will dry them sufficiently without baking them.

COCOANUT SWEET-HEARTS.

Take a large cocoanut from the shell, peel off the dark skin, and grate it fine. Sift a quart of flour, rub into it half a pound of butter, half a pound of powdered loaf sugar, a few drops of the essence of lemon and four beaten eggs. Mix it very well, and then add the grated cocoanut, with as much of the milk as will make the whole into a stiff dough. Flour your paste board, roll out the dough about half an inch thick, cut it in hearts with a tin cutter, dipping it in dry flour occasionally to prevent the dough sticking to it: lay them on buttered tin plates, (not so near as to touch each other.) grate loaf sugar over them, and bake them for a few minutes in a brisk oven: after which, lay them by to cool; then ice them very white, and when they get about half dry, touch them with a little red sugar sand, making but one spot on each heart.

ALMOND SWEET-HEARTS.

Blanch and pound to a paste one pound of sweet almonds, adding a little rose water as you proceed. Beat the whites of six eggs to a stiff froth, and mix them with the almond paste, with as much powdered loaf sugar as will make it into a stiff dough. Add a few drops of essence of lemon, roll it out on your paste board, and cut it in the shape of hearts with little tin cutters; place some sheets of fine white paper on some buttered tin plates, put your hearts on them, placing them so far apart, that they cannot unite with each other; grate loaf sugar over them, and bake them a delicate brown in a brisk oven.

ALMOND CONES.

Pound to a smooth paste one pound of shelled sweet almonds, and two ounces of shelled bitter ones, adding as you proceed, enough rose water to prevent them oiling, and that will make them white and light. Beat the whites of six eggs to a stiff froth, squeeze in it the juice of one orange, or lemon, and mix in by degrees the almond paste. Then stir in as much powdered loaf sugar as will make it into a stiff dough; flour your hands, make it into little cones, not larger than a nutmeg, put them on tin sheets, or in shallow pans, that are slightly buttered; grate loaf sugar thickly over them, and bake them a delicate brown in a brisk oven.

NAPLES BISCUIT.

Beat ten eggs as light as possible, first separating the whites from the yolks; and after they are beaten, mix them together again. Add one pound of powdered sugar, a glass of white wine, and two powdered nutmegs. Beat the whole very well, and then stir in lightly and gradually three quarters of a pound of fine flour. Stir it no more than is really necessary to mix it well, as much stirring will make the biscuit tough. Place some muffin rings on the bottom of a clean, hot oven, having them first rubbed lightly with butter to prevent the biscuit sticking to them; put in your batter by spoonfuls, filling the rings about half full, and bake them with a brisk heat.

FAYETTE BISCUIT.

Separate the whites from the yolks of six fresh eggs, beat them to a stiff froth, and mix them together again. Add to it the juice and grated rind of a lemon, and ten ounces of powdered white sugar, stirring it in very hard. Then stir in lightly and gradually six ounces of fine flour; as soon as it is well mixed, drop it hastily from a spoon into little paper cases, having them placed on tin sheets, set them immediately in a brisk oven.

SNOWBALLS.

Stir together half a pound of powdered loaf sugar, and half a pound of fresh butter, till they resemble thick cream. Beat to a very stiff froth the whites only of twelve eggs, and stir them into the butter and sugar, alternately with half a pound of fine flour; add a few drops of essence of lemon, and a glass of white wine. Butter some small round bottom tea cups, and having beaten the batter till smooth, put it into the cups, filling them about half full, and bake them in a moderate oven. When done, take them from the cups, invert them on a plate, and ice them very white with two coats of cake icing.

PUFF SNOWBALLS.

Beat the whites of eight fresh eggs to a stiff froth; add to them the juice of an orange, lemon, or a few drops of the essence of lemon, and eight ounces of powdered loaf sugar, stirring it in very hard. Then stir in very gently four ounces of the finest flour; put it in small round bottom tea-cups, having them slightly buttered, and bake them immediately in a brisk oven. When cold, invert them, ice them very white, and when about half dry, lay on each a small gilded leaf, handsomely notched.

A PYRAMID OF CAKES.

A pyramid of cake is introduced only at the finest suppers. Make them all of common poundcake, or have every cake of a different quality, if you choose. The pans in which they are baked should all be of a circular form, gradually diminishing in circumference, from the largest to the smallest size. Ice them very white, and when they get about half dry, put round each a decorament of devices and borders in white sugar, or a very delicate garland or festoon. When the icing gets perfectly dry, stack them regularly, putting the largest at the bottom, and the smallest on the top, and stick a small bunch of real or artificial flowers on the pinnacle, or top cake.

RUSK.

Take two quarts of flour, rub well into it half a pound of butter, half a pound of sugar, and six beaten eggs; add four table-spoonfuls of good yeast, commingle the whole very well together, and make it into good paste or dough, with warm sweet milk; then put it in a pan or oven, cover it, and set it by the fire to rise. When it is quite light, sprinkle your paste board with flour, rub some on your hands, and divide the dough into small cakes, knead them, and make them smooth, put them in a pan a small distance apart, having first sprinkled it with flour; set them in an oven, and bake them as light bread.

ANOTHER MODE FOR MAKING RUSK.—Sift three pounds of flour, rub well into it half a pound of powdered sugar, two powdered nutmegs, half a pint of good yeast, four beaten eggs, and enough warm sweet milk to make it of the consistence of common light bread dough; set it by the fire, where it will keep warm, till it rises well; then work into it half a pound of butter, sprinkling your paste board well with flour; make them into small rolls, put them in shallow iron pans that have been sprinkled with flour, and set them again by the fire for twenty or thirty minutes, till they begin to rise the second time, and then bake them in a moderate oven.

If you wish hard rusk, set them by till they get cold, then split them in half, lay them on tin sheets, and dry and brown them lightly in a moderate oven.

TEA RUSK.

Rub well into two pounds of flour, three quarters of a pound of powdered sugar, pass it through a sieve, add to it a gill of good yeast, make it into rather a soft dough, with sweet milk, that is luke warm, and set it by the fire to rise, sprinkling on the top a small handful of flour. When it is well risen, lay it on your paste board, flour your hands, and knead well into it half a pound of butter, make it into small round cakes, pierce the tops with a fork, and place them close together in shallow iron pans, that have been sprinkled with flour; set them into a very slow oven for twenty or thirty minutes, that they may have time to rise a little, and then bake them with moderate heat.

LITTLE SODA CAKES.

Dissolve a teaspoonful of soda, in a pint of hot sour milk. Sift two pounds of flour, rub well into it half a pound of sugar and half a pound of butter, sprinkling a wine glass of wine. Then pour on the milk and soda, and knead it a little, after which roll it into a sheet about half an inch thick, cut it into cakes with sweet cake cutters, lay them on tin sheets, and bake them briskly.

COMMON JUMBLES.

Sift two pounds of flour, sprinkle in it a powdered nutmeg, a teaspoonful of cinnamon, one of cloves, a few drops of essence of lemon, and a glass of white wine. Beat six eggs light, powder a pound of sugar, cut up a pound of butter, mix them together and work them well into the flour, adding as much milk, as will make it a stiff dough. Knead it well on your paste board, roll it into a sheet about half an inch thick, cut it in long narrow strips, half an inch wide, flour your hands, roll them gently on the paste board under your hand, till you make them round; then put them on buttered tin sheets, twist them round, regularly concatenating them together so as to form small rings; take a clean soft feather, dip it in the beaten white of egg, brush it over the jumbles, grate loaf sugar thickly on, and bake them in a moderate oven.

MATRIMONY.

Make it up as for the jumbles, roll it out about half an inch thick, and cut it into long strips about half an inch wide. Roll them on your paste board till they become round, and very smooth, then plat them evenly together, having three in a plat, lay them straight on buttered tin sheets, and bake them in a moderate oven. When they are done and quite cold, ice them very white with cake icing, making it rather thinner than common with the beaten white of egg, and flavoring it with the essence of lemon, or extract of roses. When the icing gets about half dry, variegate them over at intervals with red sugar sand, and greated rind of lemon or orange peel and stack them in a plate round a pyramidal figure.

HARMONY.

Cut up a pound of fresh butter and divide it in four equal parts. Sift two pounds of flour, rub one portion of the butter into it, with four ounces of powdered sugar; make it into a very stiff dough with cold water, and roll it into a thin sheet. Break up another portion of the butter, spread it evenly over the paste with a broad bladed knife, and sprinkle on a little flour; fold it up into a ball, and roll it out again, put on the other portions of butter in the same manner as before, rolling it out each time; lastly roll it into a sheet, cut it in circular pieces sufficienty large to cover a small patty-pan, trim the edges smoothly, crimp them neatly, and bake them in rather a brisk oven.

Beat eight eggs very light, stir them into a quart of rich sweet milk, and boil it till it becomes a curd, stirring it up occasionally from the sides to prevent its burning; then pour it in a sieve and drain the whey from it. Put the curd in a mortar, add two ounces of butter, four of sugar, a powdered nutmeg, a glass of white wine, the juice of a lemon and a few spoonfuls of sweet cream: pound it till intimately united and very smooth; then put a thick layer of it on each shell of paste, and pile whipped cream on the top.

COURTSHIPS.

Write a variety of questions, each comprising one verse, to which write as many answers, and cut them all apart. Have ready sugar-plums of various kinds; wrap a verse round each plum, taking care not to mix them. Take two kinds of glazed paper, cut it up in small circular pieces, fringe them round neatly with small scissors, put a plum with the verse in each paper, taking care to put the questions in one color and the answers in another; then twist the papers round the plums, under the curls, which press back with your fingers, so that they may entirely envelope the plums. They should be handed round together, that each one may have a solicitation with an answer, in which lies the amusement, some answers differing so far in sense to the subject of the questions. This appears very simple to be sure, but it is quite amusing to young people, for whom it is designed.

QUERIES.

Sift three pounds of flour, rub well into it one pound of powdered sugar, half a pound of butter, two powdered nutmegs, a tea-spoonful of powdered cinnamon, a glass of wine, the juice and grated rinds of two lemons, and six beaten eggs. When it is well mixed, add as much sweet milk as will make it into good stiff dough, knead it well, and roll it out thin. Have ready some almond kernels, peach kernels, raisins, small bits of citron, preserved plums, &c., &c.: wrap each article in a separate piece of paste, closing it smoothly together, and making it of an oval shape. Cut the remaining paste into various fanciful shapes, some into long slips, to be twisted and formed into rings, hoops, plats, and as many varieties of shape as you may think proper: then dust them all with flour. Have ready a pan of boiling butter, drop them carefully in, and fry them a delicate brown: after which drain them on a sieve, cool them, brush them over with the beaten white of egg, grate loaf sugar thickly over them, and set them in a warm room to dry. Then spot some of them with various colors, and commingle them in a plate together.

LITTLE QUINOMIE CAKES.

Beat to a cream half a pound of butter and half a pound of sugar, add two powdered nutmegs and a glass of wine; then stir in the beaten yolks of fifteen eggs, with half a pound of flour, beat it very well, put it into small scolloped pans, that are well buttered, and bake them in a moderate oven.

GINGER BISCUIT

Beat twelve eggs light, stir into it one pound of powdered sugar, three quarters of a pound of butter, eighteen ounces of flour and a spoonful of pounded ginger. Drop it by large spoonfuls on buttered tin sheets, and bake them in rather a brisk oven.

CRULLERS.

Beat together half a pound of butter and half a pound of powdered sugar, add a spoonful of cinnamon and mace, six beaten eggs and a glass of cream: stir in flour till it gets so thick that you can scarcely stir it at all; then put it on your paste board, sprinkle on more flour till it forms a thick dough, and knead it well; roll it out about half an inch thick, cut it in large scolloped leaves, and bake them on tin sheets in a moderate oven. Ice them when cold.

LITTLE CARAWAY CAKES.

Beat six eggs very light, stir hard into it three quarters of a pound of powdered sugar, half a pound of butter, a wine glass of caraway seeds, one of rose water, a small cup of milk and a pound of flour. When all are well mixed, drop it from a spoon on buttered tin sheets, and bake them a delicate brown in rather a slow oven.

CIDER CAKE.

Beat together six ounces of butter, eight ounces of sugar and two powdered nutmegs; add six beaten eggs, a pint of sweet cider, and enough flour to make it a thick batter. Beat it very well, put it in a buttered pan, and bake it in a moderate oven.

LITTLE CIDER CAKES.

Rub half a pound of butter and half a pound of sugar into one quart of flour: add a spoonful of cinnamon and mace; dissolve a tea-spoonful of pearlash in two large spoonfuls of boiling water, put it in as much brisk cider as will make the whole into the consistence of common dough, knead it well, and roll it into a sheet little over half an inch thick; cut it out with a tumbler or tin cutter, pierce the tops with a fork, and bake them in rather a quick oven.

CUP CAKES.

Mix together one cup of butter, two of sugar, three of flour, four beaten eggs, a spoonful of cinnamon and a few spoonfuls of rose or lemon brandy. Commingle it very well, and bake it in small buttered pans with moderate heat.

ANOTHER CUP CAKE.—Pour four table-spoonfuls of boiling water on one tea-spoonful of saleratus, let it stand to dissolve, and then stir it into a large tea-cup of sour milk; add a cup of butter and two of sugar. Beat four eggs light, stir them into the batter, &c. alternately with four cups of flour; add a powdered nutmeg and a glass of mixed brandy and wine, beat it till quite smooth, and bake it in little buttered pans, or in one large one, which you choose.

DOUGH-NUTS.

Mix eight ounces of powdered sugar with one pound of flour, add a spoonful of cinnamon, and pass it through a sieve; put it in a broad pan, pour on four large spoonfuls of good yeast, and make it of the consistence of common light bread dough with sweet milk; cover it and set it by the fire to rise. When it is very light, work in six ounces of butter, flour your hands and make it into small balls, and fry them brown in boiling lard or butter; then drain them on a sieve and grate loaf sugar thickly over them.

OLEY-KOEKS.

Rub half a pound of sugar and half a pound of butter into one pound of flour, add one pound of shred raisins, the grated rind of a lemon, a glass of wine and four beaten eggs. Dissolve a tea-spoonful of pearlash in four table-spoonfuls of boiling water, and pour it in enough hot sour milk to make it into good paste. Roll it out several times, then make it into little cones or oval shaped cakes, and fry them in hot butter. Drain and grate sugar over them.

CITRON OLEY-KOEKS.

Make a paste as above directed, omitting the raisins; roll it into a sheet about a quarter of an inch thick, cut it into small pieces, and roll them up tightly, enclosing in each a slip of citron. They should be about two inches in length, and the ends of each neatly closed: drop them in a pan of boiling butter, and fry them a delicate brown; after which drain them on an inverted sieve, and grate loaf sugar over them.

SWEET COOKIES, OR CRACKERS.

Cut up a pound of fresh butter, and rub it into three pounds of flour, sprinkling in a pound of powdered sugar, a grated nutmeg and a glass of mixed wine and brandy. Having dissolved a tea-spoonful of pearlash in a few spoonfuls of boiling water, mix it with as much sour milk as will make the whole into good paste; knead it well, and roll it out into a sheet about half an inch thick, cut it into small cakes with cake cutters, stamping each one with a print, and bake them in a brisk oven.

KISSES AND SECRETS.

Beat the white of six eggs to a stiff froth, add the juice of an orange or lemon, and stir into it powdered loaf sugar, a little at a time, till it is of the consistence of thick dough, adding a very little starch. Have ready some small paper cases, about three quarters of an inch square, put some buttered paper on tin sheets, lay on them the cases, drop in each a large tea-spoonful of the sugar and egg, make them smooth, and bake them for a few minutes in a moderate oven: then take them out of the cases, wrap round each a slip of paper containing a single verse or pun, and envelope them separately in small pieces of fine white paper that is neatly fringed, giving each end a twist.

HONEY CAKES.

Dissolve a small tea-spoonful of pearlash in four table-spoonfuls of boiling water; mix with it half a pint of sour milk, add six ounces of butter, a pint of strained honey and a grated nutmeg. Stir in flour till it gets too thick to stir with a spaddle; then lay it on your paste-board, knead in more flour till it is a good paste, and beat it slightly with a rolling-pin; after which roll it into a sheet about half an inch thick, cut it into small round cakes with a cutter, lay them on tin sheets, slightly buttered, and bake them briskly, but be sure you do not burn them, as honey cakes are very easily burnt.

HONEY GINGER CAKES.

Sprinkle two large table-spoonfuls of ginger in one pound of flour; mix together half a pound of butter and a pint of strained honey, and stir into it alternately the flour and six beaten eggs, giving it a hard stirring at the last. Put it in a buttered square pan, and bake it in a moderate oven.

ELECTION CAKE.

Take half a pint of lively yeast, mix with it half a pint of sweet milk and enough flour to make it a good batter;

cover it, and set it by the fire to rise.   This is called
setting a sponge.   Sift two pounds of flour into a broad
pan, cut up in it a pound of fresh butter, add a pound of
powdered sugar, two grated nutmegs and six beaten eggs.
When the sponge is quite light, pour it on the flour, &c.,
make the whole into a soft dough, knead it well, and
make it into small flattish loaves.   Sprinkle a shallow
iron pan with flour, lay the rolls in it close together, put
them at first in a very slow oven, that will permit them to
rise, and when risen, bake them with moderate heat.

COMMON GINGER BREAD.

Cut up half a pound of butter into a quart of West India molasses, make it a little warm, but by no means suffer it to get hot: add a tea-spoonful of pearlash, dissolved
in a tea-cupful of boiling buttermilk, a tea-cupful of powdered ginger, and enough flour to make it a common
dough; knead it well, roll it into a sheet about three quarters of an inch thick, and cut it in long slim cakes; stamp
them with a cake-print, brush over them the beaten yolk
of egg and brown sugar; lay them in shallow iron pans,
that are well buttered, and bake them in rather a brisk
oven.

SUGAR GINGERBREAD.

Powder half a pound of sugar, and stir it into a quart
of molasses, with three quarters of a pound of butter,
beaten soft, and a small tea-cupful of powdered ginger.
Add a tea-spoonful of pearlash, dissolved in a little boiling water, and enough flour to make it into good paste.
Roll it out several times, and lastly roll it into a sheet
about three quarters of an inch thick, cut it into long, narrow strips, roll them under your hand on the paste board,
till they become round; then place them on buttered tin
sheets, hold one end down with your finger, draw at the
same time the other end round, and keep wrapping it
round smoothly and closely, till you form a round cake
out of each; then brush them over with beaten yolk of
egg and brown sugar, mixed smoothly, and bake them in
rather a brisk oven.

GINGERBREAD NUTS.

Make up a dough precisely as above directed, only add one pound of raisins, shred very fine, or currants, that have been picked, washed and dried. Roll the paste about half an inch thick, cut it out in very little diamonds, and bake them in rather a brisk oven.

ICINGS, AND COLORINGS FOR CAKES, &c.

WHITE ICING FOR CAKE.

It is a very common way of making icing to allow five or six large tea-spoonfuls of powdered loaf sugar to the white of one egg; but the most correct way of proportioning it is to weigh it, and even then, when there is much made at a time, it requires some skill in proportioning, as the whites of some eggs are at least a third larger than others. Beat the whites of the eggs to a stiff froth, so much so that it will not fall from the dish in which it is beaten, when inverted. Powder some loaf sugar, pass it through a fine sieve, and mix it with the froth, allowing four ounces of sugar to one white of egg. Stir it in slowly, and but little at a time, and beat it till it looks quite smooth, adding as you proceed, a few drops of oil of lemon, or extract of roses, or the common lemon juice will answer; and you may also flavor it with orange juice, by adding a little more sugar. Or you may make it with three ounces of sugar, one of starch, and the white of one egg, flavoring it as directed. If your cakes should be scorched, or rather brown, scrape them with a knife, and brush them neatly; then put the icing on the top and sides, making it very smooth and regular with a broad bladed knife, which for this purpose is preferable to any thing else; set them in a warm room to dry, where nothing can disturb them, and when the icing gets about half dry, put on the decoraments in the most adroit manner.

ALMOND ICING.

Beat the whites of eggs to a stiff froth, flavor it with a little oil of lemon, and stir into it alternately till quite thick and smooth, equal portions of powdered loaf sugar and sweet almonds, that have been pounded to a smooth paste, and moistened with rose water as they were pounding, to make them white and light. Put it on the cakes as directed for other icing, only put it on some thicker.

PINK ICING.

Prepare your egg and sugar as before directed, flavoring it in the same manner, or with any thing else you choose; add a little cochineal coloring, to make it a fine pink, beat it till it is very regularly mixed through the icing, put it on in the same manner as directed for the white icing, and if decorated at all, let it be with something white. A dark red icing may be made by tinging it with tincture of saunders; and a very pretty icing for fruit cake may be made by coloring it with dark colored preserve juice, or with the juice of ripe cherries or strawberries, which will also give it a good flavor.

YELLOW ICING.

Icing may be colored yellow, deep or pale, with saffron juice or turmeric; it may also be colored a very pretty pale yellow, by rubbing the sugar while in lumps, on the rind of a fine colored lemon, and also a beautiful yellow icing may be made by rubbing lumps of loaf sugar hard on deep colored orange peel, which will at the same time flavor it sufficiently, without the aid of any thing else; then pound it, and prepare the icing as before directed.

TART ICING.

Beat together equal proportions of fresh butter, and yolk of eggs, beat it till very smooth, put it evenly on your tarts with a large stiff feather, grate on some loaf sugar, and dry them in a moderate oven.

ROSE DROPS.

Beat very fine, and pass through a lawn sieve, one pound of double refined loaf sugar. Beat half an ounce of dried red roses, and sift them also. Mix both well to-

gether, wetting them as you proceed with as much lemon
juice as will make it into a good paste; set it over a slow
fire, and let it get scalding hot, stirring it all the time to
prevent it scorching; then drop it from a spoon on writing
paper, set them by, where they will be undisturbed; and
when they get quite cold, they will slip off easily. Lemon drops are made in the same manner, by omitting the
roses, also peppermint, and any other drops with which
you wish the sugar flavored, may be made in a similar
manner.

PINK COLORING.

Pound in a mortar some cochineal, put it in white brandy, proportioning them as you may desire a deep or pale
pink; let it stand one hour to infuse, and strain it through
a bit of muslin. Another mode is to take fifteen grains
of cochineal, ten grains of cream of tartar, a bit of alum
the size of a small pea, and pound them together in a mortar till reduced to a fine powder; then mix it with two
wine-glassfuls of water, half a one of brandy, and simmer
it slowly for thirty or forty minutes. After which filter
it through a bit of muslin, and cork it up in a phial. When
you wish to make use of it, you have nothing to do but
to stir the tincture gradually into what you intend coloring, until you get the shade you desire.

DARK RED.

The juice of ripe cherries, or red strawberries, makes
very pretty coloring for creams, &c.; but the tincture of
saunders is the most common article used for a dark red,
and may be easily prepared by putting the saunders powder in a phial till you fill one third, and then filling it up
with white brandy, or alcohol. Stop it securely, shake
it up occasionally, and in a short time it will be ready
for use.

YELLOW.

Turmeric is frequently used for coloring yellow, but
the bloom of garden saffron will be found very convenient, and the color not inferior to any other yellow, though
for icing I prefer the peel of oranges or lemons, as they

not only produce a fine yellow color, but a nice flavor, by rubbing of the yellow rind with lumps of loaf sugar. To prepare the saffron, put the bloom, after bruising it a little, in an earthen vessel, cover it well with cold water, cover it, and let it stand a few hours to infuse, until it is a bright yellow; then filter it through a piece of muslin.

GEEEN.

There is a greater call for green coloring for pickles, &c., than for eatables of a finer quality, as it is seldom used for any thing else. Take fresh spinach, green wheat, or any nice vegetable that is a pretty green; bruise it, squeeze out the juice, strain it through a bit of muslin, and it will be ready for use. Or if it is not wanted for immediate use, simmer it for three or four minutes in a saucer, throwing in a very minute portion of alum; then strain it, and cork it up in a phial.

WARM CAKES, &c. FOR BREAKFAST AND TEA.

SALERATUS BISCUIT.

Sift a quart of flour, sprinkle into it a salt-spoonful of salt, and rub into it one ounce of butter. Pour half a tea-cupful of boiling water on a small tea-spoonful of saleratus, let it stand to dissolve, and then stir it into enough sour milk to make the flour into rather a soft dough. Knead it but very little, flour your hands, make it into small biscuits, and bake them in rather a hasty oven. In using saleratus or pearlash, for any kind of cake or bread, be sure to dissolve it in boiling water or sour milk, and make up the bread with sour milk; otherwise, it will not rise so well. Pearlash biscuit may be made in the same manner.

SHORT BISCUIT.

Rub half a pound of butter into a quart of flour, sprinkling in a salt-spoonful of salt. Make it into good common paste with cold water, knead it well, and beat it till very smooth, with a roller; then roll it into a sheet about half an inch thick, cut it into small round cakes with a biscuit cutter, and bake them in a moderate oven.

LARD BISCUIT.

Put four ounces of lard in a cup of sweet cream, warm them a little, and beat them till well intermixed. Sift a quart of flour, sprinkle in a salt-spoonful of salt, and make it into common biscuit dough, or paste, with the cream and lard. Knead it well, roll it into a sheet half an inch thick, cut it out with a biscuit cutter, and bake them in a moderate oven.

LIGHT BISCUIT.

Sift three pints of flour into a broad pan, sprinkle on a large tea-spoonful of salt, rub in a large spoonful of butter, add a gill of lively yeast, and make it into rather a soft dough with warm sweet milk. Knead it only till it becomes smooth, then make it into small cakes, as they will increase very much in size; put them in a shallow iron pan, having first sprinkled it with flour, set them by the fire till they become quite light, and then bake them in a moderate oven.

COMMON BUNS.

Sprinkle six ounces of powdered sugar into one pound of flour, add four table-spoonfuls of good yeast, and make it into common light bread dough with warm sweet milk. Set it by the fire till it is very light, then work in four ounces of butter, flour your hands, make it into small buns, and bake them in rather a brisk oven.

FRENCH ROLLS.

Sift two pounds of flour, rub into it three beaten eggs, four ounces of sugar, and four table-spoonfuls of good yeast; make it of the consistence of common light bread dough with warm sweet milk, cover it, and set it before the fire to rise, taking care to turn it round occasionally. When it is very light, put it on your paste board, knead into it four ounces of butter, flour your hands, make it into small rolls, lay them in a shallow pan that is sprinkled with flour, and bake them in a brisk oven.

FRUIT ROLLS.

Rub into one pound of flour eight ounces of currants or raisins that are seeded and shred as fine as possible, six ounces of sugar, four ounces of butter, two beaten eggs and a gill of good yeast; add enough sweet milk to make it of the consistence of common dough, knead it only enough to mix it well, make it into small rolls, put them in a pan that is well floured, cover them and set them by the fire till they are very light; then bake them in a moderate oven, and send them to the table warm.

COMMON ROLLS.

Beat three eggs very light, rub them in a pound of dry flour with a large spoonful of butter; add a tea-spoonful of salt, a grated nutmeg, two large spoonfuls of lively yeast, and make it into rather a soft dough with warm sweet milk. Flour your hands, make it into small rolls, put them in a shallow pan that is well floured, and set them by the fire to rise; after which bake them in rather a brisk oven, and send them up hot, to be split and buttered at table.

TEA BISCUIT.

Sift a quart of flour, mix with it two ounces of sugar, two of butter, and make it into good paste with sweet cream. Knead it well, roll it out into a thin sheet, cut it into cakes with a biscuit cutter or the edge of a tumbler, pierce the tops with a fork, and bake them in a brisk oven. Send them to table warm.

SODA BISCUIT.

Dissolve a tea-spoonful of soda in two spoonfuls of boiling water, and mix it with a pint of sour milk, pour it on two pounds of flour, add four ounces of powdered sugar and four of butter, knead it well, roll it into a sheet about half an inch thick, and cut it out with the edge of a tumbler, pierce the tops with a fork, and bake them in a quick oven. Send them to the tea-table warm.

MILK BISCUIT.

Rub a spoonful of butter into three pints of flour, sprinkle in a large tea-spoonful of salt, and make it into a stiff dough with cold sweet milk. Roll it thin, put on a spoonful of butter, broken up in small bits, dust on a little flour, fold it up and roll it out again; put on another spoonful of butter in the same manner; fold it up again, and roll it into a sheet about half an inch thick; cut it out with a biscuit cutter, and bake it hastily. Do not split them with a knife, but break them open with your hands, butter them and eat them warm.

CREAM CAKES.

Sift one quart of flour, sprinkle in a salt-spoonful of salt, and make it into rather a thick dough with sweet cream. Roll it out thin, break up a spoonful of butter, and spread it evenly over it, sprinkle on a spoonful of flour, fold it up and roll it into a thin sheet, cut it in square cakes, and bake them in a quick oven. Send them up warm to be buttered at table.

CHOCOLATE CAKES.

Mix with a quart of flour four ounces of butter and four ounces of sugar, make it into good paste or biscuit dough with sweet milk, and knead it well. Roll it into a sheet not more than a quarter of an inch thick, cut it in long narrow strips, mark them across with a knife, about half an inch apart, and bake them hastily. Eat them warm with chocolate.

COFFEE CAKES.

Sprinkle a salt-spoonful of salt into a quart of flour, and make it into a stiff dough with cold water: roll it out thin, put over it a large spoonful of butter, broken up into small bits, sprinkle on a spoonful of flour, fold up the paste, and roll it again into a thin sheet; then put on more butter and flour, repeating it in the same manner till you have rolled in three large spoonfuls of butter, but do no knead it in the least. Lastly, roll it into a sheet about half an inch thick, cut it into cakes about three inches wide and six long. Mark them across with a knife, so as to form diamonds, or stamp them with a cake-print, and bake them in a quick oven. Split and butter them, and eat them warm with coffee.

LEATHER HOE CAKES.

Make a common biscuit dough with sweet cream and flour, adding a little salt; roll it out several times with a rolling-pin: lastly, roll it into a sheet about three quarters of an inch thick, cut it into long narrow cakes, bake them hastily on a hoe or griddle, turning them over once; then split and butter them, stack them in a plate, and send them to table warm.

SHORT HOE CAKES.

Rub two large spoonfuls of butter in a quart of flour till well incorporated, sprinkle in a salt-spoonful of salt, and make it into common biscuit paste or dough with cold sweet milk, knead it well, and roll it out several times with a roller; then roll it into a sheet a quarter of an inch thick, cut it in oblong cakes, and bake them hastily on a hoe or griddle, having it neatly cleaned and rubbed with butter; turn them over once, and as soon as they are done, split and butter them, and eat them warm.

COMMON MUFFINS.

Beat three eggs light, stir them in a quart of sweet milk, add a tea-spoonful of salt, four spoonfuls of yeast, and enough flour to make it a tolerably thick batter. Beat it with a spoon till smooth, and set it by the fire to rise. Heat your griddle, clean and grease it with sweet lard or butter, grease the inside of your muffin rings also, place them on your griddle, and when your batter has well risen, pour into each ring a small ladleful of it, and bake them a delicate brown: then break them evenly apart with your fingers, lay in each a slice of firm butter, close them together again, and send them to table immediately.

RICE MUFFINS.

Beat four eggs very light, mix with them a quart of sweet milk, with two ounces of melted butter and a salt-spoonful of salt. Having boiled some rice very soft, mash it fine, mix with it an equal portion of flour, and stir it gradually into the milk, &c. till you form a thick batter. Place your muffin rings on a clean hot griddle, having first greased them; put in each ring two large spoonfuls of the batter, and bake them a light brown with moderate heat. When done, lay a small lump of firm butter on the top of each, and send them hastily to table.

INDIAN MUFFINS.

Beat five eggs light, stir them into a quart of milk, with a small handful of flour and a tea-spoonful of salt; then stir in as much fine Indian meal as will make it a tolerably thick batter. Having buttered some little scolloped muffin pans, place them in an oven that is moderately heated, put in each a small ladleful of the batter, and bake them a nice brown; then take them from the pans, arrange them neatly in a plate, lay on the top of each a slice of firm butter, and eat them warm.

WAFFLES.

Make a thin batter of four beaten eggs, a quart of sweet milk and flour, add a little salt, and beat it till entirely free from lumps, and very smooth. Heat your waffle irons moderately, by holding them in the fire; clean them neatly, and grease them well with fresh lard or butter; then put in your batter, filling them quite full, close the irons, confine them at the end with a ring, that is to one side of the irons, and lay them level in the fire, on a bed of clear coals, that the under side may get done as soon as the upper. Take them out, and open them occasionally, to see how the waffle is progressing, and as soon as it is of a light brown on both sides, take it from the irons by running a knife under it. In like manner fry or bake all your batter, stack four or six on a plate, pour over them a few spoonfuls of melted butter, and send them warm to table, as you fry them.

SWEET WAFFLES.

Make a batter of six beaten eggs, a quart of sweet milk and flour, add two ounces of melted butter, four of powdered sugar, and beat it till entirely smooth. Heat your waffle irons, clean and grease them, and bake them as directed for plain waffles. Stack four or six in a plate, grate on a little loaf sugar, and send them warm to table, as you fry them.

RICE WAFFLES.

Boil your rice till very soft, drain off the water, and wash the rice as fine as possible. Beat three eggs light, stir them in a quart of milk, with two ounces of melted butter, and a salt-spoonful of salt; then stir in as much of the rice paste and dry flour, in equal proportions, as will make it a tolerably thin batter. Heat your waffle irons, and bake them as other waffles, greasing the irons well each time before you put in the batter. Stack them in a plate, pour over a few spoonfuls of melted butter, and send them to table warm.

WAFERS.

Beat six eggs to a froth, stir them into a quart of sweet milk, with four ounces of butter, six of powdered sugar, a grated nutmeg, the juice of a lemon, or a few drops of the essence, and enough flour to make a tolerably thick batter. Beat it till it is perfectly clear of lumps, and entirely smooth. Heat your wafer irons moderately, clean and grease them well with butter, put in two large spoonfuls of the batter, close the irons, put them level in rather a brisk part of the fire, where they will be clear of smoke, and as soon as the wafer is of a delicate brown on both sides, remove it from the iron, by running a knife under it; sprinkle it immediately with powdered white sugar, and roll it into a scroll. Bake all of your batter in the same manner, and roll them likewise, buttering the irons well each time before you put in the batter.

LIGHT WAFFLES.

Make a thick batter of three eggs, a quart of milk, and flour, adding a little salt, and two large spoonfuls of good yeast. Set it in a warm place till it gets very light, then stir in a spoonful of flour, and three of melted butter. Heat your waffle irons of a brisk heat, butter them well to prevent the waffles sticking to them, put in batter according to the size of your irons, not filling them quite full, as the waffle will expand a little while baking; close the irons, and bake them till a light brown on both sides; then take them from the irons, sprinkle them with powdered sugar and cinnamon, and send them to table warm.

VELVET CAKES.

Make a batter as for the light waffles, and when it is quite light, stir in four table-spoonfuls of melted butter, and if not sufficiently thin, add a few spoonfuls of milk. Heat your griddle of a brisk heat, clean and grease it well with fresh lard or butter, and place it level over a bed of clear coals. Put on a large ladleful of the batter, which should be sufficiently thin to run immediately over the griddle; make it smooth, having it as large as a common desert plate, and as soon as it is of a very light brown on the under side, turn it over carefully, lest you break it; when both sides are a light brown, lay it smoothly on a plate, and put on a spoonful of melted butter. Grease your griddle again, and bake all your batter in the same manner. As soon as you get three or four baked, stack them, putting a spoonful of melted butter between each, cut them across, dividing each into six, lay a few small bits of hard butter on the top, and send them to table as warm as possible. As fast as you get three or four warm ones, butter them, stack them, cut them across, and send them to table, that they may be handed round to the company while warm.

BATTER CAKES.

Make a thin batter of two eggs, a pint and a half of sweet milk and flour, adding a very little salt, and beat it hard till quite smooth. Fry or bake them on a griddle, as directed for the velvet cakes, putting only two small

spoonfuls of batter to each cake. Make them all of a regular shape, smoothing them round the edges, and turning them over once; as soon as both sides are of a delicate brown, stack them, making three stacks in a plate;
pour over a little melted butter, and send them warm to
table.

INDIAN BATTER CAKES.

Make a tolerably thin batter of three beaten eggs, a
pint and a half of sweet milk, and fine Indian meal, mixing in a small handful of flour, and a little salt. Beat it
till quite smooth, and bake it as directed for flour batter
cakes; butter them, and eat them warm.

INDIAN FLAPPERS.

Sift a quart of fine Indian meal, mix with it a small
handful of flour, three beaten eggs, a tea-spoonful of salt,
three spoonfuls of good yeast, and enough warm sweet
milk to make it a tolerably thin batter; set it by the fire
till it looks light, and then bake them on a clean, hot griddle, that is well buttered. Allow a large ladleful to each
cake, making them quite thin, round, and the edges smooth,
and as soon as they are a light brown on both sides, stack
them in a plate, lay a slice of firm butter between each
cake, cut them across, dividing each one into four, and
send them to table warm.

RICE BATTER CAKES.

Boil a pint of rice very soft, drain the water from it,
mash it fine, mix with it an equal portion of flour, add a
tea-spoonful of salt, four table-spoonfuls of butter, three
beaten eggs, and enough sweet milk to make it a common
batter. Mix it very well, and bake it on a griddle, in
small cakes, turning them over once. Stack them in a

plate, laying a thin slice of butter between each, and eat them warm. Similar cakes may be made of nice boiled hominy.

BANNOCK.

Sift a quart of fine Indian meal, mix with it a salt-spoonful of salt, two large spoonfuls of butter and a gill of molasses; make it into a common dough with scalding water, or hot sweet milk, mixing it well with a spoon; put it in a well buttered skillet, make it smooth, and bake it rather briskly. When it is done, cut it in thin smooth slices, toast them lightly, butter them, stack them and eat them warm.

BUCKWHEAT CAKES.

Put two spoonfuls of yeast in a quart of buckwheat flour, add a little salt, and make it into rather a thin batter with cold water; set it by the fire till it looks light and the top becomes covered with little bubbles; then bake it hastily, as buckwheat batter turns sour quite soon. Have your griddle hot, place it level over a bed of clear coals, and rub it well with fresh lard or butter; put on a large ladleful of the batter, make the cake thin and very smooth round the edge, turn it over once carefully, lest you break it, and as soon as both sides are a light brown, remove it from the griddle, butter it and set it by the fire to keep warm, till you bake two or three more in the same manner, greasing the griddle well between each cake; then butter them, cut them across, dividing each in six, and send them to table warm. Bake the remaining batter in the same way, butter them, cut them across, and send them to table hot, to be handed round to the company. If by neglect you let your batter get a little sour, stir into it a small portion of dissolved pearlash, which will never fail to destroy the acid taste.

Very good cakes may be made in this manner, substituting rye flour for buckwheat.

INDIAN SHORT-CAKES.

Beat four eggs very light, and mix them with a pint and a half of sweet milk; add a tea-spoonful of salt, two spoonfuls of butter, and enough fine Indian meal to make it a thick batter. Drop it on buttered tin sheets, allowing a large spoonful to each cake, and bake them a nice brown in a brisk oven. Send them to table warm.

COMMON EGG BREAD.

Beat four eggs light. stir them into a quart of sweet milk, add a tea-spoonful of salt, two spoonfuls of butter, and enough fine Indian meal to make it a good batter, stirring it in very hard. Put it in a buttered pan, or small skillet, and bake it with a brisk heat. Eat it warm, splitting and buttering it at table.

PUMPKIN CAKES.

Having stewed a fine sweet pumpkin, mash a pint of it very fine, pass it through a sieve, and mix with it one quart of fine Indian meal. Add a small dessert-spoonful of salt, two large spoonfuls of butter, two beaten eggs, and enough sweet milk to make it a thick batter. Drop it by large spoonfuls on buttered tin sheets, and bake them a nice brown in a brisk oven.

PUMPKIN HOE CAKES.

Mix one pint of stewed pumpkin with a quart of fine Indian meal, make it into rather a thin dough with sweet milk, and work it well with a spoon. Heat your griddle rather brisk, place it over a bed of clear coals, grease it well with lard or butter, put on your dough in small thin cakes, and bake them hastily, turning them over once. As soon as both sides have a thin crust, and are of a light brown, send them to table, that they may be split and buttered while warm.

INDIAN HOE CAKES.

Sift a quart of Indian meal, mix with it a large tea-spoonful of salt, two large spoonfuls of butter, and make it a thin dough with sweet milk. Bake them as the pumpkin hoe cakes, and butter and eat them warm.

INDIAN WATER CAKES.

Indian water cakes, when made of stiff dough, and baked with a hard crust, of all cakes are the most disgusting; but when made in a proper manner, they are really good. Sift some fine Indian meal, make it a soft dough with cold water, and work it well. Heat your griddle hot, clean and grease it well, and place it over a bed of clear coals; then put on your cakes, make them small, thin and smooth, bake them hastily, turn them over as soon as the crust is a light brown, and when they are done through, which will take but a very short time, split and butter them, and send them to table immediately.

POTATO CAKES.

Having boiled some fine sweet potatoes done, peel them, mash them fine, pass the pulp through a sieve, and mix one pint of it with a pint of flour. Add two beaten eggs, two spoonfuls of butter, half a tea-spoonful of salt, and enough sweet milk to make it a thick batter. Beat it very well, drop it on buttered tin sheets, allowing a large spoonful to each, and bake them in a brisk oven till a light brown. Lay on the top of each a small lump of firm butter, and send them to table warm.

JOHNNY CAKES.

Make a thin dough of sifted Indian meal and lukewarm water or sweet milk, adding a tea-spoonful of salt, and a large spoonful of butter to each quart of meal. Work it well, as Indian meal, in whatever way it is prepared, should be worked thoroughly. Having ready a piece of board planed smooth, wet it with water, and put on a cake of the dough about three quarters of an inch thick, make it smooth and even round the edges, brush it over with sweet cream, and brown it lightly before a clear fire, propping it on one edge by setting something behind it, to support it. Then run the blade of a knife or a sewing thread between the bread and board, to loose it, turn it over, brown the other side in the same manner, first moistening it with sweet cream, and then cut it across in small cakes, split them, lay a slice of firm butter on one half of each piece, put them together again, and send them immediately to table.

INDIAN MUSH.

Like many other of our receipts, the process of making mush is quite plain and simple, yet it is often badly prepared, and to the inexperienced some instructions are necessary. Sift some fine Indian meal, make a smooth batter of it by stirring in a sufficiency of cold water. Having ready a pot of boiling water, throw in a handful of salt, and stir in your batter till it is like very thick soup. Boil it till of the proper consistence, and stir it frequently to prevent its being lumpy, and to keep it from burning at the bottom. Mush, made in this manner, will never fail to be thoroughly done and clear of lumps, which are two common failures. Cold mush may be sliced and fried brown in butter. They are very good for breakfast.

DRY TOASTS.

Cut some smooth slices from a fine loaf of light bread, trim off the hard crusts, brown them delicately on a toaster, and send them warm to table with a plate of firm butter, to accompany coffee, tea or chocolate.

BUTTERED TOASTS.

Slice and brown your toasts as before directed; arrange them in a deep plate, and pour over them a good quantity of melted butter. They are nice with tea and coffee, and are also often served up with poultry and game.

CREAM TOASTS.

Slice and brown your toasts neatly, place them on a plate, and pour over them a good quantity of sweet cream made scalding hot. Send them immediately to table.

WATER TOASTS.

Having sliced and browned your toasts, lay them in a plate. Make a few spoonfuls of water boiling hot, add a very little sugar, and slightly acidulate it with vinegar or lemon juice, pour it scalding over the toasts, and send them immediately to table. They are very fine for people of delicate appetite.

BREAD AND BUTTER.

Cut some smooth thin slices from a fine light loaf of bread, buttering each slice neatly before you cut it from the loaf. Stack them in a plate, and introduce them at the table with chipped beef, &c.

LIGHT BREAD, YEAST, &c.

—◦✦◦—

LIGHT WHEAT BREAD.

In proportioning the yeast and flour, you must be partly governed by the quality of the yeast: if it is good and quite lively, a gill will be sufficient for a quart of flour. Sift your flour, sprinkle in a little salt, add your yeast and enough lukewarm water or sweet milk to make it rather a thin dough. Knead it till it becomes smooth, but no longer; put it in an oven that has been cleaned, greased and rubbed with dry flour; throw a few embers about it, to warm it slightly, but not so much so but that you may bear your hand on it without burning you. Cover the oven, set it by the fire where it will keep a little warm, and do not disturb it more than to turn it round occasionally till it rises to double the original height; then heat it gradually and bake it with a moderate fire. When it is thoroughly done, if the crust is rather hard, take it from the oven, sprinkle it lightly with water, wrap it up in a folded cloth. If it is too large to use at one meal, do not cut it till it gets cold, as it will make it have a raw, clammy taste. If you wish to make the pores of your bread very fine and close, sprinkle in your flour a very minute portion of powdered alum.

—◦✦◦—

LIGHT INDIAN BREAD.

Having ready a pot of boiling water, throw in a small handful of fine salt, and make it into a common bread dough, with sifted Indian meal. Stir it very hard with a wooden paddle or spaddle, till well mixed; sprinkle on the top a handful of dry meal, cover it and set it in a warm place to rise. In a few hours it will look very light and crack on the top; then heat your oven as for other Indian bread, grease it with a little lard, rub it with a handful of dry Indian meal, and bake your bread with common heat. It will keep moist for several days, and will be found quite convenient, being always in readiness.

A VERY GOOD INDIAN BREAD.

Make it up as before directed, and let it stand till it gets sweet, but not till it becomes light; then, if it is a common sized loaf, work in it a small lump of butter and two beaten eggs, make it into small loaves, and bake them in a moderate oven.

COMMON HOP YEAST.

Put a large handful of hops into three quarts of water, and boil it till reduced to two quarts; then strain it, and make it a thin batter with flour. When it gets nearly cold, stir in half a pint of good yeast, fresh from the brewer's, if it can be procured; set it by the fire to rise, and when well fermented and very light, put in a few spoonfuls of brown sugar, and bottle it for use. In warm weather, it keeps best prepared in cakes; for this purpose, some people prefer fine Indian meal, and others prefer flour; either, however, will answer. Pour your yeast into a bowl or tray, and work in as much flour or fine Indian meal as will make it of the consistence of common biscuit dough; set it again by the fire to rise, and when well risen, make it into small cakes, dry them in the shade, turning them over frequently, and then put them away in dry flour for use. When you wish to make use of them, take one or two cakes, according to the quantity of bread you wish to make, dissolve it in lukewarm water, or sweet milk, and make it into rather a thin batter with flour; set it by the fire to rise, and when well risen, make your bread as before directed.

MALT YEAST.

Take a large handful of hops, one of malt, and one of rye meal; boil them twenty minutes in half a gallon of water, then strain it, and put the liquid on to boil again.

Stir into it a few spoonfuls of molasses, and half a pint of rye flour, which has been stirred till smooth, in a little water; as soon as it comes to a hard boil, take it from the fire, and set it by to cool, and when it gets to be only luke-warm, stir in a pint of good yeast, and set it by the fire to rise. In very warm weather, it should be set in rather a cool place to rise, lest it sours. Bottle it while ferment-ing.

POTATO YEAST.

Boil some white mealy potatoes quite soft, then peel and mash them fine. Take half a pint of the pulp, mix with it an equal portion of flour, and enough hop tea to make it into a batter; add a gill of good yeast, mix it well, cover it, set it in a warm place till it gets light, and it will be ready for use. Some people are fond of light bread mixed half and half with flour and mashed potatoes.

RYE YEAST.

Stir together rye flour and cold water till you make a smooth batter; then add boiling water till you make it quite thin, and set it by to cool. After which, stir in some lively yeast, allowing half a pint to each quart of the bat-tar, and set it by to rise. When it gets well to working, bottle it, but do not cork it tight at the first, or your bot-tles will burst. Keep it where it will neither freeze, or get too hot, and when you wish to make use of it, take a gill or half pint, according to the number of loaves you wish to make up, and proceed as directed for light bread. Some people are fond of light bread made entirely of rye flour, and no doubt but it is very healthy.

MILK YEAST.

Milk yeast can be prepared more hastily than any oth-er kind, and is very good while fresh, particularly for biscuit. Stir into a pint of sweet milk a small tea-spoon-ful of salt, a large heaping spoonful of flour, and one of good yeast. Set it where it will keep lukewarm, and in an hour it will probably be fit for use. Any kind of good bottled yeast, that gets a little sour, if it still looks lively, may be restored by stirring into it a small portion of dissolved pearlash. By this you may know whether it is fit for use; after the pearlash is mixed with it, if it foams, and looks livelier than before, you may know it is good, but if it remains unaffected, it is too far gone to be restored; therefore, do not use it.

SALT RISING, OR YEAST.

This kind of yeast will be found convenient when you get out of other kinds; it does not rise quite so soon as the hop yeast, yet it makes excellent bread. Make a quart of water lukewarm, stir into it a table-spoonful of salt, and make it a tolerably thin batter with flour; mix it well, sprinkle on the top a handful of dry flour, and set it in a warm place to rise, but be sure you do not let it get hot, or it would spoil it. Turn it round occasionally, and in a few hours it will be light, and the top covered with bubbles; then make up your bread into rather a soft dough, adding as much lukewarm water as will be found necessary; grease and flour your ovens well, set them where they will keep a little warm till the bread rises and looks very light, and bake it as other light bread. The softer is the dough, the more light and spongy will the bread be.

CUSTARDS, CREAMS, &c.

BAKED CUSTARD.

Boil a quart of sweet milk, flavor it with any thing you please, and set it by to cool. Beat eight eggs very light, and when the milk is cold, mix them with it, adding four ounces of powdered sugar. Stir it till well mixed, put it in custard cups, filling them quite full; set them in an oven, pour round them hot water, but not enough to reach to the tops, lest it gets in, and spoils your custards. Having heated your lid, put it on the oven, throw some coals on, and under it, and bake the custards till thick, and of a light brown. When cold, grate nutmeg over them, and send them to table with a tea-spoon for each cup. If you bake the custard in a deep dish, send with it cups, to be filled at table, and each one provided with a spoon.

PLAIN BOILED CUSTARD.

Beat six eggs very light, and mix them with a quart of sweet milk; add four ounces of powdered sugar, and a little grated lemon, or powdered cinnamon, to flavor it. Set it over a bed of coals, and stir it steadily till it comes to a boil; then remove it from the fire, or it will curdle. Have ready some custard cups, lay in the bottom of each an almond cone, or cocoanut maccaroon; pour on each a table-spoonful of white wine, and when the custard is cold, fill up the cups with it, grate nutmeg over the tops, and send them to table with a tea-spoon in each.

GOOSEBERRY CUSTARD.

Pick and rinse some gooseberries, stew them tender in a small quantity of water, with enough sugar to make them very sweet. Then mash them to a pulp, press them through a sieve, put it in tea-cups, pressing it down hard, and set it by to cool. Beat six eggs light, stir them into a quart of sweet milk, with a spoonful of powdered cinnamon, or nutmeg, and simmer it till it becomes thick, stirring it all the time. Turn the gooseberries into a small deep dish, place them side by side, pour over the custard and brown it a little in a brisk oven. Grate loaf sugar over it when cold.

APPLE CUSTARD.

Pare, core and stew till tender some fine cooking apples, adding only enough water to keep them from burning; then mash them fine, sweeten them, flavor them with cloves or grated lemon, and stir a pint and a half of the pulp into a quart of sweet rich milk; add six beaten eggs, stir it hard, put it in custard cups, set them in a Dutch oven, pour round them some boiling water, but not enough to rise to the top of the cups, and bake the custards till thick and a little brown. Grate nutmeg over the top of each, and send them to table cold.

RICE CUSTARD.

Pick and wash some rice very clean, and boil it soft in sweet milk; then drain it, and stir a pint of it into a quart of sweet milk with six beaten eggs; add five ounces of powdered sugar and half a grated nutmeg, or a tea-spoon-ful of powdered cloves; pour it in a pitcher, set it in an oven of boiling water, having it placed over a bed of coals, and simmer it till the custard becomes thick and smooth, stirring it all the time; then remove it from the fire, and stir it occasionally till it gets cold. Serve it in glass cups, grate on a little nutmeg, and lay on the top of each a lump of fruit jelly.

SNOWBALL CUSTARD.

Boil some rice very soft in sweet milk, then drain it, put it in round-bottom teacups, filling them quite full, and set them by to cool. After it is glutinated and received the shape of the cups, turn them out carefully, inverting them in a deep dish. Pour round them a rich boiled custard, but do not suffer it to come quite to the top of the balls: lay on each a spoonful of white of egg that has been beaten to a stiff froth; squeeze on a little lemon juice, and grate loaf sugar thickly over them.

BOILED GOOSEBERRY CUSTARD.

Stew your gooseberries very soft, mash them fine, and press them through a sieve; put them again in the pan, add to each quart of the pulp a spoonful of butter, six ounces of powdered sugar and six beaten eggs, stirring them in very gradually. Simmer it a few minutes, stir it all the time, and set it out to cool. Serve it up in glasses, and grate nutmeg over the top of each.

ALMOND CUSTARD.

Blanch three quarters of a pound of sweet almonds and two ounces of bitter ones; pound them to a paste, moisten-ing them with a little rose water, mix them together, and stir them into a quart of rich sweet milk. Add six ounces of powdered loaf sugar, six beaten eggs, and a tea-spoonful of powdered cinnamon: mix it very well, put it in a pitcher, set it in a kettle or oven of boiling water, and simmer it till the custard is thick, stirring it all the time; then take it from the fire, and when it gets cold, serve it up in cups or glasses. Sweeten some rich cream with powdered loaf sugar, and flavor it with oil of lemon; beat it to a froth, pile it high on the tops, and stick in each a pink or some other delicate flower.

LEMON CUSTARD.

Beat twelve eggs light, stir into them half a pound of powdered sugar, a tea-cupful of water, a large spoonful of butter and the juice of four lemons. Beat it very well, put it into cups, and bake them a few minutes, but not till they get hard. When done, grate nutmeg on the tops, lay a slice of citron on each, and send them to table cold.

A BOILED LEMON CUSTARD.

Beat the yolks of sixteen eggs and the whites of ten to a froth, mix them together, and stir into them eight ounces of powdered sugar and a tea-cupful of water; put the mixture in a pitcher, set it in a pan or oven of hot water, and simmer it gently till thick, stirring it all the time; then take it from the fire, and set it by to cool. Beat the remaining six whites of eggs to a stiff froth, and make it very sweet with powdered loaf sugar. Stir well into the custard the juice of five lemons, put it into cups, and pile the egg froth on the tops.

AN ORANGE CUSTARD.

Beat very well the yolks of sixteen eggs and the whites of ten; mix them together, and add the juice of four fine oranges, a tea-cupful of water and six ounces of powdered sugar; stir it very well, put the mixture into cups, bake them in an oven till the custard gets thick, but not hard, and then set them by to cool. Beat the whites of the remaining six eggs to a stiff froth, make it very sweet with loaf sugar, pile it on the tops of the custards, and grate on each some of the yellow peel of the oranges till the froth becomes lightly tinged with it.

BAKED COCOANUT CUSTARD.

Having broken up a cocoanut, peel off the dark skin and grate fine a pound of the meat. Beat to a froth five eggs, and stir them into a pint and a half of milk, with half a pound of powdered white sugar and the milk of the cocoanut: add a grated nutmeg and the grated cocoanut, stirring it hard at the last. Put it into cups, set them in an oven of boiling water, put on a lid that is moderately heated, put a few coals on the lid and under the oven, and bake them a few minutes till a delicate brown. Grate loaf sugar over them when cold.

BOILED COCOANUT CUSTARD.

Beat six eggs light, and stir them into a quart of sweet milk, with a pound of grated cocoanut and half a pound of powdered sugar; add a grated nutmeg, mix it well, put it in a pitcher, set it in a kettle of boiling water, and simmer it gently till quite thick, stirring it all the time; then take it from the fire and set it by to cool; after which put it into cups or glasses, pile whipped cream on the tops, and lay on each a small light leaf or flower.

VANILLA CUSTARD.

Boil a vanilla bean in a quart of rich sweet milk till it is sufficiently flavored with the bean; then take it out and set it by to cool. Beat the yolks of eight eggs and the whites of four to a froth, mix them together, and when the milk is cold, stir them into it. Add six ounces of sugar, put it in a pitcher, set it in boiling water, and simmer it gently till thick and smooth, stirring it all the time; then remove it from the fire and set it by to cool; after which put it in cups or glasses, and grate nutmeg over the tops.

BURNT CUSTARD.

Beat the yolks of ten eggs and the whites of five to a froth, stir them into a quart of milk, add four ounces of powdered sugar, a little grated lemon, and boil it in a pitcher as before directed. When it is quite cold, put it into cups, pile on each the beaten white of eggs, grate on some loaf sugar, and brown them delicately with a salamander or red hot shovel, by holding it a little above them.

CREAM CUSTARD.

Separate the whites from the yolks of twelve eggs, beat the yolks only, and stir them into a quart of entire sweet cream, add six ounces of sugar, and flavor it with nutmeg, cinnamon, bitter almonds or peach leaves. Have ready some custard cups, put in the bottom of each an almond cone or cocoanut maccaroon; fill them up with the mixture, and bake them in an oven with boiling water poured round; then set them by to cool, pile on the tops the beaten whites of eggs, having flavored it with lemon; grate on some loaf sugar, and lay on the top of each a thin slice of some nice kind of preserves.

BOILED CREAM CUSTARD.

Beat well the yolks of eight eggs and the whites of four; stir them into a quart of sweet cream with six ounces of sugar and a tea-spoonful of cinnamon, pour the mixture into a pitcher, set it in an oven of hot water, and simmer it a few minutes, stirring it all the time, but do not let it come to a boil, or it will curdle. Have ready some glass cups, put in the bottoms of them a thin slice of sponge-cake, pour on each a spoonful of white wine, and fill up the cups with the custard when cold; pile on them the beaten whites of eggs, grate on some loaf sugar, and lay on the top of each a thin slice of ripe orange or other nice fruit.

DECEPTION.

Having ready a bowl of rich sweet cream, stir into it gradually enough lemon juice to make it a little thick, make it sweet with loaf sugar, whip it with rods to a perfect froth, and pile it high in glasses.

SYLLABUB.

Cream for this purpose must be perfectly sweet and very rich. Stir in gradually enough white wine to flavor it, but not enough to curdle it; sweeten it with powdered loaf sugar, and put it into glasses. Make some cream very sweet with powdered loaf sugar, flavor it with lemon juice, whip it to a froth with rods or wires, and pile it high on the glasses.

WHIPPED CREAM.

Squeeze the juice from two large lemons and two oranges; put it into a bowl and mix with it a pint of white wine and eight ounces of powdered loaf sugar; set it by for three or four hours, and then beat it with rods or wires to a froth. Have ready some custard glasses, put in the bottom of each a cocoanut snowball or almond cones, pile on them the whipped cream, extending it as far above the top of the glass as possible, and drop over them at short intervals delicate spots of thick red or dark colored preserved juice.

PINK SYLLABUB.

Stir gradually into a quart of rich sweet cream a pint of white wine, the juice of three lemons, eight ounces of powdered loaf sugar, a few spoonfuls of currant jelly, and enough cochineal tincture or powder to color it a fine pink. Set it by for two or three hours, then whip it to a froth, and put it into glasses, piling it high.

EGG CREAM.

Beat very well the yolks of half a dozen eggs, and stir them into a quart of rich sweet milk with half a pound of powdered loaf sugar: put it in a pitcher, set it in a pan of hot water, and simmer it till it gets thick, but do not suffer it to boil. Stir it all the time it is on the fire, and after it is set off, stir it occasionally till it gets cold, adding by degrees the juice of two fine oranges, and then put it in glasses. Make a pint of sweet cream a little thick with powdered loaf sugar, flavor it with orange or lemon juice, color it a delicate yellow with saffron juice, beat it to a froth, and pile it high on the tops of the glasses.

A TRIFLE.

Cut a pound of white sponge cake in thin slices, all of equal size; lay them in the bottom of a large glass or China bowl, pour on them enough white wine to moisten them, and nearly fill the bowl with a rich boiled custard, with which a little fruit marmalade has been mingled. Take a quart of rich sweet cream, stir gradually into it six ounces of powdered white sugar, half a pint of white wine and the juice of two lemons; beat it all to a froth, take it off as it rises, and lay it on the custard, forming a pyramidal heap; then lay round it on the edge of the bowl a delicate garland.

AN ORANGE QUIDDATIVE.

Place some gingerbread nuts, almond cones, cocoanut snowballs, or sweet-hearts, in the bottom of a large glass bowl, alternately with four sliced oranges; pour on enough white wine to moisten them, set them by for one hour, and then nearly fill the bowl with cream custard. Beat the whites of twelve fresh eggs to a stiff froth, so much so that it will not drop from the dish when inverted. Make it very sweet with powdered loaf sugar, squeeze in the juice of two oranges, and pile it high upon the top of the custard, forming a conoidical figure; then grate all over it enough deep colored orange peel to make it a pretty yellow, and lay around it on the edge of the bowl a light wreath of real or artificial flowers.

FLOATING ISLAND.

Nearly fill a glass bowl with egg cream; slice some white sponge cake, spread on each slice a thin layer of raspberry or strawberry jam, stack them together, making it of an oval shape, and lay it on the top of the cream; put over it a good quantity of whites of eggs, that have been beaten to a stiff froth, and well seasoned with powdered sugar and lemon juice. Make it smooth, decorate it with small light bits of preserves, and stick in the centre of the island a small bunch of real flowers.

SMALL FLOATING ISLANDS

Nearly fill a glass bowl with float: slice up some Naples biscuit, cut them of circular form, gradually diminishing them in size; spread each one with a thin coat of nice jam or marmalade, stack them together regularly, making four mounds, and placing the smallest slices on the tops; then lay them side by side in the bowl on the float; cover them thickly and smoothly with whipped cream or beaten whites of eggs, that have been seasoned with white wine and loaf sugar; ornament them with very small bits of preserves, or little spots of colored sugar sand, and stick in the centre of each a small bunch of leaves and flowers.

A PLAIN CHARLOTTE.

Cut some slices about half an inch thick, of common pound cake, spread on them a thin layer of any nice kind of preserves, and place them in the bottom and round the sides of a large glass or china bowl. Pour in enough egg cream to nearly fill it, pile on the top a good quantity of whites of eggs that have been beaten to a stiff froth, and seasoned with lemon juice or white wine, grate loaf sugar thickly over it, and brown it delicately with a salamander.

A FRENCH CHARLOTTE.

Prepare a pint of almond custard, and set it by to cool. Put three gills of rich sweet cream into a pitcher, stir in it the beaten yolks of four eggs and three ounces of powdered sugar. Put it in a pan of hot water, set it over a bed of clear coals, and stir it all the time, till it comes to a slow boil; then stir in alternately enough scraped chocolate and pounded cocoanut maccaroons, in equal proportions, to make it like thick baked custard; let it boil a few minutes, stirring it all the time, and then set it by to cool. Cut up a large sponge, or lady cake into slices about half an inch thick; spread one half with a layer of the almond custard, and the other half with the chocolate custard. Stack them alternately in a glass dish, forming them into a conic figure, then ice it very white and smooth with cake icing, strew round it, on the edge of the dish, a handful of almond cones, and stick on the pinnacle a small bunch of orange or artificial flowers. Have two on the table at once, as they are only introduced at large parties.

A CHARLOTTE RUSSEE.

Pick the stems and leaves from a quart of the finest English red strawberries, that are perfectly ripe; mash them fine, and mix with them half a pound of powdered loaf sugar, press the pulp through a sieve, stir it into a quart of sweet cream, and beat it till very thick and smooth. Have ready a large glass bowl, put in the bottom of it a handful of ginger bread nuts, maccaroons, or sweet-hearts, put slices of cake round the sides, pour on them the cream, &c., and lay on the top several spoonfuls of white cake icing, having but one spoonful in a place.

GOOSEBERRY FOOL.

Pick three pints of gooseberries, stew them with half a pound of sugar and a very little water, merely to keep them from burning. When they get quite soft, mash them to a pulp, and set them by till cold; then stir them into a quart of cream custard, and put it in a glass dish or bowl. Make a pint of sweet cream a little thick with sugar; flavor it well with white wine, or lemon juice; color it a pale green with thick spinach juice, beat it to a froth, and pile it high on the gooseberries. Set it in ice for a few minutes before you send it to table.

A JELLY CONE.

Break up and boil some of the finest Russian gum isinglass till entirely dissolved, and when cold, will form a thick jelly; sweeten it with powdered loaf sugar, flavor it with white wine, or lemon juice, and strain it through a fine sieve. Cut up a white sponge cake into slices about half an inch thick; spread them thickly with rice or cocoanut custard, trim them of a regular form, so as to form a cone, and stack them neatly. Have your mould a size larger than the cone of cake, open it at the sides, wet them, color the insides with pink, or take a fine brush, and make pink stripes with cochineal, to run round them slantwise; place them together round the cake and custard, leaving about half an inch all round between the cake and moulds, pour in your isinglass jelly, and set it for half an hour in a tub of ice and salt. When it has conglutinated, wet a cloth in hot water, put it round the mould for a few minutes, and turn the jelly cone smoothly on a glass dish. They are only introduced at parties or fine suppers, and should be at least two on the table.

FLOAT.

Stir gradually into a pint of sweet cream a gill of white wine and the juice of one orange and one lemon. Beat four eggs very light, stir them into a quart of rich sweet milk, with six ounces of powdered sugar; put it in a pitcher, set it in a pan of boiling water, and simmer the milk, &c. gently, till thick, stirring it all the time; but be sure you do not let it boil hard, or it will curdle, and be spoiled. Then pour it into a large bowl, and set it by to cool; after which, mix with it the cream, &c., beat it very light, serve it in glass cups, or a large glass bowl, and grate nutmeg, lemon, or orange peel thickly over the top. Another way is, to keep the cream and milk separately, and beat the cream to a froth, and pile it on the top.

BIRDS IN JELLY.

Break up some of the nicest Russian gum isinglass, and boil it in water till completely dissolved, making it sufficiently thick to form a stiff jelly when cold. Then strain it, season it highly with white wine, lemon juice, and powdered white sugar; half fill a large deep dish with it, and set it by till it gets cold and firm. If you find it will not be sufficiently thick to take the shape of the mould, melt it again, dissolve some more isinglass in a very little water, strain it, and mix it with the other jelly; if the isinglass is good, the jelly will be quite transparent and lucid. Cut some yellow and white sponge cake in the form of birds, making them of different sizes, tinge some of the white ones with red coloring, spotting each with two dark spots in the proper place for eyes; draw through the beaks of some of them a thin strip of preserved citron, that is colored yellow, and draw through others a slip of green watermelon rind. Break little places in the top of the jelly, so that you can place the birds firmly on it, as though they were sitting, and their heads pointing in different ways. Then pour on the rest of the jelly, which should be only lukewarm; set it in a tub of ice and salt till it congeals, and then turn it out smoothly on a glass dish. Have syllabub or egg cream to eat with it

A DISH OF PINK JELLY.

Prepare your jelly as before directed, substituting madeira or champagne for white wine; color it a fine pink, with fruit juice, or cochineal, and having three pints, pour one third of it into the bottom of a deep dish, and set it by to cool. Then throw over it a small handful of almond cones and cocoanut snow balls; pour on another pint of the jelly, which must be only warm enough to pour, and set it by till the jelly is set. After which, strew on another handful of the cones and snowballs, pour on the other pint of jelly, and set it in a tub of ice and salt, to congeal. Then turn it out smoothly on a glass dish.

A DISH OF STRAWBERRIES.

Prepare three pints of thick isinglass jelly, seasoning it highly with white wine, lemon juice, and loaf sugar. Having strained it, pour one pint of it in a deep dish; have ready one quart of the finest red strawberries, pick them, and when the jelly that is in the dish is cold, sprinkle on regularly a pint of the berries; pour on another pint of the jelly, and set it away till it gets cold also. Then put on the other pint of strawberries, pour on the remaining jelly, and set it in a tub of ice and salt to congeal; after which turn it out on a glass dish, and accompany it with some nice kind of cream. The jelly must be perfectly transparent, that the berries may be quite perceptible.

BLANC-MANGE.

Break up an ounce of the best Russian gum isinglass, (the American gum is not sufficiently clear,) boil it till dissolved in a pint of water; add a quart of sweet milk, simmer it a few minutes, and strain it into a clean pan; mix with it half a pound of powdered white sugar, the juice of a lemon, two ounces of sweet almonds and two ounces of bitter ones, which have been blanched and pounded to a paste with a little rose water. Give it another boil up, and having wet your moulds, pour it in them, and set them by till the blanc-mange gets so firm that they will retain the shape of the moulds; then, having dipped a cloth in hot water, wrap them up in it, and let them remain in it a few minutes to loosen them, and turn them out smoothly into a glass dish. You may mould blanc-mange in bowls, deep dishes, cups, glasses, &c., and you may also mould it in figure moulds, to represent any thing you choose.

RICE BLANC-MANGE.

Break up and dissolve some Russian gum isinglass in a small quantity of water, and strain it into a clean pan. Wash and boil very soft an equal portion of rice, mash it fine, and mix them together. Make it sufficiently liquid for a thick jelly with sweet milk: if you put in a little too much, you will only have to boil it the longer to reduce it to the proper consistence. Add to each quart six ounces of powdered white sugar, a gill of white wine and the juice of a lemon: give it one boil up, stirring it all the time, and put it in your moulds, first wetting them with cold water. When they get cold and hard, turn them smoothly out.

JAUNE-MANGE.

Boil till dissolved two ounces of isinglass in a pint and a half of water, and then strain it into a clean pan; add to it half a pint of white wine, the juice of two lemons, the juice and grated peel of an orange, six ounces of loaf sugar and the beaten yolks of six eggs. Simmer it a few minutes, stirring it all the time; then take it from the fire and put it in moulds to congeal: then turn them out into a glass dish and surround them with cream, highly seasoned and whipped to a froth. For blanc or jaune-mange, select the nicest Russian gum isinglass. There is some that looks very well when dry, but by examining it closely, you will find that it has rather a tainted smell, and when it is dissolved, is quite unpleasant. Good Russian gum, when dissolved and cold, will look perfectly transparent. The American gum is dark and full of sediments when dissolved, and is not nice enough for such purposes.

ARROW ROOT BLANC-MANGE.

Boil a quart of sweet milk, and stir into it while boiling six ounces of powdered sugar and a grated nutmeg. Having dissolved a tea-cupful of arrow root powder in a very little water, add that also to the milk, stirring it in very hard; then take it immediately from the fire, stir in the juice and grated rind of a lemon, a few spoonfuls of white wine, and when it gets cool, put it in moulds to congeal.

BLUMONGE.

Blanch and pound with a little rose water two ounces of sweet almonds and two of bitter ones. Boil a quart of water, and stir into it enough rice, white starch, first wetting it with a little cold water, to make it a thick jelly: then strain it into a clean pan, and stir into it the almond paste, with half a pound of powdered white sugar and the juice and grated rind of a lemon, or a few drops of the essence. Stir it very well, simmer it a few minutes, cool it, and put it in moulds to congeal, first wetting them with cold water. Accompany it with creams.

ANOTHER WAY TO MAKE BLUMONGE.—Boil one ounce of isinglass till dissolved, in just enough water to make it a thick jelly; strain it, and put it on the fire again to boil. Mix a tea-cupful of nice white starch with a pint of sweet cream, beat it smooth, strain it, and stir it into the isinglass jelly. Add half a pound of powdered loaf sugar, a gill of white wine, and the juice and grated peel of one orange or lemon. Stir it till very smoothly mixed, and put it into tea-cups to congeal. After which, take them out on a glass dish, and accompany them with cake and syllabub, or some nice kind of cold cream.

CALF FOOT JELLY.

Boil four calf's feet perfectly soft, leaving about two quarts of the jelly, strain it, and set it by till next day; then take off every particle of grease, as the smallest portion will cause it to be a little nubilated, and also be careful to remove the sediment from the bottom. Then melt it, measure it, put it into a clean pan, or porcelain skillet,

and to each quart add a pound of loaf sugar, broken up,
a pint of white wine, the juice of two fine oranges and
four lemons, and the whites of six eggs, which have been
strained. Stir it till intimately united, and then do not
stir it any more. Boil it till it looks thick and clear; then
pour it in a jelly bag, made of white flannel, having it
suspended by a wooden frame, made for the purpose; cover it with a cloth, and set a bowl under it, to catch the
jelly as it drops. Be sure you do not squeeze the bag,
and if the first that drips through is not entirely pelucid,
pour it back, and drip it through again. When the clear
jelly is done dripping, remove the bowl, and squeeze out
the remaining jelly, which of course will not be of the
nicest quality, but will answer very well for common
family use. Set the fine jelly by till it congeals, then
break it up, and serve it in glasses. By breaking it up,
it will look much more relucent than when moulded and
served in a solid figure. Jelly may be made from pigs'
feet in the same manner.

◦◦

ORANGEO, OR ORANGE JELLY.

Break up, in a very little water, two ounces of the best
Russian gum isinglass; boil it gently till it is completely
dissolved, and looks like thick starch, mashing it with a
spoon against the sides of a pan, which will greatly facilitate the process; then strain it into a large bowl; grate
the yellow rind from one dozen large, deep colored oranges, squeeze the juice into the bowl, with the isinglass,
adding one pound of powdered loaf sugar; put it in a pan,
give it one boil up, and then remove it from the fire.
Have your moulds made precisely in the shape and size
of common oranges, making each one in two equal halves,
which will fit very closely when put together, with the
exception of a small hole at one end, that must be, to pour
the jelly into the moulds. Wet them with water, to make
the jelly come out smoothly, pour in your jelly, and set
them by to congeal. After which, open the mould, and
turn out the jelly; sprinkle the grated orange peel regularly over the moulds, wet your jelly balls with a little
jelly that is lukewarm, put them in the moulds, press them
together, and set them in ice till the jelly and orange peel
consolidates; then turn them out into a glass dish.

A DISH OF PEACHES.

Having made your moulds in the form of peaches, wet them and fill them with calf foot jelly, or any other nice clear kind. When they have congealed, turn them out: put a little pale saffron juice evenly over the moulds, sprinkle on enough cochineal or red sugar sand to give your peaches the proper shade; brush them with a little lukewarm jelly, put them again into the moulds, and let them stand in a tub of ice and salt till the jelly and colorings are conjoined; then turn the peaches smoothly into a glass dish, and send them immediately to table

---

A DISH OF RADISH.

Make your moulds to open in the middle, in two equal halves, having them exactly in the shape of a long radish, on which one inch of the green top has been left. Wet them, put them together, and fill them with hot blancmange. When they have congealed and taken the shape of the moulds, take them out, and brush the large ends with lukewarm jelly; put spinach or spinach juice evenly and thickly over the part of the moulds that is to represent the green tops; suffuse the moulds thickly, just under the green top, with cochineal coloring, gradually diminishing the shade to one third of the moulds: then put in your radishes, close up the moulds, and set them in ice till the jelly and coloring are sufficiently united. Serve them in a glass dish. You may make blanc-mange or white jelly to represent any kind of fruit by giving it the proper coloring and shade, and when dexterously made, there is nothing prettier to set off a table.

RICE SNOWBALLS.

Have your moulds made a size larger than a hen's egg, perfectly round and to open in half. Wet them with cold water, fill them with rice blanc-mange, pouring it in while hot at one end of the moulds, and set them in a cool place. When the rice, &c. is congealed, put them in ice till shortly before you send them to table; then grate loaf sugar thickly over them.

CHOCOLATE JELLY.

Having scraped very fine six ounces of chocolate, dissolve it in half a pint of boiling water. Break up and dissolve one ounce of Russian gum isinglass in just enough boiling water to make it a thick jelly; then strain it, and mix with it the dissolved chocolate; add six ounces of powdered white sugar, put it in a skillet or kettle, give it one boil up, and put it in a mould to congeal.

SAVORY JELLY.

Put eight pounds of the lean of veal and two sets of pigs' feet, that have been nicely cleaned, into a kettle of water; throw in a handful of salt, one of thyme, one of parsley, one of summer savory, and one of sage. Boil it till the meat is into rags, leaving about two quarts of jelly; strain it, and set it by till next day. Then skim off all the fat, removing at the same time the dross or dregs that may have accumulated at the bottom. Cut up the jelly, warm it and measure it, put it in a clean pan, and add a spoonful of pepper, one of mace, two of lemon pickle, a pint of white wine, and the whites of half a dozen eggs. Boil it up, and drip it through a jelly bag. It is fine with poultry and game.

CURDS AND CREAM.

If you have the preparation of rennet, it will be found more convenient than dried rennet, though the latter will answer very well. Cut a piece two or three inches square, pour on it a few spoonfuls of warm water, a large spoonful of white wine, and set it in a warm place for two or three hours. Then stir the liquid into a quart of entire sweet milk, that is made lukewarm, over a few embers. Cover the milk, and set it in a warm place till it forms a thick curd; then turn off the whey, put the curds into a glass or china bowl, and grate on a little nutmeg. Season a pint of rich sweet cream with four ounces of powdered white sugar, a gill of white wine, and the juice of a lemon; beat it to a froth with rods, and pile it on the curds. They should be prepared but a short time before they are sent to table.

LEMON CREAM.

Grate the rind from three lemons, and squeeze the juice into a bowl; sprinkle on it half a pound of powdered loaf sugar, and when completely saturated, add the grated peel and a quart of rich sweet cream, stirring it in gradually. Cover it, set it by for one hour, then beat it till light, and serve it in glasses.

STRAWBERRY CREAM.

Pick the leaves and stems from a quart of English white strawberries, mash them to a perfect marmalade, add three quarters of a pound of powdered white sugar, press it through a sieve, stir it into a quart of rich sweet cream, beat it till light, and serve it in cups or glasses. Raspberry cream may be made in the same manner.

ORANGE CREAM.

Grate the yellow peel from four fine oranges, and squeeze the juice into a bowl, sprinkle on it half a pound of powdered sugar, and the grated peel, and after standing till well mixed, stir gradually into it a quart of rich sweet cream. Set it by for one or two hours, then beat it light, and serve it in glasses. The difference in making lemon and orange cream is only in the quantity of the juice and grated rind, as it does not require as much of the lemon to give the proper flavor as of the orange. If the fruit cannot be obtained, the essence will answer.

PEACH CREAM.

Take soft peaches, that are perfectly ripe, peel them, take out the stones, mix with them an equal weight of powdered sugar, mash them to a pulp, and press them through a sieve. Have ready a quart of rich sweet cream, stir the pulp into it till it is as thick as boiled custard, beat it light, and serve it in cups or glasses. Season a pint of rich cream with powdered loaf sugar, white wine and lemon juice; tinge it yellow with saffron juice, beat it to a froth, and pile it high on the tops of the glasses.

QUINCE CREAM.

Pare and core some fine ripe quinces, stew them soft in a very little water, with an equal weight of powdered white sugar; mash them fine, press it through a sieve, and set it by to cool. After which stir it into sweet cream, making it about as thick as boiled custard, beat it light, serve it in glasses, and crown them with whipped cream. Pear and apple cream may be prepared in the same manner.

WHORTLEBERRY CREAM.

Pick and wash a quart of ripe whortleberries, and stew them with a pound of sugar; do not break them, but when they get cold, stir them into a quart of sweet cream, serve it in glasses, and crown it with whipped cream, tinged with dark colored preserve juice.

ITALIAN CREAM.

Beat the yolks of six eggs till very light and smooth; stir into them gradually a pint of wine, and let it set for half an hour; then stir in half a pound of powdered sugar, the juice and grated peel of one orange and one lemon, and let it set again for half an hour, after which stir in a quart of rich sweet cream, beat it light, serve it in glasses, and crown them with whipped cream. These cold creams, as they are called, are plain, nice, fashionable and easily prepared. They are eaten with tarts, sweet meats and cake.

OBSERVATIONS ON ICE CREAMS.

Get a tub proportioned to the size of your freezer, so that there will be a space of about five inches round the freezer, when placed in the middle of the tub, which will contain a sufficient quantity of ice to freeze the cream well, while a larger space must necessarily be filled and only be a superfluous waste.

The length of time that is required to freeze cream in a proper manner, depends greatly on the quantity of cream and the size and shape of the freezer. If it is deep and small in circumference, the process will be retarded, while it will be much accelerated by the freezer being large in circumference, as the ice must form on the sides of it. Cream will generally freeze sufficiently hard for what is called the first freezing, in two hours; that is, to make the cream of the proper consistence to put into moulds, and then to make it smooth and firm, it will require from two to three hours longer, but seldom more, which is called the second freezing or congelation.

You may mould your cream in as many fanciful shapes as you please, by making your moulds precisely the shape of what you wish to represent; but never put your cream in figure moulds till after the first freezing. Break up your ice very small, mix with it an equal portion of coarse salt, and put it in the ice tub. Having prepared your cream, put it in the freezer, set it in the tub of ice, pressing up the ice closely to it; cover it with a folded carpet, turn it round constantly, taking care not to let a drop of the salt water get in, which would injure very much the taste of the cream. Raise the cover frequently, and with a long-handled spoon scrape down the ice from the sides of the freezer. When the whole is congealed, put it into your moulds; fill up the tub with fresh ice and salt, place your moulds firmly in the ice, cover the tub with a bit of folded carpet, and let them remain in it till the ice is smooth and firm, which will seldom take more than two hours. Turn them out smoothly, arrange them tastefully on a glass dish, and send them immediately to table. If you do not use figure moulds, rinse out the freezer, put the ice again into it, cover it, put it in the ice, and let it remain untouched for two hours; then serve it in glasses, piling it high on the tops.

---◦◆◦---

PINE-APPLE ICE CREAM.

Take one large ripe pine-apple, pare it, cut it in very thin slices, mince them fine in a bowl, and sprinkle on a pound of powdered loaf sugar, stir them up, cover them, and set them by for two hours; then mash them fine and press it through a sieve: stir the juice into one quart of rich sweet cream, put it into the freezer, and when it has congealed, which will probably be in two or three hours, put it into moulds, and freeze it the second time as directed. Ice creams should always be accompanied with cake, and immediately followed by wine and cordials.

LEMON ICE CREAM.

Pare the yellow rind from three lemons, put it into a porcelain skillet, with the beaten yolks of eight eggs, a quart of rich sweet cream, and simmer it gently till the flavor of the lemons is extracted: then strain it into a bowl, and stir in it while warm three quarters of a pound of powdered loaf sugar. When it is cold, stir gradually into it the juice of the three decorticated lemons, and freeze it as directed. Cold lemon cream makes very fine and delicate ice, when made a little sweeter. As much of the sweetness is lost by the process of freezing, ice creams require more sugar than the common cold creams.

ALMOND ICE CREAM.

Blanch and pound to a paste two ounces of sweet almonds and one ounce of bitter ones, adding as you proceed a little rose water, to make them white and light; simmer the paste a few minutes in a porcelain skillet, with a pint of sweet cream; then pour it into a bowl on half a pound of powdered sugar; stir it up, cover it, and set it by to cool: then strain it, stir into it another pint of sweet cream, and freeze it.

RASPBERRY ICE CREAM.

Pick the leaves and stems from a quart of ripe English raspberries, mash them to a pulp, press it through a sieve, and mix it well with a pound of powdered white sugar; then stir into it a quart of sweet cream, and freeze it twice as directed.

STRAWBERRY ICE CREAM.

Pick the leaves and stems from a quart of ripe English strawberries, put them in a bowl, and sprinkle on them a pound of powdered white sugar. Stir the beaten yolks of six eggs into a quart of sweet milk, simmer them gently till thick, then put it in a bowl, and set it by to cool. Mash the berries fine, press them through a sieve, and when the custard is cold, stir them well together, and freeze it over twice as directed. Strawberry cream may be made as directed for raspberry cream, and raspberry cream may be made by this receipt.

COCOANUT ICE CREAM.

Take a large cocoanut from the shell, pare off the dark skin, and grate the nutmeg fine. Have ready a quart of sweet cream and three quarters of a pound of loaf sugar. Stir into the cream two table-spoonfuls of rose water, and then stir in alternately the sugar and grated cocoanut. When it is very smooth, freeze it over twice by the directions. If you serve it in glasses, pile it high on the top, and always accompany ice cream, whatever kind it may be, with some nice kind of cake: sponge-cake is generally preferred. Send round your wines and cordials very soon after a course of cream and cake.

ANOTHER COCOANUT CREAM.—Beat the yolks of six eggs light, and stir them into a quart of rich milk alternately with a pound of grated cocoanut and three quarters of a pound of powdered loaf sugar. Add the milk of the cocoanut, put it in a pitcher, set it in a pan of boiling water, and simmer it gently till thick, stirring it constantly. Stir it occasionally till it gets cold and very smooth, and then freeze it. If you use figure moulds, arrange the ice fancifully on a glass dish. Have glass cups to be filled at table, each one provided with a teaspoon.

CHOCOLATE ICE CREAM.

Scrape very fine four ounces of chocolate, mix with it a quart of rich sweet milk, and simmer it till completely dissolved in a porcelain skillet or preserving kettle: stir it frequently, and when it looks thick and rich, strain it, and set it by till it gets cold; then stir in the beaten yolks of six eggs alternately with half a pound of powdered sugar; give it a boil up, stirring it all the time, and then remove it immediately from the fire. Freeze it over twice.

PEACH ICE CREAM.

Select peaches that are very ripe and soft, peel them, extract the stones, and mash them to a marmalade. Having one quart of peach pulp, mix with it one pound of powdered sugar, a grated nutmeg and a tea-spoonful of powdered cinnamon; stir it into a quart of rich sweet cream, and freeze it as directed. If cream is not to be had, substitute a quart of rich sweet milk, stir into it the beaten yolks of five or six eggs, simmer it till the eggs are sufficiently cooked, set it by till cold, and then stir into it the peaches, &c. as before directed.

ORANGE ICE CREAM.

Beat the yolks of eight eggs light, and stir them into a quart of rich sweet milk or cream, put it in a pitcher, set it in a pan of boiling water, and simmer it gently till it becomes thick, but do not let it boil, or it will curdle. Having stirred it all the time it was simmering, pour it into a bowl, and set it by to cool. Grate the yellow peel from four oranges, and squeeze out the juice, and when the cream is cold, stir them alternately into it with three quarters of a pound of powdered loaf sugar. Mix it very well, and freeze it. Cold orange cream makes a very fine ice when made sweeter.

CHERRY ICE CREAM.

Get some fine ripe cherries, break them up, and squeeze out a pint of thick juice. Beat to a stiff froth the whites of six eggs, and mix it with the juice: put it in a porcelain skillet, set it over a few coals, and stir it till it raises the simmer. Powder a pound of loaf sugar, put it in a bowl, pour over it while scalding the juice and egg, mix it well, and set it by to cool. Have ready a quart of entire sweet cream, and when the juice, &c. is cold, stir the cream gradually into it. Freeze it over twice as directed.

CITRON ICE CREAM.

Slice very thin one pound of the finest citron melons, that are perfectly ripe. Powder a pound of loaf sugar, and put it in a bowl with the sliced citron, stratifying them, and set them by for several hours; then chop them small and press out all the juice you can through a sieve. Have ready a quart of rich sweet cream, stir the juice into it, and conglaciate it twice as directed.

PEAR ICE CREAM.

Pare and slice some fine ripe pears, stew them till quite soft in a very little water; mash them to a pulp, press it through a sieve, and set it by to cool. Have ready a quart of sweet cream, mix with it the beaten yolks of four eggs, and simmer it over some coals till it becomes a little thick; stir into it three quarters of a pound of powdered loaf sugar, and then remove it from the fire. When it gets cold, stir hard into it a pint of the pear pulp. Add the grated rind of a lemon, or a few drops of the essence of lemon, and freeze it over twice.

QUINCE ICE CREAM.

May be made in every respect by the preceding receipt. Accompany them with cake, &c.

GOOSEBERRY ICE CREAM.

Pick the stems and blossoms from a quart of gooseberries, mix with them an equal weight of sugar, and stew thew tender; mash them to a pulp, press it through a sieve, and set it by to cool. When it is cold, stir into it a quart of rich cream, and freeze it.

GRAPE ICE CREAM.

Take the white English grapes when perfectly ripe, mash them fine, and press them through a fine wire sieve, that it may keep back the skins, &c. Mix with one quart of the juice, a pound of powdered loaf sugar. When it is completely dissolved, stir in a quart of sweet cream, and freeze it.

VANILLA ICE CREAM.

Boil a vanilla bean in a quart of rich sweet milk till the milk is sufficiently flavored; then take out the bean, and set the milk by to cool; after which stir into it the beaten yolks of half a dozen eggs, and simmer it again till a little thick, stirring it all the time. Add three quarters of a pound of sugar, and freeze it.

SASSAFRAS CREAM.

May be made in every respect as directed for vanilla cream, and is very much liked. For this purpose take the red sassafras, which will color as well as flavor it.

TEA ICE CREAM.

Put two tablespoonfuls of good tea in a tea pot, pour on enough boiling water to cover it, and let it stand for half an hour to infuse. Stir into a quart of sweet cream the beaten yolks of eight eggs, and simmer it slowly till it becomes thick. Having strained the tea, stir it into the cream, and cool and freeze it as directed.

ICED CHERRY JUICE.

Beat the whites of six eggs to a stiff froth, mix them well with a quart of thick cherry juice, and three quarters of a pound of powdered loaf sugar, stir it till the sugar is dissolved, and freeze it. The juice of currants, strawberries and raspberries may all be prepared and frozen in the same manner.

ICED ORANGE JUICE.

Pare very thin the yellow peel from six large deep colored oranges, put it in three gills of water, and simmer it till the flavor is extracted; then strain it, and set it by to cool. When it is entirely cold, stir into it the whites of six eggs that have been beaten to a stiff froth, simmer it over a few coals, till it becomes thick, but by no means suffer it to boil; then take it from the fire, and when cold, mix with it three quarters of a pound of powdered loaf sugar, and a pint and a half of orange juice. When all are well mixed, and the sugar completely dissolved, freeze it as directed.

ICED LEMON JUICE.

Grate the rind from four lemons; stir it into a pint of water with the whites of six eggs, that have been beaten to a stiff froth; put it in a porcelain skillet, set it over a few coals, and stir it till it gets a little thick. Then strain it, and when it gets cold, mix with it a pint and a half of lemon juice, and freeze it.

LEMON AND ORANGE-ADE.

Make very delicate ice, but should be made sweeter than the common lemon and orange-ade, and the juice not diluted more than one fourth with cold water.

ICED JELLY.

Take any kind of nice white jelly, melt it over a few coals, add to it a little water and powdered sugar; cool it, freeze it, and serve it in glasses.

FROZEN CUSTARDS.

Take any kind of boiled custard, make it a little thinner with cream or rich sweet milk, add more sugar, and freeze it like creams. Most kinds of creams, where there is not too much acid used, are finer and more delicate when made with rich sweet cream, without the aid of eggs. Ice creams and custards should always be accompanied with cake, and followed very soon by some kind of cordial or wine, which will eradicate the unpleasant sensation of the stomach, that is often occasioned by the coldness of the ice, with people of delicate habits, and with those who have not been much in the habit of eating them.

SWEET-MEATS, &c.

PRESERVED PEACHES.

Select large plum, or clingstone peaches, that are ripe but quite firm; pare them, cut them from the stones in large slices, and weigh them. Weigh an equal quantity of loaf sugar, break it up, and put it in a preserving kettle, with a few spoonfuls of water at the bottom. The best preserving kettles are made of iron, and lined with porcelain. Set it on a trivet over a bed of clear coals, and when it boils, skim it well, and then put in your peaches; stew them gently till they are quite transparent, stirring them occasionally, but be sure you do not break or mash them to pieces. Put them in a broad earthen pan to cool, and set them by till next day. Then put them up in small queens-

ware or glass jars, lay a bit of brandy paper on top of the
preserves, and tie several folds of soft paper over the tops
of the jars.   Examine them occasionally, and if they seem
like fermenting, scald them over again, skim them, cool
them, and put them up again, in the same manner as before.

TO PRESERVE PEACHES WHOLE.

Take plum peaches, that are ripe, but firm, and not of
the largest size, pare them, pierce them with a needle in
several places, to the stone, and weigh them.   Weigh an
equal portion of sugar, make a syrup of it, as directed in
the former receipt, and when you have skimmed it well,
put in your peaches, simmer them slowly till they look
clear, and the syrup tolerably thick; then cool them, and
next day put them up in small jars, covering them with
brandy paper.   Preserves for nice purposes should always be made of the best loaf sugar, but for common
family use, they may be made of nice brown sugar, first
clarifying it by dissolving it in a little water, stirring into
it while cold the beaten whites of eggs, and then boiling
and skimming it well.

PEACH MARMALADE.

Take ripe, soft peaches, pare them, extract the stones,
and mash the peaches to a smooth pulp.   Pound enough
peach kernels to flavor the marmalade, mix them together, and weigh them.   Weigh three fourths the quantity
of sugar, put it into a preserving kettle, add a very little
water, and when it boils, skim it, and put in the peach
pulp; simmer them together for thirty or forty minutes,
stirring it the most of the time, and then cool it, put it up
in small jars, and cover them with brandy paper.

PEACHES FOR TARTS, &c.

Take clingstone peaches, that are very ripe and sweet,
pare, and slice them from the stones, stew them in a preserving kettle till quite soft, with a very little water, and
half their weight in brown sugar; mash them to a pulp,
stir it till nearly dry, cool it, put it up in small jars, and

keep them in a cool, dry place, where they will be exposed to the air. When you wish to make use of it, liquefy it sufficiently with sweet milk or water, mixing with it a little more sugar.

PEACH CHIPS.

Get large clingstone peaches, that are ripe, but firm; peel them, slice them round the stone with a sharp penknife, forming them into large thin shavings, or chips, and weigh them. Have ready a preserving kettle, with a sufficient quantity of strained honey to cover them well, boil it up, skim it, and put in your peaches; simmer them gently till they look quite luculent; then lift them out with a perforated ladle, that the honey may drain entirely from them, spread them on dishes, and expose them to the sun till dry, turning them over as they may require it, and then pack them away in jars, with half their weight in powdered loaf sugar, stratifying them, and sifting on the sugar, to make it even and regular over the chips. Secure the tops with folded paper, tying it firmly round.

BRANDY PEACHES.

Take freestone peaches, that are firm, and entirely free from blemish; wash them, and wipe them with a flannel, to free them from the fuzz, pierce them to the stones in several places with a needle, and scald them a few minutes in just water enough to cover them, and half their weight in sugar. Then drain them, spread them on a dish to cool, boil the syrup till two thirds of the water which was added has evaporated, mix with it an equal portion of white brandy, put the peaches in a wide mouthed bottle, and pour over them the brandy and syrup. Next day cork it securely.

PEACH LEATHER.

Take freestone peaches, that are ripe and sweet; pare them, mash them to a pulp after taking out the stones, and weigh it. Break up as many peach kernels as will flavor it to your taste, pound them to a paste, and mix it with the peach pulp. Weigh your sugar, allowing half a pound to every pound of peaches; break it up, put it into a preserving kettle with a very little water, boil and skim it, and then put in your peach pulp; simmer it at least thirty minutes, stirring it very well, and then spread it out in a smooth coat on dishes, and expose them to the sun till dry, turning them over once a day. Sprinkle over each piece a little powdered cinnamon and grated lemon, roll them into a scroll, and keep them in a dry place, exposing them occasionally to the air.

PEACH JELLY.

Take ripe soft peaches, pare, mash and stew them in a very little water. Put it in a jelly bag, which should be made of white flannel, squeeze out the juice, and to each pint allow a pound of loaf sugar. Break up and boil in a very little water, as many peach kernels as will flavor it well, and mix it with the jelly and sugar; put it in a preserving kettle, and boil it slowly till it is a thick jelly, stirring and skimming it as it may require. If you wish it a very stiff jelly, add a little dissolved isinglass, which will never fail to make it such, but I do not think the jelly keeps as well as when made without it. When it is done and quite cold, put it up in small glass jars, lay brandy papers on the tops, and cover them securely with folded white paper.

TO DRY PEACHES.

Select fine large cling-stone peaches that are ripe, but firm; peel them, cut them from the stones in large slices, and spread them on a scaffold in the sun, and turn them over once a day till they get dry; then put them in sacks, and expose them occasionally to the sun, to keep them clear of worms. You may dry them on a kiln more speedily, but they are not so nice as when dried in the sun. If you dry them with the peelings on, wash them before you cut them, and wipe them with a cloth to get off the fuzz.

PEACH BUTTER.

Peach butter, when made in the proper manner, is cheap and really fine. Take cider just from the press, that has been made of the best of apples, boil it in a preserving kettle till reduced to one half its original quantity. Have ready some nice dried peaches, wash them clean, squeeze out the water, and put them in the cider. Boil them till they are very soft, stirring and mashing them till they become a smooth pulp, and replenishing the kettle with fresh cider as it may require. Let it remain over a slow fire of coals till it gets hard enough to slice, but be careful to stir it almost constantly towards the last, lest it scorch. Flavor it highly with powdered cloves, ginger, cinnamon and nutmeg, put it up in stone or queen's ware jars, cover them securely by tying over the tops some folded paper, and keep them in a cool place. It will keep good a year, and will be found very nice and convenient.

PEACHES PRESERVED WITH CIDER.

For this purpose the cider should be made of very sweet mellow apples. Take it immediately from the press, boil it down one third its original quantity. Have ready your peaches, which should be pared and neatly dried in the sun; put them in the kettle of cider, and simmer them gently till they become tender and quite clear, but do not break them to pieces. Put them up in jars as other preserves, and keep them in a cool place, exposing them occasionally to the air. They will keep well a year, and will be found good for many family purposes.

TO PRESERVE PEARS.

Take large firm pears that are not fully ripe, peel them, cut each one in four, extract the cores and hard parts, and weigh them. Weigh an equal portion of loaf sugar, break it up in just enough water to dissolve it, stir in the whites of eggs, allowing one white to five pounds of sugar; put it in a preserving kettle, boil it fast till the scum rises, which remove, and then put in your pears; set them over a few coals, and boil them slowly till they look quite transparent. Raise them with a perforated skimmer, spread them on dishes to cool, and then put them in jars. Flavor the syrup with lemon juice, boil it gently till the water that was put in has evaporated, and pour it over the pears. Cover them securely with brandy papers.

TO PRESERVE PEARS WHOLE.

Select large pears of equal size, not quite ripe, and perfectly free from blemish: pare them smoothly, leaving on a short bit of the stems, and weigh them. Weigh an equal quantity of loaf sugar, which divide in half; put one portion in a preserving kettle with a little water, allowing half a pint of water to each pound of sugar; set it over some coals, and when it gets to a boil, put in your pears. Boil them gently till they look like they may be about half done; then take them out, draining them with a perforated ladle; spread them on dishes and set them by to cool. Take the syrup from the fire, mix in the other half of sugar, and when it gets cold, stir in the whites of eggs, allowing one white to five pounds of sugar; set it over a bed of clear coals, having it placed on a trivet. When it boils hard, skim it, and then put in your pears; boil them gently till quite transparent, and after cooling them, put them in jars, having stuck a clove in the blossom end of each. Boil the syrup till the water has evaporated, add a little lemon juice to flavor it, and pour it over the pears. Cover them with several folds of soft paper.

PEAR MARMALADE.

Take ripe pears, divest them of the peeling and cores, and boil them tender in a very little water. Mash them to a pulp, add three fourths its weight of sugar, and stir and simmer it gently till it gets nearly dry. Flavor it with essence of lemon, and put it up in glass or queen's ware jars.

PEAR CHEESE.

Pare and core some ripe pears, weigh them and stew them in a very little water till tender; add an equal portion of sugar, and flavor it with wine, nutmeg, lemon and cloves; simmer it gently, stirring it frequently till it gets hard enough to slice, and put it away in queen's ware jars, packing it closely. When you wish to use it, cut it in smooth slices, and introduce it at the tea table.

PEAR BUTTER.

Take sweet cider just from the press, and boil it in a preserving kettle till reduced to one third its original quantity. Have ready some fine ripe pears, that have been pared, cored and sliced; put them in the cider, and boil them gently till they are quite soft. Mash them to a pulp, season it with nutmeg, cloves, mace and lemon; set it over a few coals, and simmer it slowly till it is nearly thick enough to slice, stirring it almost constant towards the last, to prevent it burning at the bottom and sides of the kettle. Put it up in queensware jars, and if boiled sufficiently, it will keep good a year or two, and will be found fine for the tea or breakfast table.

PEAR JELLY.

Cut up some ripe pears, and boil them in a very little water till soft, adding enough lemon peel to flavor them well. Have ready a white flannel jelly bag, put in it the pears with their juices, and press through all the juice you can; mix with it loaf sugar, broken up, in the proportions of a pound of sugar to a pint of the juice. Add enough cochineal tincture to color it a fine pink; put it in a preserving kettle, and boil it slowly till it is a thick jelly; if you find it difficult to get such, add a little dissolved isinglass, simmer it a few minutes longer, cool it, put it up in small jars or glasses, and cover them with double tissue papers, that are cut exactly to fit the inside of the glasses.

TO DRY PEARS.

Select large pears that are ripe, but firm; peel them, cut each one in four, and extract the seeds and cores. Spread them thin on a scaffold in the sun, and turn them over once a day, securing them from the night and morning dews. When they are perfectly dry, put them up in small sacks, and expose them occasionally to the sun. They make excellent sauce when stewed, to accompany poultry and game, and also makes good butter, boiled in sweet cider, and made in the usual manner.

PRESERVED QUINCES.

Pare, core and quarter your quinces, weigh them, and also weigh an equal quantity of loaf sugar. Break up the sugar, dissolve it in a little water, and mix with it whites of eggs, allowing one white to four or five pounds of sugar. Put it in a preserving kettle, and when it boils, skim it, and put in your fruit. Place your kettle on a trivet, over a bed of clear coals, and boil the preserves gently till quite transparent, stirring them occasionally, but be careful not to break them, as they look much nicer to remain in large pieces. Drain them, spread them out on dishes to cool, which will have a tendency to harden them, put them up in glass or queensware jars, pour the syrup over them, and cover them with paper, dipped in brandy.

TO PRESERVE QUINCES WHOLE.

Select ripe quinces, that are free from blemish, and of equal size; pare them, extract the cores with a sharp penknife, leaving the quinces whole; fill the cavities whence the cores were taken, with slips of lemon peel, and weigh them. Weigh an equal portion of loaf sugar, and divide it in half. Boil the peelings and cores in a small quantity of water till they are tolerably tender, strain the juice into a preserving kettle, put in one half of the sugar, boil it, skim it, and then put in your prepared quinces. Boil them slowly for half an hour, drain them, put them on dishes, and set them in the open air till they get cold. Cool the syrup, mix in the remaining half of sugar, boil it up, skim it, and put in your quinces again. Boil them till they become quite pelucid, drain them, cool them, and put them up in small glass jars. Boil the syrup till it gets to be a jelly, pour it over the quinces, and cover them with brandy papers.

QUINCE MARMALADE.

Having divested some ripe quinces of the peelings and cores, cut them up, and weigh them. Weigh your sugar also, allowing three quarters of a pound to each pound of the prepared quinces. Boil the peelings and cores in a small quantity of water till they are soft, strain the liquor through a fine sieve, put it in a preserving kettle, dissolve in it the sugar, boil it, skim it, and put in your sliced quinces. Boil them soft, mash them to a pulp, simmer and stir it till it gets quite thick and smooth, and when it gets cold, put it up in jars. Marmalade for present use, may be made with half a pound of sugar to each pound of the quinces; but if you wish to keep it throughout the year, a more liberal allowance of sugar is necessary.

QUINCE JELLY.

Your quinces must be very ripe, cut them up, boil them soft, in a small quantity of water, mash them up, and pass the liquid through a white flannel jelly bag; to each pint of which add a pound of loaf sugar, broken up. Boil them slowly together till they form a thick jelly, and when cold, put it up in small jars, covering them with double tissue paper, or soft white paper, dipped in brandy.

QUINCE CHEESE.

Pare and slice from the cores some ripe quinces, and weigh them. Weigh an equal quantity of loaf sugar, put it in a kettle with a very little water, and when it is dissolved, put in your sliced quinces. Boil them soft, and mash and stir them till very thick and smooth; color it with cochineal, flavor it with grated lemon peel, nutmeg and cinnamon, and when cold, pack it away in queensware jars. When you wish to make use of it, cut it in smooth slices, and lay them on a glass or china plate. It is generally eaten at tea. If made by these directions, it will keep good for more than a year. If, by keeping it a long time, it becomes too hard, simmer it over a few minutes, adding a little water to make it sufficiently soft. A similar cheese may be made of ripe, soft peaches.

QUINCE BUTTER.

Take sweet cider, that is made of mellow apples; it should be just from the press, as it will not do after it has begun to ferment; boil it till reduced to one third its original quantity, and skim it well. Have ready some ripe quinces, which have been pared and sliced from the cores, and put them in the cider, but do not crowd them. Boil them very soft, mash them to a pulp, and then simmer them slowly over a few coals till thick and smooth, stirring it frequently, to prevent it sticking and burning to the sides of the kettle. Flavor it highly with powdered cinnamon, nutmeg, cloves, mace and grated lemon peel; and when it is as thick as common soft butter, cool it, and pack it away in jars for use.

In making these butters, much depends on the manner in which they are boiled, they should be boiled slowly, regularly, and a long time, even after the fruit becomes soft, and towards the last, they should be stirred almost constantly. When made in a proper manner, they will keep good more than a year, and will be found very convenient, being always in readiness.

TO PRESERVE CITRON.

Take the finest citron melons when ripe; pare off the rind, cut them in several pieces, take out the middle, and let them lie in salt and water for half a day; Then soak them in fresh water, changing it frequently till every particle of salt is extracted; dissolve a small lump of alum in enough boiling water to cover them: it must be very weak or it will impart to them a rough unpleasant taste. After scalding them a few minutes in the alum water, scald them in a little weak ginger tea, made of the roots. Have ready a preserving kettle lined with green vine leaves; put them in the kettle in layers of the green leaves; put a thick layer of them over the top, pour in enough water to cover them, and simmer them over a few coals for nearly two hours. Make a plentiful syrup to cover them well, allowing a pound of loaf sugar to a half pint of water; boil it up, skim it, and boil the citrons gently in it till they are so tender that you can pierce them through easily with a broom-straw, and spread them on dishes to cool and harden. Pare the rinds very thin from enough deep colored lemons, to flavor the citrons well; cut them of regular size, in any fanciful shape you please, and scald them for a few minutes in clear water, to draw out a part of the bitter taste. Cut up the decorticated lemons, boil them to a pulp, allowing half a pint of water to each one; strain the liquid through a fine sieve, and to each pint add a pound of the best loaf sugar. When the sugar is dissolved, stir it in the whites of eggs, allowing one to every four or five pounds of sugar; boil it up, skim it, and boil your lemon peel in it till soft. When the citrons are cold, put them in a jar, and pour the syrup with the lemon peel over them while scalding. Next day, cover them with folded, soft paper.

CANDIED CITRONS.

Prepare your citrons in every respect as directed for preserves, and when you boil them in the syrup, cut them in thin smooth slices all of the same size. Put them in a glass jar with stratum, superstratum of powdered loaf sugar, allowing a quarter of a pound of sugar to each pound of the citrons, and sifting on, to make it perfectly regular over the whole. Having prepared the second syrup as directed for the preserves, boil it until it will rope when dropped from a spoon; pour it over the citrons when a little warm, and cover the jar with soft paper.

WATERMELON SWEETMEATS.

Take a fine ripe watermelon that has a thick rind; take out the soft part, pare off the thin green pellicle, and cut the middle part of the rind in any fanciful shape you please. Weigh them, and to each pound allow a pound and a half of loaf sugar. Line the bottom and sides of a preserving kettle with green vine leaves; put in your rind with layers of the leaves, and put a thick layer of them over the top. Dissolve a small lump of alum in just enough water to cover them well; pour it over them and let them simmer slowly from one to two hours, according to the size and thickness of the pieces; then scald them a few minutes in a little weak ginger tea, adding a small portion of spinach juice, which will assist in making them a pretty green: spread them on dishes, and set them in the air to cool and harden. Take one sixth part of the sugar, powder it, and reserve it to sift over the melon. Take the other part of the sugar, dissolve it in water, allowing half a pint to each pound and a quarter of sugar: stir in one white of egg to every five pounds of sugar: flavor it highly with the juice and grated rinds of lemons or oranges; boil it up, skim it well, and then put in your prepared melons: simmer them till they are tender and quite transparent. Spread them on dishes, and set them by to cool. After which, put them in a glass jar, stratifying them with the powdered sugar; boil the syrup till it will rope when dropped from a spoon; pour it over them, and when cold, cover them securely. They make a very pretty decorament for creams, jellies, &c.

TO PRESERVE CHERRIES.

Take morella, or any other kind of nice ripe cherries, extract the seeds with a quill, holding them over a bowl or dish to catch the juice, and to each pound of the seeded cherries allow a pound and two ounces of loaf sugar. Put the sugar with the juice into a preserving kettle, mix in the white of egg, and boil and skim it well; boil very gently in it the cherries till they are done, and the syrup sufficiently thick and low: then cool them, put them up in jars, pour over the syrup, and cover them with brandy papers.

TO PRESERVE CHERRIES WHOLE.

Take any kind of fine, large cherries, that are not too ripe: the light red ones are prettiest for this purpose; leave on a short bit of the stems, which cut smooth, pierce them with a needle in several places to make the syrup penetrate them easily; weigh them, and to each pound allow a pound and a quarter of loaf sugar. Break up some cherries that are very ripe and sweet; squeeze out the juice, to each pint of which, add two pounds of the sugar: when it is dissolved, stir in the white of egg, boil it up, skim it, and then put in your cherries: simmer them for fifteen or twenty minutes, and spread them out on dishes in the air. When they get entirely cold, put them in the syrup and let them simmer till they look quite transparent; but be sure to not let them boil hard, or the skins will burst and the stems become loose. Spread them on dishes again till they get cold, and put them in small jars; boil and skim the syrup, pour it over them, and next day cover them with brandy papers. If they are preserved with the best loaf sugar, and these directions carefully followed, they will be so pelucid, that, by holding them up, you may see in them the full size and shape of the seeds.

CHERRY BUTTER.

Take any kind of nice cherries, which for this purpose must be very ripe. Having extracted the seeds, put the cherries with the juice and an equal weight of loaf sugar into a preserving kettle, and set it over a bed of coals. When they boil, skim them, and then simmer them till they are very soft, mashing and stirring them till they become a thick smooth mass; flavor it with wine and nutmegs, and when it is quite cold, put it up in small jars, cover them with paper dipped in brandy, and keep them in a cool place. It will keep well, and will be found fine for the tea-table.

CHERRY JAM.

Take very ripe cherries, extract the seeds, spread them out on a dish, sprinkle on them their juice and three quarters of a pound of the best brown sugar to each pound of the seeded cherries. Next day put them in a preserving kettle, with as many kernels from the cherry seeds as will flavor them well, having first pounded them to a paste. Simmer them gently till done and thick, stir and mash them to a pulp, and put it up in queen's ware jars, covering them with brandy papers.

CHERRY JELLY.

Beat up some ripe juicy cherries, (the carnation ones make the prettiest jelly,) put them with their juice into a preserving kettle, boil them slowly for fifteen or twenty minutes, and pass the juice through a jelly-bag. Measure it, and to each pint add a pound and a quarter of loaf sugar: put them in the kettle, and simmer them together till they form a thick jelly, which you may tell by taking out a little in a spoon and holding it in the air till it gets cold.   Flavor it with essence of cinnamon, put it up in small glass jars, and cover them with double tissue paper.

Cherry jelly is frequently made with one pound of sugar to each pint of juice; but as it is rather an acid fruit, to secure it from all possibility of its fermenting, it is much the surest and best way to allow a pound and a quarter of sugar to one pint of the juice, as one pint of first rate jelly is worth two of an inferior quality.

TO DRY CHERRIES.

Take large ripe cherries, extract the seeds with a quill, holding them at the same time over a dish or bowl, to catch the juice that runs from them.   Spread them thin on large flat dishes, set them in the sun, and sprinkle on the juice a little at a time, till you have put it all on them; turn them over as they may require, and when they are dry, put them up in queen's ware jars, dispersing among them half their weight of brown sugar.

They make excellent pies and puddings,—very near as good as when made of fresh ones.

STEWED CHERRIES.

Take nice dried cherries, stew them in a small quantity of water till tender; mash them fine and serve them in a glass dish, having them tolerably moist.   It is a nice concomitance to poultry and game.

PRESERVED LEMONS.

Select ripe thin rinded lemons, that are of equal size and without blemish: boil them in clear water till the rinds become tender, excavate a small portion of the stalk end of each, that the syrup may penetrate them easily, and spread them out on dishes to cool.   Make a plentiful syrup to cover them, allowing a pound of loaf sugar to each quart of water; boil it, skim it, and put in your lemons; simmer them a few minutes, put them with the syrup into an earthen jar, and set them by till next day: then turn off the syrup, boil it up, pour it hot over the lemons, and set them by till the second day.   Turn off the syrup again, add to it more loaf sugar, making in all a pound and a half to each pound of the lemons; mix with it the whites of eggs, allowing one to every five pounds of the sugar, and boil, skim it, scald your lemons in it a few minutes, drain and cool them, put them in a jar, and when you have boiled the syrup till thick, pour it over them while hot. Next day cover them securely.

LEMON MARMALADE.

Take smooth deep colored lemons, weigh them, and to each pound allow a pound and a quarter of loaf sugar. Pare the rind from one half of them, which you may reserve for other purposes; grate the yellow rind from the other half, cut up the lemons, saving the juice, and put it into a preserving kettle with the sugar and grated rind; add a very little water, and simmer it till it is a thick mass: add a small portion of white wine, boil it up again, and when cold put it up in small glass jars, and cover them with paper dipped in brandy.

TO PRESERVE LIMES.

Get your limes as near the same size as possible, and preserve them in every respect by the preceding receipt. Lay on them pieces of paper dipped in brandy, and cut to fit in the tops of the jars; tie over the tops soft paper, that will fit closely round, and keep them in a cool place. Occasionally look to them, and if the syrup looks like fermenting, boil and skim it well, pour it over the limes, and when cold cover them as before directed.

TO PRESERVE ORANGES.

Take large smooth deep colored oranges, as near the same size as possible; cut a small hole in the stalk end of each, that the syrup may penetrate the inside easily; weigh them, and to each pound allow a pound and a quarter of loaf sugar. Divide the sugar into two equal parts, and with one half make a thin syrup; put it in a preserving kettle with the oranges, boil them slowly, or rather simmer them till the peels become soft; then spread them on dishes in the open air. Mix with the syrup the other part of the sugar, add whites of eggs to clear it, boil it up, skim it, and having put the oranges in a jar, pour the syrup scalding over them, cover them, and set them by till next day: then boil up the syrup again, pour it over them, and let them stand for twenty-four hours longer; after which simmer them a few minutes in the syrup, cool them, put them in jars, boil the syrup till very thick, and pour it over them while hot. When cold cover them with brandy papers, and keep them in a cool place.

ORANGE MARMALADE.

Grate fine the yellow peel from some ripe deep colored oranges, cut up all that are decorticated, saving the juice and removing the seeds and cores; mix with the pulp the grated peel, add an equal weight of powdered loaf sugar and a very little water, simmer the whole together till it becomes thick and quite transparent. When cold put it up in small glass jars, and cover them with brandy papers.

TO PRESERVE LEMON RIND.

When you are making lemonade, saving lemon juice, &c., save the yellow rind, which must be pared very thin. Weigh them and boil them tender in a small quantity of water; then mix in an equal weight of sugar to that of the lemon rind; boil them together a few minutes till the syrup is quite thick, and then put them up in jars, covering them quite securely. They are very nice for puddings, &c.

ORANGE PEEL PRRSERVED.

Orange peel may be preserved by the above receipt, and is also fine for puddings.

TO KEEP ORANGE PEEL.

Grate as fine as possible the yellow peel from some fine ripe oranges; mix with it an equal weight of powdered loaf sugar, pack it firm in a jar and cover it securely. It is nice to flavor cake, &c. Lemon rind may be kept in the same manner.

TO DRY ORANGE PEEL.

When you eat ripe oranges, or use them in any way that you do not use the peel, pare off the yellow peel neatly, and place them daily in the air till they become dry, turning them over frequently: then put them up in a jar, cover them, and expose them frequently to the air. They may be grated fine, and answer very well for flavoring cakes and puddings, when fresh orange peel.cannot be procured.

SCOTCH MARMALADE.

Mix together equal proportions of strained honey and the juice and pulp of oranges; boil to the proper consistence, skimming it well, and cool and put it up in jars.

TO PRESERVE PINE-APPLES.

Having pared your pine-apples, cut them across in slices, about an inch thick, removing the core from each slice as you proceed, and weigh them; also weigh an equal quantity of loaf sugar, which powder fine. Stack them in a dish in layers of the sugar, cover them and set them by till next day: then put them with the sugar into a preserving kettle, adding half a pint of water to each pound of sugar. Boil it slowly and steadily till the slices of pine-apple are tender, skimming it very well; then spread them out on a dish to cool, and put them up in jars of a proper size. Boil the syrup till tolerably thick, pour it over them, and when cold cover them securely.

PINE-APPLES TO EAT FRESH.

Pare your pine-apples, cut them across in smooth slices, about half an inch thick. Sift on each slice a little powdered loaf sugar, stack them in a dish, cover them, and let them remain untouched for an hour or two before they are eaten.

TO PRESERVE STRAWBERRIES.

Select the large English strawberries, which must be ripe, but firm; pick the stems and blossoms from them, and weigh them, allowing a pound and a quarter of loaf sugar to each pound of the berries. Break up half as many ripe berries as you have weighed; squeeze out the juice and put it in a preserving kettle with the sugar, allowing half a pint of water to each pound of sugar; boil it, skim it well, and then put in your berries. Boil them a few minutes till they look clear, but be careful not to break them; raise them carefully with a perforated ladle, and spread them on dishes in the open air. When cold put them in a jar, boil down the syrup till it is tolerably thick, pour it hot over the berries, let them stand to get cold, and cover them with paper dipped in brandy.

STRAWBERRY JAM.

Take ripe strawberries, pick them carefully and weigh them; mix with them loaf sugar in the proportions of three quarters of a pound of sugar to a pound of the berries. Break them up and simmer them till they are a thick smooth pulp, stirring them frequently. When it is cold put it up in small jars, covering them with brandy papers. A very nice jelly may be made of the English strawberries, made exactly like red currant jelly.

PRESERVED RASPBERRIES.

Select the largest raspberries when ripe, and preserve them in every respect like strawberries.

RASPBERRY JAM.

Raspberry jam should be made exactly like strawberry jam, and also blackberries make a very good jam, prepared in the same manner. A nice jelly may be made of either of these fruits, made and sweetened like red currant jelly.

TO PRESERVE APRICOTS.

Scald and peel some ripe apricots, split them, extract the stones and weigh the apricots. Put them in a deep dish, with their weight of powdered white sugar, strewing the sugar between each layer of apricots, and set them by till next day; then put them with the sugar into a preserving kettle, adding a few spoonfuls of water, boil them slowly for fifteen or twenty minutes, drain them, spread them out on a dish, and set them by till next day. Put them in the syrup, boiling them again for fifteen or twenty minutes, cool them, and put them up in small jars: boil the syrup thick, pour it over them, and cover them securely with brandy papers.

PRESERVED GINGER.

Take the roots of green ginger, pare them, wash them and boil them in a large quantity of fresh water till about half tender; then wash them in cold water, and boil them again in a large quantity of water till tender; then throw them in a pan of cold water, and let them lie till you prepare the syrup. The design of shifting them so often into fresh water, is, to draw out a part of the hot, poignant taste. Having weighed your ginger, weigh some loaf sugar, allowing a pound and two ounces to each pound of ginger. Break up the sugar, put it in a preserving kettle, with half a pint of water to each pound and one white of egg to every four or five pounds; boil and skim it well, and set it by to cool; drain your ginger roots, cut them of uniform shape and size, and put them in a jar. When the syrup is cold, pour it over them, close the jar, and let it remain untouched for three days; then turn off the syrup, boil and skim it, pour it over the ginger, and let it stand for three days longer; then boil and skim it again, flavor it with lemon juice and white wine; boil it again, which by this time should be very thick; pour it scalding over the ginger, cover it closely, and when the syrup has penetrated through them, they will be fit for use.

TO PRESERVE ENGLISH GRAPES.

Take the English white grapes when full grown, just before they get fully ripe. Pick them from the pedicels, weigh them, and to each pound allow a pound and two ounces of the finest loaf sugar, which break up: mix with it half a pint of water to each pound, and the white of one egg to every four or five pounds; boil and skim it well, and then put in your grapes: boil them gently till

they are about half done, which will only take a few
minutes; raise and drain them with a perforated ladle,
and spread them on dishes in the open air. When they
are cold, return them to the syrup, and boil them slowly,
till they look quite transparent; then spread them on
dishes again, but be careful not to break them, and when
cold, put them in glass, or queen's ware jars. Boil the
syrup very thick, skim it, pour it scalding over the grapes,
and when cold, cover them with brandy papers.

GRAPE JELLY.

Take grapes that are entirely ripe, and full of juice;
pick them from the pedicels, crush them to pieces, and
boil them for a few minutes in a preserving kettle. Drip
the juice through a jelly bag, to each pint of which, add
a pound and two ounces of sugar. Boil them gently together till they form a thick, transparent jelly; then cool
it, and put it up in small glass jars, and cover them with
tissue paper. Look to it occasionally, and if it has the
least appearance of fermenting, boil and skim it again,
and put it up as before. A very good dark jelly may be
made of the common winter grapes, and brown sugar,
made as above directed.

TO PRESERVE FOX GRAPES.

Gather your grapes when full grown, but before they
get fully ripe, or the seeds and skins will be unpleasantly
hard and tough. Pick from them the stems: put the
grapes in a large bowl or jar; pour on them enough hot
water to cover them, and let them remain in it till the
water gets cold. Make a syrup of a pound and a quarter
of loaf sugar, and half a pint of water to each pound of
the grapes; clarify it with whites of eggs, and scald the
grapes in it a few minutes, but do not boil them fast, lest
they burst. Raise them carefully with a perforated
ladle, draining the syrup from them, and spread them on
dishes in the air to cool. After which, put them in a
jar, boil the syrup thick, skim it well, pour it over the
grapes, and next day cover them with brandy papers.

GRAPES FOR TARTS.

Gather the small wild grapes after they have taken a a few light frosts. Pick them from the pedicels, stew for fifteen or twenty minutes, in molasses, skimming them well, and when cold, put them in jars with the molasses: cover them, and keep them in a cool place. Examine them occasionally, and if they look like fermenting, sprinkle in a little brown sugar; give them another boil and put them up as before.

TO DRY GRAPES.

Select some of the finest winter grapes after they have taken a few light frosts. Break them off the vines, and hang the bunches up where they will be daily exposed to the air, and entirely excluded from the heat of the sun. They will keep perfectly through the winter, and when you wish to make use of them, pick them from the branches, and stew them in a little water till tender, adding as much sugar as will sweeten them to your taste.

BRANDY GRAPES.

Take fine large bunches of grapes that are fully ripe; put them in a jar in alternate layers of brown sugar, filling the jar two thirds full, and allowing half a pound of brown sugar to each pound of the grapes. Then fill it up with brandy, and close the jar securely, to keep the strength of the brandy from evaporating.

TO PRESERVE GREEN GAGES.

Take green gages that are full grown, but not entirely ripe: put them in a preserving kettle, in alternate layers of green vine leaves: fill it up with water, and scald the green gages over a slow fire. Then take them out, peel them, and weigh them. Put them in the kettle with fresh vine leaves, fill it up with water, hang it over a slow fire till the water gets hot, and set them in a corner where they will keep warm for four or five hours, keeping the kettle closely covered. Allow a pound and a half of loaf sugar to each pound of the fruit; break it up, mix with it half a pint of water to each pound and a half of sugar; drop in the white of an egg to every five pounds, mix it well, boil and skim it; and having drained your green gages, put them in syrup, and boil them gently for fifteen or twenty minutes. Then drain them, spread them out on dishes, and when they get cold, put them in the syrup, and set them by till next day. Then boil them again in the syrup for fifteen or twenty minutes; afterwards cool them, and put them in small jars. Boil the syrup thick, pour it over the fruit, and cover the jars securely with brandy papers.

TO PRESERVE TOMATOES.

Take large deep colored tomatoes that are ripe, but firm; pour boiling water on them to make the skin come off easily; peel them and weigh them. Also weigh an equal portion of the best brown sugar; mix in a very little water, merely enough to dissolve the sugar: add the white of one egg to every three pounds; and boil and skim it well. When the water has pretty well evaporated, put in the tomatoes, with half a lemon to each pound, which must be sliced very thin. Boil them gently till they look like the syrup has penetrated them sufficiently: then take them out carefully, spread them on dishes in the open air, and when cold, put them in a jar. Boil the syrup till it looks very thick and rich; pour it over them and cover them securely.

TO PRESERVE YELLOW TOMATOES.

Take the finest yellow tomatoes when quite ripe and mellow, but before they begin to get soft: take off a thin paring, leaving the tomatoes whole, and weigh them. Weigh an equal quantity of the best loaf sugar; break it up, mix with it half a pint of water to every two pounds, and the white of an egg to every four pounds; put it in a preserving kettle, boil and skim it well, and then put in your tomatoes: let them simmer gently till they begin to look clear, and then remove them from the fire; raise them carefully with a perforated ladle, letting the syrup drain from them into the kettle; spread them on dishes in the open air to cool and harden, and afterwards simmer them in the syrup till they look quite transparent; drain them again, and when cold put them up in jars. Pare the rind from some deep colored lemons, put it in the syrup with enough of the juice to flavor the tomatoes to your taste; simmer the syrup slowly till quite thick, and pour it scalding over the tomatoes. When cold cover them with brandy papers. They will be found very fine.

TOMATO JELLY.

Break up some fine ripe tomatoes; mix with them at least half the rind of a lemon to each pound of the tomatoes, and boil them slowly and steadily to a mash. Squeeze out all the juice, drip it through a thin jelly bag; to each pint of which, add a pound of loaf sugar, broken up, and the juice of half a lemon. Boil them steadily together till they form a very thick jelly; put it up in small jars, and cover them securely. This jelly will be found very nice and convenient, answering for many purposes that a thinner jelly would not.

TOMATO MARMALADE.

Gather your tomatoes when very ripe, peel them, stew them till they are all to pieces; press them through a sieve, and weigh the pulp: to each pound of which, add three quarters of a pound of the best brown sugar, the juice and grated rind of half a lemon, a teaspoonful of powdered cloves, and one of cinnamon. Put the whole into a preserving kettle, simmer and stir it till very thick and smooth, and put it up in small jars, covering them with brandy papers.

TO PRESERVE PLUMS.

Take the largest plums that are ripe, firm, and free from blemish; scald them in boiling water to make the skins come off easily: peel them, weigh, and spread them out on a dish. A very nice way to peel them is, after they are scalded, to pierce them through the skins with a sewing needle, pass it round between the plums, and thin out side skins, and with it draw them off. Allow a pound and a quarter of the best loaf sugar to each pound of the pared plums: powder it fine, sift one half of it over them, and set them by till next day. Then dissolve the remaining half of sugar in a very little water; add the sugar and juice from the plums; mix in enough white of egg to clear it; boil and skim it, and then put in your plums, with as many kernels from the plum seeds as will flavor it well, having pounded them to a paste. Boil them steadily for a few minutes, till the syrup has penetrated them sufficiently, and spread them on dishes to cool. Boil the syrup till thick and rich: put the plums in small jars; pour the syrup over them dividing it equally, and cover them with double tissue paper. Green gages may be preserved by this receipt.

TO PRESERVE PLUMS FOR COMMON PURPOSES.

Take the red thin skinned plums when fully ripe, but firm, and pierce them in several places with a needle. Put them in a preserving kettle with an equal weight of the best brown sugar, and boil them slowly till they are done, but do not suffer them to boil to pieces. Raise them carefully, drain them, spread them out on dishes to cool, and put them up in jars. Boil the syrup till sufficiently thick, skim it well, pour it hot over the plums, and when cold, cover it with papers dipped in brandy.

PLUM MARMALADE.

Take the large egg plums when ripe; scald them to make the skins come off easily; peel them, and boil them to a mash, and press them through a sieve. Return the pulp to the kettle with its weight of loaf sugar, broken up, and simmer them together, till they become a smooth, thick mass, stirring it very frequently. When cold, put it up in small jars, covering them securely with brandy papers.

TO DRY PLUMS.

Take large ripe plums, and cutting each one in two, extract the seeds; spread them on large dishes, sprinkle them lightly with sugar, and expose them daily to the sun till they get a little over half dry, turning them over occasionally. Then put them up in large jars, dispersing among them half their weight of brown sugar, and keep them in a cool, dry place. They will keep well, and will be found fine for puddings, &c.

TO PRESERVE DAMSONS.

Gather your damsons before they get fully ripe, pierce them in several places with a needle, and weigh them. Make a syrup of an equal portion of loaf sugar, and a very little water, clarifying it with whites of eggs. When it has boiled till the water is evaporated, put in your damsons, and boil them slowly and steadily till the syrup has penetrated the middle, which you may tell by taking one out, and mashing and tasting it. By this time the syrup will be very thick and rich; pour it with the damsons into a large bowl, and set it by till next day: then put them in small jars, dividing the syrup equally, and cover them securely with tissue paper.

TO PRESERVE GOOSEBERRIES.

Pick the stems and blossoms from your gooseberries, and divide them in half. Break up one half, boil them tender in a very little water, and strain the liquid through a fine sieve. Weigh the other half of the berries, and to each pound allow a pound and a half of loaf sugar. Break it up, mix with it the syrup, and boil and skim it well. Then put in your whole berries; put the whole into a pitcher, and boil them slowly in an oven of water till they are done, and quite transparent, and the syrup very thick and rich, but avoid breaking them. Put them up in small glass jars, and cover them with double tissue paper.

GOOSEBERRY JAM.

Goosberries for jam must be very ripe. Pick the blossoms and stems, or pedicles from them; stew them till tender in a very little water, and press them through a fine sieve. Weigh the pulp, and to each pound allow a pound and a quarter of loaf sugar. Simmer it gently till thick and smooth, stirring it frequently. When cold put it up in small glass jars; put a spoonful of white brandy on the top of each, and cover them with **tissue** paper.

TO PRESERVE CRANBERRIES.

Take large ripe cranberries, weigh them, rinse them, and put them in a sieve to drain. Weigh half as many berries in another vessel, break them up, and stew them tender in a small quantity of water: squeeze the jelly through a bag, and return it to the kettle. Weigh some loaf sugar, allowing a pound and a half to each pound of the whole berries; dissolve it in the cranberry juice; add the white of an egg to every five pounds, boil it up, skim it, and put in your whole berries. Boil them slowly till they are about half done; then raise them with a perforated ladle, spread them out on dishes, and set them by till next day. Then boil them in the syrup till they are done, and quite transparent; cool them again, put them up in small jars, and cover them with brandy papers.

CRANBERRIES FOR TARTS.

Weigh a pound and a quarter of brown sugar to each pound of cranberries, and divide it in half; stew the berries with one half of the sugar in a very little water till they are done and the syrup low: then put them with the syrup in a jar, disseminating evenly among them the other half of the sugar; cover them securely, and keep them in a cool dry place. They will keep well, and will be found fine for tarts, puddings, &c.

CRANBERRY JELLY.

Take ripe cranberries, break them up in a bowl or earthen pan, and set them by till next day; then boil them, strain the juice through a jelly-bag, and to each pint add a pound and a half of loaf sugar, broken up, and a small portion of calf-foot jelly or dissolved isinglass; simmer it slowly till it is a thick jelly, skimming it well and stirring it frequently: then cool it, put it up in small jars, cover them with brandy papers, and keep them in a cool place.

RED CURRANT JELLY.

Gather your currants when perfectly ripe, strip them from their pedicils, rinse them clean, and drain them till perfectly dry on a sieve. Break them up, put them in a jar, set it in a kettle of boiling water, and boil them for a few minutes; then squeeze the juice through a jelly-bag, to each pint of which allow a pound and a quarter of loaf sugar; put them together in a preserving kettle, and boil them slowly together for fifteen minutes; then put it in a jar, cover it, and set it by for three days. Afterwards boil it gently till it is a thick jelly, carefully removing the froth or scum as it rises. When it gets cold, put it up in small glass jars, and cover them with double tissue paper. Expose the jelly occasionally to the air, and if at any time it has the smallest appearance of fermenting, scald it over a few minutes, skim it, cool it, and put it up as before. White currant jelly may be made in the same manner.

CURRANTS FOR TARTS.

Gather them before they get entirely ripe, pick them from the bunches, and stew them down with an equal weight of the best brown sugar. Put them up in queen's ware jars, cover them securely, and keep them in a cool place. Examine them occasionally, and if need require it, scald them over a few minutes, skim them, and put them up as before.

TO BOTTLE CURRANTS.

Gather your currants while green, pick them from the bunches, put them up in junk bottles that are perfectly clean and dry, cork them securely, dipping the necks into melted rosin, and keep them in a cool place. It is said they will keep good a year. Gooseberries and grapes may be preserved fresh in the same manner.

BLACK CURRANT JELLY.

Gather them when ripe, pick them, break them up, and boil them for a few minutes. Squeeze the liquid through a jelly-bag, and to each pint add one pound of

good brown sugar. Boil it a few minutes, skim it, and
put it up in small jars.

WHITE STRAWBERRY JELLY.

Take the large white strawberries, which are called
the English strawberries: they must be perfectly ripe:
pick the leaves and stems from them, break them up,
put them in a jar, and boil them for a few minutes in a
kettle of water. When they have given out their juices,
sqeeze them through a jelly-bag, and to each pint add a
pound and a quarter of the finest loaf sugar. Put it
again into the jar, boil it in a kettle of water till very
thick, skimming it as it may require, and when cold, put
it up in small jars, covering them with tissue paper. It
is an excellent jelly, and if properly made, it will be perfectly white. A similar jelly may be made in the same
manner of white raspberries.

MULBERRY VEIGA.

Take the common mulberries, when fully ripe, pick
the stems carefully from them, rinse them clean and drain
them on a sieve. Afterwards mash them to a pulp, which
put in a preserving kettle with a few spoonfuls of water,
and simmer it a few minutes; then strain the liquid
through a very fine sieve, pressing it with the back of a
large spoon, to obtain all the liquor you can; to each pint
of which add one pound of loaf sugar, and simmer them
together till they form a thick jelly, skimming it occasionally. Put it up in small jars, and keep them in a
cool place. It will keep well, and if properly made, it
will rope a yard when dropped from a spoon.

TO PRESERVE GREEN CRAB-APPLES.

Gather your crab-apples when full grown, rinse them
clean, put them in a preserving kettle in alternate layers
of green vine leaves, fill it up with water, and scald them a
few minutes; then peel them, extract the cores smoothly
with a small pen-knife, put them in the kettle with a fresh
supply of leaves and water, and scald them till they begin
to look green; then take them out, drain them and weigh

them. Make a syrup of a pound and a half of loaf sugar and half a pint of water to each pound of the prepared crab-apples; mix in the white of an egg to every four or five pounds of the sugar, and boil and skim it well; boil your crab-apples gently in it till they look quite transparent; then cool them on dishes, and put them up in small jars. Boil the syrup till very thick and rich, skim it, and pour it over the crab-apples, dividing it equally: cover them with brandy papers, and keep them in a cool place.

A CONSERVE OF ORANGES.

Take fine ripe oranges, rub off the yellow peel on a loaf of sugar, and then rub in the pulp and juice; scrape off the wet part of the sugar with a knife, and in like manner grate or rub up as many oranges as you wish, scraping off the wet sugar each time, which contains the peel, pulp and juice of the oranges; then pack it away in jars, covering them with brandy papers. If made in the proper manner, it will be like a thick batter, will keep well, and be found very fine when fresh oranges cannot be procured, for creams, cakes, puddings, sauces, &c.

A CONSERVE OF LEMONS.

May be made in the same manner, and is also good for many nice purposes.

MUSKMELON SWEET-MEATS.

Take a long deep colored muskmelon that is ripe, but firm; pare the rind and take out the seeds, scraping out the soft part of the melon. Cut the firm part into large smooth slices, about half an inch thick, weigh them and spread them out on dishes. Weigh an equal portion of loaf sugar, break it up, put it in a preserving kettle with a little water and white of egg to clear it, and boil and skim it till the scum ceases to rise; then put in your melon slices, adding enough lemon juice to flavor them highly. Simmer them gently till they look clear, but be sure you do not break them. Raise them carefully with a perforated ladle, spread them on dishes, set them in the open air till cold, and put them up in small jars, interspersing among them a quarter of a pound of powdered loaf sugar to each pound of the melon. Add to the juice some thin slips of lemon peel, boil it till very thick, so that it will rope when dropped from a spoon, and pour it with the lemon peel over the sweet-meats. Cover the jars securely, and keep them in a cool place.

Pumpkin sweet-meats may be made in the same manner, only they require a greater proportion of lemon juice to flavor them.

TO PRESERVE APPLES.

Take large ripe apples that are firm and sufficiently acid to cook tender; pare them, extract the cores smoothly, and fill the cavities with fresh lemon rind, cut in very thin slips. Boil them till half done in a small quantity of water, and weigh them. Weigh an equal quantity of loaf sugar, dissolve it in the syrup in which the apples were boiled, mix in the white of one egg to every five pounds of sugar, boil it fast for a few minutes till the scum rises, which carefully remove, and then put in your apples. Add enough lemon juice to flavor them well, and boil them slowly and steadily till they are quite transparent, but be careful not to break them. Raise them with a perforated ladle, that the syrup may drain from them into the kettle; spread them out on dishes, set them in the open air till they get perfectly cold, and then put them up in jars. Boil the syrup thick, color it red with sanders or cochineal, pour it over the apples while hot, and next day cover them with paper dipped in brandy.

APPLE MARMALADE.

Pare, core and slice some fine pippin, or some other nice cooking apple; put them in a preserving kettle in layers of the best brown sugar, allowing three quarters of a pound of sugar to each pound of the prepared apples, and interspersing among them some thin slips of lemon peel: boil them slowly till very soft, mashing them to a pulp and stirring them frequently, particularly towards the last. When it gets very thick and smooth, put it up in small queen's ware jars, covering them securely with folded paper.

APPLE JELLY.

Pare and slice from the cores some fine flavored apples that are ripe and juicy. Put them in a preserving kettle. dispersing among them the paring of one lemon to every two pounds of the apples; add a few spoonfuls of water, barely enough to keep them from burning, and simmer them over a bed of coals till they are very soft and all the water has evaporated; then put them in a jelly-bag and squeeze out the juice, to each pint of which add the juice of one lemon. Measure it again, and allow a pound of loaf sugar to each pint of the mixed juice. Put them together in a preserving kettle, simmer them till they form a thick transparent jelly, removing every particle of scum as it rises: then put it in a large bowl or dish to cool, and afterwards put it up in small glass jars, and cover them with papers dipped in brandy.

APPLES PRESERVED WITH CIDER.

Take sweet cider immediately from the press, and boil it in a preserving kettle till reduced to one third its original quantity. Prepare some of the finest cooking apples, by peeling and coreing them smoothly, fill up the holes with the thin yellow peels from some smooth, deep colored oranges, and boil them gently in the cider, till they are tender and quite clear. Then raise them carefully with a perforated ladle, letting the cider drain into the kettle; spread them on dishes, and set them in the open air till they get entirely cold, which will make them tough, and quite transparent. Boil the syrup very thick, adding a little powdered cinnamon, and orange, or lemon juice to flavor it, and having put the apples in a jar, pour the syrup over them, and when cold cover them securely, and keep them in a cool place. Look to them occasionally, and if the least bit of froth rises to the top, boil them over a few minutes, skim them well, and when cold, put them up in a jar as before.

APPLE BUTTER.

Cider for apple butter must be perfectly new from the press, and the sweeter and mellower the apples are of which it is made, the better will the apple butter be.

Boil the cider till reduced to one half its original quantity, and skim it well. Do not use for this purpose an iron kettle, or the butter will be very dark, and if you use a brass or copper kettle, it must be scoured as clean and bright as possible, before you put the cider into it, and you must not suffer the butter to remain in it a minute longer than is actually necessary to prepare it, or it will imbibe a copperish taste, that will render it not only unpleasant, but really unhealthy. It is best to prepare it late in the fall, when the apples are quite mellow. Select those that have a fine flavor, and will cook tender; pare and quarter them from the cores, and boil them in the cider till perfectly soft, having plenty of cider to cover them well. If you wish to make it on a small scale, do not remove the apples from the cider when they get soft, but continue to boil them gently in it, till the apples and cider form a thick smooth marmalade, which you must stir almost constantly towards the last. A few minutes before you take it from the fire, flavor it highly with cinnamon, nutmeg, ginger, and cloves, and when the seasonings are well intermixed, put it up in jars, tie folded paper over them, and keep them in a cool place. If made in a proper manner, it will keep good more than a year, and will be found very convenient, being always in readiness.

Many people who are in the habit of making apple butter, take it from the fire before it is boiled near enough. Both to keep it well, and taste well, it should be boiled long after the apples have become soft, and towards the last, simmered over coals till it gets almost thick enough to slice. If you wish to make it on a large scale, after you have boiled the first kettle full of apples soft, remove them from the cider, draining them with a perforated ladle, that the cider may fall again to the kettle, and put them into a clean tub. Fill up the kettle with fresh apples, having them pared and sliced from the cores, and having ready a kettle of boiling cider, that is reduced to at least half its original quantity; fill up the kettle of apples with it as often as is necessary. When you have boiled in this manner as many apples as you wish, put the whole of them in a large kettle, or kettles, with the cider, and simmer it over a bed of coals till it is so thick, that it is with some difficulty you can stir it: it should be stirred almost constantly, with a wooden spaddle, or paddle, or it will be certain to scorch at the bottom or sides of the kettle. Shortly before you take it from the fire, season it as before directed, and then put it up in jars.

BUTTER, CHEESE, &c.

TO MAKE BUTTER.

To make nice, well tasted butter, the strictest attention must be paid to cleanliness with the vessels in which you keep your milk. You should have two sets of vessels, that they may be regularly scalded and sunned, every two days. Pour the water in them boiling hot, cover them and let them sit till the water gets nearly cold; then empty them, rinse them in clean cold water, and sit them in the sun during the day. Never fail to use plenty of water when preparing for milking, more especially to wash the udders of your cows after the calves have sucked, a practice that is often omitted, to the shame, and discredit of the dairy-maid. The best vessels for milk, are broad shallow pans, or earthen crocks, made of the same shape: there will rise nearly double the quantity of cream in a vessel with a large surface, as will on the same milk when put in a small necked jar or pitcher. The most convenient coverings for such vessels are pieces of plank, cut to fit the tops, and planed smoothly. If it is possible, keep your milk in a spring house, where a current of fresh water may be constantly running round it. If your situation forbids you having a spring house, and you are compelled to keep it in a cellar, have it well aired, and wet the floor every morning with fresh water, which will keep milk very good and cool, in moderately warm weather. Have high, small necked jars, expressly for your cream, and every time you put in a fresh skimming, mix the old and new thoroughly together. Churn at least twice a week in warm weather, or the butter will have an old and unpleasant taste. Be as particular with your churn as any of your other milk vessels, to keep

it well scalded and sunned.   When the butter is beginning
to separate from the fluid, it will first appear in very
small particles on the handle of the dash; but when it
has completely glomerated, there will not be the smallest
speck to be seen, and the dash will be perfectly clean:
this is the most correct way of judging when the butter
is all separated from the fluid.   Raise the butter carefully with the dash, and wash it in several cold waters,
to free it from the buttermilk, the last of which should
look entirely clear.   Salt it lightly with the nicest salt,
and work and beat it with a wooden paddle till every particle of water has exuded from it; the bulk of butter
will of course be smaller, but it will be much sweeter,
firmer, and keep doubly as well as if the water is suffered
to remain in it.

TO PREPARE BUTTER FOR TABLE.

Having worked your butter thoroughly, make each
pound in a separate cake; make them very smooth, and
of a square, or oblong shape, and stamp them with a
wooden print made for the purpose, wetting it each time
with cold water.   A few hours before you send it to table,
put it on a plate, and set it in a pail of fresh water, in
which a little ice has been broken up: this will make it
very cool, sweet and firm.   Shortly before it goes to table,
drain it and wipe the water neatly from the plate.

For large parties, butter may be made into stacks or
cones, and printed neatly, but they are never introduced
at common suppers.

TO KEEP BUTTER.

Take nice fresh butter, wash and work it thoroughly,
salt it as for immediate use, and pack it closely in stone
or earthen jars.   Make a brine of cold water and fine
salt sufficiently strong to bear up an egg; pour it over
the butter, letting it stand two or three inches deep on
the top, cover the jars securely, and keep them in a cool
place.   Each time that you take any out, cut it evenly
from the top, that the brine may remain deeply over it.
If these directions are exactly followed, the butter will
keep good and sweet for some months.   After taking the

butter from the brine, wash it in cold spring or pump water, and work it thoroughly before you send it to table: this will give it a fresh, sweet taste.

TO KEEP CREAM.

Take cream that is thick and perfectly sweet, boil it gently for a few minutes, and skim it well: stir in a pound of powdered loaf sugar to each quart of cream, and simmer it over a few coals for three quarters of an hour, stirring it very frequently. When it gets entirely cold, put it in bottles, cork them securely, dipping the necks in melted rosin, and keep them in a cool place. It is said it will keep well for several months, and may be used for many purposes when fresh cream cannot be obtained.

MILK.

The receipt written for butter will suffice for the management of milk. As soon as you are done churning, pour the buttermilk into a jar, cover it closely, set it in the spring house, and each time, before you take any out for the table, churn it up well for a few minutes with a small dash, made for the purpose, that the thick part of the milk may be well mixed with the whey. Buttermilk is very much liked when rich and new, but it is seldom eaten with any thing else than warm bread and butter. Nice sweet clabber is also fine. When the milk begins to turn sour, put it in a large tureen or bowl, and set it in a cool place. After it is clabbered, do not break it up, but send it to table whole, in the tureen or bowl in which it turned, as the whey will rise on the top very soon after it is broken up, and of course it is not so good. Sprinkle on the top of the clabber a handful of powdered sugar, and provide it with a large spoon to lift it at table. Do not stir it, but take it out by large spoonfuls without breaking what is left in the bowl. Set by it a bowl of powdered sugar and some mixed cinnamon and nutmeg, that the company may season it to suit their own taste. It is eaten as a dessert with sweet-cakes, &c. A little lemon juice mixed in just as it is beginning to turn improves the taste. Never skim the cream from sweet milk, that is to set before company; keep it in the spring house or some other cool place till a few minutes before it is sent to table; then pour it with the cream into a pitcher, drop in it a small lump of ice, and with a bunch of hickory rods or wires, whirl it round and round near the top for a few minutes till a rich froth rises, and send it immediately to the table. It is eaten with pies, tarts, &c.

TO MAKE CHEESE.

If you have the preparation of rennet, it will be found very convenient to use that in the place of dried rennet, allowing a large spoonful of the liquid to each quart of the milk. If you use dried rennet, cut a piece four or five inches square, according to its strength; pour on a gill and a half of lukewarm water, add two large table-spoonfuls of brandy, cover it securely, and set it by to steep till next morning: then, having your milk fresh from the cows, strain it into a large pot or kettle; throw round it a few embers to make it about blood warm, and stir into it the prepared rennet water, allowing a table-spoonful to each quart of milk. Much depends on the strength of the rennet, some having double the gastric juice that others of the same size have: therefore if the milk should not conglomerate and form a firm curd in half an hour, mix in more of the rennet water. As soon as the whole is formed into a firm curd, press out as much of the water as you can conveniently with a saucer, put the curd on a large cloth over a sieve to drain, having first wet the cloth in cold water, to prevent the curd sticking to it; season it lightly with salt, and put it with the cloth into a cheese-hoop; place it in a cheese-press or on a smooth plank, lay a bit of plank on the cheese, putting one corner of the cloth smoothly between, and having the plank cut exactly to fit the inside of the hoop; put a small weight on the top, and press it lightly for several hours; then increase the weight, and let it remain untouched till next morning; then take it out of the hoop, dip the cloth in water, wring it tolerably tight, spread it smoothly over the cheese, and invert it in the hoop: lay the plank again on the top, put on the weight, and let it sit till next day; then take it from the cloth, rub it evenly over with butter, and put it in a wire safe on a smooth plank, where it will be exposed to the air. Turn it over once a day till the outside becomes firm, brushing it each time with a soft cloth and occasionally a little butter. If you press your cheese too hard, it will be dry and crumbly, and if you use too much rennet, it will be tough and porous: therefore both of these extremes should be carefully avoided.

A RICHER CHEESE.

Set your night's milk in a cool place, where it will keep perfectly sweet till next morning; then skim it, and having strained your morning's milk into a clean pot or kettle, mix your cream with it, and proceed as before directed, mixing in half a pint of wine to every gallon of milk, or half as much brandy, which will answer well. You may flavor it with bitter almonds, peach kernels, rose water, or any thing you please, and you may color it, if you choose, to look very rich with a little saffron or anatto, both being perfectly harmless. When the whey is drained from the curd, break it up in a tray, sprinkle it lightly with salt, and finish it in every respect as directed in the preceding receipt The flavor may be improved by keeping them in layers of grass for several weeks after they have become dry and firm, changing the grass every day, which should be perfectly dry when it is put about the cheese.

CREAM CHEESE.

Having kept your night's milk perfectly sweet, skim it, and mix the cream with the morning's; make it lukewarm over a few embers, and stir into it enough of the preparation of rennet, to turn it to a curd in twenty or thirty minutes, adding half a pint of wine to each gallon of the milk, a little rose water, and a small portion of salt. When a firm curd is formed, drain the whey from it, put it in wet cloths, place them smoothly in small cheese hoops, and press them lightly: next day turn them, wetting the cloth, and press them lightly again for twenty-four hours; then brush them over well with butter, using a soft cloth; place them in a wire safe, or

some other convenient place where the air will have free
admission to them, taking care to turn them over every
morning, and brush them lightly with a soft cloth, and
a little butter. In one week they will be fit for use.
Scrape and brush the outsides neatly, and send them to
table whole, as they should be quite small. They are
eaten at tea, and are considered very fine. They look
very pretty pressed in hoops of a conical shape, and sent
whole to be sliced at table. When you press them in
such hoops, you must have a small hole made in the top,
or pinacle of each hoop for the whey to escape, and place
the small ends downwards while pressing.

COTTAGE CHEESE.

Take a large bowl of milk that is just beginning to
turn sour, cover it and set it in the corner where it will
keep lukewarm till it forms a curd. Then place a linen
cloth over a sieve; put in your curd, fold over the corners of the cloth to keep out the dust, and let it drain till
next morning, without pressing it in the least. Then
turn it in an earthen dish, add as much rich, sweet cream
as will make it a little soft; add a large spoonful of butter to each pint of the curd, mixing in a very little salt,
and work it with a spoon till the whole is very smoothly
mixed. Then put it in a china bowl, and set it in a
cool place till the tea-table is ready. This kind of cheese
may be made of entire sweet milk, by turning it with a
little preparation of rennet, but you must not make near
as stiff a curd as for cinnamon cheese.

TO TOAST CHEESE.

Take a cheese that is sufficiently dry and firm; peel
off the skin, and cut the cheese in smooth slices, about
one third of an inch thick. Toast them till soft in a
cheese toaster, and serve them up warm in a glass, or
china plate. If you toast them on a gridiron, clean it
nicely; grease the bars, and place it over a bed of clear
coals; turn the slices over once, and remove them as soon
as they become soft, or they will soon drop to pieces.

Another way is to cut some nice smooth slices of
bread, all of equal size; put a slice of butter on each:

grate cheese thickly over them, and brown them delicately with a salamander. Serve them warm, and eat them at supper.

GRATED CHEESE.

Of course there can be no great art in grating cheese. The prime reason why I give a receipt for it, as well as many others, is because it is a fashionable mode of serving it.

Take cheese that are well dried; remove the hard peeling; grate the cheese fine, and serve it in small plates.

A very common way to serve cheese, is to peel and slice them neatly, and lay them on a glass or china plate.

COFFEE, TEA, AND CHOCOLATE.

TO MAKE COFFEE.

To make good coffee, keep your tea-kettle and coffee boiler neatly scalded and sunned, and occasionally drop a few live coals, or a spoonful or two of wood ashes in them with the boiling water; then rinse and sun them well: this mode of cleansing them will keep them perfectly sweet.

A coffee toaster is much preferable to an open vessel for roasting coffee, as when done in the latter, much of the strength is lost in the process. It should be picked carefully, and toasted regularly, making the whole of rather a dark brown, and adding a small lump of butter, which will assist in parching it evenly. As soon as the grains become brittle, they are parched or toasted enough; then remove it instantly from the fire, or it will have a bitter taste. To have it in perfection, it should be toasted but a short time before it is made, and ground while it is yet warm: if it lies only twenty four hours after it is toasted, a part of the nice flavor will be lost. The most common rule is to allow half a pint of ground coffee to three quarts of water; but all coffee is not of the same strength, therefore this rule will not always hold good, and of course a little judgment will be required on the part of the cook. Mix with half a pint of ground coffee the white of one egg, adding as much water as will make it of the consistence of thick batter, mix it well, put it in your coffee boiler, and then pour in the water, which should be boiling. It may also be cleared with the yolk of eggs, or isinglass: if cleared with the latter, put the water boiling into the coffee boiler, put in your coffee by spoonfuls, stirring it as you proceed, and then drop in two or three small chips of isinglass. When it boils hard, and rises up to the top of the boiler, remove it further from the fire, set it on a trivet over a small bed of coals, and let it boil gently for thirty or forty minutes; then scrape down the grounds from the sides of the boiler, pour out half a cupful of the coffee, to get the grounds out of the spout, pour it again into the boiler, add a small cupful of cold water, and set it in the corner for a few minutes to settle. After which, having scalded your coffee-pot, turn the coffee carefully into it, leaving the grounds undisturbed in the boiler, and send it hot to table. If cream is used, it must be sweet and rich.

TO DRAW COFFEE.

To draw coffee, you must have a biggin, which is quite a common article, various sizes of which can be readily purchased at the tin stores. Scald your biggin properly, and having your coffee freshly toasted and ground fine, put it in the biggin, and pour on the water, which should be boiling. Eggs and isinglass need not be used when coffee is made in a biggin, as it will be sufficiently clear without their aid   Shut down the lid, set it near the fire, and as soon as the coffee has drained through the coarse and fine strainers into the pot, or receiver below the spout, it will be ready for use. (The best strainers are made of perforated tin.) Scald your coffee pot, pour the coffee into it, and send it to the table hot. Drawn coffee is thought by some to be at once food and medicine. When you have to substitute sweet milk for cream, to use in coffee, it will be found an improvement to boil the milk and make use of it while hot.

TEA.

In buying tea, try to get the best quality, selecting only such as looks firm and glossy, and has a strong fragrant smell. Tea that is very dry and crumbly, affording but little smell or taste, is sure to be weak, having lost much of its excellency. The best of green tea will look smartly green in the cup, after it is drawn, and good black tea will look dark.

The strictest attention should be paid to your tea-pots and tea-kettles, to keep them well scalded and sunned, otherwise the best of tea will be indifferent when drawn.

Scald your tea-pot well, then put in your tea, pour on enough boiling water to cover it well, shut down the lid, and set it before the fire to infuse for ten or fifteen minutes; then fill up the pot with boiling water from a tea-kettle, and send it immediately to table, with another tea-pot filled with boiling water to weaken it at table, for those who may prefer it. If you have a large company, of course you must have more than one pot of tea: then it will be more convenient to have a tea-kettle of boiling water placed on a chafing-dish and set in the room for the purpose of filling your pots; or, if you choose, just before you sit down to table, put a portion of tea in a cup, pour on a little boiling water, cover it closely with a saucer or small plate, and let it set on your tea-board to steep, and after you have filled the first course of cups, put the tea from the cup into the tea-pot, and fill it up immediately with water from a boiling kettle, that the second course of cups may be as strong as the first. Never fail to have your tea perfectly hot when you fill the cups, otherwise it will not be good.

The black tea is considerably weaker than the green: of course a larger quantity of it will be required for a drawing. Two tea-spoons, heaping full of good tea, will be enough for a pint of water.

CHOCOLATE.

Chocolate cakes are carved in little squares on one side, to each of which, if the chocolate is good, allow about three jills of water. Scrape it very fine with a knife, mix it with just enough boiling water to dissolve it, mashing it with a spoon till smooth, and then put it in a block-tin boiler, mix in the remaining water, which must also be boiling, cover it, set it on a trivet over a bed of coals, and boil it gently till reduced to about two thirds its original, giving it a light stirring two or three times: then replenish it with cream or rich sweet milk, making the boiler as full as it first was with water; watch it closely, stirring it a little till it boils up; then take it instantly from the fire, or it will boil over the top and a good part of it be lost. Whirl round in it, near the top, a chocolate mill, (or a small bunch of bended wires will answer,) till you raise a rich froth on the top, and send it to table hot, accompanied with chocolate cakes, dry toasts or hard rusks.

DOMESTIC LIQUORS, &c.

LEMON BRANDY.

Slice half a dozen fresh lemons, put them in a quart of peach brandy, cover the jar securely, and let it sit till the flavor of the lemons is extracted: then strain it, and to each pint of the liquid add half a pound of powdered loaf sugar. When the sugar is completely dissolved, put it up in small bottles, cork them securely, dipping the necks into melted rosin, and keep them in a cool place. A few spoonfuls of this will give an excellent flavor to puddings, mince pies, &c.

ORANGE BRANDY,

May be made as directed for lemon brandy, substituting oranges for lemons.

LEMON CORDIAL.

Take one dozen large ripe lemons, roll them under your fingers on a table, to increase the juice; pare off the yellow rinds, put them in three quarts of white brandy, and cover them closely. Squeeze the juice of the pared lemons on four pounds of loaf sugar, cover it and set it by till next day: then boil three pints of sweet milk, mix the sugar, brandy, &c. together, and pour the boiling milk among it; cover it and set it away for one week, shaking it up once a day; then strain it, put it into a demi-john, and let it stand four or five weeks: afterwards filter it through a piece of muslin, having it confined to a sieve, and bottle and cork it securely.

TO KEEP LEMON JUICE.

To each pint of the lemon juice, after settling, add one pound of powdered loaf sugar, mix it well, cover it and set it by till next day. Have ready some pint bottles that are clean and dry; put four table-spoonfuls of white brandy in each, and fill them up with the juice. Cork them securely, dipping the necks in melted rosin.

LEMON SYRUP.

Select one dozen large deep colored lemons, weigh eight pounds of loaf sugar, break it up in large pieces, and with it grate or rub off all the yellow rind of the lemons; put them in a bowl, pour on them three pints of boiling water, cover it and let it stand till it gets cold; then squeeze in all the juice from the twelve decorticated lemons, mix it well, put it into small bottles, corking them securely, and keep them in a cool place. A very little of this syrup, mixed with iced water, makes a cooling effervescent drink in summer.

Lime syrup may be prepared in the same manner.

LEMONADE.

Take ripe lemons, roll them under your fingers on a table till they appear like they are full of juice; then squeeze the juice into a bowl, to each pint of which allow three pints of water, or if in summer, allow two and a half pints of water and a lump of ice equal to the other half pint. Sweeten it to your taste with loaf sugar, and serve it up in small glasses.

ORANGE-ADE.

May be made in every respect by the receipt written for lemonade.

PORTABLE LEMONADE.

Take twelve ounces of loaf sugar, pulverize it with two ounces acid tartar and two drachms essence of lemon; divide into fifty papers, each for a tumbler of water.

SECOND MODE.—Loaf sugar two pounds, concrete acid of lemons half an ounce, and essence of lemons one drachm.

TO KEEP ORANGE JUICE.

Squeeze the juice from some fine ripe oranges, and to each pint add a pound of powdered loaf sugar. Put it up in small bottles, and secure the corks with melted rosin.

ROSE BRANDY.

Fill a glass jar with fresh rose leaves, pour over them as much white brandy as the jar will hold; cover them and set them by to steep till the flavor of the roses is extracted; then drain them out, fill up the jar with fresh rose leaves, cover them, and let them stand again for at least twenty-four hours; drain them out again, and in like manner fill up the jar the third and fourth time. Then strain and bottle it. It is thought by many to be superior to distilled rose water for flavoring cakes, puddings, &c. To make the liquid more odoriferous, you may add some fragrant pink leaves, sweet williams, &c.

ROSE CORDIAL.

Fill a jar with fragrant rose leaves, merely cover them with lukewarm water, and let them steep for twenty-four hours. Then squeeze out the leaves, and fill up the jar again with fresh rose leaves. Repeat this process till you have a strong infusion, and filter it through a piece of muslin, pinned to a fine sieve. Mix with the liquid half its quantity of white brandy; sweeten it with loaf sugar, flavor it with cinnamon and nutmeg, and bottle it for use.

CHERRY CORDIAL.

Your cherries should be very ripe, and full of juice. Pick them from the stems, break them up, mash a few of the seeds, put them with the cherries and juice into an earthen or queensware jar, and set it in a kettle of boiling water; boil them gently till they become soft, and squeeze the juice through a bag. Put it in a preserving kettle, with loaf sugar, in the proportions of three pounds to each gallon of the juice; boil it a few minutes, skim it well, and set it by to cool. Afterwards mix with it a pint of brandy to each three pints of the juice before it was mixed with the sugar, and bottle it for use.

CHERRY SHRUB.

Break up some fine ripe cherries, press out all the juice, and put it in a preserving kettle, with a pound of loaf sugar to each quart of the juice. Break up a few of the cherry seeds, boil them in a very little water, till the flavor is extracted, and strain the liquid into the juice and sugar. Boil it for eight or ten minutes, skim it, and cool it. Have ready some small bottles, washed clean, and dried; put in each a wine glass of brandy; fill them with the syrup, and cork them securely. It makes very delicate ice, frozen over twice, as directed for ice creams, and is also fine, mixed with iced waters.

CHERRY BOUNCE.

Mix together equal proportions of black hearts and morella cherries, which must be very ripe, and full of juice. Extract one half of the stones, and break up the other half with the cherries. Weigh the whole, and to each six pounds add one gallon of rectified whiskey. Put it in a cask, stop it closely, and let it set in a cool place for two months, shaking it up frequently for the first month. Then draw off the liquor, strain it, dissolve in it one pound of loaf sugar, or of sugar candy, to each gallon, and bottle it for use.

RASPBERRY CORDIAL.

Gather your raspberries when ripe and full of juice; pick the leaves and stems from them, break them up, and squeeze out the juice; to each three pints of which allow a pint of white brandy; put it in a demijohn, stop it close ly, and let it stand for two weeks. Then filter it through a piece of muslin pinned on the bottom of a fine sieve, dissolve in it two pounds and a half of sugar to each gallon, and bottle and cork it securely.

STRAWBERRY CORDIAL.

Pick your strawberries when very ripe, and make the cordial by the preceding receipt. Never boil delicate fruit for cordial, or the flavor will be injured.

BLACKBERRY CORDIAL.

Blackberry cordial is considered good medicine for children in cases of affections of the bowels, &c., and it is thought that the medical quality is improved by boiling the berries. Gather them when in the height of perfection, pick them carefully, as there are some very poisonous bugs that dwell among them; break them up, boil them a few minutes in a preserving kettle, adding a few spoonfuls of water. Squeeze the juice through a cloth, put it again in the kettle, having first washed it clean; add three quarters of a pound of loaf sugar to each quart of the juice, and boil and skim it for ten minutes. When it is quite cold, mix with it the brandy, which should be in the proportions of a pint to each three pints of the juice before it was mixed with the sugar; let it stand till the sugar is completely dissolved, and then bottle it for use.

RASPBERRY SYRUP.

Squeeze the juice from some fine ripe raspberries; strain it, put it in a preserving kettle with a pound of loaf sugar to each quart of the juice, boil it up, skim it, and cool it. Put it up in small bottles, putting in each a wine glass of brandy, and filling them quite full of the syrup; cork them securely, and keep them in a cool place. It makes delicate ice, and also makes a fine beverage, mixed with iced water.

STRAWBERRY SYRUP.

May be prepared by the above receipt. The berries should be perfectly ripe, put in a preserving kettle that is nicely cleaned, and only boiled a few minutes, or the flavor will be much impaired.

RASPBERRY SHRUB.

Gather fine ripe raspberries, (the English ones are best,) pick them, but do not wash them, break them up, and put them in a jar. Pour in as much good vinegar as will cover them well, close the jar, and let them steep for several days. Then strain them through a cloth, pressing them, to obtain all the juice you can; pour it on a fresh supply of berries, let them set again for several days, then boil them up, strain the liquid through a cloth, and set it by to cool. Mix with it half a pound of loaf sugar to each quart of the liquid, and when it is completely dissolved, and the liquid cold, bottle it, securing the corks with melted rosin. Strawberry shrub may be made in the same manner, and either is very nice, mixed with iced water, for a summer drink.

SYRUP OF VINEGAR.

Put two sliced lemons, two sliced oranges, a pound of sugar, and a quart of honey, with one gallon of the best vinegar; boil them together till they form a thick syrup, keeping the vessel closely covered, and then strain, cool, and bottle it. A little of this syrup, mixed with iced water in summer, makes a delicious beverage. A very good syrup may be made of the best vinegar and sugar, in the proportions of two pounds of sugar to one gallon of vinegar, and boiled till tolerably thick.

PEACH CORDIAL.

Select the ripest and finest flavored clingstone peaches, wash off the down, wipe them dry, and cut them from the stones. Break up half of the stones, extract the kernels, and bruise them slightly. Put them with the prepared peaches into a cask, filling it quite full; pour on as much of the best peach brandy as the cask will hold, stop it up, and let it stand for two months, shaking it up occasionally. Then draw off the liquid, dilute it to the strength you like it; add two and a half pounds of brown sugar to each gallon after it is diluted, and when the sugar is dissolved, filter it through a muslin rag, having it pinned on the bottom of a fine sieve. Cork it up in bottles or a demijohn for use.

PEACH LICURE.

Wipe the down from some fine ripe free-stone peaches, break them up, extract the kernels from the stones, bruise them, and put them with the broken peaches into a cask. Pour on as much good peach brandy as will cover them, (the older the brandy is the better it will be for the purpose,) close the cask, and set it by for two months, shaking it up occasionally: then draw off the liquor, mix with it strained honey in the proportions of one quart to each gallon of the liquor, filter it through a muslin rag, and bottle it for use, corking them securely.

MINT CORDIAL

Gather some young tender stalks of mint early in the morning; pick off the leaves, put them in a jar, pour on enough rectified whiskey to cover them, close the jar, and set it by for two days. Then squeeze out the mint, and fill up the jar again with fresh mint. Repeat this the third and fourth time; lastly, strain it, add two pounds of sugar to each gallon of the brandy, and bottle and cork it up for use. When you wish to make use of it, dilute it to the proper strength with water, and add more sugar.

TANSY CORDIAL,

May be made by the above receipt. The principal design of these cordials is to preserve the juice, to use when the fresh materials cannot be procured, as it is much cheaper than to use the essence, and the flavor is equally as nice.

QUINCE CORDIAL.

Select the finest ripe quinces, that are free from blemish, cut them up, put them in a strong linen bag, and squeeze out the juice. Mix with each three quarts one quart of brandy, put it in a demijohn, and in two weeks, filter it through a piece of muslin, pinned on the bottom of a fine sieve. Afterwards mix in two and a half pounds of loaf sugar to each gallon, and when the sugar is dissolved, bottle it for use.

GRAPE CORDIAL.

Take fox grapes, or any other nice kind, when fully ripe; pick them from the bunch, break them up and squeeze out the juice, to each three quarts of which allow one quart of French brandy; cork it up in a demijohn, and let it remain undisturbed for two weeks; then strain it, mix with each gallon two pounds of the best brown sugar, and put it up in bottles for use.

GRAPE SYRUP.

Squeeze the juice from some fine ripe grapes; strain it, put it in a preserving kettle with a pound of loaf sugar to each quart, and boil and skim it well. When it is quite cold, mix with it a gill of rectified whiskey to each quart, and bottle and cork it securely, dipping the necks into melted rosin.

GOOSEBERRY CORDIAL.

Pick the stems from a quantity of gooseberries, which should be grown, but not quite ripe; break them up, put them in a preserving kettle with just enough water to cover them, and boil them for a few minutes; then strain the juice through a cloth, and having washed the kettle, put in the juice with three quarters of a pound of sugar to each quart; boil it again for a few minutes, skim it well, and set it by to cool. Afterwards add a gill of brandy to each quart, and put it up in bottles.

CURRANT SYRUP.

Gather some fine red currants when fully ripe; pick them from the stems, break them up with a small wooden mallet, and squeeze out the juice. Put it in a preserving kettle, with a pound of loaf sugar to each quart of the juice, and boil it to a rich syrup, skimming it very well:

then cool it, put it up in quart bottles, having put a gill of brandy in each, and cork them securely, dipping the necks into melted rosin. This syrup makes an excellent summer beverage, mixed with iced water.

PLUM CORDIAL.

Break up some fine ripe plums, and boil them in a small quantity of water till soft, adding the kernels from half of the plum seeds, after bruising them. Strain the liquid through a cloth, and to each three quarts add two pounds and a half of the best brown sugar. Boil it up, skim it, and cool it: put in a quart of brandy to every three quarts of the syrup, and bottle it for use.

CRAB-APPLE SHRUB.

Gather your crab-apples when ripe, break them up with a wooden mallet, and boil them for a few minutes in just enough water to cover them: then strain the liquid and set it by till next day; mix with it a pound and a half of loaf sugar to each quart of the liquid, and boil and skim it well. When it is cold, put it up in quart bottles, putting in each a gill of brandy, and mix it with iced water for a summer's drink.

CURRANT WINE.

Break up fine ripe currants, having first picked them from the stems; put them in a linen bag, and squeeze out all the juice you can. Mix with it an equal quantity of water, adding to each gallon three pounds of loaf sugar. Boil it up, skim it, and put it into a cask; stop it securely, and let it remain undisturbed from two to four weeks, according to the quantity you have, a common sized barrel requiring four weeks: then draw it off carefully, leaving the lees or settlings in the cask; bottle it, and keep it in a cool place. It will not be fit for use under a year. Age improves it.

CIDER WINE.

Gather a quantity of the common grapes when fully ripe, pick them from the bunch, put them in a cask, and cover them with peach brandy; stop the cask, and let them stand for two or three weeks to infuse: then put in sweet cider, just from the press, allowing one gallon of brandy to four of cider. Stop up your cask, and if it is a thirty gallon one, having made it late in the fall, let it remain untouched till spring. About one bushel of shelled grapes is the common allowance for a thirty gallon cask. By that time the wine will be very clear; then draw it off the grapes, &c., and put it in a clean cask or demijohn for use.

GOOSEBERRY WINE.

Gather a quantity of gooseberries when ripe, pick the stems and blossoms from them, break them up with a mallet or beetle, and put them in a jar. Pour over half as much boiling water as you had whole berries, cover them and set them by till next morning: then strain the juice through a cloth, measure it, and to each gallon allow three and a half pounds of loaf sugar. When the sugar is dissolved, put the liquid into a cask of suitable size, filling it nearly full, and do not put in the bung till the liquid is done fermenting; then add a pint of white brandy to every gallon of the fermented liquor, and stop up the cask securely. At the end of four or five months, according to the size of the cask, draw off the liquid carefully, and put it into bottles, having first put some small lumps of loaf sugar into each one; then cork them closely, dipping the necks in melted rosin or sealing wax, and keep them lying on the sides, in a box of dry saw dust, or sand, which should be set in a dry, cool place. You may begin to make use of it as soon as bottled.

SECOND MODE FOR MAKING GOOSEBERRY WINE.—First, pick the leaves and stems from ten gallons of ripe gooseberries, break them up, put them into thirty gallons of water, and set them by till next day. Then strain the liquid, and to each gallon add two pounds of sugar, ferment, and afterwards bung it up.

THIRD.—Bruised berries, eighty pounds, water, ten gallons; next day strain the juice, to each gallon add two pounds and a half of loaf sugar, ferment and cork it up.

FOURTH.—Break up the ripe berries, press the juice through a sieve, to each five gallons of which add ten gallons of water, and thirty-five pounds of sugar. Ferment, and afterwards cork it up.

FIFTH.—Take a hundred pounds of gooseberries when ripe, break them up, put them in a fifteen gallon cask, with enough water to fill it, add ten pounds of brown sugar, and let it stand for four months, then draw it off, and cork it up. It will be very transparent, but tolerably sour.

RED CURRANT WINE,

May be made by the above receipt. It makes a pleasant red wine, that keeps well, but is rather tart.

RASPBERRY WINE.

Select the finest raspberries, which are ripe, and full of juice. Pick them carefully, crush them to pieces, squeeze out the juice, and measure it. Pour as much boiling water on the mashed berries as you have juice, let it stand a few hours, to extract from them the remaining juice, and then mix all the liquid together, and strain it. Dissolve in it three pounds of loaf sugar to each gallon, mixing in the white of one egg to every two quarts, and boil and skim it, till the scum ceases to rise. When it is cold, put it in a keg till it is done fermenting, leaving the bung quite loose; then put it in bottles, sealing the corks, and keep them in a cool place, buried in a box of dry saw dust. With these proportions, no brandy is necessary.

GRAPE WINE.

Take the white grape when fully ripe, pick them from the pedicels, pound them to a pulp, and put them in a large stone jar or jars. Pour over them half as much boiling water as you had whole grapes, cover them, and let them stand till next day; then squeeze out all the juice, and strain it. Mix in three pounds of loaf sugar, and the whites of two eggs to each gallon of the grape liquid, and boil and skim it till the scum ceases to rise, which will only be a few minutes. When cold, put it in a keg till done fermenting, and then bottle it, putting a lump of loaf sugar into each, and sealing the corks. Bury them in a box of dry saw dust, keep them in a cool place, and turn them over frequently.

CIDER SYRUP.

Take the best flavored cider, immediately from the press, mix with it two quarts of strained honey to each gallon of the cider, and boil them together in a preserving kettle, till they form a thick syrup, skimming it as it may require. Flavor it with essence of lemon, and of cinnamon, and when cold, bottle it, putting in a gill of brandy to each quart of the syrup. It is excellent, mixed with cold water.

ORGEAT.

Mix together three ounces of shelled sweet almonds, and one ounce of bitter ones. Pound them, a few at a time, to a paste, adding by degrees enough orange flour, or rose water, to prevent them oiling, and removing them as you proceed. In the mean time, boil with three pints of entire sweet milk a stick of cinnamon till the flavor is extracted; then take out the cinnamon, stir in half a pound of loaf sugar, and set it by to cool. Afterwards, stir in the almond paste, set it over a few coals, till it comes to a boil, and remove it instantly from the fire. Pass it through a very fine sieve into a bowl, and stir it occasionally till it gets cold. Then mix in half a pint of brandy, put it into decanters, and when you set it before your guests, accompany it with a pitcher of iced water, that they may dilute it, if preferred so. It is a good plan to keep almond paste in readiness, as it will keep good for several months, by mixing with it a small portion of loaf sugar, and packing it away in little queensware jars; then when you wish to make use of it, dissolve a small lump of it in iced water toddy, or prepare it in the usual manner, as directed.

RAISIN WINE.

Chop sixty pounds of raisins, put them in a cask with fifteen gallons of water, and let them remain for two weeks, stirring them every day: then press them out, put the liqud into a clean cask, leaving the bung loose till it is done hissing. Afterwards add four pints of brandy and bung it up closely. Some use nearly double this quantity of raisins: it makes the wine much richer to be sure, but it is quite extravagant.

BLACK CURRANT WINE.

Take the currants when ripe, pick them and bruise them, and to every twenty pounds add a gallon of brandy, twelve gallons of water and a gill of good yeast. Let it stand to ferment for eighteen days; then filter, bottle and cork it securely. It yields a thick, purplish colored wine.

MIXED FRUIT WINE.

Mix together equal proportions of white currants and red gooseberries, break them up, press out the juice, and to each gallon add two gallons of water and three pounds and a half of sugar. Ferment and bottle as other wines.

ANOTHER MODE FOR MIXED FRUIT WINE.—Take equal proportions of red and black currants, black-heart cherries and raspberries; to each four pounds of the bruised fruit add one gallon of water, steep for three days, press, and to each gallon of the liquor add three pounds of sugar; ferment and add to each ten gallons a quart of brandy. Age improves this wine. After standing some weeks, mix in an ounce of isinglass, dissolved in a little water, which will make it very clear.

CHERRY WINE.

Take twenty-five pounds of ripe cherries, bruise them, put them in a cask with five gallons of water and four pounds of sugar. After it has well fermented, draw it off and put it in a clean cask, closing the bung.

ELDER WINE.

Take the berries when ripe, press out the juice, and to each gallon add a gallon and a half of water, stirring in three pounds of brown sugar to each gallon after it is mixed, and a pint of brandy to every five gallons; put it in a cask with the bung put in loosely, let it stand for six or eight days to ferment, and then close the bung very tight. At the end of six months draw off a quart of it, mix in the whites of a few eggs that have been beaten to a froth, or a little dissolved isinglass, pour it again into the cask, mix it well, let it stand two weeks longer to refine, and then bottle it.

GINGER WINE.

Bruise six pounds of root ginger, mix with it five gallons of water, and boil it for twenty five or thirty minutes; add fifteen pounds of brown sugar, boil till dissolved, cool, strain, and put it in a cask with eight sliced lemons, one quart of brandy and a little yeast. When it is done fermenting, close the bung, let it remain untouched for three months, and then bottle it.

ORANGE WINE.

Dissolve fourteen pounds of sugar in five gallons of water, mix in the whites of three eggs, boil, skim it, and pour it while boiling upon the parings of fifty oranges. Squeeze the juice from the oranges, and when the liquid is nearly cold, mix them together, adding a pint of good yeast. Let it ferment three or four days; then strain it into a barrel and bung it loosely. In a month add a quart of brandy, and in three months more it will be fit for use. All these wines may be made without the aid of brandy, if preferred so, except elder wine.

PORT WINE.

Take twenty-four gallons sweet cider, six gallons elder berry juice, English port wine four gallons, brandy one gallon and a half, logwood one pound, and twelve ounces of isinglass, dissolved in some of the cider. Put all together in a cask, bung it up, and in three months it will be fit to bottle, but should not be used for a year, as age improves it. If a rough flavor is desired, a small portion of alum may be added.

CHAMPAIGN.

Dissolve twelve pounds of loaf and ten of brown sugar in nine gallons of water, mix in the whites of four eggs, boil it gently and skim it well, add concrete acid of lemons, or crystalized acid of tartar, six drachms, and before it gets entirely cold, mix in a pint of good yeast and ferment. When it is nearly done working, add one gallon of perry, three pints of brandy, and bung it up for three months: then draw out a quart, dissolve in it one ounce of isinglass, pour it again in the cask, to clear it, and in two weeks it will be ready to bottle. If a red color is desired, mix in an ounce of cochineal before it is first bunged.

MADEIRA.

Grind two bushels of pale malt, infuse it in twenty-four gallons of boiling water, and strain it while warm. Mix with the liquor twelve pounds of sugar candy, and when completely dissolved, stir in a pint and a half of good yeast. When the fermentation is nearly over, add five quarts of raisin wine, one gallon of port wine and one gallon of brandy. Bung it up and let it remain for nine or twelve months. Age improves it.

SHERRY WINE.

Boil sixteen gallons of water, dissolve in it thirty-two pounds of loaf sugar and ten pounds of sugar candy; boil it again, add six gallons of pale ale or malt liquid, made as for madeira, and a pint of yeast. On the third day add ten pounds of stoned raisins, and in three days more one gallon of brandy. Bung it up for four months, then draw it off in another cask, add another gallon of brandy, and in four months more bottle it.

These last four wines are imitations of foreign wines, and may be substituted for seasonings, &c.

RUM SHRUB.

Take rum ten gallons, water five gallons, concrete acid of lemons eight ounces, raisin wine four gallons, orange flour water half a gallon, and strained honey three quarts. Put all together in a cask of suitable size, and cork it up securely.

BRANDY SHRUB.

Mix together one gallon of brandy, five pints of water, half a pint of lemon juice and the rinds of two, a pint of orange juice and the peel of four, and three pounds of sugar. Put all together in a demijohn, and cork it up, shaking it till well mixed.

LONDON PORTER.

For one barrel, take a bushel and a half of malt, which must be mashed and stirred very hard with a wooden spaddle, forming it into a mush with boiling water. Whilst the water is boiling, before you pour it on the malt, add to it a pound and a half of hops, one and a half pounds of liquorice root, four pounds of sugar, a quart of molasses, one drachm of capsicum, Spanish liquorice half an ounce, linseed half an ounce, cinnamon one ounce, and heading two drachms: boil all together a few minutes, strain the malt while boiling, and proceed as above directed. When it gets nearly cold, mix in two quarts of good yeast, and when it gets well to working, add an ounce of bruised ginger, and one drachm of coculus indicus; then barrel and finish the working, refining with an ounce of dissolved isinglass.

SPRUCE BEER POWDERS.

Twenty-six grains salt of tartar, essence of spruce ten grains, and white sugar one drachm, two scruples; pulverize and mix: (this much is for each blue paper:) acid of tartar half a drachm in each white paper: these allowances to be mixed in half a pint of water.

GINGER BEER POWDERS.

White sugar one drachm, two scruples, powdered ginger five grains, salts of tartar twenty-six grains in each blue paper, acid of tartar one scruple and a half in each white paper. These proportions are for half a pint of water.

SODAIC POWDERS.

Carbonate of soda half a drachm in each blue paper, and acid of tartar twenty-five grains in each white paper: these quantities for half a pint of water. It makes a cooling beverage in summer.

CREAM DES BARBADES.

Slice four oranges and four lemons, break up four ounces of cinnamon, two drachms of mace and one of cloves; put them together in two gallons and a half of rum to digest; add a sufficient quantity of sugar to sweeten it, and cork it up for use.

CREAM DES BARBADES, ENGLISH

Slice twenty-four lemons and six citrons, bruise eight ounces of fresh balm leaves, and put the whole in a mixture of two gallons and a half of syrup of violet roses and three gallons of water; add eight pounds of sugar, digest for two weeks, and strain and bottle it for use.

CHREME DE NOYAU, ENGLISH.

Blanch eight ounces of bitter almonds, put them into half a gallon of proof spirits; add two pounds of loaf sugar and cork it up.

CREAMED ORANGES, ENGLISH.

Slice thirty-six oranges, put them into two gallons of rose syrup and four gallons of water; add ten pounds of sugar, digest for two weeks and strain and bottle it.

CEDRAT.

Take the peels from twelve fresh oranges, put them in two gallons of rose syrup, to be mixed at pleasure with punch, &c. or iced water and sugar for a beverage.

PARFAIT AMOUR is the same, colored with a little cochineal.

ORGEAT SYRUP

Blanch and pound one pound of sweet almonds, and two ounces of bitter ones; mix with it a quart of the decoction of barley, strain it, add a pint and a half more of the decoction, two pounds of sugar, and when the sugar is dissolved, mix in one drachm of orange flour water.

ANOTHER MODE.—Pound together three quarters of a pound of sweet almonds, and a quarter of a pound of bitter ones; rub them with a little water into an emulsion, strain, rub what is left of the almonds afresh on the strainer, with the strained liquor, to make it as rich as possible, add three pounds of loaf sugar, two ounces of orange flour water, and spirits of lemon peel, six drachms; strain it through white flannel, and cork it up in bottles.

ALMOND PASTE FOR ORGEAT, &c.

Blanch and pound one pound of sweet almonds with one ounce of bitter ones, and a pound of powdered loaf sugar, adding a little orange flour or rose water, to prevent them oiling; beat it well, forming it into a stiff paste, so as not for it to stick to your fingers. Put it up in small pots, covering them securely. It is used for making liquid orgeat, &c., and to mix with iced water for a summer's beverage.

RATAFIA.

Break up eight pounds of morella cherries with their seeds and kernels, or the same quantity of small black wild cherries; put them in a gallon of proof spirits, digest for one month, and strain them with expression; add to the liquid one ounce of powdered nutmeg, two pounds of sugar, and cork it up.

ANOTHER MODE.—Take a hundred and fifty peach or apricot kernels, bruise them in a mortar, put them in half a gallon of proof spirits, or as much of the syrup of the fruit, and syrup of roses, mixed in equal proportions, and reduced to proof, mix in a pound of loaf sugar, dissolve, filter and bottle it. Add citron at pleasure.

THIRD MODE.—Blanch a pound of bitter almonds, pound them to a paste, moistening them with rose water; powder an ounce of nutmegs, and put them together in a gallon of proof spirits, add three sliced lemons, and let it stand two weeks to digest; then filter it, add a pound and a half of loaf sugar, and bottle it.

PEPPERMINT CORDIAL.

Drop seventy-five drops of the best oil of peppermint on a pound of loaf sugar, pulverize it, add syrup of violet roses one pint; while pulverizing, dilute with ten pints of syrup of roses, and ten gallons of water five with three drachms of alum.

NOYAU.

Pound to a paste one pound of peach kernels, mix with them the grated rinds of four large lemons, and two quarts of clarified honey. Put the mixture into a demijohn, pour on one gallon of the best peach brandy, stop it up, and let it stand for two months, shaking it up occasionally; then filter it through a piece of muslin, or of white blotting paper, pinned on a fine sieve, which must necessarily be renewed. Cork it up in bottles, and as you make use of it, dilute it to your taste with rose water. It will keep good for years; age improves it.

MEAD.

Take sweet cider, just from the press, and boil and skim it well. Mix with each gallon one quart of clarified honey, put it in a cask, and leave the bung loose till it is done fermenting, and becomes clear. Then mix with it a quart of the best white brandy or rectified spirits to each gallon of the fermented mixture, and cork it up for use. It will keep well, and is very much liked.

CAPILLAIRE.

Dissolve some loaf sugar in cold water, allowing half a pint of water to each pound of sugar. Mix in the whole of an egg to every four pounds of sugar, and boil it to a thick syrup, removing every particle of scum as it rises. Pass it through a piece of muslin, and when quite cold, flavor it highly with orange flour water. Cork it up in bottles. It is principally used to flavor punch, &c.

CAPILLAIRE, ANOTHER WAY.—Dissolve eight pounds of loaf sugar in one gallon of water, add the whites of two eggs, boil and skim it, and when nearly cold, stir in a pint of rose water.

BISHOP.

Roast before a clear fire half a dozen deep colored oranges till a light brown; slice them up, and put them in a bowl, sprinkle them with three quarters of a pound of powdered loaf sugar, pour on half a bottle of claret, cover it, and set it by till next day; then heat the remaining half bottle of claret till it is ready to boil. Strain the orange juice, &c. through a napkin, pressing it, to obtain all the juice you can, and mix it with the hot wine. Serve it either warm or cold, in glasses, and grate nutmeg thickly over the tops.

MILK PUNCH.

Take rum, or any nice kind of brandy, and dilute it to the strength you like it, with entire sweet milk, stirring it in gradually. Sweeten it to your taste with loaf sugar, flavor it with a little capillary, and serve it up in glasses; drop a small lump of ice in each, and grate nutmeg thickly over them.

LEMON PUNCH.

Select one dozen of the finest smooth rind lemons; grate off the yellow rind, and put it in a bowl, with two pounds of powdered loaf sugar. Add the juice of the lemons, cover it, and set it by till next day; then beat the whites of eight eggs to a stiff froth, and put it in a separate bowl. Stir gradually into it a bottle of champaign, mix in the ingredients from the other bowl, and pass the whole through a very fine sieve, dilute it with water as you use it, and you may freeze it, or serve it up in glasses, with a small lump of ice in each, and grate nutmeg on the tops.

ORANGE PUNCH.

Weigh two and a half pounds of loaf sugar, put it in a bowl, and pour on it two and a half table-spoonfuls of rose water. Grate the yellow peel from one dozen fine oranges, and two lemons, and squeeze the juice into the bowl, add the grated peel, cover the bowl, and set it by till next day; then mix in a bottle of claret, or champaign, pass it through a fine sieve, and stir well into it the whites of eight eggs, which have been beaten to a stiff froth. Serve it up in glasses, putting a lump of ice in each, and grate nutmeg thickly over them; or you may freeze it, and serve it in glasses, providing each with a tea-spoon.

ROMAN PUNCH.

Take twelve fine lemons, and two oranges, roll them on a table under your hand, to increase the juice, and pare off the yellow rinds. Put them into four quarts of water, and boil them till the liquid is reduced to three quarts; then take out the parings, dissolve in the water three pounds of loaf sugar, and set it by to cool. Mix in the whites of two eggs, boil it up again, simmer it well, and strain it, and cool it; then mix in the juice of the lemons and oranges, and stir in gradually one quart of rum or rectified whisky.

ITALIAN PUNCH.

Pare very thin the yellow rinds from six oranges and six lemons, put them into three pints of water, and boil them till the water is reduced to one quart, and strain it into a large bowl. Mix in two and a half pounds of loaf sugar, three pints of boiling sweet milk, and set it by to cool; then stir in gradually one quart of rum, or of the best brandy, and the juice from the decorticated lemons and oranges. It will keep well for several months, put up in bottles, and when you wish to make use of it, serve it up in glasses, mixing in a few beaten whites of eggs, and grating nutmeg on the tops.

TEA PUNCH.

Make a pint and a half of very strong tea in the usual manner; strain it, and pour it boiling on one pound and a quarter of loaf sugar. Add half a pint of rich sweet cream, and then stir in gradually a bottle of claret or of champaign. You may heat it to the boiling point, and serve it so, or you may send it round entirely cold, in glass cups.

NEGUS.

Mix together one pint of lemon juice and three pints of iced water, pour it into a large bowl on a pound and a half of loaf sugar, and let it stand till the sugar is dissolved; then stir in one quart of champaign or claret. Send it round in glasses, with nutmeg grated thickly on.

SANGAREE.

Sangaree is a mixture of clear, cold water and wine, porter, or ale, sweetened in glasses with lumps of loaf sugar, and crowned lightly with grated nutmeg. A very good proportion is two measures of water to one of spirits. In warm weather, a small lump of ice in each glass improves it.

RUM TODDY.

Mix one third of rum with two of iced water, or if you wish it very weak, have only one fourth rum. Sweeten it with lumps of loaf sugar; serve it in tumblers, and grate nutmeg thickly over the tops. Toddy may be made in a similar manner with brandy or good whisky, and you may have peppermint toddy, annise, clove, lemon, cinnamon toddy, &c., by flavoring them with their respective essence. Some of these drinks, as well as many articles of diet for which I have given receipts, have been in common use for many years, yet by observation we are bound to believe that there are many people who are not expe-

rienced, even in some of the most simple of these preparations; therefore we find it necessary to give receipts for
them also.

EGG NOGG.

Break six eggs, separating the whites from the yolks;
beat the whites to a stiff froth, put the yolks in a bowl and
beat them light. Stir into it slowly, that the spirits may
cook the egg, half a pint of rum, or three gills of common
brandy; add a quart of rich sweet milk and half a pound
of powdered sugar; then stir in the egg froth, and finish
by grating nutmeg on the top.

APPLE TODDY.

Take half a dozen fine pippin apples, extract the cores
smoothly, and fill the cavities with brown sugar: bake
them in an oven till very soft, adding a few spoonfuls of
water at first, to prevent them burning; then draw off
the peelings, put the apples in a bowl, squeeze on them
the juice of two lemons, and set them by till they get
cold. In the mean time prepare a quart of toddy, with
one third spirits and two of water; sweeten it with loaf
sugar and pour it on your apples. Serve it up in large
glass tumblers, and grate nutmeg on the tops.

Quince toddy may be made in the same manner, substituting quinces for apples. In cold weather apple toddy
should be served warm.

Apple and quince punch are nothing more than baked
apples or quinces put into common milk punch.

MULLED CIDER.

Boil a quart of cider a few minutes, with enough cinnamon and cloves to flavor it, and strain it through a
napkin into a pitcher. In the mean time beat six eggs
light, and put them in a bowl: pour the cider while boiling on the egg, stirring it in gradually; add enough sugar to make it sufficiently sweet, and whirl round in it a
bunch of wire till you raise a froth on the top; then serve
it up immediately in glasses while it is warm, and grate
nutmeg thickly over them.

Wine may be mulled in a similar manner.

PEACH-LEAF BRANDY.

Put some green peach leaves in a jar, pour on as much white brandy as will cover them, close the jar and let them steep for three days: then take them out and fill the jar with fresh leaves. Repeat this process till you have a very strong infusion, and then strain it and put the liquid up in bottles. A little of this brandy is excellent for flavoring cakes, puddings, &c.

SPRUCE BEER.

Boil four ounces of hops and four of sassafras bark, chipped fine, in ten gallons of water; strain it, and add to it while hot four quarts of molasses, a small cup of ginger and two spoonfuls of essence of spruce. When it is nearly cold, stir in half a pint of good yeast; put it in a cask, leaving the bung loose till it has fermented and become clear, and then bottle it for use, corking them securely.

SECOND MODE FOR SPRUCE BEER.—Dissolve six pounds of sugar in ten gallons of warm water, add four ounces of essence of spruce, a pint of yeast, and cork and bottle it as directed for ginger beer. Brown spruce beer may be made in the same manner, substituting molasses for sugar.

GINGER BEER.

Mix together two and a half pounds of sugar, three ounces of good ginger and the grated peel of three lemons; put the mixture into a small cask, and pour on it two gallons of boilng water; shake it up and mix it well, and when it is only lukewarm, put it in the juice of the three lemons with a gill of good yeast, shaking it up again till the yeast is mixed through the other ingredients. Stop it up slighty, and next day bottle it, securing the corks with leather. If you can't procure fresh lemons, mix in two ounces of cream of tartar, which will impart to the beer an agreeable acid taste, and make it very lively and brisk.

SECOND MODE FOR GINGER BEER.—Mix together three pounds of sugar, two ounces of bruised ginger, one ounce cream of tartar and four sliced lemons; pour on them four gallons of boiling water, and when lukewarm mix in half a pint of good yeast. Let it stand to ferment four days, and then put it up in small bottles, tying down the corks with leather.

THIRD.—Six pounds of moist sugar, five ounces of bruised ginger, two ounces cream of tartar, half a dozen sliced lemons, seven gallons of hot water, and when nearly cold add a pint of yeast. Work it two or three days, strain, mix in one pint of brandy, bung it closely, and in fourteen days bottle it, securing the corks with leather. It makes a cooling beverage for summer.

MOLASSES BEER.

Make three gallons of water lukewarm, stir into it one gallon of West India molasses, two table-spoonfuls of ginger, one of cream of tartar, two sliced lemons and half a pint of good yeast. Next day bottle it, putting two or three raisins in each, and tying leather over the corks.

BRAN BEER.

Put two quarts of wheat or rye bran into five gallons of water, add three pints of hops and boil it for one hour; then strain it into a tub, mix in two quarts of molasses, and when it gets to be lukewarm, stir in three jills of good yeast, and cover it with a folded cloth till it is done fermenting and quite clear: then bottle it and secure the corks with leather or rosin.

M'ETHEGLIN.

Mix twelve pounds of honey with four gallons of boiling water, stir it frequently for a day or two, then add a little yeast and ferment.

Metheglin is sometimes made from the honey combs from which the honey is extracted by boiling it in water. Some people make their mead in this manner.

HONEY VINEGAR.

Mix one quart of strained honey with seven quarts of lukewarm water, put it in a keg or jug, and expose it daily to the sun, leaving the bung loose till it is done fermenting, and then cork it up tolerably tight. In a short time you will have a very pleasant tasted vinegar.

CIDER VINEGAR.

Mix with ten gallons of cider five quarts of strained honey; put it in a cask, and in six months you will have a vinegar too strong for common purposes, without diluting it with water.

WHISKY VINEGAR.

Mix together whisky and water in the proportions of four gallons of water to one of whisky; put it in a cask, and fill it up with ripe peaches. After standing two or three weeks, draw off the liquid, empty the cask of the peaches, and put the liquid again into it; cork it up slightly, leaving the bung a little loose, and in five or six months, according to the quantity you make, you will have an excellent, strong and well flavored vinegar.

ANOTHER WAY TO MAKE WHISKY VINEGAR.—Mix the whisky and water in the proportions of two and a half gallons of water to one of whisky, and to every ten gallons of the mixture add three pints of good yeast and three pounds of powdered charcoal. Put it in a cask, leaving the bung loose, and place it in a sunny part of the yard till the fermentation is over: then close up the bung tolerably tight, and in four or five months you will have a fine white vinegar, answering for many nice purposes that dark colored vinegar would not.

A VERY CHEAP VINEGAR.

Have a barrel with one head loose; set it in a snug place of the yard, and when you are drying your peaches, apples or pears, put the parings and cores in the barrel, filling it quite full; then fill it up with cold spring water, spread a cloth over the top, and let it stand for several weeks. It will not injure the taste of the vinegar to remain with the pumice the greater part of the winter: then draw it off into a clean cask, and in four or five months from the time you commence making it, you will have a pleasant tasted vinegar, strong enough for common purposes.

PREPARATIONS FOR THE SICK.

REMARKS.

Whatever may be the disease of a person, if they are dangerously ill, whether they are under the influence of medicine or no, the strictest attention should be paid to their diet. Many a horrible disease has been driven from the system by such a course, and many others fed and nourished up, by indulging too freely in the luxuries of life. Not only a strict attention should be paid to the quality of their diet, but also to the quantity, as there is no one or two things that ever caused more dangerous relapses in sickness, than the indulgence of these two evils; therefore, they should both be carefully avoided, selecting only such articles of diet as may best agree with their situations, and giving it to them in proper proportions. There is very near as much depending on the understanding and management of the nurse as the physician.

CHICKEN TEA.

Take a grown fowl, pick and clean it neatly, cut it into joints, and boil a small portion of it till tender, adding no seasonings, but barely enough salt to make it palatable. This will many times set upon a weak stomach when nothing else will.

BEEF TEA.

Take a very nice, tender piece of fresh beef or veal; cut it into thin slices, and beat them tender. Season them as for eating with salt and pepper, and broil them till a light brown on a clean gridiron, over a bed of clear coals, turning them over once or twice; then cut them into small bits, put them in a bowl, pour on some boiling water, and cover them with a plate. The nurse must be the judge as to the richness of the tea, knowing the situation of the patient. By the time it gets cold enough to drink, it will have imbibed a sufficient flavor of the steaks. This is a tea that may be used in most cases of sickness, where it is not too strong, and is generally liked.

CHICKEN BROTH.

Take a small young chicken, clean it nicely, cut it into joints, and boil it very tender, leaving at least one quart of the liquor when done. If the chicken be half grown, it will make three pints of broth rich enough for a sick person. Beat up a large spoonful of flour in half a pint of entire sweet milk, and stir it gradually into the liquor. Boil it a few minutes longer, and take it from the fire, seasoning it lightly with salt and pepper; and if the patient is fond of the flavor, you may add a few sprigs of parsley. When you make broth of a grown chicken, only use half of it at one time.

SQUIRREL SOUP.

Having cleaned a fat young squirrel, cut it into quarters, and boil it very tender, carefully removing the scum. If well boiled, it will make a quart of good soup. Mix up half a pint of stiff batter with half a beaten egg, sweet milk and flour; drop it into the liquor while it is boiling, dropping it from a dessert-spoon, that it may remain in lumps or small dumplings. Boil it till the dumplings are done, which will only take a few minutes, season it lightly with salt and pepper, as sick people are not generally fond of soups very highly seasoned, and if they were, they are not good for them. Add a little parsley, or thyme, if preferred by the patient, and serve it up moderately warm. Chicken, pheasant, partridge or rabbit soup may be made in the same manner.

PARTRIDGE TEA.

You may make partridge tea as directed for chicken tea; or you may broil the partridges neatly on a gridiron, seasoning them highly with salt water and pepper, and basting them lightly with butter; then cut them up into small bits, put them in a pitcher, and pour on some boiling water, allowing a pint to each partridge; add a little nutmeg and lemon juice, or grated lemon peel, and cover it with a plate, to keep in the steam. By the time it gets cool enough to sup, it will have extracted from the partridges the most of their juices. It may be taken warm or cold, but is generally preferred warm. Such teas are very nutricious, and principally designed for weak, debilitated patients, who are not able to take stronger nourishment.

BROILED PARTRIDGES.

If the patient is allowed to eat a bit of meat for a relish, broiled partridges, and other small birds, are superior to any other kind of fresh meat. Clean them nicely, rinse them in cold water, and wipe them dry with a cloth. Broil them on a clean gridiron over clear coals, basting them with a little weak salt and water, and a small portion of pepper, until they are sufficiently seasoned, and at the last baste them slightly with fresh sweet butter. Squirrels and very small chickens may be broiled in the same manner. A chip of dried beef or venison is very good to give a relish to teas. They are generally preferred rare, but if not very dry, they may be slightly broiled, after washing the slices in hot water, and wiping them dry with a cloth, to take off the superfluous salt, which would be disgusting to a sick person. Such relishes are generally served with tea, and a bit of waffle, or batter cake, or dry toast.

BATTER CAKES.

Batter cakes, or waffles, for a sick person, should be made with very little egg; one egg to a pint of milk is quite enough. Beat it light, mix in your milk and a little salt, and make it into a thin batter with flour; beat it well with a spoon, and strain it through a fine sieve, to get out all the little lumps of dry flour, which is very hard to break down in thin batter. Have your griddle hot, clean it nicely, and place it level over a bed of clear coals;

grease it slightly with butter, merely enough to prevent the cakes sticking to it; put on your batter in very thin small cakes, turn them over as soon as the under side is a light brown and before they get hard; serve them up hot and slightly butter them.

Cakes made in this manner generally agree with sick persons.

PARTRIDGE PANADA.

Having cleaned your partridges neatly, rub them with salt and boil them very tender in a small quantity of water: then remove the skin, mince the meat fine from the bones, and pound one half of it in a mortar. Return it to the liquor, which should be about half enough to make the whole as thick as common panada, or thick soup; add a small portion of butter, pepper and nutmeg, and serve it up with dry toasts.

Chicken and squirrel panada may be made in the same manner.

RICE.

Pick and wash your rice carefully, and boil it very soft in milk and water, mixed half and half: then drain it and mix in a small portion of butter, sugar and nutmeg. Or, if the patient is suffered to eat milk, boil the rice in clear water, season it lightly with salt, and eat it warm with cold sweet milk.

RICE MILK.

Boil your rice quite soft, but do not mash it: mix it with sweet milk, making the whole about the consistence of thick soup; add a little water, lest it should be too rich, sweeten it to your taste, and boil it up again. Serve it warm, and grate a little nutmeg on the top.

BOILED MILK.

Boil a pint of sweet milk with a little cinnamon till it has imbibed enough of the flavor. Beat very light half of one egg, mix with it a small portion of salt, a gill of sweet milk and enough flour to make it a stiff batter;

drop it by spoonfuls into the boiling milk, that it may remain in lumps, and boil it till the dumplings are done. Season it with sugar and nutmeg, or butter and pepper.

MILK TOAST.

Boil a pint of sweet milk, and throw into it while boiling a small handful of light brown toasts, not larger than half a dollar: add a little sugar and nutmeg, and serve it up.

MILK PORRIDGE.

Mix a large table spoon heaping full of flour with a gill of sweet milk, beat it till smooth, and stir it into a pint of boiling sweet milk; boil it up again, stirring it all the time, add a little sugar, lemon juice and nutmeg, and serve it up with rusk or dry toast.

RAISIN PORRIDGE.

Seed half a pint of raisins, shred them fine, and stew them tender in a small quantity of water, adding enough sugar to make them tolerably sweet: then stir in gradually enough sweet milk to make it the consistence of thick soup, boil it a minute or two longer, and remove it from the fire.

HOTCH-POTCH.

Rub a large spoonful of butter in a small handful of flour till completely saturated, and stir it into a pint of boiling water. Boil it till thoroughly done, stirring it occasionally; add a few spoonfuls of sweet milk, a little nutmeg or ginger, and sweeten with sugar. If rightly proportioned, it will be tolerably thick and full of small lumps. It is excellent food for a sick person.

CUSTARD.

Beat two eggs very light, stir them into three gills of sweet milk, with enough sugar to sweeten it, and bake it a light brown in cups. Grate nutmeg on the tops.

If the eggs are beaten sufficiently light, the custard will be perfectly harmless.

CLOTTED MILK.

Beat one egg as light as possible, and stir it into a pint of cold milk; set it over a few coals, stir it till it comes to a boil, and then remove it from the fire. Season it to your taste with spice, lemon and sugar, and serve it up with dry toasts.

ARROWROOT JELLY

Mix two spoonfuls of arrow root powder in a teacup of cold water, stirring it till quite smooth. When it is completely dissolved, stir it into a pint and a half of boiling water; add a little grated lemon and powdered loaf sugar, and boil it three or four minutes longer, stirring it all the time. If the patient's system is in a relaxed state, a little wine and nutmeg may be added. It is also very good made with sweet milk instead of water, but it is much richer, and does not always suit a weak stomach best.

BREAD JELLY.

Take the crumb of a small light loaf, toast it brown, pour on enough boiling water to cover it well, and let it stand till completely saturated; then beat it smooth, add enough sweet milk to make it a little liquid, boil it a few minutes, and strain it into a bowl. Season it with grated lemon or nutmeg and loaf sugar.

TAPIOCA JELLY.

After washing the tapioca in two or three waters, steep it for five hours in fresh water. Boil it in the same water with some bits of lemon peel till sufficiently thick and quite clear; then take out the lemon peel, and season the jelly with loaf sugar and lemon juice or a little wine, according to the taste and situation of the patient.

RICE JELLY.

Mix up a cup of rice flour in a little milk: when smooth, stir it into a quart of boiling water, add a few slips of lemon peel, and boil it till it is a thick jelly; then strain it, and season it with loaf sugar and lemon juice, or nutmeg and wine.

SAGO JELLY.

Wash a tea cupful of sago thoroughly in two or three cold waters, and soak it for one or two hours in a bowl of water; then put it in a quart of water with a few slips of lemon peel, and simmer it till the sago looks clear: after which take out the lemon peel, season the jelly with loaf sugar and a little wine, and simmer again for a few minutes. If it is thought improper to use wine, and milk is advisable, boil the sago in sweet milk and season it with loaf sugar only.

CHICKEN JELLY.

Take a grown fowl, clean it nicely, cut it up and pound it in a mortar, breaking all the bones. Sprinkle on a little salt, and boil it in a covered vessel till done very tender, raising the lid and removing every particle of scum as it rises; then strain the liquid through a cloth, and if the system of the patient is in a relaxed state, season the jelly with loaf sugar, wine, nutmeg and lemon juice; but if there is fever and the bowels constipated, omit the wine, &c. and season it with salt and a little pepper.

BEEF JELLY.

Take a piece of tender beef, remove every particle of fat, cut the lean in small chunks, and beat them tender: boil them till the meat is into rags, skimming it well, and then strain the liquid into a clean pan. Season it with sugar, nutmeg and wine, or salt and pepper, as the case may require.

A similar jelly may be made of the lean of fresh mutton, and both may be thickened a little with flour, if preferred so.

MULLED BUTTERMILK.

Beat two eggs very light, and stir them into a quart of fresh buttermilk; set it over the fire, and stir it constantly till it comes to a boil; then remove it instantly from the fire, or it will curdle and turn to whey. Pour it in a bowl, and season it with sugar and nutmeg.

BUTTERMILK WHEY.

Take buttermilk that is quite sour; (fresh buttermilk is not good for this purpose, not affording a sufficient quantity of acid;) put it in a pan over some coals, and to each quart add half a pint of water. Boil it hard for fifteen or twenty minutes, then take it from the fire, let it stand to settle, and draw off the whey. It is generally taken cold, without any seasoning. If it is not sufficiently sour, a little lemon juice may be added.

GROUND RICE MILK.

Stir two large spoonfuls of ground rice in enough sweet milk to make it a smooth batter, and then stir it into a pint of boiling sweet milk; add a spoonful of butter, and boil it steadily for a few minutes, stirring it all the time; then pour it into a bowl, and season it with loaf sugar and grated lemon.

WINE WHEY.

Heat a pint of sweet milk to the boiling point; then stir in a glass and a half of any kind of good sour wine, and set it by the fire, where it will keep hot and remain undisturbed till the curd forms: then drain off the whey into a bowl, and season it with loaf sugar and nutmeg.

Whey may be made in this manner with lemon juice or well flavored vinegar: that in many cases is preferred to wine whey.

EGG GRUEL.

Beat two eggs light, and stir them into a pint of sweet milk; set it over a few coals, and stir it constantly till it gets scalding hot, but do not let it boil, or it will curdle and be like a boiled custard. Season it with loaf sugar and lemon juice, or nutmeg, whichever is preferred.

INDIAN GRUEL.

Mix up two large spoonfuls of fine Indian meal with as much water as will make it a smooth batter, and stir it into a pint of boiling water; boil it a few minutes till

thoroughly done, stirring it all the time; add enough salt
to make it palatable, and serve it up. It is generally
taken a little warm, and is excellent to carry off medicine.

FLOUR GRUEL.

Boil a pint of water and a little salt, and stir in as
much flour as will make it a thin jelly, having first made
it into a smooth batter with cold water. Seed and shred
a small handful of raisins, boil them a few minutes in the
gruel, and sweeten it to your taste with loaf sugar.

A similar gruel may be made of rye or oat meal, and
is in many cases preferred to the flour gruel, owing to its
medical qualities. If preferred by the patient, you may
add a little fresh butter to all these gruels.

RENNET WHEY.

Mix a little rennet water or preparation of rennet with
a quart of sweet milk, and let it set by the fire where it
will keep lukewarm, till the curd forms; then turn off the
whey, and mix in a little lemon juice and loaf sugar, if
preferred so.

CALF'S FEET BROTH.

Having cleaned a calf's feet nicely, boil two of them
till the meat is ready to drop into rags, and there remains
one quart of the liquor. Strain it, and season it with sugar, nutmeg, and lemon juice, or you may season it with
a little salt and pepper, and slightly acidulate it with
vinegar.

APPLE WATER.

Bake some fine acid apples till very soft; then cut them
up, and put them in cold water to steep, allowing two apples to each tumbler of water. Let them steep till the
water becomes cold, and it will be ready for use. This
water is excellent for a weak stomach, that cannot retain
soup, &c. Apple water is frequently made of raw apples,
sliced up, and hot water poured over them, but I think it
is not so good for the patient as when the apples are
cooked.

LEMON WATER.

Cut up a fine fresh lemon, and steep it for a short time in a glass of water; then drain off the water, and sweeten it lightly with loaf sugar. It is very cooling and refreshing to sick people.

ORANGE WATER may be made in the same manner, and is also good.

PEACH WATER.

Mix two or three table-spoonfuls of peach marmalade or jelly with a little lemon juice, and a few bitter almonds or peach kernels, which have been pounded to a paste, and then dilute it to the proper strength with cold water.

APRICOT WATER,

May be made in the same manner, mixing with the other ingredients preserved apricots. The strength of these waters should be adapted to the taste of the patient.

PLUM WATER.

Take some fine ripe plums, extract half the kernels from the seeds, and boil them with the plums, in a very little water; then strain the juice, sweeten it to your taste with loaf sugar, and set it by till it gets cold. A very good plum water may be made by mixing the juice of the preserved plums with cold water. These waters make a pleasant beverage, and are also good to eat with light bread and butter. The juice of cranberries, or any other acid preserves, makes a pleasant drink, mixed with cold water. And even a little cold water alone is excellent in fevers, when the system is not too strongly under the influence of medicine.

TAMARIND WATER.

Put tamarinds into a pitcher, cover them well with cold water, and let them steep for twenty or thirty minutes.

RASPBERRY SYRUP WITH VINEGAR.

Mash a pound of ripe raspberries in a glazed or earthen pan. Mix with them half a pint of white wine vinegar, and set it in a cool place for twenty-four hours; then pass the liquid through a hair sieve, but without any forcible pressure. Put it in a porcelain skillet, or preserving kettle, with three quarters of a pound of loaf sugar. Just let it come to a boil, remove the scum, and set the syrup by to cool. Stir it constantly till it gets cold, and then cork it up in a bottle. A little of this syrup, mixed with cold water, makes quite a pleasant and cooling beverage.

FLAVORED WATERS.

Many innocent and refreshing drinks may be made for the sick by mixing syrups, &c. with fresh water. Syrup of vinegar, raspberry and strawberry syrup, currants, lemon, lime, cherry, and grape syrups; the different kinds of shrubs, orgeat paste, capillaire, &c., all make excellent beverages, mixed with cold water. To be sure, in every case of sickness, cold water is not advisable; therefore, if the patient is weak and low, and under the care of a physician, his advice should be taken. For all these syrups, &c., see their respective receipts.

PEACH SYRUP.

Take nice dried peaches, wash them clean, and boil them tender, in plenty of water to cover them well; then press out all the juice, and set it by to cool. It is generally preferred cold, without any seasonings.

CHERRY SYRUP.

May be made in the same manner, by substituting dried cherries for peaches; and also pear syrup, made of dried pears, is excellent, and quite harmless.

PRUNE SYRUP.

Stew the prunes gently, in a good quantity of water, till the stones will slip out easily; then squeeze the syrup from them, and sweeten it or not, as you like. Physicians consider the prunes themselves to be safe nourishment in most kinds of fevers.

CAUDLE.

Beat one egg light, and stir it in half a pint of cold water. Set it over a few coals, and stir it constantly till it comes to a boil, and then remove it instantly from the fire. You may season it with sugar and spice, or nutmeg, and if you choose, slightly acidulate it with vinegar or lemon juice. It is very good, seasoned with salt alone. Sup it with dry toast.

HOMMONY.

Take small hommony, wash it clean, and boil it till very soft, in a good quantity of water; then drain the water from it, and season it with salt only, butter and salt, or butter and molasses. Or you may season it lightly with salt, and eat it with sweet milk. It is quite harmless seasoned in either of these ways.

MUSH.

Put some water in a skillet, and make it boil hard; mix up a little fine sifted Indian meal, with enough cold water to make it a smooth batter, and stir it into the boiling water. At first it should only be like good thick soup, and boiled down to the proper consistence, stirring it frequently; then it will be sure to be thoroughly done, and clear of lumps. Salt it lightly, as sick people are not fond of highly seasoned victuals, and if it should lack any, it will be an easy matter for them to season it to suit their own taste. Serve it up warm, to eat with cold sweet milk. If the patient is very weak, you may mix with the milk a small portion of cold water; even then it will be quite nourishing, and is considered by physicians a safe diet in most kinds of sickness.

Flour Mush may be made in the same manner, and is generally eaten with butter and molasses. Rye mush is considered almost a restorative to weak lungs, eaten with West India molasses.

MOLASSES AND WATER.

Make an excellent drink, mixed one third or fourth molasses, and the remaining part cold water. It is said to be very good for sick people, particularly for those who have weak lungs. If you choose, add a little lemon juice, which will give it an agreeable acid flavor, and not injure the medical qualities.

BARLEY WATER.

Take a quarter of a pound of common, or pearl barley, and wash it clean. Put it in a sauce-pan, with two quarts of water, and boil it soft, or till the liquid is reduced to one half; then strain it, dissolve in it while hot, enough liquorice to give it a strong flavor, and sweeten it to your taste with loaf sugar.

GINGER TEA.

Ginger tea is at once food and medicine. Break up some of the root ginger, and boil it in clear water till just strong enough to be palatable; then cool it, and you may drink it so, or sweeten it as you like; or you may sup it with cold buttered biscuit. It is excellent for a weak stomach. Pepper tea is also good. Put a little capsicum or powdered red pepper into a cup, fill it up with warm water, sweeten it, and drink it on going to bed. It is a very good remedy for a bad cold, and for its simplicity, it is rejected many times when it ought to be used.

MINT TEA.

Pick the leaves and stalks of spare mint, rinse them clean, put them in a pitcher, and pour boiling water on, cover it, and let it stand for a few minutes to infuse; then turn the tea from the leaves, sweeten it lightly with loaf sugar, and serve it warm. It is a sovereign efficacy in settling a sick stomach after taking an emetic. Sage tea is also good. Balm makes a very cooling tea; it is good to use in fevers as a constant drink.

MOLASSES POSSET.

Mix together half a pint of West India molasses, a teaspoonful of powdered ginger, two spoonfuls of vinegar, and two ounces of fresh butter. Put all together in a sauce-pan; set it over some coals, and let it get scalding hot, stirring it all the time, but do not suffer it to boil. A little of it is very good for a bad cold or sore throat.

PREPARED HONEY.

Mix very well together one pint of strained honey, the juice of three lemons, and three table-spoonfuls of black pepper. A table-spoonful of it, taken on going to bed, is excellent for a sore throat.

STEWED VINEGAR.

Take some good vinegar, dilute it to the strength you like it with water, season it highly with butter, honey and ginger, and boil it for a few minutes in a covered vessel. Take a tea-cupful of it warm on going to bed. It is a good remedy for a bad cold or sore throat.

PANADA.

Cut up two milk biscuits, or three crackers, into small bits. Put them in a bowl, add a large spoonful of butter, broken up, and a pint of boiling water. Cover it, and let it stand for a few minutes; then season it to your taste with sugar, and grate on a little nutmeg or ginger. If the situation of the patient will admit of it, you may flavor it with a little wine.

LIGHT BREAD PANADA.

Boil a pint of water, and stir into it a large spoonful of fresh butter, and a little grated nutmeg or lemon. Pare the crust from a small piece of light bread, break up the crumbs, and put it in a bowl, with the juice of half a lemon. When the boiled water is about half cold, pour it on the bread crumbs, and let it be eaten in a few minutes, or it will soon become saturated, and be like a mush or batter. Panada may be made in the same manner with rusk.

COCOA.

Boil a pint of water, and pour it on one ounce of good cocoa, which is the chocolate nut before it is ground. Cover it, and set it by the fire on a few embers, to steep for one hour; then sweeten it to your taste, and sup it warm with dry toast.

CONFECTION OF ALMONDS.

Take of sweet almonds four ounces, blanch and pound them to a paste with a little rose water; add three ounces of powdered white sugar, three drachms of powdered gum Arabic, and beat the whole into a homogeneous mass; to be used at pleasure, triturating it with water till an emulsion is formed.

TOAST AND WATER.

Take Indian bread, that has been made up with cold water only. Pare off the crust, slice the crumbs, and toast them brown on both sides. Have ready a large glass tumbler of fresh water, drop the toasts in it, filling it quite full, and let it stand to soak a few minutes. When you drink off the water, the glass may be filled up again with fresh water. Do not fill it up more than two or three times, or let it stand too long, as it will turn sour, and of course not be fit for use. It is best to make fresh toasts very frequently, where they are much used.

VEGETABLE SOUP.

Vegetable soup should not be given in all sickness, though in some light cases it may be safely used. Take equal proportions of celery, turnips, onions and potatoes; prepare them in a proper manner, and boil them in clear water, with a little salt, till the liquor is sufficiently flavored; then strain the soup into a bowl, mix with it while hot, a small portion of butter and pepper, and drop in a few brown toasts.

TOMATO SOUP.

Peel half a dozen large ripe tomatoes, slice them up, and boil them in a quart of water, with a little salt, till the liquor is sufficiently strong; then strain it into a clean pan, add a little butter, pepper, and a small handful of toasts; boil it up again, and serve it.

FLAX SEED TEA.

Boil two table-spoonfuls of flax seed in a pint of water till the most of the mucilage is extracted from them; then strain it hot on four ounces of sugar candy, that is broken up, and one ounce of pulverized gum Arabic. Boil it up again, and squeeze in the juice of a lemon, or two spoonfuls of vinegar. It is very good for a cough, or inflamed bowels, taking half a tea-cupful at a time, and repeating it several times during the day; its mucilaginous quality is quite soothing and healing. The gum Arabic may be omitted, by using a greater proportion of flax seed. The bark of the slippery elm tree, steeped in cold water, makes a tea that is thought by many people to be superior to the flax seed tea, in cases of cough, inflamed bowels, &c.

COUGH SYRUP.

Take as much elecampane and cumfrey roots as you can grasp between your thumb and finger; wash them clean, split them up, and put them in a skillet, with a quart of water. Add a small handful of horehound, and boil them together till the water is reduced to one half; then strain the liquid, rinse out the skillet, put in the liquor again, with an equal portion of strained honey, and boil them gently together, till they form a thick syrup nearly as thick as the honey was before you mixed it with the liquid. Take a spoonful of it two or three times a day. It has been found an efficacious remedy for coughs nearly approaching to consumption.

PAP FOR CHILDREN.

This kind of diet is excellent for small children, particularly where they have to be raised mostly without the breast. Put some entire sweet milk in a skillet, and stir into it while boiling, enough flour to make it of the consistence of thick soup, having first mixed it with enough sweet milk to make it a smooth batter. Boil it till it is thoroughly done, stirring it frequently; and then sweeten it with sugar, and grate on a little nutmeg or ginger. You may make pap in the same manner, substituting water for milk; then add a little butter to the other seasonings.

SIMPLE REMEDIES.

Not knowing but that these receipts may fall into the hands of some people who live at a distance from a physician, causes the author to select a few simple remedies that she has known to prove effectual in relieving the sufferings of the patients.

BURNS.

A very common and good remedy for a fresh burn is an application of the spirits of turpentine and raw cotton. The cotton should be batted out with cards, wet thoroughly with the turpentine, and laid immediately over the burn; there should be fresh applications as often as the cotton becomes dry, till the fire is thoroughly extracted. Linseed oil is very good, applied in the same manner. Also, raw Irish potatoes, scraped fine, and applied frequently. And amongst all the other remedies, fresh lard and raw cotton, frequently applied, is not inferior to any of them to extract the fire from a burn, and I think it possesses a soothing quality superior to any other remedy I ever knew tried. After frequent applications of turpentine, the burn and the skin around it will sometimes look red and inflamed, from the use of the turpentine, for which there is nothing better than a free use of fresh lard, spread thickly over raw cotton, both to draw out the inflammation, and calm irritation. When a burn is slow to heal, there is nothing better than an application, morning and evening, of a liniment, made of equal proportions of linseed oil and lime water. If there appears any proud or fungous flesh over the sore, sprinkle on it occasionally a little burnt alum, which will soon destroy it.

A FRESH CUT.

When the wound is made smoothly, close the edges, press them together, and bind it up with dry lint; then pour on enough laudanum to wet it thoroughly, and if it is not interrupted, it will heal up in a few days. A wound from a snag, or any thing else, where the flesh is torn, should be carefully probed, and every particle of the snag, dirt, &c., removed. Then lay the edges as smoothly as possible together, and bind up the wound as before directed. You may wet it occasionally with a little tincture of myrrh. It will be found very good.

TO STOP BLOOD.

There are various remedies for stopping blood, such as the scrapings or fleshy part of soal-leather, sponge, cobwebs, &c.; but it is generally believed by good physicians that the kreosote is superior to any thing else. Dilute it with water, pour it on lint, and apply it immediately to the wound, binding it up tolerably tight. It has been found an efficacious remedy when many others have failed.

TOOTH-ACHE.

The kreosote is the best remedy for tooth-ache that has ever been published. Take a small bit of raw cotton, wet it slightly with kreosote, and put it immediately in the hollow of the tooth. It will nine times out of ten give instantaneous relief, though in a few hours the application many times will have to be repeated. If you put too much on the cotton, it will blister your mouth, but it will not leave a bad sore. A small bit of opium, of gum camphor, or a few drops of the oil of cajeput, dropped on a little cotton and put on the defective tooth, will give temporary relief. The opium and camphor should be put in the hollow of the tooth, if there be any. Never have a tooth drawn when the inflammation is very high, if it can possibly be avoided, as the result often proves troublesome, and sometimes, though rarely, fatal. Be careful not to take cold in your jaw, whence the tooth was extracted: it often causes more pain than was occasioned by the tooth.

SNAKE BITE.

The best thing I have ever known tried for the bite of a snake, is tobacco juice. Boil the tobacco till the juice is very strong, and bathe the bite thoroughly, and as soon as you possibly can. Bind it up with some of the tobacco leaves, bathe it frequently with the juice, and occasionally apply fresh leaves. Give the patient enough table salt, mixed in a little water, to vomit him freely before you suffer him to eat any thing. Some chew tobacco, and swallow enough of the ambeer to vomit them speedily. To be sure, it makes them very sick for a few minutes; but it is excellent to defend the stomach from the poison. To assist in keeping down the swelling, you may bathe the defective limb occasionally in strong salt and water. I have known very bad bites, thus treated, cured in a very short time, and after the first few hours the patient experience but little inconvenience.

CROUP.

The croup is generally rapid in its progression, and is one of the most dangerous diseases that attack young children: therefore it will be safest to commence doctoring as soon as it makes its appearance. If the child is violently attacked with croup, bathe it well in warm water, scarify and cup it between the shoulders, and vomit it with a tea prepared thus: Take as much elecampane as you can grasp between your thumb and finger; split it up and boil it in a pint of water till the tea is quite strong, or till it is reduced to one half; drop in a piece of alum, a size larger than a pea, and the same quantity of castile soap; then strain it and make it very sweet with strained honey. Let the child drink it a little warm, and give it freely till it vomits two or three times. It is an excellent emetic for a babe: it of course makes them very sick for a while, but it is soon over, and it does not leave the system so weak and languid as apothecaries' medicines do. I have seen them throw up a quantity of thick glairous phlegm, much resembling the white of an egg. If the child is very weak, and it is with difficulty it can throw up the phlegm, it will assist it much to tickle its throat with a soft feather, and will not hurt it in the least.

In the mean time, scoop out the heart of a large onion, fill up the cavity with garden saffron flowers, and flour of sulphur, or a small lump of the roll. Wrap the onion up securely in brown paper, wetting it, and roast it in hot wood ashes, till the onion is very soft; then take off the envelopes, and squeeze every particle of syrup from the onion, &c., into a saucer. As soon as the child is done vomiting, commence with the onion syrup, and give it a tea-spoonful every hour, until the hives appear on the skin, or till the child begins to amend. It is quite innocent, and is particularly efficacious in relieving the sickness at the stomach, and determining the hives to the surface. In spasmodic croups, a free use of paregoric will be found of great service, but do not use it without some precaution, as it is strongly impregnated with laudanum. And I have known some happy results from applying small bags of ashes between the shoulders, moistened with a little water, and put up as hot as could be borne. This may be repeated as often as the ashes become cool, or till the child is relieved of the spasms. The spasms are said to be in the lungs, and you may tell it from the other kind of croup by the child appearing very restless, often screaming out, and straitening, or rather throwing itself back. If these directions be strictly followed, however ill the child may be, they will seldom fail to effect a cure.

COSMETICS, PERFUMERIES, &c.

POMATUM.

Take one pound and a half of beef's marrow, an ounce and a half of cinnamon, storax, calamus, benzone, and Florentine orris root, each one ounce, and cloves and nutmegs, each one drachm. Put them in a jar, cover it, set it in a pot of boiling water, simmer till the marrow is dissolved, and strain it while hot.

SECOND MODE.—Take mutton suet one pound and a half, storax, calamus, benzone, orris root, cypress root, cinnamon, cloves and nutmegs, each nine drachms, simmer and strain as above directed.

THIRD MODE.—Mutton suet, two pounds, white wax, half a pound, essence of bergamot and of lemon, each three quarters of an ounce, oil lavender and oil marjoram, of each two drachms. Simmer and strain as before directed. Pomatum, mixed with pearl white or magistery, is said to turn the hair black.

PEARL POWDER.

Magistery of bismuth and French chalk, scraped fine, mixed together in equal proportions; used as a cosmetic.

ALMOND BLOOM.

Take Brazil dust one ounce, and water three pints, boil and strain, add of isinglass six drachms, grana sylvestra two ounces, (or cochineal powder two drachms,) alum one ounce, and borax three drachms; boil again, and strain through a piece of muslin. It is used as a liquid cosmetic.

ALMOND PASTE, TO BEAUTIFY.

Blanch and pound four ounces of almonds, mix with them two ounces of lemon juice, three of almond oil, one of water, and six of proof spirits.

SECOND MODE.—Blanch and pound one pound of bitter almonds, mix with them the whites of four eggs, and enough rose water to make it of the consistence of soft soap, mix it thoroughly, and put it up in small pots.

BROWN ALMOND PASTE.

Blanch a pound of bitter almonds, and pound them to a paste with a pound of raisin pulp, adding enough proof spirits to liquefy it sufficiently. These pastes are used as cosmetics for washing the hands, instead of soap; they have a tendency to soften the skin, and prevent its chapping.

WINDSOR SOAP.

Take hard curd soap, melt and perfume it with essence of currie and bergamot.

WHITE SOAP.

Take half a pound of white soap, half a pound of starch, four drachms essence of lemon, and eight ounces rose water. Dissolve and simmer it a few minutes, stirring it all the time, and make it into cakes.

RED MOTTLED WASH BALLS.

Cut white soap into small squares, roll the pieces in vermillion, and press them together again, forming them into balls, without mixing them more than is necessary to unite the edges smoothly.

BLUE MOTTLED WASH BALLS may be made in the same manner, substituting blue powder for vermillion.

—◦✦◦—

CREAM BALLS.

Mix together seven pounds of white curd soap, and one pound of pounded almonds; beat them thoroughly together, perfume it with any thing you please, and make it into small balls.

—◦✦◦—

WHITE WASH BALLS.

Cut up a pound of white Castile soap, mix with it three pints of rose water, one ounce solution of salts of tartar, and the whites of two eggs; boil them together in a porcelain skillet till hard, stirring it very often, add one scruple oil rhododendron, one drachm essence of jasmin, half a drachm essence nerali, and ten drops oil of cloves. Make it into two ounce balls.

—◦✦◦—

MILK OF ROSES.

Prepared kali, twelve grains, oil almonds, two ounces, essence bergamot, four drachms, rose water, six ounces, Florentine orris root water, four drachms; these to be well mixed, and corked up in a bottle.

SECOND MODE.—Melt with a slow heat white wax and Castile soap, each one ounce, and spermaceti four drachms; add rose water, six pounds, rose syrup, two pounds, Jordan almonds, pounded, one pound, and oil of lavender, one drachm.

THIRD MODE.—Bitter almonds, blanched and pounded, one pound, distilled water, twelve ounces, elder flower water, eight ounces; make it into an emulsion, and add oil tartar, prepared liquid, six ounces, and benzone, four drachms; mix them well. These preparations are used as cosmetic washes.

TOOTH POWDERS.

Pulverize and mix four ounces orris root, oss sepiæ, two ounces, cream of tartar, one ounce, oil of cloves, sixteen drops, and lake, sixteen drops.

SECOND MODE.—Catechu, one ounce, Peruvian barks, cream of tartar, and gum acoriac, each four drachms, dragon's blood and myrrh, each two drachms.   Pulverize and mix them thoroughly.

THIRD MODE.—Rose pink, twenty ounces, touchwood, or spunk, oss sepiæ, cream of tartar, of each eight ounces, myrrh, four ounces, orris root, two ounces, and essence of bergamot, one drachm.   Pulverize and mix as directed.

FOURTH.—Oss sepiæ, four ounces, cream of tartar and orris root, each two ounces, burnt alum and rose pink, each one ounce.

FIFTH.—Magnesia, orris root, rose pink, prepared chalk, of each two ounces, natron, six drachms, and oil of rhododendron, two drops.   Prepared as before directed.

LIP SALVE.

Take four ounces of white wax, five of olive oil, four drachms of spermaceti, twenty drops oil of lavender, and two ounces powdered alkanet root; put the whole in a porcelain skillet or jar, melt, strain, and then simmer with a slow heat till it forms a good salve, stirring it hard.

SECOND MODE.—Best olive oil two ounces, white wax and spermaceti each three ounces, and six drachms alkanet root: melt these ingredients together, stirring them all the time; strain and add oil of rhododendron three drops.

THIRD.—Oil almonds six ounces, spermaceti three ounces, white wax two ounces, alkanet root one ounce, and Peruvian balsam two drachms.   Melt slowly and strain.   These salves are all red.

LIP WHITE SALVE.

Oil almonds, spermaceti, white wax and white candy, all of equal quantities: melt them together slowly, stirring it hard.

SPIRITS OF LAVENDER.

Mix with a pint of rectified spirits of wine one ounce of oil of lavender and two drachms of ambergris; shake them very well together, and cork it up in phials.

COMPOUND SPIRITS OF LAVENDER may be made by adding to the above mixture enough of the oil of cloves and nutmegs, in equal proportions, to flavor it well.

LAVENDER BRANDY.

Put a quart of lavender flowers in a pitcher; fill it up with white brandy, and let it steep till next day; then squeeze them out, fill up the pitcher with fresh flowers, and repeat the process till you have a strong infusion of the flowers: then strain and cork it up in a bottle.

BRITISH LAVENDER.

Oil lavender two ounces, essence ambergris one ounce, spirits of ammonia one pint, and syrup of violet roses one quart: mix them very well, and cork it up in phials.

EAU DE COLOGNE.

Essence of bergamot one ounce and a half, essence de cedrat one drachm, essence neroli one drachm, essence lemon three drachms, oil rosemary half a drachm, spirits rosemary one pound, and a half, melissa water one pound, and syrup of violet roses six pounds: mix all together, keep it in a cold cellar or ice-house for several days, and then bottle and cork it securely. Used externally as a cosmetic, and made into a ratafia with sugar.

COLOGNE WATER.

A very good cologne water may be prepared thus: Mix together two drachms oil of lemon, two of cinnamon, two of lavender, one drachm tincture of benzoin, and four of oil of bergamot; shake the oils till well mixed, pour them in a quart of spirits of wine, and cork it up in bottles.

HUNGARIAN WATER.

Mix in a bottle one pint spirits wine, one ounce oil of rosemary and two drachms essence ambergris; shake them up daily for one week, and afterwards cork it up in phials.

AROMATIC VINEGAR.

Take of the dried tops of rosemary and dried sage leaves each four ounces, dried flowers of lavender two ounces, and two drachms of cloves; put them in a quart of distilled vinegar, macerate for one week afterwards, express the liquor and filter it.

ANOTHER MODE is to steep rose leaves, pinks and lavender blossoms in equal proportions, in distilled or white wine vinegar, and express and filter as before directed.

THIEVES VINEGAR.

Take equal proportions of lavender blossoms, rosemary, rue, sage, wormwood, mint and thyme; put them in an earthen jar, cover them with good vinegar, close the jar, and set it in the sun for two weeks; after which squeeze out the liquid, filter and bottle it, putting in each bottle a sliced clove of garlic. It is very good to sprinkle in the chambers of sick people, or in sultry rooms to prevent faintness.

PERFUME POWDERS.

Powder one ounce of orris root, and sift it; drop eight drops of oil of rhododendron on half an ounce of lump white sugar, powder it also, and mix it again with the orris root powder. It is used for smelling and to perfume drawers, trunks, &c.

OIL OF FLOWERS.

Take any kind of fragrant flowers, from which you wish to extract the flavor; macerate them in the best Florence oil, repeating the process with fresh leaves till the oil is as odoriferous as you wish it; then express the oil, filter and cork it up in phials. It is used for the hair instead of pomatum.

MISCELLANEOUS RECEIPTS.

—◦◊◦—

INDELIBLE INK.

Pound together a lump of pearlash, about the size of a partridge's egg, and a lump of gum arabic, a size larger: put it in a very small phial, fill it up with rain water, cork it, and let it stand to digest. This mixture is for washing the linen, to prepare it for the marking ink. Put into a small phial three quarters of an inch of lunar caustic, fill it up with good vinegar, and cork it also. This preparation is for the marking ink. Let them both infuse for two or three days, shaking them up frequently, and they will be ready for use. To prepare the linen for the reception of the ink, you must wet the part on which you intend to write, with some of the gum liquid, and dry it thoroughly in the sun; then with a fine pen put on the letters you wish with the caustic preparation, and dry it also in the sun.

ANOTHER PERMANENT INK.—This preparation is a solution of nitrate of silver, made as thick as common ink with sap green or cochineal. The liquid with which the linen is to be wet, previous to marking, is a solution of soda, boiled with a small portion of gum arabic.

THIRD MODE FOR MARKING INK.—Dissolve two drachms of lunar caustic in six ounces of distilled or rain water, and mix with it two drachms of dissolved gum arabic. This is for the marking ink. Dissolve half an ounce of soda in four ounces of water, and add a small portion of dissolved gum arabic. This is for wetting the linen. Set them in the sun for two days, shaking them up occasionally, and proceed as before directed.

—◦◊◦—

GREEN SYMPATHETIC INK.

Saturate spirit of salt, or aqua regia, with zaffre, cobalt ore, free from iron, and dilute it with distilled water.

What is drawn upon paper with this liquor, will appear green when warm, and lose its color again when cold unless it has been heated too much.

BLUE SYMPATHETIC INK.

Dissolve cobalt or zaffre in spirits of nitre and precipitate by salts of tartar: wash the precipitate and dissolve it in distilled vinegar, avoiding an excess of the acid. Writing of this will also lose its color when cold, and appear again when warm, unless too much heated.

SALT OF SORREL.

Take the real salt of sorrel, mix with it half its weight of cream of tartar, and commingle them together in a mortar. This preparation is commonly but erroneously called salt of lemons. It is excellent for removing ink spots from the hands, and also iron rust from cloths.

BEEF'S GALL.

Take gall from the beef as soon as it is killed, and hang it where it will not be disturbed till next day; then pour off the clear fluid, and cork it up in a phial. A little of it mixed with warm water is excellent to remove greasy spots from clothes.

TO DRY HERBS.

The flavor of all herbs is in full perfection just before they begin to blossom: afterwards they begin to decline in sweetness. Gather them on a dry day, cut them into small bunches, and dry them in a slow oven, turning them over frequently. Be careful not to apply too much heat, or the flavor will be too much impaired. When dry, pick off the leaves, powder, sift and cork it up in bottles. It will be found good for flavoring many dishes.

TO SAVE SEEDS.

Many people save vegetables of an inferior quality for seeds. This is a very mistaken idea; for the finest and forwardest of vegetables should be selected for that purpose. All vegetables that have seeds on a stalk, may be greatly improved by trimming off all the small branches as they make their appearance, and suffering only the main stalk or caulis to grow and bring forth the seeds. Seeds thus saved will increase every year in size, and bring much finer and earlier vegetables than when the small branches or sprouts are suffered to grow up and bring forth seeds with the main stalk.

TO MAKE STARCH

The most economical starch is made of wheat bran, and is not inferior in any respect to the starch made of wheat. Put the bran into large tubs, pour on enough clear cold water to make it a batter, and set it in the sun till it ferments properly, which will take from one to three days, according to the temperature of the weather. Strain it through a fine sieve into a clean tub, and set it by for the starch to settle at the bottom; then team off the yellow water, pour on a pailful or more of the fresh water, mix the starch with the water, strain it through a cloth, sufficiently thick to keep back every particle of bran, and let it stand again to settle: after which pour off the water and fill up the tub again. Do this till the water ceases to be colored; then take the starch, which will have settled at the bottom of the tub, break it up, put it on large dishes, and expose them daily to the sun till the starch becomes perfectly dry, stirring it up frequently; then put it up in small linen bags.

TO MAKE STARCH FROM WHEAT.

Soak your wheat in water till the grains become soft, changing the water every day, otherwise it will have a bad smell: then break up the grains, rubbing them thoroughly with your hands, and throwing the husk into another tub as you proceed. When you get it all rubbed out, pour on the husk some clean water, wash them well in the water, to get out all the remaining starch; squeeze them out, and pour the water, &c. into the tub with the other starch; strain the whole through a cloth into a clean tub, and when the starch or white substance settles to the bottom, proceed as before directed.

TO MAKE SOAP.

Ashes that are taken off the hearth every morning, are not good for soap, as the lye is sure to be weak. Without good strong lye it is in vain to try to make good soap, for in every attempt there will be a failure. To have good lye, the ashes should be burnt thoroughly, and kept as clean as possible. When it has dripped from the gum, put it in a large iron pot or kettle, make it boiling hot, and if it will not readily eat off the soft part of a feather, when dipped into it, boil till it will: but if it will not eat the feather without boiling it down, the soap will not be good. Have the grease, whatever kind it may be, clean, put it in the lye while it is boiling, and boil it steadily till it becomes a thick soap, stirring it frequently. It is impossible to give an infallible rule as to the proportions, as so much depends upon the strength of the lye and the quality of the grease. If it is too strong of lye, it will not thicken fast, and will sting your tongue smartly on tasting it; then put in more grease. To try when it is done, take some of it up in a spoon, and hold it in the open air till it gets cold. By this rule you may tell when it is as thick as you desire it. Or, you may drop some from the paddle into a cup of cold water: if it is not any thing like done, it will readily unite with the water; but if it is done, or nearly so, it will remain in little cakes at the bottom of the cup: according to the thickness of the soap will the texture of the cakes be. Then you may dissolve it in the water, and if it is too weak, the grease will float on the top: then of course you must add more lye and boil it down again. This is the best way of making common soft or mushy soap for washing clothes.

To make hard cake soap, when your lye is strong enough to cause an egg to float on the top, put in your grease three quartes s of a pound of clean lard or tallow, which is the usual allowance to each gallon of lye. Boil it steadily and as fast as you can, without its boiling over the top, as it is very apt to do after it becomes thick: therefore, as it thickens, moderate the boiling by withdrawing a part of the fire. Stir it very frequently, and in a few hours, if the proportions exactly suit, you will have good soap. Try it as directed for the soft soap:

if it is too weak, add more lye, but if too strong, more lard is required, or it may be made to thicken by adding a little cold water. Age improves soap greatly, and the stronger it is, in reason, the better will it be when it is one or two years old. When you ascertain by cooling a a little, that it is sufficiently thick, put in common salt in the proportion of one pint to three gallons of the soap. When it is completely dissolved, stir it well, pour the whole into a tub and set it by till next day; then put it in the kettle, melt it and cool it again, and when it is quite cold, cut it out in square cakes.

An inferior soft soap may be made by mixing together clean grease and strong lye, exposing it daily to the sun for a week or two, according to the quantity, and stirring it frequently. Another way to make soft soap is to have some clean lard or tallow in a kettle, make it boiling hot, and stir hard into it enough of the strongest lye to make it into good soap. This is the most speedy way of making soap, and for present use it answers very well.

CEMENT.

Beat up the white of an egg, and stir hard into it enough unslaked lime to make it a thin paste, having first sifted it through a piece of muslin. Have your glass or china washed clean and wiped dry; rub on each broken edge some of the paste, put the pieces smoothly together, and set them by till they get thoroughly dry. You must use the lime paste perfectly fresh, or it will not do any good.

A bit of Russian gum isinglass, boiled in spirits of white wine, is said to be good cement for broken glass or china.

TO CLEAN SILVER PLATE.

Stir a large spoonful of powdered alum into a quart of strong hot soap suds; put in your spoons, &c., and let them be in it till it gets nearly cold; then wash them in clean water, wipe them dry with a cloth, and rub them well with a flannel and pulverized chalk.

ANOTHER WAY TO CLEAN PLATE.—Mix together white orgal or crude tartar, common salt and alum, in equal proportions: put a small portion of this powder into boiling water, and scald your silver in it a few minutes. It will give it a brilliant whiteness superior to any thing else.

COFFEE AND TEA POTS.

Having washed them clean, fill them with hot water, throwing into each a small shovel of hot embers; shut down the tops and let them stand till the water gets nearly cold; then empty them, scald them with clean water, and set them up to air, turning back the tops. This, done once a week, will keep them perfectly sweet.

TO CLEAN BRASSES.

If neatness is strictly attended to, you may keep your brasses in good order by rubbing them occasionally with rotten stone and oil. If by carelessness you suffer them to become cankery, put them in a brass kettle, with a plenty of water to cover them well, throw in a few hot wood ashes and some soft soap, and boil them for fifteen or twenty minutes; then rinse them clean, wipe them dry with a cloth, and rub them thoroughly with spirits of turpentine and a piece of flannel. If thoroughly rubbed, however dirty they may have been, they will look entirely bright and new.

TO CLEAN KNIVES AND FORKS.

Wash your knives and forks clean in hot water, and wipe them dry with a cloth, avoiding wetting the handles, or after using them awhile, they will become loose, and many times come off. Then rub them bright with rotten stone, or you may clean them with soft brick, that has been pounded and passed through a sieve.

BRITANNIA WARE.

Rub them well with linseed or sweet oil and a woollen cloth, then wash them clean in hot soap suds, wipe them dry with a cloth, and rub them thoroughly with a piece of flannel and pulverized chalk or magnesia. Cleaned in this manner, they will retain their beauty to the last. Tin coffee-boilers, &c., cleaned in this way, look much brighter than when cleaned in any other way.

ANOTHER MODE FOR CLEANING BRITANNIA.—Having washed it very clean in warm suds, rinse it clean and wash the outside of it with bronzing liquor, which is nothing more than blue vitriol dissolved in water; then rub it dry.

VARNISHED FURNITURE.

Pulverized rotten stone, rubbed on with linseed oil, and then wiped off clean with a silk cloth, will never fail to give a smooth, glossy appearance to defaced varnished furniture. If there are white spots on it, rub them over with spirits of turpentine, or linseed oil, and hold a few live coals in a shovel or warming-pan, a piece from the furniture so as to warm the spots a little, and then rub them with a soft cloth. This will generally remove the spots.

New furniture may be kept in good order by rubbing it occasionally with a little linseed oil and a linen rag.

PAINTED ROOMS.

Rooms that are painted with fady colors, should be cleansed with a piece of linen, wet with a small portion of linseed oil. Cleaned thus, the painting will retain its beauty much longer than when cleaned in the usual manner with soap suds, as strong suds will fade some colors very much, particularly green.

Dark painting, such as will not fade, should be washed with warm suds, wiped dry, and then rubbed with a linen rag and linseed oil.

TO CLEAN HEARTHS.

Freestone hearths, to retain their beauty, should be cleaned with nothing else than warm soap suds. After rinsing them, rub over a portion of freestone powder, and brush it off when dry. If always cleaned thus, they will look entirely new, and retain their beauty to the last. The powder can be readily procured in large quantities at the stone cutters'.

If dark hearths are desirable, rub them over occasionally with lamp oil, and then wash them clean with warm suds. This will make them look dark and very clean, suiting very well for a family room. To clean brick hearths, wash them clean, and wipe them dry; then brush them over with a mixture of red lead and sweet milk, boiled together till tolerably thick. Or you may brush them over with black lead, having first mixed it with a little water and soft soap, and boiled a few minutes. A very neat and inexpensive way to clean brick hearths is to rub them smoothly over with a mixture of sour milk and soft brick, that has been pounded and passed through a sieve.

TO MAKE CANDLES.

It is said that there is nothing better to make candles burn with a clear light, and prevent the tallow dripping, than to steep the wicks for a time in lime water, mixed with a little saltpetre, and then dried thoroughly. See that your tallow is entirely free from dregs, and if very soft, mix with it a portion of beeswax, and when melted, mix in a little powdered alum and spirits of camphor. It is said it will make them very hard and durable.

WAX CANDLES.

To bleach your wax, melt it in a large pot or kettle, and pour in a good quantity of hot water, which must be kept so by putting coals about the kettle. When the wax is melted and quite hot, it will rise to the top, and having ready a pan of soap suds and a large shallow plate, dip the plate into the suds and then in the wax; raise it up hastily, and there will have adhered to it a thin sheet of wax. Slip it off carefully, and proceed again as before, repeating it till you have dipped out all the wax; then lay them on a scaffold in the sun, and turn them over once a day till they are bleached perfectly white, which will only take a few days in warm weather.

The thickness of the sheets of wax depends greatly on the quantity of heat that is applied to the kettle: if the wax is very hot, the sheets will not be thicker than a common leaf. Melt it and dip it, or mould it as other candles. You may have them perfectly white, or any colour you please, by mixing the different colorings with the wax when melted.

WAX FLOWERS.

Prepare the beeswax as directed for candles, leaving it, after it is bleached, in the thin sheets; take any kind of flowers, as they come in season, take some of them to pieces, and cut out the wax leaves by the natural ones; then paint them with fine paint, using a camel's-hair brush, give them the proper shade, and put them together by the whole flowers: dip some little bunches of thread into melted wax, coloring the wax with any thing to suit the stamens and pistils of the flowers. When they are done, confine them on wires with thread and wax, pressing them firmly to the wires. This requires practice and dexterity to perform it in a proper manner. Make the leaves of green paper, or paint them green, which you choose. They are put up in glass boxes, and look very beautiful when skilfully performed.

INDEX.